PREFACE

The overall objective of the *Cases in Organizational Behavior* casebook is to help students become effective leaders within effective organizations. The casebook can be used as a single text or serve as a supplement to a standard organizational behavior textbook. The casebook consists of 32 field-based cases. The cases describe complex organizational problems that require the attention of the decision maker described in the case. The cases involve a wide variety of organizational settings—industries, organizational size, and the countries involved. I suggest various assignment questions that should guide the students in preparing the case for class discussion. The cases are designed to develop an understanding of, and appreciation for, the various challenges, dilemmas, and constraints that decision makers face in real organizational settings. For example, how do you create a context that allows people to perform at their potential? How do you get the cooperation or commitment from others? How do you implement change so that organizations improve their position on the competitive landscape of their industries? How do you create a burning platform for change? How do you overcome resistance to change? How can team effectiveness be increased? What makes a great team leader? How do you use coaching to increase personal effectiveness? Together, the 32 cases provide the students opportunities to hone and practice various skills, including decision-making skills, application skills, planning skills, coaching skills, and oral communication skills. The cases are all based on actual events that occurred, although at times the decision makers and the organizations they work for have been disguised.

The casebook is divided into four modules. All modules and the cases focus on the behavior of people in organizations. The modules are building effective organizations, leading people, team management, and change management. I should point out that there are several integrative issues that each decision maker or leader faces in dealing with the organizational problems described in the case. Examples of such integrative issues include globalization, managing a diverse workforce, moral or ethical dilemmas, motivation, and leadership. These and other topics are integrated throughout several cases and are not emphasized in a single module or case. For example, there are several international cases, both in the building effective organizations and change management modules. Also, ethical issues or dilemmas are front and center in numerous cases, for example, in the managing people and change management modules. And most of the cases have leadership implications.

A brief introduction to each module is provided, as well as a short description of the cases. Have fun!

ACKNOWLEDGMENTS

I wish to thank Nicki Smith and Devkamal Dutta for their help in editing the book.

CASES IN ORGANIZATIONAL BEHAVIOR

THE IVEY CASEBOOK SERIES

A SAGE Publications Series

Series Editor

Paul W. Beamish
Richard Ivey School of Business
The University of Western Ontario

Books in This Series

CASES IN BUSINESS ETHICS
Edited by David J. Sharp

CASES IN ENTREPRENEURSHIP
The Venture Creation Process
Edited by Eric A. Morse and Ronald K. Mitchell

CASES IN OPERATIONS MANAGEMENT
Building Customer Value Through World-Class Operations
Edited by Robert D. Klassen and Larry J. Menor

CASES IN ORGANIZATIONAL BEHAVIOR
Edited by Gerard H. Seijts

CASES IN THE ENVIRONMENT OF BUSINESS
International Perspectives
Edited by David W. Conklin

Forthcoming

CASES IN GENDER AND DIVERSITY IN ORGANIZATIONS
Edited by Alison M. Konrad

GERARD H. SEIJTS
The University of Western Ontario

CASES IN ORGANIZATIONAL BEHAVIOR

SAGE Publications
Thousand Oaks ▪ London ▪ New Delhi

For information:

Sage Publications, Inc.
2455 Teller Road
Thousand Oaks, California 91320
E-mail: order@sagepub.com

Sage Publications Ltd.
1 Oliver's Yard
55 City Road
London EC1Y 1SP
United Kingdom

Sage Publications India Pvt. Ltd.
B-42, Panchsheel Enclave
Post Box 4109
New Delhi 110 017 India

Printed in the United States of America.

Library of Congress Cataloging-in-Publication Data

Cases in organizational behavior/edited by Gerard H. Seijts.
        p. cm.—(The Ivey Casebook Series)
Includes bibliographical references.
ISBN 1–4129–0929–5 (pbk.)
    1. Organizational behavior—Case studies. 2. Management—Case studies.
I. Seijts, Gerard H. II. Series.
HD58.7.C358 2006
302.3′5—dc22   2005003582

This book is printed on acid-free paper.

05   06   07   08   09   10   9   8   7   6   5   4   3   2   1

Acquisitions Editor:	Al Bruckner
Editorial Assistant:	MaryAnn Vail
Production Editor:	Laureen A. Shea
Copy Editor:	Gillian Dickens
Typesetter:	C&M Digitals (P) Ltd.
Proofreader:	Libby Larson
Cover Designer:	Edgar Abarca

CONTENTS

Introduction to the Ivey Casebook Series   vii
Paul W. Beamish

Preface   ix

1. Building Effective Organizations   1
Trojan Technologies Inc.: Organizational Structuring
    for Growth and Customer Service   8
Blinds To Go: Staffing a Retail Expansion   13
Five Star Beer—Pay for Performance   20
Jinjian Garment Factory: Motivating Go-Slow Workers   30
S-S Technologies Inc. (Compensation)   36
OP4.com: A Dynamic Culture   43
WestJet Airlines (A): The Culture That Breeds a Passion to Succeed   52

2. Leading People   63
Coaching for Exceptional Performance Workshop   71
Martin Brass Company (A) Tom Fuller, Vice-President, Manufacturing   75
Intel in China   77
Chuck MacKinnon   84
Elise Smart   97
Macintosh Financial: Sexual Harassment (A)   103

3. Team Management   109
Hazelton International   116
An International Project Manager's Day (A)   124
eProcure—The Project (A)   126
Spar Applied Systems (A)   132
Richard Ivey School of Business—The LEADER Project (A)   142
Richard Ivey School of Business—The LEADER Project—Kiev Site (B)   154
Antar Automobile Company—Part I: The Automation Project   159
The Leo Burnett Company Ltd.: Virtual Team Management   161

4. Change Management   177
Cushy Armchair   188
Crafting a Vision at Daimler-Chrysler   190

ABB Poland   192
China-Canada Lean Swine Project—Changing Local Habits   201
Salco (China)   212
Deloitte & Touche: Integrating Arthur Andersen   222
PETA's "Kentucky Fried Cruelty, Inc." Campaign   230
Maple Leaf Foods (A): Leading Six Sigma Change   246
Black & Decker-Eastern Hemisphere and the ADP Initiative (A)   260
Sandalias Finas de Cuernavaca, S.A.: Total Quality Management (A)   270
Victoria Hospital Redesign Initiative   283

About the Editor   **295**

INTRODUCTION TO THE
IVEY CASEBOOK SERIES

As the title of this series suggests, these books all draw from the Ivey Business School's case collection. Ivey has long had the world's second largest collection of decision-oriented, field-based business cases. Well more than a million copies of Ivey cases are studied every year. There are more than 2,000 cases in Ivey's current collection, with more than 6,000 in the total collection. Each year approximately 200 new titles are registered at Ivey Publishing (www.ivey.uwo.ca/cases), and a similar number are retired. Nearly all Ivey cases have teaching notes available to qualified instructors. The cases included in this volume are all from the current collection.

The vision for the series was a result of conversations I had with Sage's Senior Editor, Al Bruckner, starting in September 2002. Over the subsequent months, we were able to shape a model for the books in the series that we felt would meet a market need.

Each volume in the series contains text and cases. "Some" text was deemed essential in order to provide a basic overview of the particular field and to place the selected cases in an appropriate context. We made a conscious decision to not include hundreds of pages of text material in each volume in recognition of the fact that many professors prefer to supplement basic text material with readings or lectures customized to their interests and to those of their students.

The editors of the books in this series are all highly qualified experts in their respective fields. I was delighted when each agreed to prepare a volume. We very much welcome your comments on this casebook.

—Paul W. Beamish
Series Editor

The book is dedicated to my parents, Piet and Nel, and my wife, Jana. I thank them for their ongoing love and support.

1

BUILDING EFFECTIVE ORGANIZATIONS

Brent Schlender (2004) encouraged readers of *Fortune* to try the following thought experiment: "What are the most significant innovations of the past 50 years?" Answers that come to mind may include the following: the VCR, the personal computer, genetically engineered medicine, telecommunications satellites, fiber optics, cell phones, the Internet, the ATM, the microwave oven, the cardiac stent, and the bar code. All these innovations have added value to our lives. But Schlender noted that the innovation that has brought those "miracles" is the modern corporation—companies such as GE, Intel, Pfizer, Microsoft, IBM, GM, and so forth. He argued that "without them and their proven ability to marshal and allocate resources, organize and harness the ingenuity of people, respond to commercial and social environments, and meet the ever more elaborate challenge of producing and distributing goods and providing services on a global scale, we would have far less innovation—and less wealth" (p. 104). Companies that have become successful and leaders in their respective industries have mastered the art of managing people and resources. And that accomplishment, Schlender argued, makes the corporation "the latest jewel in the crown of human endeavour."

Jay R. Galbraith (1995), among the leading experts on organizational design and now at the Marshall School of Business, noted that organizational design decisions are critical to organizational effectiveness. That is, for companies to be truly effective requires that they be structurally aligned (see Figure 1.1). Misalignment among the building blocks of an organization is an impediment to organizational effectiveness. And designing effective organizations is a key task of the leader.

Michael Watkins (2003), a Harvard Business School professor, wrote that "the higher you climb in organizations, the more you take on the role of organizational architect, creating the context within which others can achieve superior performance. No matter how charismatic you are, you cannot hope to do much if the key elements in your unit are fundamentally out of alignment. You will feel like you are pushing a boulder uphill every day" (p. 130).

The focus in this module (and the seven cases) is on helping students to appreciate the importance of organizational design and to offer tools and ideas that will help them create effective units or organizations.

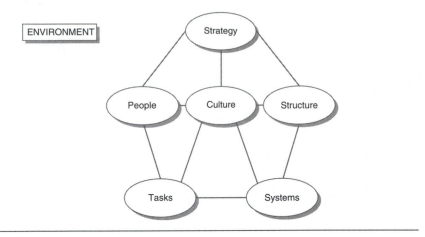

Figure 1.1   Organizational Design Framework

Leaders should start to think like organizational architects; their task is to create the context in which individuals can achieve their potential. Figure 1.1 identifies the six elements of organizational design.

- Strategy

Strategy refers to the chosen direction for an organization, or an organization's "formula for winning." Leaders should be concerned with the question, "What is our business, and how do we compete?" There are a multitude of strategies that organizations can adopt. Two examples include lowest-cost producer and differentiator. Organizational design experts have argued that in thinking about (re)designing organizations, we should always start with strategy. For example, how is our organization positioned vis-à-vis our competitors? How can we add value? What are our goals?

- Structure

Structure refers to the (in)formal system of tasks and reporting relationships that controls, coordinates, and motivates employees so that they cooperate to achieve the organization's goals. In essence, the organizational structure is the anatomy of the organization; it includes such things as organizational charts, the informal networks that exist, the differentiation versus the specialization dilemma, organizational forms, and decision rights.

- Systems

Systems are the processes and policies that complement the structure. Examples of systems include the ways data are shared, communication, human resources (HR) policies, and budgeting. The processes and policies that exist within an organization can be seen as the physiology of the organization.

- Critical tasks

Leaders have to define the jobs and role requirements that will help to achieve the organization's goals. Critical tasks also include the technologies and tools that are required for employees to complete their jobs or tasks.

- People

What characteristics—or knowledge, skills, and abilities—are required to accomplish tasks and achieve the organization's goals? This element of the organizational design module contains the human resources element—the pool of knowledge, skills, motivation, needs, values, and attitudes on the part of people.

- Organizational culture

Culture refers to the set of core values, norms, and assumptions that controls or guides the way people and groups in an organization interact with each other and with people outside the organization. Organizations often have different cultures, even those that operate in the same industries; the airline industry is a good example.

The various components of the organizational design model need to "fit" or be aligned with one another. There are two kinds of fit:

- External fit (environment—strategy)

External fit addresses the question, "To what extent is the strategy that the organization adopted a reasonable response to environmental demands?" For example, all things considered, does it make sense to enter new markets? The question of external fit is of interest to organizational strategists; it is not the topic of organizational behavior.

- Internal fit (among components of the organization)

Internal fit addresses the following three questions: (a) Do the components of the model of organizational design allow for the effective implementation of the strategy and for performing the core activities of the organization? (b) Do the components of the model of organizational design allow for the effective use of the organization's resources? (c) Is there a consistent message? For example, are the components of the model of organizational design reflective of the values underlying the organization?

Misalignment among the components will hurt organizational effectiveness. For example, a lack of fit among the various components can render even the best thought-out organizational strategies useless. John Kotter (1996) provided three common mistakes in the design of organizations.

The vision is to:	The organizational structure is such that:
Give more responsibility to lower-level employees Increase productivity to become a low-cost producer Speed everything up	Layers of middle-level managers criticize and question employees Huge staff groups at corporate headquarters are expensive and constantly initiate costly programs Independent, functional silos do not communicate and thus slow everything down

There are at least four implications that the model of organizational design suggests. It is important that leaders understand these implications. First, a change in strategy affects all other components of the model. As one (or more) element of the model changes, so too must others change to maintain fit or alignment. For example, the result of organizational change is more than just a refocus of strategies, business model, or goals. The entire design of the organization needs to be evaluated. Does the design still support the attainment of the organization's goals?

Second, there is no "one size fits all" organizational design that all organizations should implement. A "good" organizational design for a particular organization is one that has high external and internal fit. Companies within the same industries can have different configurations and yet be highly successful.

Third, leaders have a tendency to focus on the "formal" systems to facilitate behavioral change and make sure that tasks are performed. For example, rewards are often seen as a driver of behavioral change; in reality, they are a reinforcer. All components of the organizational design model should be used as levers of behavioral change or individual performance. Too often, however, leaders focus on structure and rewards in isolation of culture, tasks, coaching, communication, and so forth.

Fourth, culture affects, and is affected by, all components in the model of organizational design. A big impediment to creating organizational change is culture. Culture changes slowly and must be managed in the long term through appropriate changes in strategy, structure, systems, tasks, and people.

The seven cases in this module deal with organizational design issues. For each of these cases, I urge students to think about the following four challenges or questions:

- Analyze the design of the unit or organization. Is there a fit among the components of the organizational design model?
- Identify specific areas for improving fit.
- Design plans for correcting the lack of fit.
- Think about how to best implement those plans.

Some students may feel that issues of organizational design are not relevant to those who are not in leadership positions. This is an incorrect assumption. For example, Watkins (2003) noted that even those people who do not have the authority to lead change so that alignment is achieved should take an active interest in organizational design: "A thorough understanding of organizational alignment can help you build credibility with people higher in the organization—and demonstrate your potential for more senior positions" (p. 131).

A brief description of each case is provided next, and specific assignment questions are suggested.

TROJAN TECHNOLOGIES INC.: ORGANIZATIONAL STRUCTURING FOR GROWTH AND CUSTOMER SERVICE

A group of Trojan Technologies Inc. employees grappled with the issue of how to structure the business to effectively interact with their customers and manage the company's dramatic growth. The London, Ontario, manufacturer of ultraviolet water disinfecting systems believed that strong customer service was key to its recent and projected growth and had come to the realization that changes would have to be made to continue to achieve both simultaneously. Recent problems encountered included difficulties being experienced in training, career development, recruiting, customer service, and planned geographic and product line expansions. The group hoped to develop a structure to address these issues. The executive vice president was to lead the development and implementation of the new structure. The transition to the new structure was to coincide with the new fiscal year.

Assignment Questions

- Consider the organization's fundamentals in terms of products and customers. Describe the importance of customer service and support, and consider the implications for the company's functions that directly interact with customers, given the historical and projected growth in the company.

- Given the decision to structure the company for growth using business teams, how would you decide the composition and delineation of the teams to achieve the growth and customer service objectives of the company?
- What concerns do you have with changing company structure, and how would you address them to ensure the new structure was successful?

BLINDS TO GO: STAFFING A RETAIL EXPANSION

Blinds To Go is a manufacturer and retailer of customized window coverings. The company has been steadily expanding the number of stores across North America. In the year 2000, the company was experiencing tremendous growth, with plans of adding 50 stores per year in Canada and the United States. The vice chairman is concerned with the lack of staff in some of these newly expanded stores. With plans of an initial public offering within the next 2 years, senior management must determine what changes need to be made to the recruitment strategy and how to develop staff that will help them achieve the company's growth objectives.

Assignment Questions

- Why is Blinds To Go having difficulty attracting and retaining retail staff?
- Are the elements of the organizational design at the retail store level "aligned" to facilitate the retention of new employees? Why?
- What recommendations would you give Blinds To Go to improve their staffing practices?

FIVE STAR BEER—PAY FOR PERFORMANCE

In June 1997, Tom McMullen (president of the Alliance Brewing Group) and Zhao Hui Shen (general manager of Five Star Brewing Co. Ltd.) met to discuss the "pay for performance" systems that Zhao had been implementing at Five Star's two breweries over the past several months. The president needed to determine whether these systems were properly designed to ensure that they are producing higher quality product at progressively lower costs. If not, he needed to consider how he might suggest that these and other systems be changed to achieve cost and quality objectives.

Assignment Questions

- Assess the organizational design of Five Star. In developing your assessment, consider the strategic, structural, human resource, and task elements at play, particularly as they relate to Zhao's performance-based compensation systems.
- Analyze Zhao's "bonus" compensation systems in detail. What likely impact will these systems have on quality at Five Star? What impact will they have on the sales force?
- As Tom McMullen, what suggestions would you give Mr. Zhao on how to improve these systems? What organizational design changes can realistically be made that will enhance quality and promote acceptance of the systems? How would you implement these changes?
- As an outside consultant to McMullen and Zhao, what would you recommend they do to change Five Star's culture from a "volume culture" to a "quality and profitability culture"?

JINJIAN GARMENT FACTORY: MOTIVATING GO-SLOW WORKERS

The case illustrates a typical labor-intensive industry that is characterized by furious competition and low employee loyalty. Jinjian Garment Factory is a large clothing manufacturer based in Shenzhen with distribution to Hong Kong and overseas. Although Shenzhen had become one of the most advanced garment manufacturing centers in the world, managers in this industry still had few effective ways of dealing with the collective and deliberate slow pace of work by the employees, motivating workers, and resolving the problem between seasonal production requirements and retention of skilled workers. However, the owner and managing director of the company must determine the reasons behind the deliberately slow pace of the workers, the pros and cons of the piecework system, and the methods he could adopt to motivate the workers effectively.

Assignment Questions

- Is the piecework system the most suitable wage system for factories in the Shenzhen garment manufacturing industry?
- What are the pros and cons of the piecework system?
- What industry is most suitable for the piecework system?
- How do you solve the dilemma facing the garment industry—that of seasonal production requirements versus retaining skilled workers?
- Do you agree with the severe quality punishment policy prevailing in the Shenzhen garment industry? If not, is there a better way to deal with the quality problem?
- If you were Mr. Lou, what would you do to increase worker productivity?

S-S TECHNOLOGIES INC. (COMPENSATION)

The owners of S-S Technologies Inc. were concerned with the rapid rate of growth facing their company. The company had revenues of $6.3 million and employed 30 highly skilled workers. These numbers were expected to double or triple in the next couple of years. To determine how well the company was structured to achieve its future goals, they hired a consultant they had worked with successfully in the past. The consultant's major role was to make recommendations as to the appropriate organizational design (culture, people, layers of management and administrative systems) in the event that the company grew from 30 to 60 or even 120 employees. Among other issues, questions regarding compensation were surfacing, and the owners wanted to address these questions as soon as possible.

Assignment Questions

- What are the key success factors (things that the company has to do well) for S-S Technologies to attain high growth, high profits, and high morale?
- Describe S-S Technologies' compensation plan. Does it contribute to attracting and keeping key employees? What factors account for the highly skilled and committed workforce at S-S Technologies?
- How long can S-S Technologies continue with its existing compensation plan? Why?
- What recommendations would you make to Brock and the consultant regarding (a) base pay, (b) bonuses, and (c) "equity" for partners?
- What process would you recommend to obtain acceptance of the new compensation plan?

OP4.COM: A DYNAMIC CULTURE

OP4.com, an Internet portal for teenagers, had just celebrated 6 months of existence. The cofounders of OP4.com knew that the internal culture had to reflect the identity of its Web site, so they wanted to cultivate a savvy, hip staff. They used unique methods to evaluate a prospect's fit into the company and some unorthodox training and feedback systems. With profitability being the next key step, they had to determine how to maintain this culture through the next stage of growth—one that would result in the creation of business units and formal reporting structures for staff.

Assignment Questions

- How would you characterize the organizational culture at OP4.com?
- How was this culture developed and maintained?
- What role, if any, does OP4.com's culture play in the organization's effectiveness?
- How should Ray Matthews and Stuart Saunders manage the transition to a new organizational design?

WESTJET AIRLINES (A): THE CULTURE THAT BREEDS A PASSION TO SUCCEED

WestJet Airlines, a regional carrier that provides low-fare flights with exceptional service, has achieved remarkable success. It has made profits ever since its inception in 1996. Its market capitalization has surpassed that of Canada's national airline. The founders believe that the company's culture is the key to continued success and that they cannot afford to mismanage it. "We're in the hospitality business and our culture is everything to us," stated Don Bell, cofounder and senior vice president of customer service. However, three potential threats to WestJet's culture and its success emerged. First, industry watchers voiced concerns about WestJet's future, arguing that an economic downturn could hurt the carrier dependent on leisure travelers. Second, its expansive growth could make it hard, if not impossible, to keep the "fun" culture alive. In light of the tremendous growth, the founders must determine how WestJet could grow while maintaining its unique and vibrant culture. Third, other airlines had noticed the success of WestJet and were in the process of attempting to mimic its service.

Assignment Questions

- What is WestJet's competitive advantage? What are the sources of that competitive advantage?
- Is the culture at WestJet as important to the success of the organization as its management team believes it to be?
- How serious is the threat from conventional airlines that want to imitate the WestJet culture? What does it take to imitate organizational culture?
- What does WestJet need to do to keep its success going as it is expanding its fleet?

REFERENCES

Galbraith, J. R. (1995). *Designing organizations: An executive briefing on strategy, structure, and process.* San Francisco: Jossey-Bass.

Kotter, J. (1996). *Leading change.* Boston: Harvard Business School Press.

Schlender, B. (2004). The new soul of a wealth machine. *Fortune, 149*(7), 102–110.

Watkins, M. (2003). *The first 90 days: Critical success strategies for new leaders at all levels.* Boston: Harvard Business School Press.

Trojan Technologies Inc.: Organizational Structuring for Growth and Customer Service

*Prepared by Greg Upton under the
supervision of Professor John Eggers*

Copyright © 1999, Ivey Management Services

Version: (A) 1999-08-19

In March 1998, a group of Trojan Technologies Inc. (Trojan) employees grappled with the issue of how to structure the business to effectively interact with their customers and to manage the company's dramatic growth. The London, Ontario, manufacturer of ultraviolet (UV) water disinfection systems believed that strong customer service was key to its recent and projected growth, and had come to the realization that changes would have to be made to continue to achieve both simultaneously. The group hoped to develop a structure to address these issues. Marvin DeVries, executive vice-president, was to lead the development and implementation of the new structure. The transition to the new structure was to begin as of September 1998 to coincide with the new fiscal year.

THE BUSINESS

Technology

Since 1977, the company had specialized in UV light applications for disinfecting water and wastewater. In essence, Trojan's products killed microorganisms using high-intensity UV lamps. Water was channeled past the lamps at various speeds, based on the clarity of the water and the strength of the lamps, to achieve the required "kill" rate.

Trojan's UV technology had proven to be an environmentally safe and cost-effective alternative to chlorination, and was gaining wider recognition and acceptance. Even so, a significant market remained to be tapped, as the company estimated "...that only five per cent to 10 per cent of municipal wastewater sites in North America use UV-based technology... [and] of the approximate 62,000 wastewater treatment facilities operating worldwide, only 2,500 currently utilize UV disinfection systems."[1]

Trojan Technologies Inc.[2]

Trojan was established in 1977 with a staff of three with the goal of developing a viable UV wastewater disinfection technology. Following several years of work, the first UV disinfection system (System UV2000™) was installed in Tillsonburg, Ontario, in 1981. It took another two years, however, before the regulatory approvals were in place to market the technology for municipal wastewater treatment in Canada and the United States. During this time, the company generated revenues through the sale of small residential and industrial cleanwater UV systems.

By 1991, the company had sales in excess of $10 million, and had introduced its second-generation technology in the System UV3000™ wastewater disinfection system. As the company's growth continued, a staff of 50 was in place by 1992. The following year, due to capital requirements created by the company's strong growth, an initial public offering on the Toronto Stock Exchange was completed. Also in 1993, a branch office was established in The Hague, Netherlands, expanding Trojan's reach across the Atlantic.

1994 saw the launch of the System UV4000™, the construction of a new head office and sales exceeding $20 million. In 1995, a branch office was opened in California to service the enormous market for wastewater treatment in that state. Two years later, an expansion doubled head office capacity to house 190 staff and to meet the demand for sales of more than $50 million.

Well into 1998, the expectation was that sales would reach $70 million by year-end and continue to grow by more than 30 per cent per year over the next five years, reaching $300 million by 2003. The company was in the process of planning additional capacity expansion in the form of building and property purchases adjacent to head office, and expected to quadruple its headcount by 2003 to more than 1,000 employees.

Products

In 1997, 93 per cent of Trojan's sales were of wastewater products (System UV4000™ and System UV3000™). These systems were designed for use at small to very large wastewater treatment plants and more complex wastewater treatment applications with varying degrees of effluent treatment. The remaining seven per cent of sales were cleanwater products (primarily the System UV8000™ and Aqua UV™) for municipal and residential drinking water and industrial process applications. Growth in the coming year would be driven by increased sales of the wastewater disinfection products in both current and new geographic markets. In the longer term, new products such as the A•I•R• 2000™, which was to use UV light with an advanced photocatalytic technology to destroy volatile organic compounds in the air, were expected to further Trojan's sales growth.

Products were typically assembled from component parts at Trojan head office. The complexity of the product design, manufacture and service arose from the integration of skills in electronics, biology, controls programming and mechanical engineering. The company owned patents on its products and was prepared to defend them to preserve its intellectual capital.

Customers

Trojan sold its wastewater treatment products to contractors working on projects for municipalities or directly to municipalities. Typically, the process involved bidding on a project based on the Trojan products required to meet the municipality's specifications, and, therefore, engineering expertise was required as part of the selling process. Project sales typically fell in a $100,000 to $500,000 range, and given the large value of each sale, the sales and marketing function was critical to the company's success. However, for marketing to be effective, this new technology had to be well-supported. Municipalities purchasing the wastewater disinfection systems required rapid response to any problems, and expected superior service given the consequences of breakdowns for the quality of water being discharged from their facility. Municipalities also had the ability to discuss Trojan and their UV products with other municipalities before deciding to make their purchase, further underlining the importance of warranty and aftermarket service to customers to ensure positive word-of-mouth advertising.

Trojan's smaller product line, the cleanwater segment, focused on a different customer base from wastewater, and it was difficult to generalize about the nature of this segment's customers. These customers ranged from municipalities to industrial companies to individuals.

INTERACTION WITH CUSTOMERS

The Process

The main points of customer interaction in the wastewater product line included:

1. Quote/bid process
2. Configuration of project structure
3. Project shipment and system installation
4. Technical support and warranty claims
5. Parts order processing

Each of these is described briefly below:

The quote/bid process was a major function of the marketing department, with support from the project engineering department. Although the marketing department took the lead role in assembling the appropriate bid and pricing, the customer would on occasion wish to speak directly to the project engineering department on specific technical questions related to the function of the UV unit within the particular wastewater setting.

After winning a bid, the configuration of project structure involved working with the customer on the detailed specifications for the project and applying the appropriate Trojan systems in a configuration that would meet the customer's needs. The project engineering department took the lead role in this work, and either worked through the marketing representative in transmitting technical information to and from the customer or communicated directly with the customer's technical personnel.

Once the project had been configured, it was scheduled for manufacture by the operations department. On completion, and when the customer was ready to integrate the UV system into their wastewater facility, the service department completed the installation and start-up of the unit. The service department would also be involved in demonstrating the proper use of the system to the customer.

After the system was in use by the customer, further interaction came in the form of technical support. The service department would deal with phone calls, site visits and warranty claims and was the primary contact point for the customer. By its nature, most service work at this stage of the process was completed on an "as-needed" basis by the first available service representative. As a result, it was difficult or impossible to have the same service representative available to respond to a particular customer on every occasion. The service department, therefore, kept a detailed file on each UV installation and all customer contact to ensure the most informed response on each service call.

The final stage of customer interaction was the ordering of replacement parts by the customer after the warranty period was complete.

This was handled by a call centre at Trojan head office in London that was separate from the other departments that had dealt with the customer. The call centre was staffed to receive orders for Trojan replacement parts, but not to provide technical support as with the service department, and would generally not access customer service files in taking the order.

In summary, customers would deal with as many as four different departments during their interaction with Trojan. During the early days of Trojan's growth, the "close-knit" nature of Trojan's workforce allowed a seamless transition between "departments." However, as described below, the company's continued growth began to complicate the transition between departments.

Customer Support in the Early Days

In the 1980s and early 1990s, when Trojan had less than 50 employees and worked on a limited number of wastewater bids and projects during the course of the year, customer support was a collective effort across the entire company. In fact, it was not unusual that virtually everyone in Trojan knew the details of all the major projects in process at any given time. There was a common knowledge base of customer names and issues, which resulted, in DeVries' words, in an "immediate connectivity" to the job at hand. At times, during those early days, there were as few as two employees in a "department." Under these conditions every project received immediate and constant attention from start to finish, ensuring the customer was satisfied and potential issues were addressed in a proactive manner.

Challenges Created by Growth

As the company grew, departments grew. Very quickly the number of projects multiplied and it became impossible for everyone to know all the customers and active projects, or even all the people in the organization. As departments grew from two to five to 10 people, communications became focused internally within the departments. This made it progressively more difficult to ensure timely and effective communication on project status between departments, and the "immediate connectivity" described by DeVries began to break down. The situation was described by many as one where "things began to slip between the cracks" in terms of customer service excellence, because it was no longer possible for employees to shepherd a project through the company from start to finish as had been done in the early days. Once a particular department had finished their component of a project, they immediately had to turn their attention to the other projects they had ongoing, creating the potential for a lag before the next department picked up the customer file.

Project Engineering

Project engineering was one example of a department that had begun to experience problems maintaining service levels to the end-customer as a result of growth. By 1997, there were seven engineers in the department handling the regular support to the marketing department and acting as "specialists" for the various technical components of the products. When engineers were hired into this group, there was no formal training or apprenticeship program in place. The new hire would simply follow along as best he or she could and attempt to learn the complex product line through observation and assistance from others in the department. This type of training was strained by the demand for project engineering services brought on by Trojan's growth.

A "specialist" role, in addition to their support of the marketing department's project bids, had evolved within the project engineering group. To handle specific technical requests, this informal addition to the project engineer's role had occurred somewhat spontaneously within the department. For example, if one of the project engineers had developed a detailed understanding of the electronics included in the System UV4000™ products, that employee acted as the reference point for most detailed queries on this subject and was considered the "electronics specialist." There was no specific training or support to develop these specialists for their roles in place in 1997, nor was hiring particularly targeted at filling the

specialist roles described above, as it was a secondary role for the department. As a result of the dual roles and the company's rapid growth, project engineers could not take responsibility to guide a project from bid through customer queries to production and commissioning of the project. The demand for assistance on many bids, coupled with the need to respond to queries in their "specialist" area on active projects prevented project engineers from acting as a steward on specific projects as they passed through the company. Instead, the department operated more as a pooled resource that was accessed as needed by the marketing department to support bids and by the service group to assist with product support.

Service

The growth of the company and the establishment of new product lines had caused an amplified growth in the service group, because for each new project installed there was a long-term source of potential queries and service needs. The service group covered a broad spectrum of needs, from the initial setup of UV systems to emergency responses to equipment problems or queries (which frequently required site visits). A formal training program had been instituted during early 1998 when the new service manager recognized the need to quickly develop new employees to ensure they could contribute a strong technical background and familiarity with the product. An existing service group member typically instructed new employees for approximately one week, and new employees learned the balance "on the job" through observation and discussion of issues with other service employees. Again, company growth had caused some difficulty in ensuring that new employees received adequate training before they were needed to actively service customer inquiries.

There was a fundamental structuring conflict within the service area on how to best serve the customer. On one hand, customers appreciated the ability to contact one person whenever they had a concern or question. Also, customers frequently needed quick response times to their site for in-person assessments and action by the service employee. This appeared to suggest a need to place service employees physically as close to the end-customer as possible, especially given the company's expanded geographic marketing area. However, the timing of service work was very uncertain. Whereas the project engineering department had some ability to prioritize and schedule their workload, the service department typically had to respond to customer calls immediately, and the geographic distribution of calls was not predictable. Therefore, if Trojan received significant service requests in California, the company could be forced to respond by sending all available service employees there. The uncertainty of the timing and geographic distribution of service calls lent itself more to the centralized pooling of resources that Trojan currently used.

As Trojan had a significant geographic distribution of sales, service work involved substantial travel. In fact, the constant travel presented an additional risk of "burnout" that was unique to the department. To address this, and to ensure a reliable response to calls for assistance from customers, a head office call centre was created in 1998. The call centre was staffed by service technicians who could respond to many customer situations over the phone and by using sophisticated remote monitoring of the UV installments in some cases. The call centre also provided a place where experienced service personnel who were at risk of "burnout" from constant travel could use their expertise. Also, the call centre provided another opportunity to train new employees before dispatching them directly to customer locations on service calls.

RELATED ISSUES

Career Ladders

In a small company, career progression and satisfaction typically comes with successes achieved that significantly affect the organization. There was generally not the expectation or the possibility of significant promotion or role development, but this was offset by the potential for involvement of everyone in several major components of company activity. This was certainly the case at Trojan in the early days. As the company grew, however, a need to distinguish between and recognize the various levels of experience developed. The current department structure did not provide for much differentiation of job requirements within the departments, and, therefore, did not recognize the significant difference in experience levels between new and veteran employees.

Training Issues

As Trojan's sales continued to grow, the need to increase staffing was accelerating. In the early days, the addition of a person to the company was informal and supportive. The new employee would be introduced to everyone and would easily be able to approach the appropriate person to ask questions and to learn their role within the company. Given the rapid expansion of the company, this informal introduction to the company and its processes was rapidly becoming insufficient to allow new employees to become effective in their new position. Training, therefore, needed to be addressed in many areas.

DECISIONS

Given the issues developing as Trojan grew, the structuring issue was becoming steadily more important. The structuring team under DeVries envisioned a regional, team-based approach to customer interaction that would replicate the structure used by the company in the early days. One of the difficulties in implementing such a structure, however, would be ensuring that the groups still operated as though they were one company, sharing knowledge and resources as appropriate. Another would be determining what level of centralized support would be appropriate, bearing in mind the need to avoid duplicating activities at head office that should be handled by the regional teams. Employees were now aware that there would be a change in the company structure, and there was a need to come to some conclusions on the new structure quickly to reduce anxiety about the change within the organization.

NOTES

1. From Trojan 1998 annual report.
2. The information in this section was primarily gathered from Trojan 1997 annual report.

BLINDS TO GO: STAFFING A RETAIL EXPANSION

Prepared by Ken Mark
under the supervision of Professors
Fernando Olivera and Ann Frost

Version: (A) 2001-10-09

INTRODUCTION

"Staffing stores is our most challenging issue as we plan our expansion across North America," exclaimed Nkere Udofia, vice-chairman of Montreal-based Blinds To Go (BTG). "There are locations now where we've got physical store buildings built that are sitting unstaffed. How are we going to recruit and develop enough people to meet our growth objectives? What changes should our company make?" It was August 2, 2000, and Udofia knew that if Blinds To Go was to continue to grow 50 per cent in sales and add 50 stores per year, the issue of staffing would be front and centre.

THE DEVELOPMENT OF
THE BLINDS TO GO RETAIL CONCEPT

This retail fabricator of window dressings began as a one-man operation. Growing up in the Côte-des-Neiges district in Montreal, Canada, David Shiller, the patriarch of the Shiller family, started in business in 1954. Stephen Shiller, his son, joined the business in the mid-1970s, convincing his father to focus on selling blinds. Called "Au Bon Marché," as it was known in Quebec, the Shillers

began to create the production system that allowed them to cut the normal six- to eight-week delivery time frame for custom blinds to 48 hours. The customer response was overwhelming and the business took off.

Stephen Shiller exclaimed:

> We gave them food, kept them busy while they waited for their blinds to be ready. The factory was literally next to the store and we offered our one-hour delivery guarantee, which kept our customers happy. Our St. Leonard store, the prototype for the current Blinds To Go stores, opened in 1991. Prior to that, people used to drive for up to 100 miles to come to our stores.

> At that point, in early 1994, we realized what a hot concept we had on our hands—our sales were higher for each consecutive store opened, and none of our competitors could replicate our model. They were either manufacturers or retailers: none were both. None could hope to deliver the 48-hour turn-around we promised, had our unique sales model, which is 100 per cent commission-based, or had our attention to customer needs.

By June 2000, Blinds To Go operated 120 corporate-owned stores across North America (80 U.S. stores, 40 Canadian stores), generating in excess of US$1.0 million in sales per store (having a staff of between six to 20 people per store). Blinds To Go expected to add an average of 50 new stores per year for the next five years, 80 per cent of which was targeted to be U.S. expansion stores.

RETAIL OPERATIONS

It was senior management's belief that quality of staff was even more important than store location, the surrounding customer demographics or advertising. Stephen Shiller, president, tested this belief with the East Mississauga, Ontario, store.

In 1999, the East Mississauga store had experienced declining sales and high employee turnover. Analysing the demographic data surrounding the store left management with the impression that the store was a victim of poor location and cannibalization from another BTG store 10 miles away. However, Stephen Shiller, suspected that the real problem was in the quality of the store's staff. Stephen Shiller commented:

> We let the store continue on its downward sales trend as we trained a management team for this store. Although I was quite sure that the quality of people was at fault, I was determined to use this as a lesson to show the rest of the company how important it was to have first-class talent. After six months of waiting, we put in an "A" management team and trained staff. In one week, we doubled our sales and we tripled our sales in one month. That was a lesson we must never forget.

There were four staff roles in the stores—the sales associate, the selling supervisor, the assistant store manager and the store manager. The sales associates were the most junior employees and their job was to follow a set plan to help walk-in customers purchase a set of blinds. If they proved to be consistent sales performers, they would be promoted to selling supervisors or assistant store managers. Selling supervisors were assistant managers in training and usually had been one of the best sales associates. Assistant managers were in charge of the store when the store manager was not scheduled to work. The store manager was directly responsible for overall store operations,

including closing sales, motivating and developing staff, and handling customer service issues such as repairs and returns.

Generally, a very good sales associate was promoted to selling supervisor six to nine months after hiring date. To become a store manager generally took another six to 18 months. However, because of the enormous variation in personal potential, these progression targets were by no means fixed.

The BTG selling process involved a very high level of interaction with the customer, which set a very high level of service expectation. At the retail stores, the emphasis on customer satisfaction and sale closure led to a higher volume of orders relative to their retail competition. Outlined in the Blinds To Go University Manual (training program for new sales staff) were the following four operating guidelines:

- Service and Satisfy every Customer
- Never Lose a Sale
- Make the Customer Feel Special
- Bring the Manager into Every Sale to Give the Customer "Old Fashion Service"

Salespeople were expected to bond with a customer through a personal greeting, then ask open-ended questions about their product needs. The purpose of the next few minutes of interchange between associate and customer was to understand the customer's primary concerns and work towards a sale by resolving those issues. Next, associates emphasized to the customer the quality of the product, large selection and warranties. At this point, the associate would listen to any customer objections, and try to address them. The associate would price the product(s), then introduce the customer to the store manager. After walking the store manager through the order, the associate would deduct any relevant coupons, then attempt to close the sale.

All employees of BTG, even up to the president, prided themselves on being able to sell blinds to customers. During store visits, it was not uncommon to see senior management helping out the staff in dealing with an overflow of customers.

COMPENSATION OF RETAIL STAFF

The commission-based structure fostered a high-energy, sales hungry culture at Blinds To Go. Todd Martin, the director of retail planning and operations, explained:

> We know people come to us because they need blinds. An example of our culture in action is a manager who is unhappy with closing eight of 10 sales, because with the tools at his disposal, he should be able to close all 10. Even if the customer is just looking because they want to buy a house in six months, we can take their worries away from them. He should be able to sell to 10 out of 10 customers.

Todd Martin also believed there was a healthy competitive environment among sales associates. He offered:

> In the store, there are no rules on grabbing customers—in my two years here, I've never seen a problem with staff fighting for customers.

As BTG grew from a one-store operation, the Shillers kept a commission pay structure for its salesforce, believing that it best motivated performance. From experience, they knew that a suitable salesperson could, with the commission structure, make more money at BTG than at a comparable retail outlet. The focus had been on hiring energetic, personable people who loved the thrill of a sale.

A CHANGE IN COMPENSATION RESULTS IN SALES DECLINE

In 1996, the Shillers decided to change the compensation system from full commission to salary. This change was the result of a recommendation from a newly hired vice-president of store operation who had been the vice-president of a major U.S. clothing retailer. Her intention was to attract more recruits for Blinds To Go's expansion phase by standardizing store operations and compensation. At that time, there were already 15 stores and expansion was underway. Based on her prior experience at the U.S. retailer, she led the change from full commission to paying sales associates a wage of Cdn$8 per hour. This was intended to make sales associates less entrepreneurial and more customer-service focused. Store manager compensation was also revised to reflect a higher base salary component relative to commissions. A more casual uniform was mandated in place of the business casual attire that was being worn at stores. In an attempt to differentiate the roles of sales associates and store management, it was decided that the store manager would no longer be involved in the sale. Though skeptical of this recommendation, the Shillers reluctantly agreed to proceed as suggested, rolling out these changes in 1996.

Sales declined between 10 per cent to 30 per cent in both new and existing stores from 1996 to 1997. Overall staff turnover increased to more than 40 per cent from a pre-1995 figure of 15 per cent. This problem was further exacerbated by the fact that rapid store expansion into Toronto, Philadelphia and Detroit had required the deployment of skilled store staff, thinning the ranks of existing stores. The Shillers attributed this decline in performance primarily to the change in the compensation structure.

BTG REVERTS TO COMMISSION-BASED COMPENSATION

Unsatisfied with this turn of events, a change was made in the leadership of the stores' team. A variation of the commission-based compensation plan was brought back in May 1998 (see Exhibit 1). Udofia explained why he believed that commission was key to the sales culture of Blinds To Go:

> When we made the 1996 change, the base salary of $8/hour made it much easier to staff the store, but we were attracting a lower caliber of people—our best commission-based people did not like it and left. Having learned our lesson, we went back to our roots, brought back the old culture and experienced a sales turnaround. But, we've never 100 per cent recovered from it and are still playing catch-up today.

Corporate Formula	Original	1995 to 1996	Current
Sales Associate	$3 to $5/hr + 3% sales	$8/hr	$6 to $8/hr minimum, OR 6% sales (whichever was higher)
Managers/Assistants	$10,000 to $20,000/yr + 1.5% – 3% of overall store sales	$25,000 to $40,000/yr + 0.25% – 0.5% of overall store sales	$10,000 to $20,000/yr + 1.5% – 2.5% of overall store sales

Actual Results	Original	1995 to 1996	Current
Sales Associate Top 20% of Class ($14,000/sales/week)	$620/wk	$320/wk	$840/wk
Sales Associate Average Success ($10,000/sales/week)	$500/wk	$320/wk	$600/wk
Sales Associate Marginal Performer ($6,000/sales/week)	$380/wk	$320/wk	$360/wk
Sales Associate Poor Performer ($3,000/sales/week)	$290/wk	$320/wk	$240/wk
Manager Top 20% (2.5% of store sales)	$75,000/yr	$52,500/yr	$67,500/yr
Manager Average Success (1.2% of store sales)	$50,000/yr	$40,000/yr	$50,000/yr
Manager Poor Performer	$35,000/yr	$35,000/yr	$40,000/yr

Exhibit 1   BTG Pay Structure History

Since the return to commission-based compensation in 1998, store sales improved across the board, and within a few months, stores were posting between 10 per cent to 30 per cent increases in sales from the previous year (see Exhibit 2).

This dramatic turnaround was accomplished with the aid of several other initiatives. First, all U.S. district sales managers (DSMs) were brought to Toronto to see top-performing stores, thus establishing a performance benchmark. Next, a BTG employee stock option plan for store employees (all full-time sales associates were made partners and given shares in the company) was implemented along with a sales award and recognition program. Also, weekly development

	Pre-1994	*1995 to 1996*	*1997 to 2000*
New stores/year	N/A	25	20
New store average sales	$1 million	$0.7 million	$1.2 million
Versus comparable store sales year ago	3%	−20%	+15%

Exhibit 2   Sales Turnaround

conference calls between senior management and the district sales managers and training managers were set up for the purpose of constant updates and to facilitate group learning. Finally, a manager/assistant training program was tested in the U.S. in early 1998.[1]

The 1998 shift back to commission caused another huge turnover in BTG stores. This was unfortunate, because, from a staffing perspective, BTG had still not fully recovered from the previous compensation change. The need for additional staff was further aggravated due to BTG's continued push for growth and the tight U.S and Canadian labor markets (four per cent unemployment) in which it operated.

Another concern was that a commission-based compensation structure would not work in the U.S. Martin explained:

> The U.S. folks seemed uncomfortable with 100 per cent commission. They seem to prefer a straight wage or salary. Thus, we have not figured out our compensation system, but for now, it's largely commission based. We know that for the people who are good, they will figure out what they need and go get it. Commission for us is like an insurance policy on our hires—the better you are the more you make. If you don't like servicing the customers, you leave.

Along with the reversion to the proven BTG compensation structure, Blinds To Go emphasized the practice of promoting their managers from within. Senior management believed that sales

managers had to be properly motivated and provided them with a combination of store sales commission and opportunities for rapid advancement in the growing organization. However, being a top salesperson did not necessarily guarantee promotion, as Blinds To Go also looked at a matrix of sales, drive, presence, and people skills. Martin explained: "So even with the top salespeople, they have to be solid in their other attributes to be chosen for management. If the person is driven, he or she will ask for what it takes to be promoted."

ATTRACTING QUALITY RETAIL SALES CANDIDATES

BTG was looking for people who possessed certain sales-driven qualities. Martin explained:

> We look for people who have the "gift of the gab," no ego, are honest, like sales, are driven and hungry for an opportunity, and have good leadership and good people skills. People have to possess these core values. We're partners—we want other people who want to be our partners. We pay for performance. You bet on yourself. You get rewarded because you're performing. Entry-level sales associates get 1,000 stock options after 90-days. At another successful retailer start-up that has since gone public, their people only received 500 options each.

Having recognized that quality of staff was paramount, BTG devoted resources to ensure that it hired the right people as it was estimated that 80 per cent of their expansion needs would be for new U.S. stores. BTG store staff was very diverse. In terms of gender, it was a 50/50 split between men and women. Among associates, high school was the most common education level, followed by college students, then college graduates. In Ontario, Canada, 20 per cent of the associates were recent immigrants who had college or professional qualifications. The average age of associates was distributed over a typical bell curve between the ages of 18 to 50.

Over the last few years, BTG had tried several recruiting methods to varying degrees of success. There were several formal and informal programs that worked to entice qualified personnel to apply to BTG.

Employee Referral

Having current staff refer friends and family to BTG seemed to be the most effective way to attract a candidate already briefed on the BTG concept. A recent addition to create an incentive to refer was the "BMW" contest where staff could win the use of a BMW car for a year if they referred 10 eventual hires that stayed for at least three months. Employee referrals alone did not currently satisfy BTG's hiring needs.

Internet Sourcing

BTG used the Internet in two ways: BTG solicited résumés at its blindstogo.com site; DSMs and recruiters actively searched online job sites like Monster.com and other job sites to contact potential candidates.

DSM Compensation Readjustment

To put more emphasis on staffing in early 2000, DSMs' incentive bonus was changed from a sales target to new staff quota target. Historically, district sales managers had received an incentive bonus based on sales. Thus, a large part of the DSM's role had evolved to include recruiting responsibilities—the DSM now had to hire 10 new sales associates a month.

BTG Retail Recruiters

Professional recruiters were hired in early February 1998 and had been paid annual salaries ranging from $30,000 to $60,000. Recruiters generate leads through cold calls (in-person and via telephone), networking referrals, colleges, job fairs, the Internet, and employment centres. Even though they were given some training and recruiting objectives, the initial recruiters had averaged around four hires per month (against the company objective of four hires a week). "Overall, the performance was sub-optimal," lamented Martin. "By paying them a base salary, we divorced performance from pay and they became administrators." For recruiters, a switch was made in early 2000 to a mix of salary and commission. "They will still need to average four hires a week—but we've increased our training and the 'per hire' commission will focus them on results," Martin concluded.

Newspaper Advertising

BTG used weekly newspaper advertising for nine months starting in mid-1998. Although this method generated a sufficient number of candidate leads, senior management believed that this medium did not generate the quality of candidates that it needed—newspaper advertising attracted people who did not possess the skills and core values that BTG was looking for.

Store Generated Leads

Each BTG had a "help wanted" sign on its window, and walk-in traffic, along with customer referrals, resulted in some sales associates becoming hired. Overall, this was very successful only in stores located in densely populated areas with foot traffic.

THE HIRING PROCESS AT BLINDS TO GO

Once potential candidates were persuaded to apply, a store visit was arranged. The purpose of this visit was to acquaint the potential candidates with the BTG environment and for them to get an overview of the job of a sales associate. Subsequently, the DSM administered a telephone interview. If the candidates were selected to proceed beyond this screen, two additional face-to-face interviews awaited them—one with the DSM and another with the store manager. BTG hired associates against these six criteria:

1. "Gift for Gab"
2. Outgoing personality
3. Energetic and motivated
4. Honest
5. Likes sales or dealing with people
6. Positive

If the candidate was selected to be a sales associate, then references were checked and offers extended.

THE RESULTS OF HIRING PROCEDURES

Before collecting data, it was the impression of senior management at BTG that the most effective method of attracting quality candidates was employee referral, followed by Internet sourcing, and then DSM recruitment. To confirm their suspicions, BTG tracked the yield of different hiring methods for June and July 2000 and, as of the end of July, had these results to show:

Recruiting Method	June	July	Total (2 mth)
Cold Call (Recruiters)	9	0	9
Walk-Ins	31	16	47
Internet	9	3	12
Employee Referral	39	20	59
DSM Hires (Direct/Rehires/College)	8	8	16
Total	**96**	**47**	**143**

Martin explained that the highest ratio of leads to hire was in the employee referrals. This was partially attributed to the fact that referrals generally pursued employment with BTG, excited by the opportunity that a friend or family member who was a BTG employee had recounted. Cold calling was thought to have the lowest close rate because the recruiter had to first educate, then convince potential recruits. But cold calling was thought to be time-efficient if the recruiter was good. Recruiters were focused on non-store sources (cold calling, Internet, schools, etc), store sources (store walk-ins and employee referrals) were handled by the DSM. Recruiters were now paid $20,000 a year with a bonus of $150 to $500 for each successful hire, defined as a hire who stayed at least three months.

STAFF TURNOVER

BTG also began tracking staff turnover and had created a turnover list from existing data. A large percentage of staff voluntary turnover occurred in their first four months. The higher turnover after eight months was partly due to termination because of sales underperformance. Also, sales associates who were not progressing as fast as their peers would inevitably be dissatisfied, leaving for other jobs.

BLINDS TO GO FUTURE NEEDS

BTG needed these additional staff to proceed with its expansion plan of 50 stores per year and to fill current store requirements.

Number of staff leaving and length of stay (numbers from June and July 2000)

Length of Stay	1 to 4 Months	5 to 8 Months	8+ Months
Total	**29**	**12**	**13**

Position	Current Complement	Extra Personnel Needed for Expansion (per year)
Sales Associate	1,000	500
Selling Supervisor	150	50
Asst. Store Manager	150	50
Store Manager	150	50

Udofia had one more pressing concern on his mind:

We're planning an initial public offering in the next one to two years. The key to our success is our ability to recruit and develop enough people to meet our growth objectives.

He wondered what strategy he should follow to meet the staffing challenge ahead.

NOTE

1. This program eventually evolved into the Legends Training Program, where the best training managers at BTG were relocated to new regions to motivate, train and coach new store employees.

FIVE STAR BEER—PAY FOR PERFORMANCE

Prepared by Tom Gleave under the supervision of Professor Brian Golden

Version: (A) 1998-10-08

In June 1997, Tom McMullen (President—Alliance Brewing Group) and Zhao Hui Shen (General Manager—Five Star Brewing Co. Ltd) met to discuss the "pay for performance" systems which Zhao had been implementing at Five Star's two breweries over the past several months. McMullen needed to determine whether or not these incentive systems were properly designed to ensure that the breweries would produce higher quality beer at progressively lower costs. If not, he needed to consider how he might suggest that these and other systems be changed in order to achieve Alliance Brewing's cost and quality objectives.

FIVE STAR'S ASIMCO CONNECTION

The majority owner of Beijing Asia Shuang He Sheng Five Star Brewing Co. Ltd. (Five Star) was the Beijing-based investment group, Asian Strategic Investments Corporation (ASIMCO). The primary shareholders of ASIMCO were Trust Company West, Morgan Stanley—Dean Witter Reynolds and senior management. The senior management team consisted of the following people:

Jack Perkowski (Chairman and CEO)—a former investment chief at Paine Webber (New York City) and graduate of both Yale University (cum laude) and the Harvard Business School (Baker Scholar).

Tim Clissold (President)—a physics graduate from Cambridge University who turned accountant with Arthur Anderson in the 1980s. Clissold had worked in England, Australia, China and Hong Kong for Anderson before entering London's School of Oriental and Asian Studies where he became fluent in both spoken and written Mandarin.

Michael Cronin (Chief Investment and Financial Officer)—also worked as an accountant for Arthur Anderson throughout the 1980s in Australia, the UK and Hong Kong. Previously, Cronin had worked for over five years at 3i, Europe's largest direct investment organization.

Ai Jian (Managing Director)—a Chinese native and graduate from Northwestern Polytechnical University in Xian, China. Ai's previous working experience included senior posts in the foreign relations department of China's Ministry of Foreign Trade and Economic Cooperation. He was a native Mandarin speaker and also fluent in English.

The motivations underlying ASIMCO's investment in the Chinese beer industry were twofold. First, the industry was experiencing high, sustainable growth rates. This high growth was spurred by the increasing levels of disposable incomes in China, to the point where it was expected that the Chinese beer market would become the world's largest (overtaking the U.S.A) within the next several years. Second, the industry was highly fragmented and was undergoing a significant restructuring. This high degree of fragmentation was a consequence of China's legacy

of central planning. Given its increasing adoption of market-driven mechanisms, China's central government was encouraging (or passively allowing) the rationalization of certain industries, including the beer industry. The industry consensus was that the number of breweries was expected to be reduced from over 800 to less than 600 nationwide over the next several years while managing to steadily increase overall beer volume. This meant that surviving firms would need to seek economies of scale, maintain high quality production and ensure development of strong management teams as the competition intensified.

ASIMCO's investment strategy was to identify Chinese companies that had the potential to be globally competitive and to support these firms with capital, western management skills and leading-edge technologies. The partners they sought were expected to be aggressive, profit-oriented and industry leaders. Whenever a potential opportunity was discovered, ASIMCO would marshal its skills and international resources to perform due diligence, negotiate contracts and obtain necessary approvals. ASIMCO would subsequently provide capital, western management expertise and technological know-how to the joint venture and devise an exit strategy designed to realize the value created.

ASIMCO viewed itself as an agent of change in helping to transform formerly inefficient state-owned enterprises into market-driven and export-ready competitive firms. By June 1997, ASIMCO had entered into 13 automotive parts manufacturing, two automotive parts distribution and two beer manufacturing joint ventures. The sum total of these investments, all of which were majority positions, was about U.S. $360 million. All minority positions were held by various Chinese partners. The Five Star joint venture was ASIMCO's largest single investment in its portfolio with a total capital outlay of U.S. $70 million for a 63 per cent stake in the company. The minority interest partner was the First Light Industry Bureau (FLIB) with a 37 per cent stake. The FLIB was a division of the Beijing municipal government and had ownership

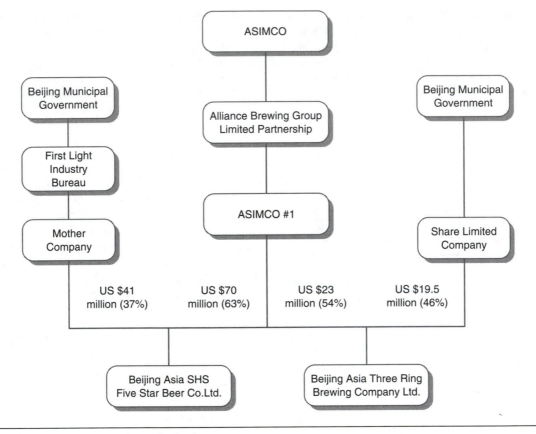

Exhibit 1   ASIMCO's Ownership in Brewing Joint Ventures

interests in many diverse business activities. ASMICO's other joint venture in brewing was a 54 per cent interest in the Three Ring Beer Company, an investment valued at U.S. $23 million. Both of the brewing joint ventures were formalized in January 1995. (See Exhibit 1— ASIMCO's Ownership in Brewing Joint Ventures.)

ALLIANCE BREWING GROUP

Alliance Brewing Group (ABG) was a management services group which was specifically established to provide support to both of ASIMCO's brewery joint ventures. This gave ABG the mandate to support three different, yet related, brewing facilities. These breweries were as follows:

Brewery	Owner	Annual Capacity
Shuang Sheng	Five Star	90,000 tons
Huadu	Five Star	180,000 tons
San Huan	Three Ring	130,000 tons

Note: Total production for the three breweries was currently running at about 250,000 tons per year.

ABG was organized into separate corporate level support functions which included marketing, brewing and quality control, operations services, financial control and new business development. The President of ABG was Tom McMullen, an American expatriate who formerly worked in the consumer packaged goods business in the U.S. after graduating from the Wharton School of Business. (See Exhibit 2—ABG Partial Organization Chart.)

The overall goal of ABG was to help both brewing companies realize their return on invested capital targets. With respect to Five Star, this was expected to be accomplished through the achievement of five key objectives, which included (in order of priority) the following:

1. improved product and packaging quality.

2. reduced production costs in an effort to gain better margins.

3. the development of professional sales, marketing and distribution systems.

4. the development of a system which rewarded good performance and punished bad performance.

5. an increased understanding between Five Star's two breweries that separate production facilities did not mean separate companies. Rather, they were part of the same brewing company.

According to McMullen, one of the more meaningful signs of progress that ABG was able to make over the past year was the development of rational and integrated financial reporting systems. These new systems took more than one year to develop but eventually allowed both Chinese and expatriate managers to "talk from the same page." As evidence of the importance of the need for reliable and timely financial

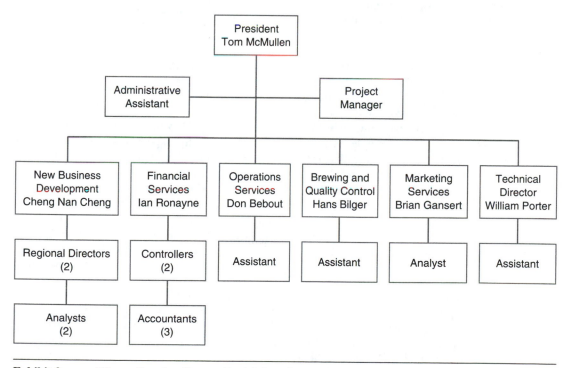

Exhibit 2   Alliance Brewing Group—Partial Organization Chart

information, particularly with respect to the need for Chinese management to understand the importance of meeting budgeted targets, ABG had installed its own financial personnel at both of its beer companies.

FIVE STAR'S RECENT HISTORY

Five Star was one of the oldest brewing companies in China, with its origins dating back to 1915. Like most breweries in China, Five Star originally served its local markets, the main one being Beijing and the surrounding Hebei province. This focus on local markets developed as a consequence of competing interests from local governments which, in turn, led to the industry's fragmented structure. Over the years, however, Five Star was able to gain some market share in areas beyond the immediate region. This market penetration was accomplished through the establishment of licensing agreements between Five Star and other regional brewers throughout the country.

Prior to the early 1990s, the company enjoyed a majority share of the local Beijing market. This market position had developed because Five Star had a lengthy history in the region and, as a state enterprise which was wholly owned by the Beijing municipal government, was conferred special privileges. For example, in 1957, Chinese Premier Zhou Enlai decreed that Five Star was to be the exclusive beer supplied at all State banquets, thus bringing the company name to national prominence.

By the early 1990s, Five Star's market position began to deteriorate as it found itself competing in the same territories in the Beijing area with one of its largest licensees, Three Ring Beer. In 1993, Five Star entered into a licensing agreement which allowed Three Ring to produce and market Five Star beer for sale in specific territories on the northeastern outskirts of Beijing. However, Five Star soon found that Three Ring was "stealing" sales by deliberately encroaching on Five Star's exclusive territories within the core areas of the city. Three Ring was successful in securing significant market share due to its offer of lower pricing (for virtually the same products) and the lack of wholesaler and retailer loyalty. ASIMCO acquired a majority stake in both brewing companies in January 1995. This left ABG with the challenge of ensuring that the two companies refrain from directly competing with each other.

The progressive intrusion by Three Ring was compounded by the deteriorating quality of Five Star's products. It was only after it acquired ownership control that ASIMCO discovered that Five Star was experiencing greater quality difficulties than originally thought. Perhaps most disturbing of all was the consistently poor performance and apathetic attitude of Mr. Xu, Five Star's former General Manager. According to Tom McMullen:

> Xu was completely lacking in competence in virtually all respects. He was simply a victim of the old state-enterprise culture which encouraged senior managers to have a minimum of initiative and innovation. He perceived himself to be a king in his castle, while ABG in general, and me in particular, were seen as interlopers. Unfortunately for him, he discovered the hard way that his position was less secure than he believed.

Admittedly, McMullen had much less control than he originally expected when he signed on with Five Star. Having worked in the U.S for over 20 years, McMullen was accustomed to the idea that employees could be hired, disciplined and terminated as deemed necessary. However, in China, such activities were regulated to a much greater extent and often involved political considerations. For example, the person in charge of the human resource management and training functions at Five Star was Mr. Qi, resident member of the Communist Party of China. (See Exhibit 3—Five Star Beer Organization Chart; See also Appendix: Labour Market Conditions and Human Resource Development Practices in China.)

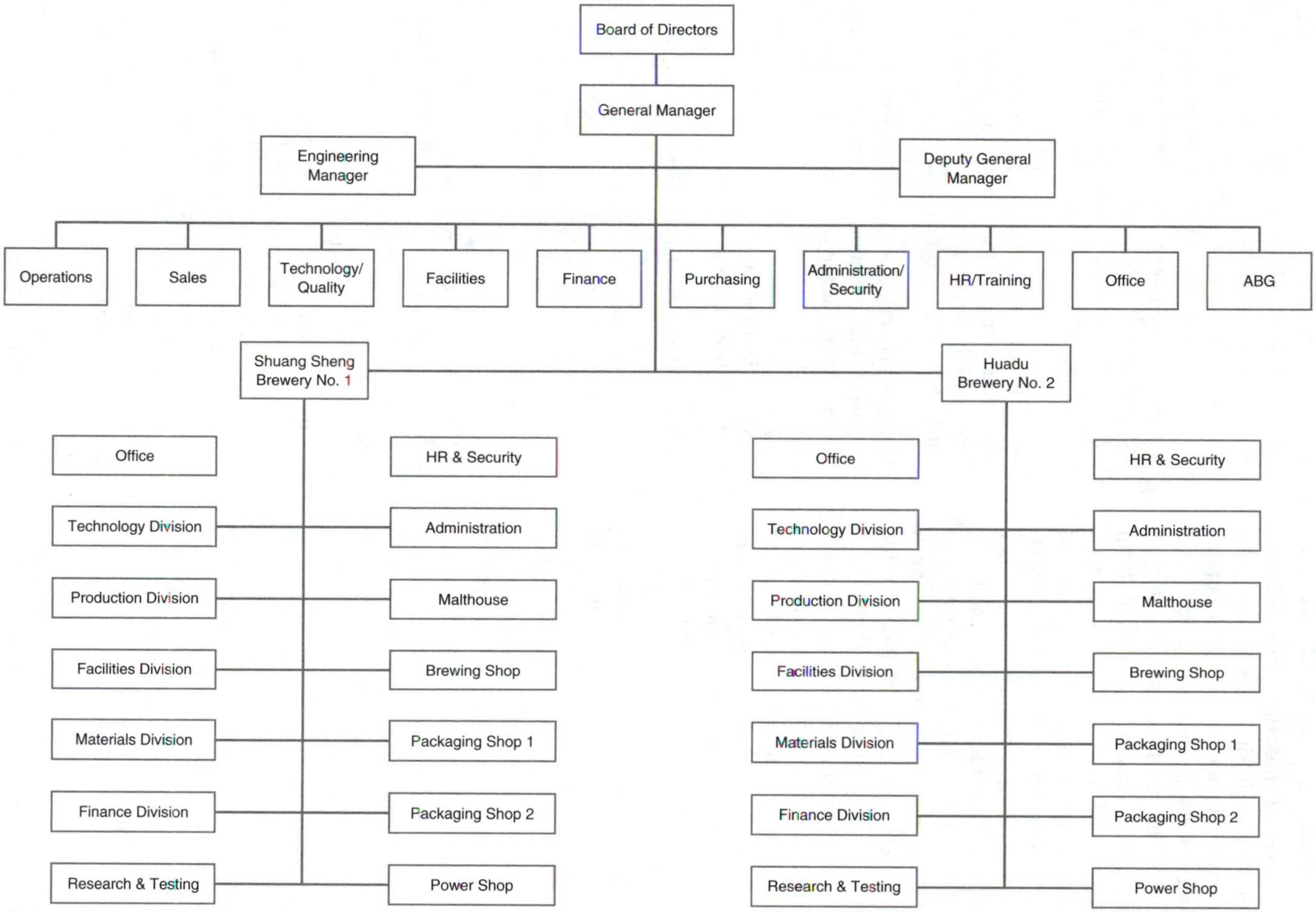

Exhibit 3 Five Star Beer Organization Chart

THE IMPERATIVE FOR QUALITY

The high degree of industry consolidation, coupled with increasing Sino-foreign joint venture activity involving numerous world famous beer companies (such as Heineken, Beck's and Budweiser), meant that Five Star was beginning to experience greater competition from very capable rivals. This created a critical need for Five Star to provide higher quality beer and packaging. The common criteria by which product quality was evaluated included consistency in taste, clarity, carbonation, fill levels and labelling. The challenge of achieving consistency across all of these quality dimensions was great. Numerous incidences of foreign matter inside bottles, as well as unfilled or short-filled bottles and cans, had been documented. Many packaging issues had also been identified and typically included poorly labelled or poorly sealed bottles and cans. One particularly poignant incident occurred shortly after the joint venture was formed and signalled to ASIMCO and ABG the need for drastically improving Five Star's quality. In this instance, a customer found a bottle which was half-full that had been released with a ripped label that was glued on sideways, despite having passed at least four inspection workers. Upon hearing the news of this episode, Tim Clissold (ASIMCO President) declared:

> It is beyond rational thought how our workers allowed this bottle to be sent out for public consumption. And when inquiries were made as to how this type of thing could happen, the line manager simply laughed with embarrassment. This is the result of the old central planning mentality in which there was no connection between reward and effort. These workers had no proper incentive or disincentive to ensure full product quality. The workers could not be fined or punished, nor were they entitled to extra wages for extra work completed.

The bottle in question was permanently displayed in ASIMCO and ABG's combined offices as a reminder of the need for ensuring diligence at every stage of the production and marketing process.

After realizing that quality issues facing Five Star were considerable, ASIMCO and ABG moved quickly to resolve the problems. ABG's professional staff was to focus on reducing costs, but a priority emphasis was placed on quality. Three key brewing professionals, the only non-Chinese to take an active role at any of the breweries, led the effort. They were:

> Don Bebout (VP—Operations Services), an American with over 19 years of experience working for Miller Brewing. He was particularly skilled in the areas of packaging and labelling.

> Hans Bilger (Master Brewer & ABG's Quality Manager) had a lifetime of brewing experience. In his native Germany, he grew up helping his father run a family-owned brewery before embarking for the U.S. where he spent nearly 30 years involved in a variety of positions, both with U.S. brewing giants and microbreweries.

> William Porter (Technical Director) was also an industry veteran from the U.S. where he worked for over 20 years at such breweries as Miller, Lone Star and Pabst. Although Porter's "home" brewery was with the Three Ring brewing joint venture, he was often called upon to offer technical advice to Five Star.

These three ex-pats were each provided with dedicated assistants, all of whom were fluently bilingual. This assistance was essential since none of the three ex-pats spoke Mandarin. Among the three assistants, Zhou Yue reported directly to Don Bebout and held a graduate degree in fermentology. She had previously worked for several years at China's National Institute for Food and Fermentology. Similarly, Bi Hong, assistant to Bilger, was a genetics technologist and had also worked for the National Institute for Food and Fermentalogy. She also received 13 months of brewery training while studying in France.

A major concern of ABG's operations and quality staff was the need to achieve higher quality targets while "milking" the existing equipment.

When ASIMCO took its majority stake in Five Star, the company was believed to possess some of the best equipment of any brewery in China, although some of it required refurbishing due to lack of regular maintenance. Given the recent influx of well-funded foreign brewers, Five Star appeared to be at a technological disadvantage when it came to ensuring product and packaging quality.

The Need for Management Control and Motivation

Regarding the level of management control and commitment that is necessary for ensuring consistent quality, Hans Bilger (Master Brewer) offered the following remarks:

> The skills needed to produce quality beer on a consistent basis are minimal. What you need are the monitoring procedures, the discipline to adhere to those procedures and the clear reporting of information to the appropriate people. The tasks of monitoring operations, recording data and communicating results on a regular basis are not sophisticated. The problems arise when management does not take control by ensuring that procedures are followed or that information is shared. For example, line workers are expected to regularly record the temperatures in the brewing vats. This is done often enough, but the results are frequently not communicated to the people who use this information. This is a symptom of the silo mentality around here. There really is no cross-functional coordination. And in the event that any results are communicated, you end up getting what you want to hear and not the real story, even when there is a problem. This shows that our quality problems are management-related and that the senior managers at the brewery need to become committed to quality.

> Quality is a way of life. It is a mindset. The senior managers at the brewery have yet to fully understand these concepts. Part of the problem could be that they are rewarded on volume output, not quality output. This is because brewing in China is a low margin business and, therefore, breweries need to pump out the volume in order to make any profits. This means that some managers are reluctant to take

any measures which will impede their ability to produce as much as they can.

Ideally, I would like to see Five Star have an independent quality department reporting directly to the General Manager, not to the Deputy GM and Chief Engineer as is now the case—despite what the formal organization chart suggests. Both the "Number 1" and "Number 2" breweries would have their own divisional labs which would feed their results to Five Star's quality assurance office on a regular basis. This quality assurance department would also be given policeman-like powers. Someone has to be able to say "this is not good enough," and then have the authority to take corrective action. Unfortunately, this type of arrangement goes against the strong tradition of hierarchical reporting in China.

Hiring Mr. Zhao

In response to the need to replace Mr. Xu, and after a thorough recruiting process, ASIMCO and ABG agreed to hire Zhao Hui Shen. Mr. Zhao, formerly a factory manager at a piano manufacturing plant where he had worked for over 20 years, came highly recommended by the FLIB. Clissold was skeptical about hiring Zhao due to his obvious lack of brewing industry experience. However, Zhao won Clissold's confidence when confronted about this apparent liability by stating that, "you will not hire me to make the beer, you will hire me to manage the people who make the beer."

Zhao was expected to work impartially for the Five Star joint venture company. He was also expected to draw upon the resources of ABG in an effort to improve the overall quality and productivity of Five Star's brewing operations. Within the joint venture company, Zhao reported to the Board of Directors. The Board's membership consisted of Jack Perkowski, Ai Jian, Tom McMullen, Mr. Zhao and a representative from the FLIB.

Zhao was viewed by many others at ABG and Five Star as representing a new generation of Chinese manager. This was because he had taken a very aggressive and hands-on approach to managing the business, a style which was a distinct departure from the state-owned enterprise culture of the past. Zhao commented:

> You have to change the way of thinking from traditional enterprise methods. Nowadays we must think of management by objective. I want people to think about how they can achieve their goals, not how to waste time thinking of excuses for not achieving them and then relying on the government for money.

Zhao's Performance-Related Pay Systems

One of ABG's key objectives was to help the breweries adopt a "pay for performance" culture. ABG believed that it must try to get people to care about their work and about themselves, particularly since jobs were taking on an entirely new role in Chinese life. ABG was seeking to instill a culture which would see employees take greater control over their destinies.

When it came time (in January 1997) to begin the development of specific pay for performance systems, Zhao requested the assistance of ABG. However, ABG was unable to offer extensive support at that time due to limited resources and its other priorities. In March 1997, ABG offered to assist Zhao in developing the systems, but Zhao then declined the offer because he did not want ABG to change what he had already initiated. He did, however, offer to reveal his key objectives to ABG. This led McMullen to acknowledge that the issue of establishing a pay for performance system may have been a higher priority for Zhao than it was for himself.

In developing the compensation systems, Zhao believed that monetary punishment could be used as a strong incentive for better performance, something McMullen referred to as "using more stick than carrot." One such example of this approach involved the bottle-filling line, where one of the key measures of quality was to ensure that all bottles were filled to the proper level. To ensure that properly filled bottles were distributed from the brewery, each filling line was assigned two people to manually check for empty bottles, while four additional people were used to manually check for short-fills. When the bottles were filled they were date-stamped and coded so that the product could be traced to its original filling and labelling lines. In the event that a empty or short-filled product was found in the marketplace (whether it be by Five Star's sales people, distributors or final customers), all six people on the originating filling line would be fined a total of 500 renminbi, or about 83 Rmb each.[1] This fine would be deducted from their salaries in which each line worker received an average compensation of about 1000 Rmb per month, an amount which was almost double that of similar positions in Chinese wholly owned breweries.

There was some debate in the plant as to whether or not this was an effective system. Hans Bilger (Master Brewer) felt that this approach was too harsh. He believed that, at a filling rate of 12,000 bottles per hour over a six-hour shift, the employees would become too tired to identify all empty bottles or shortfills. On the other hand, Yang Xiang, a bilingual technician working for the Operations Service group, felt that this type of system was "to some extent fair." He felt that somebody must take responsibility for these types of errors and that it might be more effective if the line supervisors were fined, not just the line workers.

Another example of a disincentive for poor performance involved a fine levied on the brew house for poor sanitation in the rice mill under its responsibility. The beer that Five Star brewed typically consisted of 30 per cent rice grain and 70 per cent malt. A rice mill was utilized on-site to provide the appropriate supplies. A common problem in the mill was the high level of dustiness, due primarily to the lack of care in cleaning, as well as an occasionally malfunctioning dust collection system. This presented a danger of insect infestation which, apart from affecting beer quality, also posed a threat of flammable explosion. In the spring of 1997, after Bilger submitted one of his periodic inspection reports which gave the mill a failing grade, seven line workers in the mill and associated brew house were deducted 100 Rmb each from their next pay cheque. As was the case in the previous example, the affected employees also earned 1000 Rmb per month.

One of Zhao's more widely discussed systems involved the sales force. Given that Five Star was seeking to re-establish its market position within the greater Beijing area, a strong emphasis was placed on boosting sales and thus increasing market share. Although sales people began by earning a starting salary of only 600 Rmb per month, they could earn up to 10 times this amount depending upon their sales performance. Unfortunately, Mr. Zhao had encountered some difficulty recruiting people who were prepared to receive compensation based largely upon their own efforts. Additionally, there were widely held suspicions among some of the ABG operations and quality staff that this particular system had invited abuse in the proper recording of sales. Although these staffers had "heard rumors" of this type activity, they had no concrete evidence. Any inquiries about the company's latest sales performance were met with "stony silence."

The implementation of Zhao's various performance-related pay schemes had given rise to a general debate among ABG's operations staff. The nature of the debate centered around which direction or approach would best motivate employees to strive for quality. The divergent views expressed by the operations staff were highlighted by the contrasting opinions between William Porter and Hans Bilger. Porter contended that cash payouts were a more effective incentive for improving performance than the recognition for a job well done. He believed that the employees would "far sooner have more renminbi in their jeans than a pat on the back." Bilger, on the other hand, suggested that pride of workmanship and the recognition of a job well done were more powerful motivators than cash rewards. His reasoning was that China was a status-conscious society where a high value was placed on securing the favorable opinion of one's peers and superiors. Despite a significant amount of spirited discussion, no clear consensus had emerged among ABG's operations staff as to whose view was more compelling.

DECISION

The next Board meeting was scheduled for mid-July 1997, at which time McMullen wished to offer the members an update on the design and implementation of the pay for performance systems at Five Star. Therefore, as McMullen contemplated how he might suggest to Zhao different ways for improving these systems, he needed to consider several important factors. First and foremost, he needed to consider the cultural, historical, social and business contexts in which Five Star and ABG found themselves. McMullen was keenly aware that the receptivity to pay for performance systems was only beginning to be slowly accepted in China. Moreover, he needed to recognize the far greater knowledge that Zhao possessed about Chinese behavioral habits and culture. Therefore, he could not presume that what would be effective in North America would be effective in China. McMullen was also intrigued by the debates which had surfaced among his own operations staff. Did the notion of "punishments" have some merit in China? Would workers respond most to cash rewards or were they more likely to be motivated by some form of recognition? The only thing which seemed clear to McMullen was that the motivation and quality problems had no easy solutions.

NOTE

1. The June 1997 exchange rate was about 8.28 Rmb = U.S. $1.00.

APPENDIX: LABOR MARKET CONDITIONS AND HUMAN RESOURCE DEVELOPMENT PRACTICES IN CHINA

China's labor market in 1997 was experiencing significant structural changes as market-oriented reforms took hold. State policy efforts to establish a new social welfare system and to implement state-owned enterprise (SOE) reform have had a profound effect on labor market conditions and human resource management practices in both domestic and foreign-funded enterprises. The first national labor law came into effect in 1995 and brought with it a lower level of government intervention in human resource management (HRM) at the enterprise level and more equal treatment for domestic and foreign enterprises. It is expected that this law will eventually allow all types of firms to acquire greater control over wage setting as well as the power to hire, discipline and dismiss workers, areas which have traditionally been highly regulated by government. In the meantime, China's labor market remains under-developed: labor mobility is restricted, and HRM is a new concept. Therefore, both domestic and foreign enterprises are now operating in a highly uncertain environment which reflects a combination of the old planned economy practices with those of newer western approaches to HRM.

In 1994, China's labor force totalled 615 million, or approximately 51 per cent of the country's total population of 1.2 billion. This labor force is expected to grow by an average of 20.9 million persons per year between 1995 and 2006. Importantly, no national social welfare system has been established in China. Social welfare has traditionally been the responsibility of the SOEs, the dominant form of industrial organization in the Chinese economy since the "liberation" of 1949.

However, as market forces take greater hold in China, the SOEs will find it increasingly difficult to maintain these responsibilities for delivering a wide range of social services including subsidized housing, education and health care.

Until recently, HRM in China has been defined by the tenure employment structure of the planned economy. In the old SOE system, labor was regarded as a passive input in the production process rather than a productive factor. As a result, traditional human resource management included only personnel administration activities, such as registering the recruited workers, recording increases in wages and promotions (by seniority), filing job changes, and maintaining workers' files. Although training was provided, most of it involved indoctrinating workers with the Communist Party's prevailing policies. The focus was on the use of workers rather than their career development. Compensation was not directly linked to performance and served as little incentive for better performance. From an enterprise's overall performance perspective, it is clear that these practices were not aligned with a strategy to be productive and competitive in a market-oriented economy.

Source: The Conference Board of Canada, Opportunities and Risks for Canadian Business in China. 1996.

JINJIAN GARMENT FACTORY: MOTIVATING GO-SLOW WORKERS

Prepared by
Tieying Huang, Junping Liang
and Paul W. Beamish

Version: (A) 2004-05-21

On December 15, 1999, at 11 p.m., Mr. Lou Baijin, the owner and managing director of Jinjian Garment Factory, was still in his Shenzhen office in deep thought and red-eyed

from lack of sleep. In the adjacent workshop were more than 200 of his factory workers. Like Mr. Lou, they had been working 12 hours a day for seven days, non-stop, in order to finish in time a large Christmas order for an important European customer. From his experience, Mr. Lou could tell from the speed and sound of the sewing machines in the workshop that the workers had slowed their pace. Although they might be tired because of the long hours of overtime they had worked the last week, it was more likely that their slowness was deliberate. As a general practice in this industry, the workers had a tendency to slow their working pace in order to force management to increase the price of their piecework. If the orders were not delivered on time, Mr. Lou would have to ship the order by air freight at extra expense or risk losing valuable customers. The question of how to motivate workers, which had haunted Mr. Lou for a long time, became more urgent now. When he glanced at the entrepreneurship book, which had been on his desk for more than a month and which he had read several times, Mr. Lou forced a smile and painfully realized that the book had not provided a solution.

LOU BAIJIN AND HIS GARMENT FACTORY

Mr. Lou was born in the town of Louta in Zhejiang province in 1956. He graduated from junior high school in 1973 and was expected to make his living as a farmer. In 1976, he became a mineworker in a neighboring province. Then, in the early 1980s, Mr. Lou returned to his home town and became a salesman. He travelled extensively in China to promote the use of raw chemical materials for the enterprise sponsored by his village.

In 1991, Mr. Lou came to Shenzhen (the most prominent special economic zone of China) and searched for jobs there. He wasn't very lucky at first. In order to save on living expenses, he lived on two boxes of fast food each day for half a year. Mr. Lou finally became a commission-based salesman for an electronic factory.

By 1996, manufacturing costs in Shenzhen for garments were very high; consequently, many factories migrated to the hinterland of Mainland China. Unlike those factories' owners, Mr. Lou saw an opportunity. He took his life savings and

bought 30 secondhand sewing machines at a very low price and established his first factory in Shenzhen.

In the beginning, the factory employed about 50 workers. The main business came from taking small orders, as a subcontractor, from larger factories that had direct access to Hong Kong and overseas garment buyers. Mr. Lou's business grew very fast from that point forward. By 1999, Mr. Lou's factory had 150 sewing machines and more than 250 workers and had begun to compete directly with surrounding factories for the orders of Hong Kong and overseas customers.

THE GARMENT MANUFACTURING INDUSTRY IN SHENZHEN

Shenzhen was one of the most advanced garment manufacturing centres in the world. Garments produced there were sold at department stores in many upscale locales, including Bloomingdale's and Nordstrom in the United States. The garment manufacturing industry had prospered along with the development of the Shenzhen special economic zone during China's broad economic reforms that began in 1980. Hong Kong was the centre of the world garment-manufacturing industry during the 1980s and 1990s. When China opened its economic door to foreign investment, Shenzhen was the first place in China for Hong Kong garment manufacturers to transfer this labor-intensive industry. Hong Kong had been gradually losing its competitive advantages to other Southeast Asian countries because of the increased production costs there.

Shenzhen was inexpensive in terms of land and labor but also manageable since it was a neighbor of Hong Kong, and people spoke the same language. Hong Kong business people could go to work in Shenzhen as commuters because of the location and convenient transportation.

In less then a decade, more than a thousand garment factories were established in Shenzhen. The majority of the garment factories were either owned or managed by Hong Kong residents. The Shenzhen garment industry was literally a direct extension of the Hong Kong garment industry.

WORKING ENVIRONMENT

Hong Kong was a capitalist society known in Mainland China for its minimal social welfare and labor protection laws. Because Hong Kong was the model of the Shenzhen garment industry, the management system of the garment industry in Shenzhen copied the factory environment found in Hong Kong in the 1970s. These were known as "sweatshops" by economists and sociologists.

Workers in the Shenzhen garment industry were willing to work overtime during the peak season, and the average workday was more than 12 hours. The workers rested for only one or two days each month during the six-month peak season because they were able to work only four to five hours per day, if at all, during the slow season. Over 90 per cent of the wages were based on piecework performance, which closely linked individual effort and reward. Because the other 10 per cent of wages given by the employers, (such as food subsidy, holiday allowance and special bonus for overtime) barely covered the living expenses for workers themselves, the piecework wage fostered strong motivation for workers to work long and fast. The laws for minimum wage and labor protection in China had been established for less than a decade and had not been strictly adhered to because of the difficulty of enforcement, especially in private sectors such as the garment industry. In particular, 95 per cent of the garment workers in Shenzhen were peasants who did not have permanent residency status in the city. (China was one of the few countries in the world with a resident permit system among its citizens.) If a person was not a permanent resident, it was virtually impossible to get social welfare or labor protection from the local government.

The average monthly income for a skilled garment worker in Shenzhen was US$150 during the peak season. The average living accommodation for each person was three to four square metres, with usually eight or more people sharing one room. In spite of such conditions, the promise of a job in the industry still attracted many peasants to Shenzhen. In fact, some workers even gave monetary deposits to their factory just to retain the opportunity to work. Once they found a job in Shenzhen, most did not choose to raise a family there since they could not afford the high living cost. Instead, they went back to their home province after eight to 10 years of hard work in Shenzhen, and their savings enabled them to build a new house and live a relatively easy life.

GARMENT MANUFACTURING

Shenzhen garment manufacturing was a labor-intensive industry with a relatively low capital investment required for entry. About 90 per cent of the garment-making equipment in Shenzhen was imported from Japan, but even with the most advanced garment manufacturing equipment, the work still involved a lot of manual labor (sewing, ironing and button tacking, etc), that could not be automated, especially with ladies' clothing, which required more dedication than men's clothing. In most garment-making procedures, workers had to operate the machine by hand. Usually the work was divided into more than 10 procedures to efficiently produce even a simple shirt. Hence, a garment factory needed many workers.

The capital requirement of garment manufacturing was very low compared to the labor requirement. "You can be a boss for only US$5,000," said Mr. Lou. Setting up required a small amount of capital to buy several sewing machines, rent a house (even an apartment) and hire several workers. The industry continued to attract numerous new entrepreneurs.

SEASONALITY AND HIGH WORKFORCE TURNOVER

Although the supply of garment workers was unlimited, some of the workers were unskilled as they were peasants coming straight from the farm. Skilled workers were a valuable and scarce resource during peak time, September to February.

The need for work in the factories was seasonal. During peak time, garment factories in Shenzhen usually work 12 hours a day, 28 days per month to produce clothing for Christmas and spring seasons when consumers purchased most of their wardrobes. During other times of a year, even skilled workers did not have sufficient work.

During the peak season, proficient workers were so scarce that factories would do almost anything to keep them. The factories knew that having more skilled workers would make them more competitive. Therefore, retaining skilled workers was one of the most pressing problems the factories faced. Because of insufficient orders and furious competition in the slow season, factories were usually unprofitable, even when paying minimum wage to workers and this usually meant a bottom-line loss for the company. Large factories with long-term views usually could keep a minimum stable work force during the slow season, while small factories usually closed in order to save costs. The tricky part was that no one could tell for sure whether the losses in the slow season would be recovered during the coming peak season since 90 per cent of the garments produced in Shenzhen were exported to foreign markets, and garment factories in Shenzhen had little knowledge or control over demand.

Many workers had a long holiday during the slow season when they usually went back to their home town. When they came back at the beginning of the peak season, some might find a new job in a different factory if they were not satisfied with the existing one. The turnover rate of the workers was very high because of the unstable nature of the garment industry.

Effective Management of Workers

Production costs, which were derived from cutting, manufacturing and trimming a garment, were known in the trade as CMT. Because of competition within the industry in Shenzhen, the CMT of Shenzhen had decreased almost by half in the past 10 years. Foreign garment buyers usually imported the fabric and provided design patterns for the factories to produce apparel for a particular foreign market. The cost of the fabric was usually higher than the CMT. This put the garment manufacturers in Shenzhen at risk because the expensive fabric could sometimes be destroyed in the process of making a garment, and CMT received from the order was usually not enough to recoup such losses.

Because of the labor-intensive nature of the industry, normally the wage of the workers was about 60 per cent of CMT of a garment, which meant that 60 per cent of the revenue of a garment factory went to workers as wages. Mistakes such as destroying fabric in the garment making process or late shipments meant the owners did not make a profit, since they had to bear the cost of the fabric and high air transportation costs when a job was not completed on time for sea shipment. Therefore, effective management of workers, who not only accounted for 60 per cent of the revenue but who also decided the fate of an order, had become central to survival in the garment-making business.

Because of the nature of the export-oriented garment business in Shenzhen, the normal order size was relatively small, while the number of orders was large. The typical size of a Shenzhen garment factory ranged from 100 to 200 employees, and a typical factory could produce about 200 orders per year. In order to satisfy the most current fashion, most designers liked to alter their patterns at the last minute, which gave the manufacturers very short production lead-times. This meant that the garment factories in Shenzhen had to be able to produce a new style of clothing on an average of every three to four days.

In spite of such a short production time, the factory had to achieve two aims: (1) produce the garment according to a quality standard acceptable to customers, and (2) ship the product on time. (Late fashion is no fashion!) These two factors were also essential for a garment factory to survive.

THE PIECEWORK SYSTEM

The piecework system employed by the factories in Shenzhen was well suited to the nature of the work. For example, the retail price of a lady's dress might be US$30, and the cost of CMT (cutting, making and trimming) for it in Shenzhen might be US$3 (the fabric, accessories and patterns were supplied by the customer). The manufacturing process of this dress had more than 15 procedures, and the three dollars was distributed to the workers first. The price of sewing the collar might be five cents, the price of fitting on a sleeve might be three cents, the ironing of the dress might cost four cents, etc. Each worker was assigned to a specific job and earned an exact amount derived from the number of finished pieces times the price of that particular job to finish the procedure (piecework). One's pay was strictly linked with one's performance. Normally, more skilled and more industrious workers earned more than average workers did.

Due to the nature of division of garment-making processes, a garment factory was made up of several self-contained work units, called production teams, which usually contained 10 to 15 sewing workers and were able to produce a garment independently. A team leader, appointed by management, had absolute authority to assign the different working procedures of making a garment among the team members. Besides the unit price of piecework and the efficiency of a worker, production team leaders might also have some influence on the income of workers, as they could assign good jobs, more often, to their favored team members at the cost of jeopardizing the morale of the teams. This situation was more severe in Shenzhen's garment factories than in other cities because Shenzhen was a migrant city and many factory workers might come from the same village town or may even be related to each other.

After the deductions of the workers' cost, the balance of the US$3 CMT was distributed to the overhead of the factory. What was left was the profit for the factory owner.

DETERMINING THE PRICE OF PIECEWORK

Because each procedure for making a particular style was unique, the price of the same procedure when making a garment could vary. For example, the work required to make a round-shaped collar was different from that of a square-shaped collar so the prices for these two jobs were different. The same worker might earn $0.03 for making one round collar and $0.02 for a square one, although the two jobs belonged to the same production procedure.

Even for the same style of garment, if the order size was different, the price of making the garment might also vary. Generally speaking, productivity was increased when workers became more familiar with a particular garment. Larger orders were easier to produce than smaller ones owing to the learning curve associated with each order. Thus, owners and management (customers also required lower CMT price for larger orders) would lower the piecework price for each production procedure of a larger order and increase the prices when the order was small. The prices might also be different based on different fabrics for the same orders. For example, silk garments were normally more difficult to make than polyester ones.

In theory, if garment factories had enough time and resources, it was possible to accurately predetermine the piecework price of every procedure for every style based on the complexity, average daily salary of workers and the manufacturing efficiency of average workers. This was similar to what Frederick Taylor did in the early 1900s in the United States when he objectively measured the actions necessary for each work task. In reality, until the production of a garment order was finished, it was impossible for a garment factory to make an accurate and fair determination on the piecework price for a procedure due to the nature of the fashion business. This was because the quantity of most of the garment orders was relatively small (which was uneconomical to measure accurately), the short production lead-time of garment manufacturers offered no time for accurate measurement, and non-standard products for each fashion season had too many different styles, which were too difficult to measure reliably.

Therefore, it was a general practice for garment factories in Hong Kong and Shenzhen to decide the piecework price after the completion of an order. Usually at the end of the month, when workers received their salary, they knew the exact price of the piecework for a particular order they had finished.

Though it was difficult to know the exact price of piecework for an order before production, both management and workers, owing to past experience, would have a rough idea of the range for the prices before they began. Thus, how to divide the slim CMT fee of a garment among them was a prime focus of workers and owners, and each side tried to get a larger share because a few cents difference on a piecework price would make a big difference, both to owners and workers.

Because of the norm of "work first; pay later" in this trade, disputes over piecework prices between workers and factory owners happened quite often. Workers always believed management would take advantage of them by lowering the price of their piecework if they worked too fast since no owner was willing to pay more to workers than their market salary.

Yet, the piecework system still did not necessarily favor the factory owners. Workers knew they might offer more work for less pay if they worked too fast. They were too smart to be cheated. Sometimes the workers deliberately and collectively slowed their working pace in order to get management to increase the piecework price because of their low productivity. Therefore, factory owners often found themselves in the dilemma of either being late for sea shipment, which led to an expensive airfreight fee, or paying more to workers by increasing the price of piecework.

Severe Punishment Policy of Quality Assurance System

Stern punishment policies prevailed in Shenzhen to control for quality problems arising from the process of garment manufacture. Because

the income of the workers mainly came from piecework, to increase their income, they had to work longer hours at a faster pace. But increases in production efficiency, could to some extent, decrease quality because it tended to increase the occurrence of errors. So, to assure the quality of the garments, factories in Shenzhen adopted severe punishment systems (such as deduction of a worker's own salary) to compensate for the damage induced by the worker. This policy played a crucial role in assuring quality, on-time delivery and low waste rates.

To avoid punishment for errors, workers usually tried to cover their mistakes and avoid responsibility. Whenever a mistake was discovered, the parties involved blamed each other. When the workers were caught, the factory could then deduct the wages to compensate the loss to the company.

Quality problems could not always be easily traced to the responsible parties. In fact, the management of a factory usually caused more mistakes due to mismanagement. Workers, owing to the piecework salary system, had no way of receiving compensation for the loss of their working time due to management mistakes. That was one of the major reasons the job satisfaction among garment workers was among the lowest and turnover rate the highest of all industries in Shenzhen.

What Can Mr. Lou Do to Motivate His Workers to Work Faster?

Mr. Lou's factory was a typical Shenzhen garment factory. He had the same agonizing experiences in managing workers as others in the industry. As he listened painfully to the slow pace of the sewing machines, Mr. Lou knew that he would be responsible for a US$15,000 air freight cost to this customer because there was no way for his factory to catch up to meet tomorrow's deadline for this order. What a waste! US$15,000 was one-fifth of his total profit last year. Mr. Lou had to do something to change the deliberate slowing down of his workers. Otherwise he would have to consider selling the factory and changing to another profession. What could he do about this?

S-S TECHNOLOGIES INC. (COMPENSATION)

Prepared by Professor Al Mikalachki

Copyright © 1997, Ivey Management Services   Version: (A) 2002-10-11

In January 1994, Rick Brock and Keith Pritchard, owners of S-S Technologies Inc. (SST) were concerned with the rapid rate of growth facing their company. SST had revenues of $6.3 million in 1993 and employed 30 highly skilled workers. These numbers were expected to double or triple in the next couple of years. To determine how well SST was structured to achieve its future goals, Brock hired a consultant he had worked with successfully in the past. The consultant's major role was to make recommendations as to the appropriate organizational design (culture, people, layers of management and administrative systems) in the event that SST grew from 30 to 60 or even 120 employees. Among other issues, questions regarding compensation were surfacing, and the owners wanted to address these questions as soon as possible.

COMPANY INFORMATION

S-S Technologies Inc., incorporated in 1992, was a 100 per cent Canadian-owned company, which focused on industrial software and hardware development. Previously, the same business had operated for 12 years as a division of Sutherland-Schultz Limited, a large integrated engineering and construction company. When Sutherland-Schultz changed ownership, the new owner sold the SST portion of the company to Brock. Ultimately, SST was owned by its CEO Rick Brock, former president of Sutherland-Schultz, and by Keith Pritchard,[1] president of SST. A brief organization chart is provided as Exhibit 1.

SST had considerable expertise in the factory automation market. The company brought together

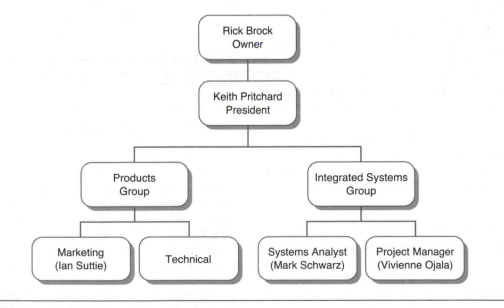

Exhibit 1   S-S Technologies Organization Chart

engineers and technicians with different but synergistic expertise to focus on projects that other systems integrators were unable or unwilling to handle. Out of these efforts, several unique communication and simulation products evolved. The company recognized the opportunities these products represented, and expanded its capabilities to successfully bring these products to the global automation market. Over the last three years, SST had grown an average of 33 per cent per year (the Products Group had grown an average of 64 per cent, and the Integrated Systems Group an average of 30 per cent), as shown in Exhibit 2.

OPERATING GROUPS

As Exhibit 1 indicates, SST was divided into two distinct operating groups: the Products Group (PG), and the Integrated Systems Group (ISG), each with its own characteristics.

Products Group

PG was involved in the development and marketing of the company's hardware and software products. The products were sold around the world through licensed representatives, distributors and direct sales. There were two key types of products:

- **Direct-Link Interface Cards** were totally programmable interfaces designed to make it easier and quicker to exchange data between personal computers and industrial computers/programmable controllers. In layman's terms, the product allowed office computers to communicate with factory floor computers (commonly termed PLCs, or Programmable Logic Controllers). SST designed and manufactured the interfaces for both the factory floor computers and desktop computers, as well as complementary diagnostic software to ensure the computer networks were performing optimally. The Direct-Link cards received the *Canada Award for Business Excellence in Innovation* from Industry, Science and Technology Canada in 1991.

- **PICS (Programmable Industrial Control Simulator)** was a hardware and software package that allowed a personal computer (PC) to simulate, in real-time, an automated factory floor environment. To use PICS, a PC (running the PICS software) is connected directly to a PLC via a Direct-Link card. An experienced software developer then programs, under the PICS environment, a set of routines that send input to and receive output from the PLC, allowing the PC to act as if it were one or more automated factory machines. The PLC is, in essence, "tricked" into thinking it is

Year	Integrated Products	Systems	Total*
1990	$931,000	$1,100,000	$2,685,202
1991	$1,638,000	$1,200,000	$3,570,797
1992	$2,763,000	$1,300,000	$4,521,987
1993	$4,036,000	$2,270,000	$6,306,000
1994**	$5,200,000	$3,500,000	$8,700,000

Exhibit 2   S-S Technologies Revenue
*Includes other sources of income and expenses
**Projection

actually running the automated factory floor, allowing the user to ensure that the PLC software is performing properly. The system can be used for debugging new industrial software, retooling, and employee training, all of which result in substantial time and cost savings for the user.

These products, developed by SST, were often the result of a solution to a technical problem no other company could solve. PG also had a number of other products and ideas under consideration for possible launch in 1994 or 1995.

PG's key success factors were applied research, product service and marketing. New products were needed to maintain pace with a rapidly changing plant electronic environment. In case of faulty products, a replacement had to be provided quickly. Also, product awareness by system integration engineers, complemented by an efficient and effective distribution network, was vital for PG's growth.

Integrated Systems Group

ISG was involved in three distinct, yet often interrelated areas of services: consulting, system engineering and customer support. ISG employed computer professionals and engineers who were assigned to the development of software and hardware solutions for complex factory floor systems. Clients were provided with tested, reliable and sophisticated solutions for data collection, custom control software, batching systems, diagnostic systems and programmable controller simulation. ISG also implemented and commissioned packaged control software, and provided project management for large and technically complex projects. ISG customers included industrial manufacturers and institutional organizations.

ISG's key success factors were to complete projects on time, on budget and of high quality. To date, ISG had received excellent feedback from clients. ISG's performance depended highly on the quality of its employees. Its goals

were for manageable growth, focusing on projects within the company's scope and skills.

ENVIRONMENT

In early 1990, the North American economy was in a recession. Although recovery was widely predicted, some results of the recession were permanent. Companies sought to maintain margins during this recession through downsizing and reducing production costs. SST's Products Group benefited from this trend because PICS and Direct-Link cards offered ways of reducing the cost of automating a plant, a move which often reduced production costs. The market for PG grew despite the recession. The recession also meant that many companies eliminated or drastically reduced their in-house engineering capabilities and sought to subcontract this work, a trend that benefited ISG.

SST's TOP MANAGEMENT AND HUMAN RESOURCES

SST was directed by its two owners:

- Richard R. Brock, P.Eng., was the CEO of SST. During his eight years as president of Sutherland-Schultz Limited, Brock recognized and nurtured the potential of the Products Group (PG) and Information Systems Group (ISG), which eventually formed S-S Technologies Inc. He continued to be involved in all aspects of the new company, and brought to it his extensive knowledge of business management and development.
- Keith Pritchard was the president of SST. Pritchard had risen through the company ranks, starting as a systems analyst, becoming project manager, then group manager, and, finally, president in 1992. Pritchard also developed the PICS product that accounted for $500,000 of company sales. His unique set of skills in both management and technical areas made him an excellent leader for the company.

SST had a flat organizational structure that allowed it to respond quickly to technical and market changes. Anyone who had a door left it open; employees felt free to take their concerns to whomever they believed could help. Decisions were often made using a consultative approach that empowered those involved, which led to "ownership" of problems and their solutions.

Projects were assigned to individuals or teams, depending on the size. The individuals and teams were self-managed. Responsibility for project scheduling, budgeting and execution was left largely in team members' hands. Such responsibility created commitment to the project for those who worked on it and led to the high motivation evident within the company.

Overhead resources, such as marketing and administration, were kept to a minimum. For example, there were only four people on the marketing team, which managed over $4 million in revenues. Administrative support was provided by two or, at times, three people. Even the controller (Doug Winger) shared his time with two other related organizations (SAF and Wilson Gas). SST was truly a lean organization.

Resources—PG

PG had highly competent, highly motivated technical teams. The technical people were leaders in their respective fields, with extensive and varied educations and backgrounds. They worked well together to meet Research and Development (R&D) challenges, and to respond quickly and effectively to customers' inquiries. Many team members were involved in the original product development and expressed a personal commitment to PG's continued market success.

- Linda Oliver, B.Math., the lead programmer for the PICS product, had worked on the project as a designer and programmer since its inception.
- Bruce Andrews, Ph.D., was involved in the ongoing development of the PICS product, especially the communications tasks and testing; he also wrote the manuals.

- Lorne Diebel, C.E.T., developed a reputation as a communications "guru." Lorne often travelled to far-off sites, on a moment's notice, to debug a customer's application problem.
- Jonathan Malton, B.Sc., a talented hardware designer, had been instrumental in advancing the Direct-Link cards from the old "through hole" format to the new "surface mount" technology.

Newer members were added to PG as the pace of R&D increased and customer support became more demanding. Newcomers brought their own areas of expertise, and worked alongside the more senior team members, whose enthusiasm for their work was infectious.

As a result of its progressive and applied R&D program, the technical team members were advanced on the learning curve. This allowed SST to keep ahead of the competition. As a result, large PLC vendors often came to SST to solve their communication and simulation problems, rather than investing in the learning curve themselves.

The marketing team had grown over the past few years as PG revenues grew. People from both a marketing and a technical background combined to create a well-rounded, effective marketing department:

- Ian Suttie, P.Eng., a leader in the market group, was involved in design review, marketing, distribution and sales of all products. His main function was to set up a network of distributors and representatives to reach all major markets in the United States, Europe and beyond.
- Colleen Richmond had experience in marketing with other high-tech firms. She handled all the trade shows, promotional material and advertising activities.
- Steve Blakely was the inside salesperson, and came to SST with a technical background. He responded to enquiries for information, and was the first contact within SST for customers having technical difficulties.
- Colleen Dietrich was recently hired by SST to determine the extent to which leads generated through the various advertising media used by PG eventually resulted in sales.

The marketing team worked well together, buoyed by PG's success. However, they were stretched to the limit, and team members admitted they were unable to do everything they wished to do because of personnel constraints. All known product complaints were acted upon; however, there was no formal audit of customer satisfaction.

Resources—ISG

ISG's most important resource was its people. The engineers and technicians were not only technically competent, but were highly motivated and loyal. The following is a brief summary of ISG people and the skills they brought to the company:

- Mark Schwarz, P.Eng., an accomplished systems analyst and leader in the group, wrote sales proposals, estimated projects, and did most of the marketing for ISG. He was very good at business development, seeking out large, extremely complicated projects, and often helping the customer define the scope and approach to the project. Convincing a customer that you could handle their large, technically complex job was tricky business, but Schwarz exhibited a talent for it. Schwarz also had a talent for scheduling personnel and was interested in ensuring that everyone had something interesting to do.
- Vivienne Ojala, P.Eng., an experienced and talented project manager, designer and programmer, as well as leader in the group, was more than capable of handling all aspects of design and project management for the $2 million-plus projects ISG hoped to attract. She was excellent with customers who preferred her "straight" talk to the "techno-babble" others gave them. Ojala made the customer confident that the project was in good hands, which is very important when you have asked a manufacturer to give you a production system that could determine business success or failure. Ojala was also good at training those who worked on her projects, as well as developing people in general.
- Peter Roeser, P.Eng., was a systems analyst with special skills in the area of communications and various operating systems.

- Brian Thomson, P.Eng., was an expert in the area of real-time software development. He also managed projects.
- Ted Hannah, P.Eng., was a project manager and systems analyst with extensive skills and experience.
- Bruce Travers, who marketed ISG capabilities in Ontario and provided technical direction for projects, had over 20 years' experience with industrial applications of information systems.

Due to the diverse skills of its people, ISG was able to tackle large, complex systems integration projects that most of the competitors could not. ISG had in-house expertise covering nearly every technology that would be applied to a project. Also, because ISG was not tied to a single supplier of PLCs or PCs (as many competitors were), it was able to be more flexible and innovative in the solutions that were presented to customers.

Another important ISG resource was its excellent reputation and relationship with a large Canadian manufacturer, which had given ISG substantial repeat business. As well, ISG had completed many projects for several large North American companies and had never failed to deliver on its promises.

ISG was advanced on the learning curve. New customers benefited from the fact that ISG had faced many challenges before, and solved them successfully. ISGs experience was more rounded, and, hence more innovative and current than an in-house engineering department that had only worked in one type of factory.

Consultants' Interviews

The consultant interviewed all SST employees. Some of the observations, which resulted from his interviews, are grouped below by issues:

i. Hierarchical Structure

Pritchard viewed Suttie, Schwarz and Ojala as group leaders. However, PG members generally saw themselves as reporting to Pritchard and saw

Suttie as performing the marketing function. When apprised of this situation by the consultant, Pritchard said it would take time for Suttie to establish his position.

The ISG situation also proved somewhat confusing. A number of ISG members saw Schwarz as a leader. However, there was some confusion as to his position vis-à-vis Ojala, who had recently returned to SST after leaving to work for a much larger technology company in Montreal. Ojala tells the story of Pritchard begging her to return to SST, a story that Pritchard confirms. Ojala saw herself as reporting to Pritchard (and so did Pritchard). Her "formal" relationship to Schwarz had to be worked out.

Before Ojala left SST (she was away for five months), both she and Schwarz reported to Pritchard directly. When Ojala left, many of her responsibilities, such as some of the proposal writing and personnel scheduling, were given to Schwarz. Now that Ojala was back, to everyone's relief, there was the question of how to structure her role, particularly in relation to Pritchard and Schwarz. Ojala would not report to Schwarz, and Schwarz would not report to Ojala.

In a short period of time, Schwarz and Ojala took on leadership positions in ISG. Informally, they divided the tasks of scheduling, hiring, training and managing customers. They worked in different industrial sectors and tended to deal with different groups of ISG engineers. However, they jointly made management decisions that affected ISG goals and maintained a free flow of people and ideas between the ISG groups related to each of them.

ii. Commitment and Motivation

The consultant was overwhelmed by the high commitment to SST and the task motivation expressed by employees. The people loved the work environment, the lack of politics, the quick response to their technical needs (equipment and/or information), and the lack of talk-for-talk's-sake meetings. They were confident in their future and happy to come to work. For the consultant, this was a refreshing contrast to the downsizing gloom and doom that permeated many other companies he worked with in the 1990s.

The employees set their own working hours. They had to put in 40 hours per week, but could do this at any time. The flexible working hours allowed them to engage in other activities that occurred between 9:00 a.m. and 5:00 p.m., such as their children's school events. Employees kept track of their overtime and were paid either straight time or took the equivalent in extra holidays. Each employee recorded his/her overtime weekly, and passed on the information to Pritchard. Previously, employees had noted the overtime information mentally. Pritchard had them write it out and report it weekly, because he observed that their mental calculations erred on the side of the company (they remembered fewer hours than they worked overtime).

iii. Personnel Function and Communications

New employees were generally assigned to a project manager, who informally took on the induction and training role. In that way, new employees immediately tied into a task, and it was left to them to learn the culture and expectations of SST by osmosis. Should the employees not perform well, or fit into the culture, their employment was terminated.

Periodically, Pritchard would have a meeting of all employees to inform them of SST's progress, success and direction. Given these meetings, Pritchard was surprised to learn that only a few employees were aware of SST's goals and strategy.

One issue mentioned by a couple of employees dealt with performance appraisal and company benefits. Performance appraisal was conducted by Pritchard; however, he did not keep a record of the meeting, and it was not done at regular intervals. Also, anyone interested in learning about benefits or salary ranges for various jobs did not know whom to contact. In contrast, all employees knew whom to contact for technical information. In fact, performance appraisal, compensation and benefits were managed in an ad hoc manner.

iv. Compensation

Compensation, base pay and bonuses, was the most contentious issue that arose from the interviews. Base pay tended to be at the low end of the spectrum for engineers. New engineers joining SST compared their salaries to those of other graduates and, also, to statistics provided by engineering associations, which published comparative data. They believed that the comparison showed them as significantly underpaid.

Bonus payments also generated concern. Historically, when SST was part of Sutherland-Schultz, the company had a few good years and generous bonuses were paid. However, when the recession hit, the construction side of Sutherland-Schultz slumped considerably and, although PG and ISG held their profitability, the company as a whole could not afford to pay bonuses. In fact, SST people were laid off, and some of those who remained felt cheated. Now that SST was on its own, there was an opportunity to tie bonuses directly to the company's performance. Management wanted the bonus system to achieve the following goals:

- To develop a cooperative team spirit.
- To foster cooperation between ISG and PG, and to limit interpersonal competition.
- To provide extra reward for unique contributions.
- To not reward weak performance.

v. Partnering

Given the experience of losing Ojala to another firm (albeit temporarily), Brock was anxious to develop a "partnering" system in which those crucial to the company's success could participate. He wanted to make people like Suttie, Schwarz and Ojala feel like owners or partners committed to the company, so they would not be lured away by the promise of greener pastures; after all, the job market for people of this calibre was extremely promising. This was true not only of those in management positions, but also of the best systems analysts and programmers: people like Linda Oliver and Lorne Diebel.

Brock contemplated having part of the partners' bonus to consist of stock in the company. The problem was that these people were all young, with growing families, and could not afford to have their money tied up in stock when they had mortgage payments and day-care costs to worry about. Generally, their immediate concern was cash flow, as they knew their long-term earning potential was excellent. Brock's concern was how to structure the partners' compensation to keep key people on-side, while allowing room for more partners to be brought in as the company grew. The company had recently hired a half-dozen talented engineering and computer science students, all of whom had the potential to become the next Schwarz, Suttie or Ojala. On top of all this, Brock still had his own return on equity to consider.

Culture	People
• Open communications at all levels • Flexible working hours • Few policies • Profit-sharing at all levels • Quick decision-making • Encourage initiative, not bureaucracy	• Highly motivated • Highly skilled (Tech) • Entrepreneurial • Team players • High performers • Committed to SST

Exhibit 3   S-S Technologies' Desired Culture and People

Where Do We Go From Here?

Brock, Pritchard and the consultant wanted to design a compensation system that would contemplate an expansion to double or triple SST's existing size. They knew the existing SST culture attracted and nurtured highly motivated and committed employees who expanded the company successfully and rapidly. The trio's task was to design a compensation system that would support the existing SST culture and the kind of people they wanted to attract (Exhibit 3). They also wanted to develop an action plan that would ensure buy-in to the new compensation system.

Note

1. Pritchard had a minority share in SST.

OP4.com: A Dynamic Culture

Prepared by Ken Mark under the supervision of Professor Fernando Olivera

Version: (A) 2001-01-23

Introduction

Feeling full of energy after having a productive company meeting that focused on updating OP4.com's vision statement, Ray Matthews, co-founder and Internet chief executive officer (iCEO) of OP4.com paused to reflect on the growth that his company had achieved. It was May 30, 2000, and Vancouver-based OP4.com, an Internet portal for teenagers, had just celebrated six months of existence. With the goal of creating the Internet's leading portal for teenagers, Matthews knew that OP4.com's internal culture had to reflect the identity of its Web site: hip, cool, spontaneous, witty.

Now that OP4.com's Web site activities were gaining momentum and media attention, Matthews wanted to maintain this unique culture through the next few crucial months of rapid growth and change. Tom Pressello, co-founder and business chief executive officer (bCEO) explained the impetus for change:

> Content sites in general are becoming more closely scrutinized by investors. To facilitate a drive towards profitability, we have recently divided the company into four divisions, each responsible for generating revenue. In addition, we've got to start thinking about revenue streams on content—wireless, syndicated content, models for sustaining our business. I'm sure that because of this change, our culture has to adapt to this reality.

The Internet and the Development of Teen-Oriented Web Sites

With the advent of instant messaging tools, communities of Internet interest groups began forming around the world. Web companies like TheGlobe.com, iVillage and Lycos began developing virtual communities where like-minded individuals could congregate. Communication between people became even more advanced with the development of chat capabilities—a mini-industry comprised of companies like iChat and ICQ began facilitating real-time conversation transmitted electronically. Aside from sheer novelty, a significant driver of this change was cost—these services were often provided free of charge to anyone with an Internet connection, often as a means to develop loyalty amongst users. Because many of the early pioneers and adopters of Internet technology were teenagers, companies focusing on the teenaged demographic began to target this niche market. The goal of community sites was, in general, to gather a particular target group in large numbers such that the collection as a whole became attractive to advertisers. Relative to other media such as television, print or radio, it was inexpensive to set up a Web site and as a consequence, large numbers of community sites sprang up in the mid 1990s, attempting to develop into full-fledged business entities by catering to the consumption needs of their audiences and/or by selling advertising.

The percentage of U.S. teenagers online aged 12 to 19 would jump from 11.5 million to 20.9 million between 2000 and 2002.[1] During that same period, conservative estimates indicated that the percentage of children and teenagers online (more than once a week) as a segment of the teenaged population, would jump from 26 per cent to 47 per cent.

Without a doubt, the teenaged North American population was more Internet-enabled than any other demographic group. This demographic group had virtually grown up with the Internet and was very at ease with its technology. They had gained a powerful communication tool with e-mail, and could be in constant, real-time communication with their friends anywhere in the world.

THE CREATION OF THE YOUTH PORTAL OP4.COM: OUR PLACE 4 EVERYTHING

OP4.com was the brainchild of Stuart Saunders and Ray Matthews, both in their early thirties. Saunders, a full-time motivational speaker, had worked directly with thousands of teens across Canada and the United States. Based in London, Ontario, Saunders was the co-founder in 1990 of Leadership Innovations, a leadership company that provided leadership training and motivational speakers to the North American high school

market. Vancouver-based Matthews was a former school teacher, award-winning educator, author and entrepreneur.

Wanting to attract the attention of teenagers and provide them with a place to voice their opinion, OP4.com's objective was to build itself to be a portal, an Internet site that would attract and retain a large percentage of its visitors by providing multiple communication and information functions and products (see Exhibit 1). OP4.com allowed teenagers to discuss topics with each other through electronic chat rooms, use e-mail and bulletin boards and submit articles. The OP4.com concept would need to have immediate appeal to this demographic group in order for its business model to work. OP4.com wanted to position itself as the premier youth-oriented site in North America, with proprietary content as a cornerstone.

Saunders commented: "I started this to have a positive Web community for kids. I had the vision but not the dollars and cents—I was thinking strictly of the kids." Saunders' vision for the site led to the creation of three content sections: expression, entertainment and empowerment. Saunders felt that these sections represented all facets of teenaged life and the issues that teenagers faced.

Expression—This section allowed users to voice their opinion and for others to read and critique them by submitting responses. Spontaneity was encouraged and there was a relatively short span of time between article submission and posting on the site. This was a forum where youth could write off-the-cuff but personal pieces on spirituality, coping, activism and more. These pieces were limited to 300 words or less and OP4.com's content editors reviewed these pieces, checking for major spelling or grammatical errors. This editing process allowed OP4.com to screen out hate postings and overtly vulgar, undesirable articles.

Entertainment—This section contained reviews of movies, music, books, sports, television and Internet sites of interest to teenagers. Aimed at keeping visitors updated on the North American entertainment scene, reviews were both written by OP4.com staffers and submitted by members.

Exhibit 1 OP4.com Site Screen Capture

Source: www.op4.com; November, 2000.

Also included were interviews of music bands conducted by OP4.com staff.

Empowerment—This section included self-help, motivational pieces—articles which were meant, in the words of OP4.com staffers, to change their world. For example, there were articles titled A Call to Action, People Doing Good, AIDS and Teams Doing Wonderful Things. The content of this section was generated internally by interviewing selected role models in the youth community. In some cases, articles were solicited from featured youth leaders.

According to Saunders and Matthews, two key factors differentiated OP4.com from other teen sites. The first was the fact that their consumer aggregation model was unique: it relied on Leadership Innovations' speakers to market to its audience. Since Saunders' other company, Leadership Innovations, reached hundreds of thousands of students each year through a combination of motivational speeches, summer leadership camps and weekend leadership conferences, there existed the opportunity to promote OP4.com via speech mentions and bookmarks that were handed out at the end of every speech or event. Saunders felt that Leadership Innovations' endorsement of the site would encourage his audience to visit it.

The second point of differentiation was the quality of its written content: it published its own staff articles and monitored the quality of solicited content on its site with the goal of developing a consistent, wholesome brand image.

The business viability of content sites had been called into question in mid 2000, with business analysts declaring that content sites were unlikely to survive as business entities unless these sites showed investors a tangible path towards profitability.

THE SENIOR STAFF AT OP4.COM

The three founders of OP4.com complemented each other's personalities. Between Saunders, Matthews and Pressello, there was a mix of vision and attention to detail and a range of different skills that each brought to the company, including financial management, people management, idea development and project execution.

Stuart Saunders, iPresident, Co-Founder and Director of Aggregation

Beginning as a high school motivational speaker in the late 1980s, Saunders had built the largest youth-oriented leadership company in North America (in terms of youths reached). Currently managing a speakers' bureau of motivational speakers, leadership summer camps, running seminars and workshops, Saunders and his London, Ontario-based team estimated that they reached over 10 million students per year in Canada and the United States.

"Although I am currently the president of OP4.com," Saunders offered, "I know that sometime soon, OP4.com will have to bring on someone more experienced to help run this company. Currently, I spend about 30 to 40 hours a week on this project, aside from the time I spend promoting the site during my speeches."

Ray Matthews, Co-Founder and iCEO

Forming Balance Fashions Inc. in 1986, Matthews grew the small company into a multi-million dollar direct sales fashion company that had since expanded to include more than 1,000 sales representatives across Canada.

The concept of direct sales with Balance Fashions took off and by January 1990, Matthews had his Balance National Program counting over 140 sales representatives nationwide. Matthews wrote "The Dirt on Success," a strategic entrepreneurial seminar series that was presented to more than 250,000 individuals in

North America. Most recently, Matthews was the founder of villagenetwork.com, a virtual community site for artists that was sold to Art Vision International.

Matthews commented:

> In my position as iCEO, I aim to be the visionary, always encouraging my team and multi-tasking. I'm not strong at linear patterns and minute details—that's why we have Tom Pressello, the bCEO, who handles the corporate financing, chief financial officer-type decisions. He starts at "no, it can't be done," then works to "yes." I'm the opposite, starting at "yes, it can be done" then working to "no."

Tom Pressello, Co-Founder, bCEO and Chief Financial Officer

Prior to joining OP4.com's Vancouver head office, Pressello, age 31, was a consultant in the strategic planning and corporate finance areas for technology start-ups and turn-arounds. A graduate of the Business Administration program from a prestigious Canadian business school, Pressello had also been the vice-president of finance for a generic pharmaceutical company and had worked in merchant and corporate banking.

> As bCEO, I'm like the stereotypical "Dad" in the family, keeping a tight control over business and finances, and Ray is the stereotypical "Mom"—motivating, nurturing, cheerleading. We butt heads, but that tension keeps us working well with each other. At OP4.com, my job is to lead the company from a financial viewpoint—I challenge all our suppliers on their costs to us. They know that they cannot squeeze me for extra profits and I think they respect me for that.

STAFFERS AT OP4.COM

Saunders ran OP4.com's office in London, Ontario and oversaw a staff of six "seeders," who were hired as facilitators in OP4.com's chat

Meet the OP4i Team

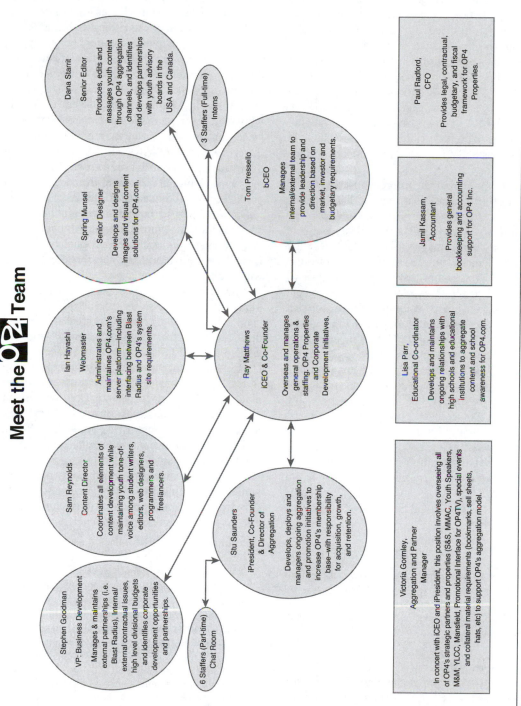

Dana Starrit
Senior Editor

Produces, edits and massages youth content through OP4 aggregation channels, and identifies and develops partnerships with youth advisory boards in the USA and Canada.

3 Staffers (Full-time)
Interns

Spring Munsel
Senior Designer

Develops and designs images and visual content solutions for OP4.com.

Ian Hayashi
Webmaster

Administrates and maintains OP4.com's server platform—including interfacing between Blast Radius and OP4's system site requirements.

Sam Reynolds
Content Director

Coordinates all elements of content development while maintaining youth tone-of-voice among student writers, editors, web designers, programmers and freelancers.

Stephen Goodman
VP: Business Development

Manages & maintains external partnerships (i.e. Blast Radius), Internal/external contractual issues, high level divisional budgets and identifies corporate development opportunities and partnerships.

6 Staffers (Part-time)
Chat Room

Tom Pressello
bCEO

Manages internal/external team to provide leadership and direction based on market, investor and budgetary requirements.

Ray Matthews
iCEO & Co-Founder

Overseas and manages general operations & staffing, OP4 Properties and Corporate Development initiatives.

Stu Saunders
iPresident, Co-Founder & Director of Aggregation

Develops, deploys and managers ongoing aggregation and promotion initiatives to increase OP4's membership base—with responsibility for acquisition, growth, and retention.

Paul Radford,
CFO

Provides legal, contractual, budgetary, and fiscal framework for OP4 Properties.

Jamil Kassam,
Accountant

Provides general bookkeeping and accounting support for OP4 Inc.

Lisa Parr,
Educational Co-ordinator

Develops and maintains ongoing relationships with high schools and educational institutions to aggregate content and school awareness for OP4.com.

Victoria Gormley,
Aggregation and Partner Manager

In concert with iCEO and iPresident, this position involves overseeing all of OP4's strategic partners and properties (S&S, MMAC, Youth Speakers, M&M, YLCC, Mansfield, Promotional Interface for OP4TV), special events and collateral material requirements (bookmarks, sell sheets, hats, etc) to support OP4's aggregation model.

Exhibit 2 Organizational Chart

Source: Company files.

47

rooms. Consisting entirely of part-time, high school-aged staff, the seeders would be present at all chat room discussions, mediating any disruptions, answering questions, bridging conversation gaps. Since London was located several thousand kilometres away from Vancouver, Saunders wondered if he would continue to run the seeders from his London office. OP4.com had been split in this fashion at the beginning due to the fact that Matthews was located in Vancouver and Saunders had his company located in London.

Matthews knew that, in order to cater to the interest of teenagers, it was critical that someone close to that age group managed the site's content. OP4.com wanted to display through its Web site a young, dynamic image of itself. Matthews' first hire was Sam Reynolds, 24, as content director, or as she was commonly called, "Content Queen." He then hired the three members of the content team—Dana Starritt, Libby Shumka, Jessica Cowley—and next the marketing staff. Last, he hired Web administrator, Ian Hayashi, and Spring Munsel, the senior designer to support the site for Flash, HTML and Java (these were the programming languages that enabled Web site creation).

Matthews located his employees by using his network of contacts, preferring to seek out people he already knew and trusted. One issue he faced was finding good Web talent who had experience in programming languages, were fluent in Internet-style communication and had a proven track record. Also needed were people with contacts who would be able to solicit advertising and business.

Reynolds commented:

> There's lots of recruitment at this stage of our company. It's who you know, personal contacts and referrals. Personal contacts are great—everyone knows at least someone and you know that if someone comes recommended, there will be no problem.

By offering university internships, OP4.com found many of its younger writers. This was not only due to the fact that OP4.com as a start-up had limited cash resources, but also because the interns were close to the age demographic it was trying to reach. Two interns were aged 19 and 20.

Matthews knew it was critical to bring people in who fit into the dynamic culture he was trying to build. By asking them a series of questions during their interview, such as what was their favorite movie and why, he was able to determine their fit. Matthews also looked for people who would thrive in a changing environment. Dana Starritt was the senior editor. Her first interview with Matthews was supposed to be at the office but, due to unforeseen circumstances, the venue changed twice more from a downtown bookstore to the Cactus Club (a downtown Vancouver bar). Through his observation of her cool reaction to these changes, Matthews was able to determine that Starritt would be a good fit for his company since she felt comfortable with spontaneity and change.

In Matthew's search for staff for OP4.com's Vancouver office, he was specific on the mix of people he would hire. "There are four 'styles' that we look for," said Matthews, "and we wanted to build OP4.com with a balanced staff." Using popular American icons to describe these styles, he continued, "There is the Analyzer, much like Mr. Spock (Star Trek), the Driver, embodied by Donald Trump (businessman), Socializer, for example Meg Ryan and Robin Williams (actors), and Relators, like Oprah Winfrey (talk show host)."

Over time, it became clear that any new hires would need to fit with the young dynamic culture that was developing and that this culture was critical for the success of OP4.com

Sam Reynolds observed:

> It's an uncomfy oxymoron if we're pitching a site to youth from a stuffy, stagnant corporate culture. Here, there is no break between the culture of youth in general and the culture of our team. In the Internet industry, it's an employees market and one can't assume that people will come begging for jobs. On the other hand, these people will spend long hours at work—you will not be invited to play on our team unless your vision is synchronous with ours. We want to make people as comfy as they can be.

DEVELOPING A YOUTH-ORIENTED CULTURE AT OP4.COM

With his first few hires, Matthews knew that he had created a solid foundation upon which to build a company. Reynolds and Starritt embodied the youth culture he was seeking to build and Matthews knew that he could count on them to train his next hires.

"We want to ensure that everybody is accessible to the team and vice versa," Matthews stated. "We share our musings constantly, have weekly strategic action plan discussions and celebrate the results achieved that week. I want to keep my team well-informed." Given that OP4.com had ramped up very quickly, Matthews felt that it was imperative the vision statement was revisited every six months in order for the staff to feel that their involvement and ideas were important.

Matthews' approach to managing was one of "managing by walking around." He wanted to be involved with his people at the ground level, to find out what they were working on, to get a sense of the whole operation by being in the "trenches," so to speak. To make new employees feel that they were part of the team, OP4.com had a welcome letter when the employee first arrived, appreciation cards, flowers and beer were sent, and weekly meetings were held to make sure the employee adjusted well.

A ritual that had been instilled from the beginning was the "robust discussion," used to welcome team members to OP4.com. Jessica Cowley, staff writer, was "honored," along with two other new members, with a team-bonding session where each team member shared their personal thoughts. No topic was taboo and this exercise was aimed at creating a sense of trust amongst team members. The objective of the session was to develop emotional relationships between team members and foster the feeling of trust within the team. "There's a real sense of safety, security and acceptance of differences at OP4.com," Cowley stated. "You can feel the culture through the variety of ways in which we treat each other, approach each other, support each other. It's all very forward-looking—from

the rituals we have, weekly meetings, running jokes, socializing outside of work time, we really enjoy each other's company."

To provide examples of leadership ideals, incidences of successes were passed down to new members. The valiant efforts of the company secretary who drove to the airport to ensure that the courier package would be submitted in time had become a company legend. Matthews believed that the lack of a formal employee training program was, in part, made up by these anecdotes which served the purpose of culture building at OP4.com.

"We're also empathic as a company and this is definitely reflected through our Web site as our users see us as an anonymous and safe forum for 'coming out of the closet,' for example," remarked Reynolds. "No one needs to use his or her real name on the site. To help our staffers appreciate this aspect, we had our team write a secret on a postcard—their deep and darkest secret—and drop it, addressed to 'The Postman,' in the mailbox."

OP4.COM'S UNORTHODOX TRAINING AND FEEDBACK SYSTEMS

As in most other start-ups, OP4.com's management team worked long hours to develop the site, often trouble-shooting minor problems which arose on a constant basis. The many demands on everyone's time meant that very few formal meetings could be set and it was up to new employees to learn from observation, by making mistakes or from a combination of both.

When asked about formal training Reynolds laughed (hard) and replied:

> Training? It's been off the cuff. Just jump off the deep end and we'll see you in two weeks! No, seriously, there's tons of support. Personally, I sit people down and go through priorities and long-term goals. Here is something interesting. There were four people who started on May 1. I wanted to teach them that the Web site needs to be cared for on a permanent basis and to illustrate that point,

we went on a field trip to a home furnishing store. Each person picked out plants and we let them know that they had to care for the plants, just as they would for the Web site.

On another occasion, we got the staffers buying postcards, writing five personal goals on them, addressing and sending the postcards to themselves. When we wanted them to get used to thinking quickly—in this business, you have to be quick on your feet—as a second assignment, we gave them three words, hammer, velvet, emancipation, and told them to write a creative piece in one minute, then send it to a team member. Along with creative writing, this exercise also served to cultivate their peer editing skills.

Public recognition was used as a mechanism to provide feedback to OP4.com employees. At the end of team meetings, Matthews would take the time to publicly recognize someone worthy of praise. Matthews felt that "dramatizing what success looks like" was far more powerful than monetary rewards. It was his belief that this affirmation of good work performed meant more to his employees because they were publicly recognized for it.

REWARDING INITIATIVE WITH RESPONSIBILITY

Matthews knew that in a start-up situation, opportunities for new business partnerships or new online ventures could arise at any time. Because of his preference for spontaneity, he was open to employee suggestions about new project ideas. Thus, Matthews allowed his employees to approach him with ideas for projects and if the ideas were deemed feasible, it was likely that Matthews would hand over to that employee direct ownership of the project.

When an employee suggested exploring co-marketing initiatives with a wireless company, Matthews endorsed her proposal and re-arranged her duties to reflect this new focus. On another occasion, Reynolds allowed an intern to assume content production and publishing duties when he sought to assume this responsibility.

MATTHEW'S REACTION IN THE FACE OF EMPLOYEE MISTAKES

Matthews realized that not all ventures would work out and that employees would be prone to making mistakes of various magnitudes. He was comfortable with this risk and made it clear to his staff that he trusted them to make the right decisions. However, when pressed about how he would deal with staffers if serious mistakes were made, Matthews responded:

> Here is a story I read in a newspaper once. Things had gone wrong at a large software corporation and an engineer, through his mistakes, had just cost the corporation $5 million. Being also the head of the research and development department, the engineer paid a visit to the president and tendered his resignation. The president listened to the engineer's announcement, thought about it for a few moments and replied; "Why would I fire you if it just cost me $5 million to train you?" That, in a nutshell, explains how I would handle potential mistakes by my fellow staff members.

REWARDING STAFFERS AT OP4.COM

OP4.com, like most Internet start-ups, had a pool of stock options for their employees, believing that providing the potential for rich rewards was a key motivating factor for employees. Options allowed an employee to purchase company stock at a very low price, often less than 10 cents per share. The whole notion behind stock options was that at the initial public offering or in the event the company was purchased, the vested options would be worth hundreds if not thousands of times the amount initially paid for them. Because of this potential payout, stock options were intended to encourage employees to put in more effort. Ideally, they would feel a bigger sense of ownership and, along with the rest of their co-workers, work hard to increase the value of their company.

OP4.com was still a small company with under 20 people and no formal promotion processes were in place. Promotion was an ad hoc process—people who took the initiative and developed a new program were rewarded for it with more responsibility, but not necessarily a title which conferred more seniority (though another perk of working at this start-up was the option of choosing your own work title— examples of which were "Code Samurai" [Ian Hayashi], "Community Hactivist" [Dana Starritt] and the aforementioned "Content Queen" [Sam Reynolds]).

Reynolds observed, "If there is something new, do it, then find someone to replace what you were previously doing. We're taut and stretched and at this stage of growth, we need to bring people on."

MAINTAINING THE CULTURE THROUGH THE NEXT STAGE OF GROWTH

From meetings with OP4.com's investors, Pressello knew that their next major goal had to be profitability. To achieve this, the founders began to draft formal reporting structures to manage their staff and prepared to divide the company into business units that would be responsible for generating their own revenue streams— content/wireless, OP4 media projects, OP4 marketing, OP4 Web site and education program/ community programs. OP4.com anticipated that it would start to hire more people as their programs developed.

Steve Goodman, vice-president of corporate affairs offered:

> We may put together a magazine, or explore other projects in television, radio or wireless. At this stage, it's like having a bank account with no job— the advertising revenues we have will not sustain us long-term. This restructuring into business units is our first step towards generating self-sufficient revenues.

What was also very important to Matthews was that the unique culture he had built up at OP4.com remain intact as the company grew. Matthews had just finished his Tuesday morning session on building culture where the team had

Business Unit (all Vancouver)	Purpose	Staff Members
Content/Wireless	Produce content for site and seek out/manage wireless partnerships.	1 director (Sam Reynolds), 4 editors, 1 designer
OP4 Media Projects	Develop new concepts in media to generate excitement amongst target audience with the objective of youth aggregation.	3 staffers
OP4 Marketing	Market OP4.com to youth market.	2 staffers to Toronto
OP4 Web Site	Manage the "look and feel" of the OP4.com Web site and chat.	Matthews, Saunders, Pressello and 6 staffers
Education Program/Community Programs	Working with high schools to solicit content.	2 staffers

revisited the vision statement. The upcoming weeks would be crucial because Matthew wondered if the still-nascent state of OP4.com's culture at its Vancouver head office would survive this restructuring.

NOTE

1. Source: Jupiter Communications, 2000.

WestJet Airlines (A): The Culture That Breeds a Passion to Succeed

Prepared by Ken Mark under the supervision of Professor Gerard Seijts

Version: (A) 2004-07-09

INTRODUCTION

It was April 17, 2001, and WestJet's market capitalization had just surpassed that of Air Canada's, the country's leading airline. "We're in the hospitality business and our culture is everything to us," stated Don Bell, co-founder and senior vice-president of customer service of Calgary-based WestJet Airlines. Bell was adamant on maintaining WestJet's culture in the face of increased company growth and competition. All of WestJet's founders believed that culture was the key to their airline's continued success and that they could not afford to mismanage it. However, Bell knew that the tremendous growth at WestJet would put pressures on its unique culture. He wondered how WestJet could grow and maintain its vibrant culture.

THE HISTORY OF WESTJET AIRLINES[1]

The roots of WestJet Airlines go back to 1994, when entrepreneur Clive Beddoe (president of the Hanover Group of Companies) discovered that it was cost-effective to purchase an aircraft for his weekly business travels between Calgary and Vancouver. During the time his company was not using this aircraft, Beddoe made it available for charter to other cost-conscious business people through Morgan Air, owned and operated by Tim Morgan. The response to this venture caused Morgan—along with Calgary businessmen Don Bell and Mark Hill—to realize that there was an opportunity to satisfy the need in Western Canada for affordable air travel coupled with good service by starting an airline.

Beddoe, Bell, Hill and Morgan believed that there was not only a market for a low-fare carrier in Canada, but that they could succeed at bringing this service to the country. Through researching other successful airlines in North America, the team examined low-cost carriers throughout the continent, including the primary examples of Southwest Airlines and Morris Air (which later became part of Southwest Airlines), both operating in the United States. David Neeleman, president of Morris Air, was contacted for assistance on writing a business plan, and along with Morgan, Hill, Bell and Beddoe, became the founding team of the concept that became WestJet Airlines.

Over the next months, the team worked with Neeleman to develop a comprehensive business plan and financial model. This information was the blueprint for the start-up of a three-aircraft, low-cost, low-fare, short-haul, point-to-point airline to serve markets in Western Canada. With the business plan in hand, a number of local business people were approached, and within 30 days, the needed capital (Cdn$8.5 million) was raised.

After this, developments moved quickly in bringing WestJet to life. In July 1995, WestJet's first staff members moved into the company's first office in downtown Calgary. In November of that year, the team purchased two Boeing 737–200 aircraft and added a third to the fleet in January 1996. In late January of 1996, the team completed a second offering to retail and institutional investors and raised over Cdn$20 million to commence operations on February 29, 1996.

The airline started operations flying to the cities of Vancouver, Kelowna, Calgary, Edmonton and Winnipeg. Since then, the company has continued to expand, bringing more Western Canadian cities into WestJet's world. In March of 1996, WestJet added Victoria to its route network.

WestJet was started in an "ideal" environment—Western Canada—where the main competition came from Canadian Airlines, which had experienced financial troubles. Although Canadian initially tried to match WestJet's rock-bottom fares (and attempted to compete in various other ways), it could not afford to compete against the upstart's low-cost structure (e.g., WestJet provides no meals, offers no frequent flier programs and has incredible turnaround times at the gates).

In June 1996, the airline purchased its fourth Boeing 737 aircraft and added service to the new market of Regina. In August that year, Saskatoon was added. In June 1997, Abbotsford-Fraser Valley was added, making WestJet the only scheduled carrier to operate at that airport. March 1999 saw the addition of the two new destinations of Thunder Bay and Prince George, and in September 1999, WestJet added Grande Prairie to its service area.

WestJet met a major business goal when, in July 1999, it completed its initial public offering of 2.5 million common shares. The share price at closing was Cdn$10. It was an exciting day for all WestJetters, representing the achievement of a major goal and raising the necessary capital for expansion of the company in the coming years. The capital raised from the offering, Cdn$25 million before post-closing adjustments, would be used for the purchase of additional aircraft, as well as the building of new head office and hangar facilities in Calgary, in order to meet the needs of the company's expanding workforce.

In 1999, unprecedented changes and restructuring were seen in the airline industry in Canada (e.g., plans for a merger between Canadian Airlines and Air Canada, small carriers that discovered viable market niches, and carriers that failed within a short time-span), offering a window of opportunity for WestJet to expand its service beyond its existing route structure. In December 1999, WestJet announced that it would be extending its successful low-fare strategy across Canada. Steve Smith, WestJet's president and chief executive officer in 1999, justified the expansion by stating:

> Our success over the past four years has proven that the travelling public will embrace any expansions to our airline's route network and schedule, while continuing to maintain the low-fare structure and exceptional customer service that has become synonymous with the WestJet name.

In March 2000, WestJet added services to Hamilton and began to build the John C. Munro Hamilton International Airport as its eastern hub. In April 2000, WestJet added Moncton to its network and in June 2000, Ottawa was also added. Bill Lamberton, WestJet's vice-president of marketing and sales, noted that these schedule enhancements included services added as a result of the addition of the third-generation aircraft for 2001. He stated:

> This new aircraft will allow us to enhance our long haul schedule to provide greater connections between our Western hub in Calgary and our Eastern hub in Hamilton. As we continue to expand our airline, we will look for new cities to add to our

network, new niche routings, as well as better connections, so that more and more Canadians will be able to benefit from our low-fare, high-volume service.

Hamilton was chosen as the Eastern hub for several reasons. First, it was a niche route, meaning no other airline operated from the airport, hence making WestJet the airline of choice for people who lived in this Southern Ontario area. Second, costs were an issue. For example, landing fees for Toronto were steep. Third, efficiencies were a consideration. For example, WestJet could land an aircraft in Hamilton, deplane and board guests, refuel, restock and load and unload bags within 20 minutes. At Pearson International Airport in Toronto, it would be hard to taxi to the gate in this time! The more time in the air, the more efficient and profitable airlines can be. Moncton was also a niche market. Halifax had significant competition, whereas Moncton had little.

THE FOUNDERS

Clive Beddoe, Don Bell, Mark Hill and Tim Morgan founded WestJet and, in April 2001, remained part of the executive team. Beddoe was the president and chief executive officer as well as chairman of the board of directors. Bell and Morgan were senior vice-presidents, and Hill was vice-president. Bell was responsible for the airlines' customer service areas including reservations, information technology (IT), customer service, and frontline services including flight attendants and airports. Bell and Beddoe were credited with creating the carrier's bottom-up management structure and energizing the staff. Morgan, a former pilot with Canadian Regional Airlines, was responsible for maintenance and flight operations. Hill was in charge of strategic planning.

All four entrepreneurs were substantial shareholders in the company—2000 data indicated that, combined, they owned nine per cent of the airline, a stake worth Cdn$85 million.

COMPANY PERFORMANCE

Since the beginning, WestJet had been consistently ranked among the most profitable airlines in North America. WestJet had been profitable since its inception in 1996. In an industry where 90 per cent of startups fail financially, WestJet grew from two planes in 1996 to 21 in 2000. Revenues in 2000 were Cdn$332.5 million, and expected revenues in 2001 were Cdn$460 million. Despite more competition, higher fuel costs and a slowing of the North American economy, the airline's earnings per share for the first quarter of 2001 increased to 13 cents from 10 cents during the same period in 2000.

All employees shared in company profits. WestJet's generous profit sharing plan allocated bonuses based on profit margins: if the airline's profit margin was 10 per cent, then 10 per cent of the net income would be spread among employees, prorated to salary. This profit sharing plan had a ceiling of 20 per cent of net income, and cheques were handed out twice a year.

In November 2000, more than Cdn$8 million was handed out to employees, with the average cheque amount being Cdn$9,000. One manager quipped, "That's why we have motivated people." But Beddoe insisted it was not just about money, saying, "They know their contributions have gone above and beyond anything we've asked of them, and that's what generated the profits."

In addition, right from the start, many of WestJet's employees owned equity in the company. WestJet matched every dollar their employees invest in company stock. For example, in 2001, 83 per cent of the airline's staff members were shareholders. Many of the original employees invested prior to WestJet's initial public offering and have more than Cdn$400,000 in stock value. The first 20 pilots at WestJet became millionaires.

In exchange for profit sharing and the stock purchase program, WestJet's employees worked for 95 per cent of the industry's median salary in their job category.

WestJet took pride in the customer service it provided to its guests. Since the Air Travel Complaints Commission began tracking passenger complaints in 2000, it had received only two from WestJet guests. In the same time period, the Commission logged 769 complaints from Air Canada passengers. This translates into 24,000 guests flown per complaint for Air Canada versus one million guests flown per complaint for WestJet (all data pertain to domestic flights).

Satisfaction with the job and colleagues among the 1,700 people working for WestJet was high. Bell explained:

> As for reality versus expectations, I found that, in general, an employee's actual experience on the job is better than what he or she had anticipated. For example, call centre customer service associates said that they found their job experience better than expected, and their colleagues warmer, kinder and more willing to help than expected. Most of them rate eight or nine out of 10 for pride in the organization. That shows me that we have to remind people how good we are. It's the one or two per cent that causes a cancerous environment. The day we find that employees' on-the-job experience is worse than what we believe it is, we're finished.

CULTURE

Beddoe insisted that WestJet's corporate culture was the primary reason for the airline's superb performance. "The entire environment is conducive to bringing out the best in people," stated Beddoe. "It's the culture that creates the passion to succeed."

Siobhan Vinish, director of public relations and communications, described the culture as a very relaxed, fun, youthful environment in which creativity and innovation are rewarded. For example, in the call centre where people take bookings (called the "Sales Super Centre"), the representatives had the authority to override fares, make decisions not to charge fees for cancellations and bookings, and waive fees for unaccompanied minors, on a case-by-case basis. People were trained to understand the ramifications of the

decisions that they made. Senior management trusted the representatives in looking out for the interests of the company, customers and shareholders. Nevertheless, overrides were tracked and monitored each month. Additional training and coaching were provided if patterns emerged (e.g., overriding change fees on a consistent basis).

Pilots were considered to be "managers," and were encouraged to think with the executive team. One example of WestJet implementing a suggestion from its pilots came from significant fuel savings as a result of taxiing with one engine instead of two.

Prior to launching WestJet, Beddoe and his colleagues had no experience running a scheduled airline. One of the industry's biggest problems was dealing with a largely absentee workforce, spread all over the country, working at airports, hangars or in the air. Beddoe stated, "What occurred to me is we had to overcome the inherent difficulty of trying to manage people and to hone the process into one where people wanted to manage themselves."

Thus, the founders set out to create a company that was managed from the bottom up. WestJet gave workers a high degree of latitude to perform their jobs without interference from supervisors. Beddoe continued, "I don't direct things—I just try to persuade. We set some standards and expectations, but don't interfere in how our people do their jobs."

Vinish explained:

> The flight attendants are asked to serve customers in a caring, positive and cheerful manner; how they do that, however, is left up to them. Resource books are provided for them to refer to, and there is a team of people who continually updates these books.

In addition, Bell offered:

> A lot of the stuff is intuitively obvious—we don't focus on culture. We believe that culture is defined by the actions of executives. I may focus on empowerment and trust, Clive on profit sharing, and another one focuses on fun. This forms

the circle of influence. It's very fragile—all our combined actions contribute and form part of our brand—whenever we start to do things offside, it affects the culture. We think of our customers as guests. We have agreements and partners, as opposed to contracts and employees. Profit sharing and stock purchase plans are important, but that's the icing on the cake. They're critical components of our company, but they don't define the culture.

People with a great attitude always see the glass as half full. We're an opportunity culture versus an entitlement culture. We create opportunities for people. For example, lots of people have made a lot of money but have given WestJet a lot in return. In contrast, at Air Canada, a lot of money is paid to get a little work done. This is because unions stripout opportunity. We're creating wealth and sharing that wealth.

In a feature article in *Canadian Business,* December 25, 2000, it was noted that:

Some executives entertain lavishly on the company dime. If Clive Beddoe tried to, he would probably get lynched. Consider what happened when the president and CEO of WestJet Airlines Ltd. threw a catered barbecue one weekend for the company's senior and middle managers at his private fishing lodge on the Bow River, downstream from Calgary. News of the party spread quickly through the company, and when Beddoe returned to work the following Monday, a WestJet maintenance worker stormed into his office. Pounding on Beddoe's desk, the employee demanded to know why the boss was blowing company profits on hamburgers and beer for the folks at head office. WestJet has a generous profit-sharing plan, and the maintenance guy figured his cut was being squandered on a soiree he wasn't even invited to. Beddoe told him not to worry. "I pointed out that I paid for the party out of my own pocket," says Beddoe, grinning. "He was a little humbled, but I congratulated him on his attitude. He's like a watchdog, and he hates inequities. That's the spirit of WestJet."

The company's accountants (located in WestJet's head office under the sign "Beanland") said that profit-sharing plan was front and centre and transformed each employee into a "cost-cop," constantly scouting for waste and possible savings.

Derek Payne, treasury director, boasted, "We are one of the few companies that has to justify to employees its Christmas party every year."

All employees had a sense of humor and played practical jokes on one another. Morgan, vice-president of operations, was also a pilot for WestJet. For new people who had never worked at an airport, Morgan would send them to "run and get the keys for the airplane." Of course, an airplane does not need keys, but the attendant would rush into the office, pick up the key with a huge tag that said "airplane" and rush back through the aisles to loud applause from passengers.

Another quality that set WestJet apart from its competition was the team spirit of its management and staff. On a visit to the night shift in the maintenance department, CEO Beddoe, dressed in coveralls, offered to go outside in sub-zero temperatures to change an airplane tire. He had to push the toolbox across the tarmac in 30-degree weather, check the tire pressure and change the tire. Eventually, Beddoe succeeded at the task. WestJet's people tended to give for the collective well-being of each and all, and there was an egalitarian spirit. It also showed that work at WestJet is a team effort. These values began at the top and trickled downward.

Bell, who oversees customer service at WestJet, routinely helped out the representatives in the Super Sales Centre when there was high call volume.

Sandy Campbell, the chief financial officer stated, "There's peer pressure among the employees. They recognize who buys into this program and who doesn't, and peer pressure is an amazing thing."

The culture is so customer-centred and so well defined that, at WestJet, employees sometimes joked that WestJet is more "Southwest" than even Southwest.

Beddoe concluded:

We have a philosophy of trust here. Sometimes you get burned when you trust people, but most times you don't. Workers have pride in what they do because they are the ones making the decision about what they're doing and how they're doing it. They are not just functionaries. They actually take ownership of their jobs.

OVERALL PRODUCTIVITY

The benefits of creating WestJet's type of environment appeared substantial. WestJet avoided the cost of a significant layer of supervisory people. Next, it achieved a higher level of productivity per person. WestJet operated with about 59 people per Boeing 737 aircraft, compared with more than 140 at a typical full-service airline such as Air Canada.

The airline's focus on controlling costs and its specific cost-cutting measures had been well publicized. It flew only one type of aircraft, the 125-seat Boeing 737, offered a single class of service, utilized the Internet as much as possible to sell tickets, operated without paper tickets, offered no frequent flyer programs, provided no meals and minimal in-flight service, had no airport lounges or link-ups with other airlines, and aggressively hedged against rising fuel costs. This can be contrasted, for example, with Air Canada and its 16 different planes from nine different manufacturers, which resulted in much higher maintenance and training costs. WestJet's cost-cutting measures resulted in operation costs being almost half those of Air Canada's.

To reinforce its cost-cutting strategies, the company stressed teamwork. With no unions to insist on job descriptions, all employees had wide discretion in their day-to-day duties. WestJet's pilots often went into the cabin and tidied up between flights. Even Beddoe would help out when he was aboard. Job behaviors such as these meant annual savings of up to Cdn$2.5 million in cleaning costs and facilitated quick turnarounds, often within a half-hour. The record was an incredible six minutes.

Striving towards savings, Bell added:

Once, I created a "report card" for the company with two or three colors in the design. Employees asked me why it was not in newsprint.

Most important of all are the actions of the executive team. People trust the executive in doing a good job. I need to link the impact of savings onto profit sharing. Cdn$8 million in savings does not mean anything to employees until you link it to their pocket book.

Because of these strong cost-cutting measures, WestJet could make money with ticket prices 50 per cent below the industry average. In an interview with the *Financial Times,* November 21, 2000, WestJet officials stated that its low costs meant it could break even when its planes were just 63.3 per cent full. In the second quarter of 2000, WestJet averaged 76.2 per cent capacity.

WestJet increased fares three per cent at the start of 2001, but resisted the temptation to raise prices even further or reduce the number of its cheapest seats, even though it flew at near capacity. Rather than fight for market share with larger carriers, WestJet's strategy was to use low prices and unrestricted tickets to lure people who would otherwise drive, take the bus or train or stay home. "To move our pricing higher quickly just means our whole philosophy of market stimulation doesn't work," said Bill Lamberton. It would also mean that there would be more room for a new competitor such as CanJet Airlines or Royal Airlines Inc. to enter the market with lower prices in an effort to capture the market segment that WestJet is pursuing.

HIRING

WestJet received between 3,000 and 4,000 résumés every week. Most of the new hires were new to the airline industry. "We prefer it that way," stated Beddoe. "This is a new culture, a new vision. It's better to start with a clean slate."

WestJet looked for two character traits—enthusiasm and a sense of humor. This was a theme borrowed from Southwest Airlines, which was known for its practical jokes and free spirit. It was common aboard WestJet's Boeing 737s for the flight attendants to crack jokes, hold contests (e.g., singing contests and aisle bowling games) with the passengers. Most passengers did not seem to mind the jokes and, in fact, most came to expect it.

The specific hiring process varied from department to department. Behavioral interviews were used to assess a fit between the person and the WestJet culture. WestJet made a conscious effort to provide realistic job previews to job applicants. Job simulations were also part of the hiring process. For example, WestJet held group interviews for flight attendants, in which it explained what WestJet was about, what WestJet stood for and what in particular WestJet was looking for. One interview session included making a lighthearted, creative presentation to the group, describing what the person would bring to WestJet.

Vinish and Bell stressed that the hiring and orientation period is of critical importance to WestJet. Bell offered:

> People by nature are negative, but there are some who are criminally enthusiastic. I do things called fireside chats. I talk to new hires about culture and what makes us tick. This is their orientation into our culture, our mission and our values. I want to find out what company people want to work for.

MAINTAINING A UNION-FREE WORKFORCE

WestJet did not have a union. Instead, WestJet's senior management team created the Pro-Active Communication Team (PACT), an employee association that allowed management to keep in touch with its employees, addressing their concerns before they became a problem. PACT provided WestJet employees with the services they might want to receive through a union, without the hassles, rules and adversarial environment that a union typically brings.

PACT covered the entire company with a number of chapters representing the different work groups. Each chapter had at least one representatives who sat on a council. Besides

dealing with personnel issues, PACT aided in setting salary scales. Said Beddoe, "It takes away the opportunity for conflict because the employees are part of the solution, not the problem."

If an employee group, such as the flight attendants, wanted to leave PACT, it has to get approval from 75 per cent of its members. Beddoe added:

> It ensures we have a successful relationship with our people on a long-term basis. It took me two years to convince our people to embrace the concept of PACT because everyone here is so anti-union. But the staff voted 92 per cent in favor of it. We have since had some extremely successful resolution to issues that have cropped up.

COMMITMENT TO MAINTAINING THE CULTURE

A vibrant corporate culture was so central to WestJet's success that preserving it was Bell's and Beddoe's main obsession. Not fitting in with the WestJet culture could have dramatic consequences. The sudden resignation of Steve Smith in September 2000 was a case in point. Smith was hired in early 1999 to take over Beddoe's job as CEO. Beddoe stayed on as chairman of the board, but wanted someone to take over the day-to-day operations and represent the carrier as it evolved from a private concern into a public company. Smith was running Air Canada's regional airline, Air Ontario, at the time, and WestJet's board of directors liked his amiable, energetic personality.

But it became apparent almost immediately that Smith did not fit with WestJet's culture. For example, Smith would override decisions made by WestJet employees who were "empowered" for over four years. Company sources said that Smith had a top-down management style and was accustomed to dealing with hostile unions. Beddoe stated:

> Steve got off on the wrong footing with PACT. He treated PACT like a union and they resented that

immediately. He came from a background where you weren't open and straightforward, where you don't play all your cards at once. Well, we don't do that. We tell it like it is. We tell the employees what our issues are, and we try to work to a solution. We don't hold back half the deck.

Beddoe maintained that Smith's interaction with PACT improved over time, but the bad feelings lingered. There were other issues. According to one source, Smith locked horns with Beddoe and the board over how quickly the airline should grow. In his first business plan for WestJet, Smith called for revenue and earnings to grow at 27 per cent per year. The board ordered him to maintain the airline's current growth rate, in the 45-per-cent to 50-per-cent range. A source from WestJet stated, "When he first arrived, Steve had no sense of how much momentum the company had and how aggressively to grow it. You'd have to dismantle the thing to grow at only 27 per cent."

Employees became agitated, morale suffered and the culture that built the airline was at risk.

Vinish had spoken to Beddoe about how he would communicate the sudden resignation to WestJetters and the public. Beddoe did not want to announce that Smith was "moving on to better things." If he had said that, and if he had not mentioned anything about culture, Beddoe believed he would lose credibility with his employees. After all, he was the one who was the foremost proponent of open communication, and candid communication is what the executive team expected from its employees. Thus, Beddoe decided to talk candidly about the differences between Smith and the WestJet culture. Beddoe believed that this would show that management had credibility to "say it like it is." He explained:

There is no question in my mind that if I had left it three or four months or even six, it would have been a precipitous event, because then we would have lost the core of the executive team, and by that I mean the senior management team of the company.

Beddoe was greeted with high-fives, hugs and hurrays from everybody once he walked back into the executive office to take over Smith's responsibilities.

Steve Smith denied that a cultural rift led to his departure and "vehemently disagrees" with WestJet's assessment.

COMPETITION AND EXPANSION

As recently as 1999, Beddoe was content to be in Western Canada. But the merger of Air Canada and Canadian Airlines changed the situation for him. WestJet's board decided to expand eastward before new carriers, such as Halifax-based CanJet, cornered the low-fare market. WestJet started flying out of Hamilton, Ontario, in the spring of 2000, and served Ottawa and Moncton and had plans to enter Montreal.

By using Hamilton as a hub, WestJet avoided head-to-head route competition with Air Canada as it tried to establish itself in the East. CanJet, in comparison, was fighting Air Canada on its home turf at Toronto's Pearson International Airport, and it admitted in late 2000 that it was struggling. One industry insider predicted that CanJet would not even be around in 2002.

Other airlines noticed the success of WestJet and were in the process of attempting to mimic WestJet, that is, its culture and operations. Canada 3000 merged with Royal and CanJet in April 2001. Air Canada intended to enter the discount market through forming a strategic partnership with Toronto-based Skyservice to fend off competition from WestJet and Canada 3000. Skyservice owned 80 per cent of Roots Air. However, WestJet appeared not to be too worried about other airlines introducing no-frills versions. Vinish explained:

Air Canada would have to reduce their costs in order to be successful. This game is all about costs—Air Canada has operated for many years in their current state—for them to go into the low-cost market is difficult. Air Canada has many operational requirements. For example, we don't hire cleaners. If I decide to fly to Saskatoon, my promise to my fellow employees is that I help to clean the plane. We don't have a mentality that says, "That's not my job, I'm not prepared to do that." Air Canada has a union—an employee would not be able to get up and serve coffee to passengers even if he or she wanted to. Such behaviors are not encouraged at Air Canada because serving coffee is somebody else's job. Low fares need low costs. Low costs need concessions from people in order to do that.

Historical data indicated that setting up a competitive, profitable low-fare subsidiary had proven to be a problematic endeavor for the conventional airlines. Several of these airlines had tried and failed.

Beddoe was more blunt, stating that Air Canada's plan "is another disaster in the making."

CONTINUED GROWTH

Beddoe continued, "We fly only five per cent of the available seat miles in Canada. We've only just started. Look at Southwest Airlines. It's still growing, and its stock today is the highest it has ever been."

Amid the vast changes taking place in the airlines landscape in Canada, WestJet had big expansion plans. In August 2000, it ordered 36 of the next-generation Boeing 737-700 series aircraft, with an option to pick up 58 more. That would give the carrier a fleet of 94 aircraft. With the new planes, WestJet intended to start flying non-stop from Calgary to Hamilton. This plan would enable WestJet to add frequency and non-stop flights to its schedule, further enhancing customer service.

Other possibilities included a future alliance with JetBlue, the discount airline launched in 2000 by Neeleman, who built and then sold another successful Southwest clone, Salt Lake City–based Morris Air, before becoming one of WestJet's founding shareholders. Neeleman's latest venture, JetBlue, is active in the northeastern United States. WestJet co-founder Hill observed, "They're in New York, and we're in southern Ontario. We operate off the same reservation system. We know each other well. Anything is possible down there. I wouldn't discount it."

CONCERNS

Industry watchers voiced concerns about WestJet's future, arguing that an economic downturn could hurt a carrier dependent on leisure travellers, and its expansive growth would make it hard, if not impossible, to keep the "fun" culture alive. Beddoe countered by saying that WestJet was prudent as well as ambitious. It had protected itself against rising fuel prices with hedging contracts. He also noted that British Columbia had been one of the fastest-growing markets, even though the province had been in a recession.

Moreover, because 58 of its 94 new jets are optional orders, the growth rate can be slowed to a rate equal to two new jets a year once its older jets are retired. The management team at WestJet believed that, in a depressed economy, it could manage performance expectations by communicating openly with its people, by being honest with them.

As for the corporate culture, Beddoe offered that Southwest, on which WestJet was based, has kept its culture alive 25 years even as its workforce swelled to 30,000. He agreed that protecting the culture is essential. "It's focus No. 1. Our risk, in my view, is internal, not external, and that's why we put so much emphasis on it."

Vinish added:

What is the impact on our culture as we continue to grow? We all could fly into Calgary and find the WestJet culture. How can we perpetuate the culture in Moncton? We've thought about that. We need to send WestJetters to go and spread the feeling out there.

Bell concluded by saying that culture was paramount at WestJet, that as it grew, it was essential it kept its unorthodox, irreverent feel. He was concerned about not overextending WestJet so that its success would come to a halt. It would be unfortunate, he thought, if WestJet developed into a big and bureaucratic organization, unable to sustain its culture because of its success.

NOTE

1. Taken from www.westjet.com, April 15, 2001.

2

LEADING PEOPLE

The topic of leadership is a huge one. This part of the casebook focuses on two critical elements of leadership—getting commitment to a course of action and coaching.

We all aspire to influence others for "breakthrough results" and to "win at work." No matter where leaders wish to take their organization or department or team, they will need the support and commitment of their employees if they are to succeed. However, getting people to commit to challenging goals or change initiatives is often a daunting task.

Before addressing the actions that leaders can take to earn commitment to their vision or breakthrough goals, it should be clear that there is a difference between commitment and compliance. Although both are related to performance, commitment is far more valuable than compliance. For example, Michael Abrashoff (2002), former commander of the destroyer *USS Benfold,* explained that threats, position, and money do not earn commitment; instead these lead to compliance. Compliance, in turn, produces adequacy, not greatness. And Jim Collins (2001), author of *Good to Great,* wrote, "Good is the enemy of great. We don't have great schools, principally because we have good schools. Few people attain great lives, in large part because it is just so easy to settle for a good life. The vast majority of companies never become great, precisely because the vast majority become quite good—and that is their main problem" (p. 1).

The implication is that leaders have to be cognizant of the fact that different people commit to a course of action for different reasons. People do things because they

- have to, or need to; for example, people know that there are costs associated with leaving the organization or with not following the directions or requests of their immediate supervisor. These costs may include negative performance appraisals, lost opportunities for promotion, not receiving good assignments, not being "in on things," and so forth.
- ought to; because some people feel obliged to stick with a course of action or remain with the organization (e.g., a felt need to reciprocate).
- want to, or desire to; when they have an emotional attachment to, identification with, and involvement in the organization or the change that is under way. This is the kind of motivation or commitment that we like to see in people. A desire for great performance leads to the highest level of persistence and subsequent performance.

Gaining commitment to a course of action is the essence of good leadership. For example, former First Lady Rosalyn Smith Carter once stated that "a leader takes people where they want to go. A great leader takes people where they don't necessarily want to go but ought to be." Research and anecdotal evidence have provided us with a clearer picture of what leaders can do to facilitate commitment to goals. I list seven examples of what good leaders *do*. Focusing on behaviors allows us to make changes in our own "doings" so that we can become more effective leaders. The "seven Es of effective leadership behavior" are as follows:

- Envision the future

Vision refers to the organization's fundamental reason for being, beyond making money. Vision provides focus; it is about what the organization can be, beyond what it is today. Hence, leaders must constantly seek new opportunities or ideas for the organization to make it even better. For example, Bill Gates recognized the value of computer software, and Howard Schultz anticipated that lots of people would buy coffee that was made as if it were a type of gourmet cooking. There is no doubt that a compelling or challenging vision can motivate or inspire people. Jack Welch, the former CEO of General Electric, once said, "Good business leaders create a vision, articulate the vision, passionately own the vision, and relentlessly drive it to completion."

- Enlist others

Most leaders are seldom able to achieve much by themselves. Organizations such as GE, Southwest Airlines, WestJet Airlines, Springfield Remanufacturing, and Johnsonville Sausage discovered long ago that leaders who make room for others often achieve great results. Their success is partly attributable to leaders who invited employees to contribute to, and take ownership of, their organizations' achievements. Ronald Heifetz, lecturer in public policy and cofounder of the Center for Public Leadership at Harvard, stated that "the lone warrior model of leadership" is "heroic suicide" (Heifetz & Laurie, 2001). Those who lead through issuing orders send their followers this message: "don't think, just do." To not use the intellectual horsepower of employees seems like a terrible waste. The message therefore is simple: Leaders need to enlist the support of others, and strong communication and persuasion skills are critical in this regard. This is true in particular if one considers that work today gets done in an environment where people do not just ask, "What should I do?" but "Why should I do it?"

- Energize followers

Leaders must generate enthusiasm for high performance; it is important to create a sense of excitement and to maintain that excitement or optimism even in the face of the setbacks and obstacles that are all too common in periods of organizational change.

- Enable performance

Enabling performance means that leaders should focus on developing the person, not just the scoreboard. If they focus on the first, then the second will follow. Leaders have to provide the resources (e.g., knowledge, skills, or equipment) to help people become successful. Enabling performance also means that they have to make sure that there is organizational alignment. This means that the vision, the organizational structure, the people and their skills, the tasks that are to be performed, and the organizational systems all reinforce each other. Too often, however, leaders overlook the importance of aligning these organizational building blocks.

- Encourage effort

Leaders need to help people develop the courage and confidence to achieve "stretch goals." How to set goals is explained below.

- Empower the team

I believe that people own the responsibility for delivering great performance. The task of a leader is to create the work environment where people can take ownership for great performance. Good leaders provide the resources that are needed to "win," as well as give people the confidence and freedom to do their job, make decisions, and innovate. The organizational culture at WestJet Airlines, for example, is centered on this principle. WestJet leaders are "socialized out" of a problem-fixing mode and encouraged to trust their people to solve the problems that they run into at the ticket counter, sales center, or elsewhere.

- Exhibit the values

There is no doubt that leaders must possess the "right" set of values to lead and foster commitment. For example, in his book *Who Says Elephants Can't Dance,* Lou Gerstner (2002) writes that the leader's actions must be consistent with his or her words and that if a leader isn't living and preaching the culture and isn't doing it constantly, then the espoused culture just doesn't happen.

A task of the leader is to *coach* others for effective performance. Goal setting and feedback are critical elements of coaching. Research has shown that for goals to be effective, they need to be SMART—that is,

- Specific; well defined, or clear to the individual. Letting people know what we expect them to do helps eliminate the danger of work being incorrect or late. Those people with specific challenging goals perform better than those who do not set goals or those who embrace abstract goals such as "to do my best."
- Measurable; know how close or distal completion of the goal is. People must have a clear indication that either more effort is needed to attain the goal or that more effective task strategies have to be discovered and implemented.
- Agreed upon; agree on what the goals should be with all the stakeholders; this leads to goals that are clearer in purpose as well as better accepted. However, getting such agreement can be difficult when stakeholders are numerous and diverse.
- Realistic; so that individuals have the resources, knowledge, and time to attain their goals. People will feel satisfied when they achieve goals that are meaningful and challenging. Goals that are too easy or too difficult often de-motivate.
- Time framed; so that individuals have enough time to achieve the goal—but not too much time, as procrastination can affect performance.

Providing feedback on how to improve performance is critical to helping people achieve their goals. Research has shown that for performance to improve, both goals and performance feedback are needed. Goals without feedback or feedback without goals are far less effective in facilitating high performance than goals and feedback. But many employees do not receive feedback on their job performance; some bosses consider that the annual review is the only time to talk about expectations and performance. It is hard to see how this annual event helps people to do their job better. Informal coaching and feedback should happen whenever appropriate; this means more than once a year. Exceptional leaders give recognition or praise, and they do so a lot. They do not stand on the sidelines and speak only "when the play goes wrong." They shout encouragement day in and day out. Good leaders show appreciation as often as possible and acknowledge even small improvements.

What are some of the things that leaders should consider doing to get commitment to the goals that are set or assigned? Four "strategies" include the following:

- Showing personal commitment or mental toughness; this means holding on to that picture of excellence that leaders have for their team when lots of people around them are saying that "it can't be done." Being visible, giving directions, providing task-relevant information, encouraging, and modeling the behaviors that leaders expect from others are some of the behaviors that illustrate personal commitment.
- Solicit input; leaders are well advised to ask employees how they feel about an assignment and see if they have any questions or concerns. "Do you feel it's reasonable to complete the work in the time frame that I have outlined?" "What bothers you?" Asking questions allows an employee to provide feedback and helps the leader to understand the employee's motivations or concerns. There can be little doubt that a critical leadership characteristic is being willing to listen to others. However, as Oren Harari (2002) observed, at times, it appears that when leaders ascend the corporate hierarchy, they become afflicted with a curious problem— their ears get smaller and their mouths get bigger. Leaders who "shut up and listen" not only learn a lot but also often create an environment in which others are more willing to listen to them.
- Communicate; people often resist change and fail to commit to goals because they do not understand the organizational realities that have created a burning platform for change. An example is Sears, Roebuck and Co. Sears faced a crisis in the 1990s, and it encountered multiple challenges in recovering. To understand the perceptions of the salespeople, Tony Rucci, executive vice president of Human Resources and Administration, visited a large number of stores. He was surprised to learn the following: He asked associates how much profit Sears made on a dollar of revenue—the average answer was 45 cents. However, the correct answer was less than 1 cent. With such misperceptions present, it is no surprise that it was hard for people to see the need for change. And no wonder it was very difficult for Sears's leaders to create a burning platform for change, to encourage people to make personal sacrifice, and to get people to commit to change goals. Sears was forced to communicate and to do lots of it.
- Leaders must explain to employees how their goal or jobs contribute to the overall effectiveness of the unit. Consider the words of Jack Stack, a general manager at International Harvester, credited with transforming a diesel engine remanufacturing plant. In a Harvard Business case named "Jack Stack," he wrote,

> The most crippling problem in American business . . . is sheer ignorance about how business works. What we see . . . is a whole mess of people going to a baseball game and nobody is telling them what the rules are. . . . That baseball game is business. People try to steal from first base to second base, but they don't even know how that fits into the big picture. What

we . . . try to do is break down business in such a way that employees realize that in order to win the World Series, you've got to steal x number of bases, hit y number of RBIs and have the pitchers pitch z number of innings. And if you put all these variables together, you can really attain your hopes and dreams. . . . Don't use information to intimidate, control, or manipulate people. Use it to teach people how to work together to achieve common goals and thereby gain control over their lives. (Jack Stack B, case number 9-993-010, p. 2)

The message? A good leader motivates people by making clear how their work fits into a larger vision for the organization; he or she must make sure that people understand that what they do matters and why. People will perform their jobs much better if they see it within the context of a larger goal. Or, in the words of Herb Kelleher (1997), "The important thing is to take the bricklayer and make him understand that he's building a home, not just laying bricks" (p. 23).

Leaders with the best results do not rely on only one leadership style—they use a variety of styles in a given week depending on the business situation. For example, Daniel Goleman (2000), a leadership development consultant, wrote, "Imagine the styles then as the array of clubs in a golf pro's bag. Over the course of a game, the pro picks and chooses clubs based on the demands of the shot" (p. 80). Goleman identified various leadership styles: coercive, authoritative, affiliative, democratic, pacesetting, and coaching. He found that of the various leadership styles, the coaching style is used the least often. His findings also indicated that many leaders felt "they don't have the time in this high-pressure economy for the slow and tedious work of teaching people and helping them grow" (p. 87). Managers who ignore the lessons of goal setting, providing feedback, helping employees to find ways to further improve performance, and working on getting commitment are passing up opportunities to "win at work."

Coaching for Exceptional Performance Workshop

Informal coaching opportunities occur in the course of daily activities. In this workshop, students are provided with ways to improve their responsiveness to these opportunities. The format is a series of sessions in which students and each member of their teams, in turn, play the role of the director of operations for a software products business. Two staff members drop in to see the director, on their initiative, to ask for ideas, help, guidance, or a decision on an issue. The director knows key details about each staff member's background and development needs but does not know in advance what the specific issues or concerns are. It is necessary to explore these issues or concerns before any decision can be made. The students' performances are videotaped and critiqued in terms of identifying each staff member's problem(s), the effectiveness of responses to the immediate problems, and contribution to that staff member's longer term growth or awareness through coaching. The accompanying seven role-plays (included in the Instructor's Manual, as are detailed instructions regarding the setup of the workshop) provide background information on each of the staff members.

MARTIN BRASS COMPANY (A) TOM FULLER, VICE-PRESIDENT, MANUFACTURING

Tom Fuller, vice president of manufacturing, is faced with a series of disputes between his direct subordinate, Harry Smith; the maintenance supervisor; and one of the maintenance foremen, Jim Jones. The situation is threatening to disrupt maintenance operations, and Fuller feels it is time to intervene. His problem is what to do and how to do it. This case is to be used in conjunction with "Martin Brass Company (B), Harry Smith, Supervisor, Maintenance Dept." and "Martin Brass Company (C), Jim Jones, Foreman, Maintenance Dept." The B and C cases are included in the Instructor's Manual.

Assignment Questions

- How do Harry Smith and Jim Jones view themselves and each other?
- What gives rise to these perceptions? How do you explain the behavior of these two men?
- As Jim Jones, Harry Smith, or Tom Fuller, determine your preferred outcomes.
- Determine the strategy and action plan you would initiate to achieve the preferred outcomes. Be prepared to execute your plan in a role-play.

INTEL IN CHINA

The newly appointed division head must examine organizational or communication problems within a division of a billion-dollar semiconductor manufacturer. The manager made a decision to discontinue a project that an employee had been working on diligently for 2 months. The employee responded emotionally to the decision, creating the potential for conflict within the department. Being new to the department, the manager made the decision in the context of ambiguity, time pressures, and as one of a host of decisions he felt pressured to make. Cross-cultural issues also come into play given that the manager, although originally from China, was educated and gathered extensive experience in the West and was thus considered an expatriate by his employees. The manager must also examine the effect of organizational culture on an employee's behavior.

Assignment Questions

- How would you have handled the situation with Li? If this question is posed to a class with Chinese and students from the West, it should elicit some interesting and varied responses from each group.
- Do you believe the incident with Li was indicative of broader internal communication difficulties, and, if so, what could Tang do about it?
- Tang largely ignores his rank or his experience in the United States and hopes that by making it a nonissue, it perpetuates a feeling that he is "one of a bunch of Intel employees, working hard to avoid dissonance in relationships." How realistic do you consider this attitude to be in dealing with the potential for cross-cultural conflict? There is no "right" answer to this question—it is meant to stimulate class discussion by inviting students to share their opinions.

Chuck MacKinnon

Chuck MacKinnon, on accepting his new position as a managing director with the Merchant Bank of Canada, found himself confronted with two significantly different mandates from his two immediate superiors as well as significant strategic and people problems with his loosely tied group. His immediate supervisor said that the new group was supposed to be great, his new position fun. In the view of his boss's boss, the group had major problems. He soon discovered that he had more problems than he had anticipated. How was he to deal with a dysfunctional group when his superiors disagreed about whether or not there were problems and were also personally antagonistic?

Assignment Questions

- From the evidence in the case, describe the people management practices of the Merchant Bank of Canada.
- Evaluate MacKinnon's handling of the following:
  - his mandate from Margaret and Eldon,
  - the people problems in the group,
  - the implementation of the new strategy, and
  - team building.
- Should MacKinnon stay on and lead the group? If he does, what should he do now?
- Design an action plan for a future leader—whether or not it will be MacKinnon—to deal with the group's problems.

Elise Smart

Elise Smart must decide what performance assessment to give one of her employees who has, uncharacteristically, failed to meet one of her key objectives for the year. The situation is difficult for several reasons: The causes of the unacceptable performance are not clear; the employee has previously received excellent appraisals, including a recent one by the vice president; and the employee was absent for a good part of the year on maternity leave. The various factors that influence sustained performance (ability, motivation, resources, role clarity, reinforcement) are examined, as well as steps leaders can take in improving performance of those for whom they are responsible.

Assignment Questions

- What factors should Elise Smart take into account in deciding what performance rating she should give to Darlene Ketchum?
- Do you think that the decision about the performance rating is likely to have a positive or negative impact on Ketchum's subsequent performance and development as an information technology professional?
- If you were in Smart's position, what rating would you assign? Why?
- Prepare to confront Ketchum with your appraisal and to role-play the subsequent interview. To prepare for this, clearly outline your objectives and how you will approach the session.

Macintosh Financial: Sexual Harassment (A)

Macintosh Financial is a subsidiary of U.S.-based Apple Financial and is the sixth largest asset management company in Canada. The assistant supervisor of client services is confronted by a customer service representative who has been experiencing ongoing sexual harassment from a coworker. The assistant supervisor must investigate the situation and determine what to do next. Supplemental cases—"Macintosh Financial: Sexual Harassment (B)," "Macintosh Financial: Sexual Harassment (C)," and "Macintosh Financial: Sexual Harassment (D)"—follow the sequence of events (and are included in the Instructor's Manual).

Assignment Questions

- Would you consider the reported incident as a sexual harassment incident? Why? As Andy Crane, did you engage in sexual harassment? What are the responses of Brenda Matheson and Kelly Taylor to these questions?
- Who do you think is responsible for the occurrence of the incident?
- What is your evaluation of Kelly Taylor's response up to the end of the case? What would you have done differently?
- As Kelly Taylor, what are the criteria for your action plan?

References

Abrashoff, D. M. (2002). *It's your ship: Management techniques from the best damn ship in the Navy.* New York: Warner Business Books.

Collins, J. (2001). *Good to great: Why some companies make the leap . . . and others don't.* New York: HarperCollins.

Gerstner, L. V. (2002). *Who says elephants can't dance: Inside IBM's historic turnaround.* New York: HarperCollins.

Goleman, D. (2000, March/April). Leadership that gets results. *Harvard Business Review,* pp. 79–90.

Harari, O. (2002). *The leadership secrets of Colin Powell.* New York: McGraw-Hill.

Heifetz, R. A., & Laurie, D. L. (2001, December). The work of leadership. *Harvard Business Review,* pp. 5–14.

Kelleher, H. (1997). A culture of commitment. *Leader to Leader, 4,* 20–24.

COACHING FOR EXCEPTIONAL PERFORMANCE WORKSHOP[1]

Prepared by Professor Jane Howell

Version: (A) 2000-05-29

OVERVIEW

The objective of the Coaching for Exceptional Performance Workshop is to improve your responsiveness to informal coaching opportunities that occur in the course of daily activities.

The **format** of the workshop is a series of sessions in which you (and each member of your team in turn) will play the role of Terry Hepburn, the director of operations for the software products business of the Multi Product Manufacturing (MPM) Company. Two of your staff members will drop in to see you, on their initiative, to ask for your ideas, help, guidance or a decision on an issue. You have only six minutes to see each staff member in this informal coaching session since you have to leave for another important meeting at head office.

Terry Hepburn knows key details about each staff member's background and development needs, but does *not* know in advance what the specific issues or concerns are. It will be necessary to explore these issues or concerns before any decision can be made. Depending on the situation, the staff member may be looking for your ideas, guidance or emotional support rather than for an actual decision.

The **quality** of your coaching performance as Terry Hepburn will be critiqued in terms of: your identification of each staff member's problem(s); the effectiveness of your responses to the immediate problems; and your contribution to that staff member's longer-term growth or awareness through coaching.

HOW THE ROLE PLAY WORKS

Every member of your team will play the role of Terry Hepburn in turn. When each person does so, the other team members will play staff roles.

Each of the staff roles is typical of those you might meet in any organization:

- an over-conscientious manager who is very critical of staff and who can't delegate;
- an insecure supervisor who is very reluctant to make decisions and take responsibility;
- a frustrated supervisor whose ambitions have not been taken seriously and who has been passed over for promotion;
- an ambitious and talented analyst who pushes hard for recognition;
- a very competent manager who is eager for promotion;
- a brilliant engineer who lacks interpersonal and conflict resolution skills;
- a dedicated production supervisor who believes manufacturing should be the company's number one priority.

You will also take a turn playing the role of one of these staff members for the purposes of visits to other team members when they are acting as Terry Hepburn. You should play your staff role with conviction and sincerity.

Your facilitator will set up the sequence of coaching interviews, and give you further details of the staff character you are to play.

SUMMARY

There will be as many 12-minute rounds as there are members on your team.

In one round, you will be Terry Hepburn, director of operations; you will meet with two of your staff members and deal with the issues they bring to you.

In two other rounds, you will be a staff member visiting Terry Hepburn to discuss an issue you have.

MULTI-PRODUCT MANUFACTURING (MPM) COMPANY

An organization chart of the MPM Company can be found in Exhibit 1. A brief description of the job responsibilities and functions follows.

Mickey King   Vice-President, Photo Media, Software and Chemical Group

Terry Hepburn Director of Operations, Software Products Business

Terry's Staff

Kelsey Scott   Telesales Supervisor: supports all group products (four telesales coordinators and one specialist)

Kim Hughes   Market Development Manager: supports all group products under Mickey King's sector (three analysts, including Pat Cox)

Jody Hickson   Project Sales and Marketing Manager, Software Products Business: two

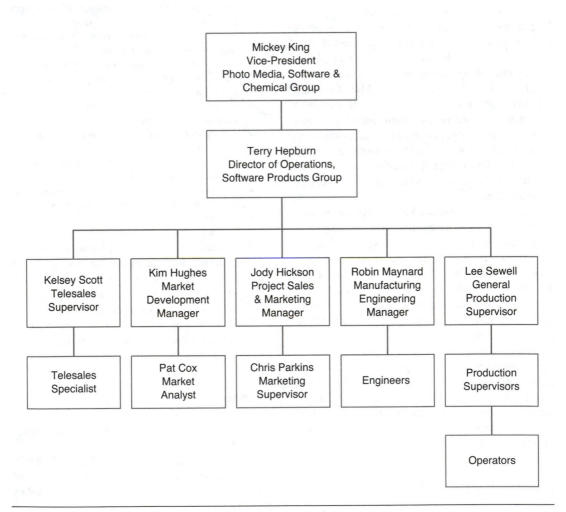

Exhibit 1   Multi Product Manufacturing Company Organization Chart

regional sales managers, one marketing supervisor (Chris Parkins), one secretary/assistant

Robin Maynard — Manufacturing Engineering Manager, Software Discs: responsible for technical aspects of manufacturing the product, i.e., quality improvements, cost improvements (five engineers)

Lee Sewell — General Production Supervisor: responsible for all aspects of manufacturing software discs (three shift supervisors and 10 process workers)

Functions

Telesales

- expand sales revenue through selling to C and B accounts in Mickey's group
- implement special project assignments that expand sales for various businesses

Market Development

- develop new markets and track competitive activity
- liaise with MPM Company's key distributors

Project Management

- responsible for all aspects of marketing and sales of current business and developing new business opportunities

Engineering

- support manufacturing in both day-to-day and long-term troubleshooting with respect to the technical aspects of manufacturing the product, i.e., quality improvements, cost improvements
- to investigate, recommend and implement modifications to processing equipment

Manufacturing

- manufacture the product, meeting cost, quality and service goals

WHAT YOU ALREADY KNOW ABOUT YOUR STAFF MEMBERS

Kim Hughes—Market Development Manager, Photo Media, Software & Chemical Group

Kim, age 35, has been employed by MPM Company for 14 years, seven years in the current position. Kim leads a group of three analysts, including Pat.

Kim is meticulous and accurate at administrative tasks, completes assignments on time, and avoids risks at all costs. Kim tends to over-supervise staff members in order to guarantee that their work is perfect. Due to poor delegation skills, lack of rapport with staff members, and drive for perfection, Kim works overtime practically every evening. In your opinion, Kim has peaked as far as promotion potential is concerned.

You assigned Kim to assist your boss, Mickey, on a feasibility study for a new information system to track sales leads.

Pat Cox—Market Analyst for Kim in Market Development

Pat, age 27, joined MPM Company as a market analyst 18 months ago. Pat shows intelligence and initiative, and tries to broaden his/her knowledge of departmental activities. Pat has made several creative procedural recommendations, which have been successfully implemented.

Pat is ambitious and easily bored with routine work. Kim has complained about Pat's careless attention to detail.

Terry believes Pat will be ready for promotion or transfer within six months.

Kelsey Scott—Telesales Supervisor, Photo Media, Software & Chemical Group

Kelsey Scott, age 31, has worked in the manufacturing industry for 10 years, the last six with MPM Company. Kelsey's tenure in the telesales supervisor role is three months. Kelsey's performance as an analyst was adequate and Kelsey was promoted to the current role as the best of a weak group of candidates.

Kelsey lacks self-confidence, is reluctant to make decisions, and avoids confronting staff with mistakes. Kelsey constantly brings simple problems to Terry to solve.

Jody Hickson—Project Sales and Marketing Manager, Software Products Business

Jody Hickson, age 31, joined MPM Company four years ago, and has been in his/her current role for two years. Jody has been designated as a high potential employee. Previously, Jody was an executive account manager at Xerox The Document Company, and has developed a rich network of contacts in the local business community over time. Recently, Jody has been hinting to you at every opportunity that the timing is right for a promotion to a higher-level sales management position.

Chris Parkins—Marketing Supervisor, Software Products Business

Chris Parkins, age 41, has 18 years of marketing experience, 12 years with MPM Company, eight years in the present position. Chris lacks a university education, but is totally familiar with marketing practices. Chris's current performance is satisfactory.

Your major concern about Chris is lack of ambition and creativity. Chris could be marginally effective as a manager although you have serious doubts about Chris's ability and motivation to advance.

Robin Maynard—Manufacturing Engineering Manager, All Products in Mickey's Group

Robin Maynard, age 42, has been with MPM Company for four years, working for Terry in Mickey's businesses. Robin is a brilliant engineer but needs to work on interpersonal skills. Robin has a tendency to be short with people and unable to empathize. Robin views engineering as the most important function in the company and therefore undervalues other colleagues' contributions.

Lee and Robin have difficulty resolving their own disputes and tend to look to higher management for solutions.

Lee Sewell—General Production Supervisor, Software Products Business

Lee, age 38, joined MPM Company 10 years ago and has been in his/her current position for three years. Lee has broad exposure to manufacturing across the company and takes great pride in achieving monthly production and revenue targets. Lee is fastidious about safety and ensures all precautions are taken in the manufacturing process. At times Lee can have too narrow a focus on "process" at the risk of losing sight of costs.

Lee has difficulty with the way engineering prioritizes its projects and feels manufacturing process issues must be first and foremost at all times.

NOTE

1. This workshop is a revision and extension of the Coaching Workshop prepared by Citicorp.

Martin Brass Company (A)
Tom Fuller, Vice-President, Manufacturing

Prepared by Professor Al Mikalachki

Version: (A) 2000-11-09

Martin Brass, a manufacturing company located in Kitchener, Ontario, made electrical control systems. It employed slightly more than 300 people and was structured in traditional, functional departments such as manufacturing, maintenance, quality control, scheduling, purchasing and shipping.

Over the last year, Tom Fuller, vice-president of manufacturing, had been faced with an on-going and escalating interpersonal conflict between Harry Smith, the supervisor of the maintenance department, and Jim Jones, a maintenance department foreman. The latest saga in this conflict resulted in Smith and Jones engaging in an argument in front of other employees. The argument centred around Jones refusing a request for non-scheduled service by one of the manufacturing departments. In doing so, Jones said that Smith had instructed him to work on scheduled service requests only. When the manufacturing foreman spoke to Smith directly, Smith not only agreed with the request, but publicly told Jones that he showed poor judgement in not servicing what "any fool could see was a priority request." Humiliated and embarrassed, Jones complained to Fuller of this "public tongue lashing by that s.o.b., when I was following his orders in the first place." When Jones left his office, Tom Fuller thought:

> Hell, it is times like this that make me wonder why I ever wanted to be vice-president of manufacturing. It seems that the greatest problem in this company is with people. Why can't two good men learn to get along with each other? If I don't quickly find an answer for the conflict brewing between Harry Smith and Jim Jones, the whole department is going to fall behind schedule.

Background on the Participants

Tom Fuller

Prior to joining Martin Brass 15 years ago, Tom Fuller had received both an undergraduate and a master's degree in engineering from two prominent North American universities. The company placed a great deal of emphasis on technical competency and Tom moved up through the organization, becoming plant manager and later vice-president of manufacturing. Although he had a strong technical background, he had previously received no formal management training. During one of the courses which Tom began to take regularly in order to improve his management capabilities, he became interested in McGregor's Theory X and Theory Y, which defined two types of managers. The Theory X manager, who believes that employees are not really interested in work, monitors them closely. The Theory Y manager, who believes that under the right conditions work can be enjoyable, treats employees in a way that gives them more opportunities.

Harry Smith

Harry Smith, a graduate civil engineer with 26 years of service at Martin Brass, supervised the maintenance department, which included machine, building and electrical maintenance. His technical expertise was essential to the successful operation of this facility, and he was dedicated to his job and to the company. Most people in the organization considered him to be a top-down manager, and there were indications of interpersonal conflicts in the past. His personal activities included membership in technical organizations such as the association of professional engineers, a foreman's club and a management club, as well as an ongoing pursuit of a master's degree at the local university. Harry, age 52, and his wife had no children.

Jim Jones

Jim Jones, foreman of building maintenance, had 19 years' service with Martin Brass, and reported directly to Harry Smith. After completing public school and apprenticing for six years as a tool and die maker, Jim worked 22 years in that trade. Before assuming his current role at Martin Brass, he had been an assistant foreman of the tool room. A very proud man, Jim made the company aware that he was not willing to leave his supervisory position to go back to being a tradesman. His work record indicated that he had experienced no interpersonal problems with his co-workers. For the last 14 years he had been an elected councillor on the local municipal school board, where he had served as chairman for the past three years. Jim was dedicated to this role and proud of the board's achievements, although the activities demanded a great deal of his time. However, Martin Brass had gained business as a direct result of Jim's interests because it had become a supplier to the school board. Jim, also age 52, was married with three sons—a chartered accountant, a minister and a high-school student.

ANOTHER FOREMAN'S VIEW

As Tom Fuller mulled the problem over in his mind, he decided he should hear an outside view on the problem. With this in mind, he called on Jeff Sprout in production, a foreman who knew both Harry and Jim well, to comment upon the situation. After a little hesitation, Jeff Sprout presented his viewpoint:

> Harry Smith is one of the weaker members of our top management staff. He has no respect for any person. With Harry Smith, it's only what is in it for Harry Smith that concerns him. He's been a problem for a long, long time. He had a foreman a few years ago who was one of the finest men that anybody will ever find in any job anywhere. Harry absolutely abused him and rode him until the fellow quit.

> Jim Jones has talked to me so often about Harry Smith that I'm fed up with hearing his stories. It's the same story over and over again. I've been hearing it from Jim for years now. He spent 30 minutes with me yesterday just telling me the same story over again. You see Jim Jones does an excellent job for the municipal school board, but he can't do anything right for Harry Smith. Harry Smith rides him and abuses him and Jim doesn't know what to do with him. I told Jim that he ought to invite Harry out to dinner, get him away from the plant, and lay it on the line. "Tell him just exactly what you think and if that doesn't work," I told him, "the next time Harry says anything to you in the company, you just talk right back and say, 'Now listen here, mister, you can't talk to me that way. If you want to fight we'll go out in the yard and we'll have a fight.'" But Jim said that he couldn't do that because he'd be afraid he'd lose, and I said I was afraid he would too.

> Harry has undercut and pushed Jim around for so long that Jim can't do anything right. Yesterday, I had some maintenance work that I wanted done in my department and I asked Jim to do it. He said he had direct orders from Harry not to touch anything that wasn't in the schedule, and consequently he wouldn't be able to do it for me because Harry had laid it on the line that the schedule was not to be budged. So Jim said that if I wanted anything, I would have to go to Harry. Therefore, I went to Harry and, oh, Harry was nice as pie to me and said, "Of course, sure, we've got to have that done." Then he went down and lambasted poor old Jim with both barrels. Jim said to him, "But Harry, I thought you told me we weren't to change anything on the schedule today." However, Harry just blasted Jim up and down until he was really a sorry sight. Then Jim came to me and said, "What am I to do?" Well, these sorts of things have been going on for a long, long time.

THE DESIRED OUTCOME

As Tom thought about Jeff's description of the conflict and wondered about a possible resolution, he knew the result he wanted to achieve:

> Ideally, I would like to have the situation resolved in a way that has both Harry and Jim developing a good relationship with each other; and with both men continuing to work for Martin Brass

Company. The business that Jim Jones has brought to the company is significant. I would like to see him happy in his job if that means that Martin Brass continues to be a supplier to the school board. At the very least, if Jim does leave the company for any reason, we have to make sure he parts on good terms.

INTEL IN CHINA

*Prepared by Donna Everatt
under the supervision of Professors
Kathleen Slaughter and Xiaojun Qian*

Version: (B) 2002-11-07

In October 1999, Charles Tang, newly appointed manager of marketing programs of Intel China in Beijing, had just emerged from an emotionally-charged meeting with Yong Li, an account manager in Tang's division. The meeting, attended by Li's direct supervisor, Qing Chen, was convened by Tang to discuss Li's feelings regarding a decision Tang had made to discontinue a project that had been assigned to Li by his previous supervisor. Despite what Tang considered to be sound business logic supporting his decision, Li's resistance left Tang wondering whether there were extenuating factors he needed to consider. Tang also wondered whether the blow-up with Li was an isolated incident, or whether it signalled deeper organizational or communication problems in his newly acquired division.

INTEL

In the mid-1960s, Intel introduced the world's first microprocessor, sparking a revolution in the technological industry. Intel was an unequivocal success story—its strategy of "driving new technology, serving global markets, and increasing customer preference for the Intel brand, while delivering excellent financial results to our stockholders" had served them well over the years. By 1996, driven by strong sales of the Pentium® processor, Intel was on their seventh consecutive year of record earnings of both sales and revenue, and had reached the US$20 billion in revenues milestone. 1997 was another year of record revenues (an increase of 20 per cent) and record net income of almost US$7 billion, up 35 per cent over 1996. However, 1998 brought weaker than anticipated demand for personal computer (PC) products, which lead to lower first quarter revenue and earnings. Dr. Andy Grove, the founder and enigmatic leader of Intel referred to first quarter 1998 results as "disappointing," and stated that the "PC industry seems to have gotten ahead of itself, building more product than customers wanted." First quarter 1998 revenue of US$6 billion fell seven per cent, net income and earnings per share declined 36 per cent from the first quarter of 1997. The company widely expected revenue for the second quarter of 1998 to be flat, and year-to-date performance during the year had reflected this expectation.

Intel's global mission was nothing short of being the "pre-eminent building block supplier to the new computing industry worldwide." Thus, a major part of Intel's strategy was their commitment to creating microprocessors that the software of the next millennium could tap into. Concurrently, Intel followed a strategy of encouraging the developments of software engineers so they could push the envelope in software design to ensure that users would receive the benefits of the most advanced hardware Intel was developing. To help strengthen the Pentium® brand name, Intel focused on emerging markets with programs that stimulated demand for Intel products. Intel had succeeded tremendously in their branding campaign, and was considered one of the world's top 10 brands. Indeed, in 1997, over half (56 per cent) of Intel's revenue was generated outside of the United States, with the Asia-Pacific region and Japan accounting for almost a third of Intel's revenue. In 1999, Intel considered China to be their single most important market.

INTEL PEOPLE'S REPUBLIC OF CHINA (PRC)

Intel PRC Corporation established a representative office in China as early as 1985; however, it was not until 1993 that Intel felt the time was right to more fully enter the Chinese market with the establishment of two wholly-owned foreign enterprises. The first, Intel Architecture Development Co., Ltd. (IADL) was responsible for the sales, marketing and development of Intel's products and services in China. IADL's 250 employees were located in 13 offices throughout China; however, the Shanghai office with 100 employees and the Beijing office with 80 were the largest. The second, Intel (China) Technology Co. Ltd., was the entity of Intel's assembly and testing plant operations.

IADL employed more than 80 engineers who worked with local and multinational software vendors to develop innovative consumer and business applications to PC users in China. IADL's charter was to "accelerate technology adoption

in the PRC by providing technical and marketing support to local software developers." Initiatives included a developer support program, which included seminars, matchmaking events, training and conferences for Chinese software engineers and a donation of more than RMB$1.5 million of Pentium II processor-based development systems to assist leading Chinese software developers in bringing advanced software to local and international markets.

IADL's mandate was critical to Intel's growth, as senior management was aware that regardless of their research and development (R&D) expenditures, without software applications that could take advantage of the latest hardware developments, the user would not receive the advantage from that innovation. Thus, according to Tang, Intel's role in China was to act as a matchmaker, bringing all pieces of technology together to help China's PC users to understand how computing could help them in a comprehensive way. Tang explained that Intel looked at technology from a "total solution standpoint."

> By the time we start developing a new chip, we're already looking at what applications it will support and what solution it provides to the user. Thus, by the time the chip is ready to go into market, the platforms, the solutions are all ready so it is co-ordinated. This way, we're all moving forward and everybody wins.

By 1999, Intel had become involved in "just about every operation in the IT industry in China" and were aggressively marketing Intel-branded products throughout the country. Though still at its early stage of development, China's computer market had been growing twice as fast as the world average, and was poised to become the second largest computer market in the world by the end of the century. With its large population and fast economic growth, China's potential was extremely attractive to multinationals. As a global leader, Intel was well-positioned to capitalize on this opportunity and Charles Tang was one of the most important players in advancing Intel's presence in China.

CHARLES TANG

Tang had not returned to China since his departure eight years prior and his home country had changed dramatically during that time. Beijing had undergone a rapid period of extensive growth and the ubiquity of shiny modern buildings and presence of so many foreign firms was a shock to Tang. However, despite the changes in Beijing that he saw, Tang had the advantage of being previously exposed to the reality of life in Beijing, which could overwhelm many expatriates—the crowded streets, the pungent aromas emanating from the street markets, traffic congestion, punishing heat, and air quality for example. Tang commented that he had known of other Chinese nationals who had returned to the mainland, and despite the fact several months had elapsed, they still did not feel comfortable being in China and never really could adjust to life there after having lived in the United States or Europe. Though he initially felt "like a tourist," after having spent just one weekend wandering through the street markets, alleyways and pathways through the heart of Beijing, he was convinced he had made the right decision and had not looked back since.

Tang was one of the first three employees who were transferred to China from other Intel sites in 1993 to more firmly establish Intel's operations in the mainland. Tang gained experience in many areas, including a two-year stint in Shanghai to help establish Intel Architecture Laboratory there. During his time there, Tang established Intel's software developer support program—an integral part of Intel's China strategy. The account managers (AMs) in Tang's department played a critical role in this support effort. Their prime mandate was to forge and nurture relationships with prestigious Chinese software developers and vendors. By 1999, Tang reported directly to the president of Intel PRC and oversaw critical areas such as government relations, as well as industry and community programs, which included donations to many of the top universities in China to support research and teaching activities, as well as donations of equipment, upgraded on an annual basis.

The scope of Tang's development projects ranged from the grassroots community level such as a program that would sponsor Chinese high school students to attend a popular international science and technology fair in the United States, to investigating strategic investment opportunities. Tang also played a leading role on Intel's corporate advisory board, a body that was comprised of some of the most prominent Chinese influencers, both from the IT industry and academia. The board's broad mandate was to "spearhead industry programs by working with trade associations and industry leaders to influence the development of programs throughout the region to promote indigenous development of the industry by transferring Intel's acquired experience and expertise locally."

YONG LI

Yong Li was one of four AMs, each of whom had individual projects in addition to their primary responsibility. According to Tang, an AM's required skill set included the ability to interact as an Intel ambassador with senior managers and owners of the software firms with whom Intel was developing relationships. This involved effectively communicating Intel's IT strategy, "not from a technical viewpoint but rather from a strategic perspective," while ensuring full customer satisfaction on a daily basis. Another critical strategic component of the AMs' responsibilities lay in their ability to consistently recognize the possibilities of advancing the mutual interests of IADL and their clients—a key part of Intel's strategy in China. An AM's ability to exceed his clients' expectations was determined by his effectiveness in mobilizing Intel's internal resources, which involved extremely strong people skills and the ability to consistently demonstrate a mature, professional and diplomatic manner.

THE ISSUE

When Tang took over Intel's Beijing division, he was eager to familiarize himself with the operation of each department, and to aid him in this, he reviewed the files of all employees to understand their roles. Using his best judgment, Tang reassigned work as he deemed necessary, to ensure that each employee was working, both individually and within a team, toward advancing the strategic goals of the department and thus Intel in China. The same rationale was behind a reassignment of various departmental managers, and in the process, Tang reassigned the AMs under Qing Chen, a Beijing native. Though she had worked for a multinational before joining Intel, this was her first managerial position.

Tang's attention was drawn to Li's project upon reviewing Li's employee file. Though Tang felt the basic concept behind the project to be sound, he felt that it had expanded to such an extent from that which was initially proposed that it was not reasonable to expect that Li could realize the project's goals without it interfering with his primary duties of servicing his account base. The scope of the project had mushroomed in part due to the perspective of Li's previous supervisor who, according to Tang, was a very ambitious person who "approached everything on a grand scale with massive goals."

Initially, the project assigned to Li was the creation of a manual providing local software vendors with tips on running their enterprise, such as marketing various software products or how to manage or set up distribution channels, for example. However, Li approached the project with such unchecked zeal that it quickly transformed from a manual to a book form, with a chapter dedicated to comprehensive business planning issues, beginning with such basics as how to incorporate a business in China, sourcing venture capital, and the development of a comprehensive marketing plan tailored for software products.

Tang described the project as a "portable MBA-type book, covering essentially every topic a software company would need to know to do business in China." This was such an ambitious project, and Tang estimated it could take up to one year to complete, not including the two months of research Li had already conducted. Upon review of the file, Tang concluded that Li, a new and relatively young employee, without significant exposure to the business world or the software industry, did not have the background or expertise for this type of book. Tang felt that the project would be better suited to a writer who specialized in issues in the software industry. Given that there were many other projects that could be assigned to Li, which were of a more appropriate scope and focus, Tang instructed Chen to inform Li that work on the project was to be halted immediately, and that Li should be assigned a new project.

When Chen informed Li of Tang's decision to cancel the project, Li "totally rejected her," and he was not willing to even listen to the rationale behind the decision. Chen turned to Tang for assistance as she was at a loss as to how to reconcile Tang's demand with Li's desire to continue with the project and his agitated state that it had been cancelled. Tang decided that given Li's reaction, the best course of action was to bring them all together, and he scheduled a meeting as soon as he could to resolve the issue. Tang was conscious of handling the situation in such a way that did not undermine Chen's authority, as he felt that the empowerment of direct supervisors was critical. On the other hand, Chen confessed she was confounded by Li's reaction.

LI'S PERSPECTIVE

During his brief history with Intel, Li had dedicated himself to exceeding his clients' service expectations. Indeed, Tang readily acknowledged that Li had excelled at developing relationships with senior management in the companies in his assigned account base. Tang agreed that this was no small feat, as Tang's client base included some of China's most influential software firms, and in some cases had been so successful that he had created strong *"guanxi"* with senior management at those firms. *Guanxi* was the basis on which business in a Chinese context thrived. Loosely translated as "relationships," *guanxi* was such an integral part of doing business in China, that it was essentially impossible to do without it. Thus, when *guanxi* was established, it was protected at great cost, as it was widely considered to be the single most important factor in a successful business transaction. Its value in a Chinese business context could not be underestimated.

Li's success, therefore, in the realm of his primary duties was indisputable; however, he also applied himself equally to conducting research for his project and took ownership of it very seriously. Upon hearing that Tang had cancelled his project, he voiced his opinion immediately to Chen, saying that the two months of work he had conducted on his project were "wasted." Moreover, it was Li's strong contention that Tang altered not only one of his projects, but the essence of his responsibilities in one broad stroke, without due consideration, thereby undermining his efforts to date. Li continued:

> This is typical of expat managers—they come along and don't really care about what the workers are doing. They don't show respect and change the workplace according to their whim without providing explanation, and without warning.

Li felt that Tang had caused him to "lose face." Causing another to "lose face," could result in irreparable damage to the interpersonal relations between those two parties.

TANG'S PERSPECTIVE

Though he had heard through Chen that Li was very upset, Tang was previously unaware of the extent to which Li felt he had "lost face." Tang was thus largely unsure of how his actions could have affected Li at such an emotional level, and he took a few moments to consider his perspective of the situation. Tang acknowledged that Li was successful in establishing strong relationships with his clients. However, Li won various concessions for his clients through a demanding style toward his colleagues and a single-mindedness of purpose. Another talent that Tang acknowledged Li brought to his AM position was his ability to "think big." However, Li's assertive manner was not commonly found in traditional Chinese workplaces, and some of his colleagues, both within his department and throughout other departments which Li relied upon, were uncomfortable with Li's level of zeal. Complicating the situation was Tang's assumption that Li had not been formally indoctrinated to the Intel culture.

To demonstrate the Intel culture, Tang explained that Intel's employees throughout the world were characterized by their energy and youth, and thrived in a dynamic and creative environment. Tang further explained that in order to sustain intense levels of innovation, a degree of dissension and constructive criticism was encouraged; however, policies that helped advance Intel's 64,000 employees globally in the same direction were required. Tang explained a crucial part of Intel's culture—which was in place to achieve this end—the "disagree and commit" philosophy.

> If a consensus has been established that a particular course of action or a decision is appropriate, any individual employee would not only have to commit to that decision, but if he or she were responsible in any way in implementing it, this concept would dictate that they act as if they were in 100 per cent agreement with the decision. This means that once the course of action had been decided, it should not be discernible who was for, and who was against the decision before it was made. This is a condition of employment at Intel. It is the professional code on which I was brought up on at Intel.

Given Li's reaction, Tang wondered whether he had communicated to Li, and potentially his other employees, the quintessential role that this philosophy played in Intel's culture.

Tang reflected upon what other factors he should consider in analysing Li's behavior beyond his inexperience and apparent ignorance of Intel doctrine and considered potential underlying cross-cultural issues that might help to explain Li's behavior, while at the same time increase his understanding of all his employees. Although Tang had grown up in China and pursued his undergraduate degree in China, he had received a graduate degree from study in the United States as well as almost a decade of Western experience. Thus, he found himself in a precarious balance between two cultures. This created a rather unique situation for Tang—internally, he was perceived as an expatriate, yet because of his precise fluency in Mandarin and obvious comfort in Chinese culture, Tang felt he was perceived externally as a local Chinese.

TANG—AN EXPATRIATE OR A LOCAL?

When Tang first returned to China, when meeting with local government officials, he had a difficult time in persuading them that he was directly authorized to make decisions. First, at 33, he was significantly younger than most senior managers at multinationals in Beijing. Second, most often local Chinese did not hold positions of such power in multinationals.

To establish his credibility externally, Tang used a clever and effective technique. When Tang first met with the officials, he noticed that when he proffered his opinions directly, many of the local officials did not have confidence that Tang was empowered to make decisions. After trying a more direct approach, when a decision was consequently required, Tang told the officials that "I should check with my boss" but offered his decision in the interim. In subsequent meetings, it became clear to the local officials that Tang's "boss'" decision correlated precisely with Tang's personal decisions, time and time again. Thus, in time, he succeeded in establishing his credibility.

On other occasions, when he encountered a reticence among senior external managers or officials, he used another technique, equally effective. Tang would say, "I'll see if I can set up a meeting with my boss to discuss this issue, but may I have some background information to impart to him on which he can base his decision." This would allow Tang to obtain the required information on which to base his decision, which he would disclose at the following meeting. In these ways, Tang artfully managed his credibility as a local Chinese with external stakeholders. However, internally, Tang was perceived as an expatriate.

Tang was aware that being perceived as an "outsider" could undermine his ability to persuade his department that they were all part of the same team. Complicating the issue was not only Tang's expatriate status (one of few at the time), but as an expatriate, Tang received a superior pay and benefit package than local (Chinese) employees. Tang saw where he had advanced in relation to his employees as "just going through a different process to get to where we are, but now we're all at the same place—part of the Intel team." According to Tang:

> Work really doesn't have anything to do with whether you're an expatriate or local Chinese—it has to do with your ideas, how you understand strategy, technology and marketing—that's work. As long as you focus on that, and once your employees begin to focus on that, perceived differences really become a non-issue.

Tang dealt with the potential for conflict because of his rank or his experience in the United States by largely ignoring it, but Tang did not view this as an abdication of his responsibilities. On the contrary, Tang believed that by working hard and proving himself trustworthy, his employees would come to see that "we're all working together." According to Tang:

> How people look at you and how they feel about you has everything to do with how you make them feel about you. If you want to be seen as different, and if you want them to see you as different, they will. If you want to distance yourself from them you can. However, if you want them to see you as one of them, they will.

Tang was cognizant of some basic tenets on which the foundation of organizational behavioral differences as generally found between Chinese and Western firms were based, and acknowledged that both his Western education and experience as well as his exposure to Eastern business cultures affected his interpretation of the situation he was facing with Li. What challenged Tang also, with regard to managing Li, was how much of a departure Li's behavior was from what Tang considered to be a traditional Chinese business culture. Tang wondered whether he should question some of his beliefs about Chinese communication patterns and organizational behavior. Had things changed drastically since he had been away or was Li's behavior out of the ordinary?

Organizational Differences

Differences in Communication Patterns Between the East and the West

Generally speaking, Chinese organizational structures were more vertically layered than Western firms, resulting in dense reporting lines and bureaucratic administrative mechanisms. Moreover, Chinese organizations were most often led by a strong autocratic figure who took an active role in daily operations as well as the strategic direction of the firm. Whereas in some Western firms the organizational structure, supported by cultural influences, encouraged a degree of dissension and disagreement to advance the firm's organizational effectiveness and strategic direction, generally speaking Chinese firms operated on a principle of unquestioning adherence to the direction as dictated by senior management.

In contrast to Eastern management style, in Tang's opinion, Western organizational and communication systems promoted a more open discussion between managers and their employees. Tang's management experience suggested to him that employees in the West had a higher propensity to be more open and possessed a greater willingness to listen to their bosses if they had established a proven track record of being reasonable and open-minded. In contrast, Tang felt there seemed to be more suspicion among employees toward their supervisors in an Asian business context, as they managed with a much more closed style.

Though Tang considered his management style to be a mixture of Eastern and Western characteristics, he felt that many Western management principles manifested themselves more strongly. For example, he considered being open with his employees an integral part of managing, and indeed had succeeded in encouraging many of his employees to treat him as a confidant. On several occasions, he had been approached by members of his team and had held closed-door, one-on-one discussions regarding various aspects of their personal and professional lives. Tang was proud of the role he was able to take in acting in this capacity for his employees. On a broader level, Tang did his best to ensure that his employees' needs and concerns were addressed. For example, Tang ensured that his employees' salaries were commensurate with their responsibilities, and competitive as compared to other multinationals for employees working in a similar capacity. Tang considered actions such as this to be critical in establishing his employees' trust in him. It was actions such as this that reinforced Tang's belief that his employees were more comfortable approaching him than they may have been with an expatriate manager from North America or Europe.

The Decision

In this context, Tang was confounded by Li's reactions. Why did he respond so emotionally and what could he now do about it? Li was otherwise a promising employee who had forged valuable *"guanxi"* with his accounts. Tang did not want to risk losing him. Moreover, on a personal level, Tang cared about the welfare of his employees and, thus, it was upsetting to him that he may have caused his employee some distress.

Tang considered whether in light of Li's emotional attachment to the project he should allow him to continue with it, as in the scheme of things it was a relatively short-term project. Or was there a way to modify the project, finding a compromise between his needs and Li's desire to continue with the project? Tang was eager to have his employees contribute in such a way that would advance the strategic direction of his department, and felt strongly that whatever decision he made should be guided by that general principle. Tang knew that perhaps the easiest means to achieve this end would be to coerce Li to follow the "disagree and commit" philosophy

at Intel and redirect Li's attention altogether to a more appropriate project. However, he was concerned about Li's reaction to this move, given his emotional state.

Tang also considered the idea that perhaps this issue pointed to a larger one. Were the systems that facilitated vertical communication sufficient or should he consider implementing a more effective, more formal internal communications strategy? But Tang did not have time to consider this issue at the present moment—he glanced at his watch, jumped up and hurriedly placed his laptop in his briefcase to rush to a meeting.

CHUCK MacKINNON

Prepared by Kate Hall-Merenda under the supervision of Professor Jane Howell

 Version: (A) 2002-09-30

The day after his group's 1994 Christmas party, Chuck MacKinnon, a managing director with the Merchant Bank of Canada (MBC) in New York, wondered how both his group and his career had become so seriously derailed. The night before, he had witnessed the virtual disintegration of a group that he had worked diligently to mould into a fully functioning team. Chuck knew his career and his personal life, as well as the group's survival, depended on how he addressed the multitude of people problems which he thought had been resolved, but which he now knew had only been lying in wait, just below the surface. As he pondered the previous night's events as a denouement of 18 months dedicated to trying to bring his group up to speed for the changing marketplace of the 1990s, he wondered not only what he should do, but if he was the right person to do it.

CHUCK MacKINNON

After graduating from Georgetown University with his Bachelor of Science in Foreign Service, Chuck MacKinnon immediately went to work for Corporate Bank International (CBI), partially because CBI offered him the opportunity to work and earn his MBA in Corporate Finance, which he received in 1980. From 1980 to 1991, he held progressively more responsible positions within CBI, including a stint in Hong Kong. Then, in 1992, following CBI's merger with the Merchant Bank of Canada, MacKinnon was offered and accepted a position managing a full service branch of MBC in Saudi Arabia.

The Saudi Arabian months, Chuck's first exposure to the MBC, were fraught with difficulties. Managing a matrix organization with many units having dotted line reporting relationships to other areas around the globe was a challenge, but the larger challenge was solving a myriad of people problems that had been left unresolved by the previous manager.

Not long after his arrival in Saudi Arabia, Chuck discovered that the senior expatriate manager in the branch frequently left the bank to lunch in a bar in the American compound and did not return, and that his predecessor had allowed it. Chuck called Pete Dimarco, his boss in the United States, advised him of the situation and wondered aloud why it had been permitted to go on for so long. He could not have anticipated that he would receive a call from Bill Perkins, yet another MBC senior manager with interests in Asia, who "went ballistic" about Chuck not calling him first. As he reflected on the situation, Chuck noted:

> Immediately I was put off by how the Bank was not dealing with these problems, seemingly allowing them to happen, and accepting it; and then even getting angry with it being surfaced. . . . From the beginning I was never on solid ground on how we wanted to deal with this kind of stuff. We say the right things, but the messages once you get below the surface are not the same.

And there were other problems. Chuck caught some of his staff bribing government officials; having tax refunds directed into their personal accounts; cheating on credit cards; putting foreign exchange tickets in their personal desks; and having outside business interests that were in conflict with their jobs at the Bank. He resolved many of these problems by "firing a lot of people"; then he had union problems, but he persevered, trying to resolve the problems in the branch. His perseverance lasted until he started receiving death threats from a client who had bribed a Bank employee in order to get money out of the country illegally and whom Chuck had subsequently reported to the Bank of Saudi Arabia. According to Chuck:

> I thought that I had cleaned it up, that I had gotten the right people in place and that things were

running fine and that maybe, after all this pain, given the cultural issues, it was time for somebody else to come in and take it to the next step.

Chuck was looking for a new lease on life when a phone call came from Eldon Frost in Montreal offering him a corporate banking job in New York City with the Merchant Bank of Canada. Eldon portrayed the New York group as "working wonderfully, making money." In fact, he said, "it's a great business, you'll have a lot of fun." Chuck, thinking of his wife and two-year-old child, jumped at the offer.

ONE JOB, TWO MANDATES

In August 1993, Chuck stepped into his new position as Managing Director, Financial Institutions, with MBC in New York, looking for a fresh start. His job was to manage MBC's relationships with a multitude of financial institution clients as well as to lead a team in marketing MBC's and CBI's corporate financial services and products. His first few weeks on the job were sufficient to convince Chuck that his group had a number of people problems as well as an outdated business strategy. Yet, when he broached the subjects of adopting a new strategy to deal with changing business conditions or making changes within the group with Eldon, Eldon's mantra was "this group is great. Hey, your group is making 10 million bucks a year; it's working wonderfully!"

Although he did support Chuck's idea of a new strategy, Eldon was unwilling to let go of the group's traditional products. He did not see the market the same way as Chuck did; he had a different perspective. Eldon's market was the world, where a shortfall in revenues in one country could be made up by strengthening revenues in another. Chuck's world, the United States, was very different; there was no "contingency" location for making up revenue shortfalls. In spite of these differences, or because of them, Eldon could not see any reason for change;

he believed "our group is different, we don't need to change, we're happy, we're separate, don't worry about it."

Eldon was driven by the concept of keeping everyone happy. He had survived a major corporate downsizing and had adapted by keeping his head down and making no noise. Perhaps, Chuck speculated, that was why Eldon's attitude was, "Don't rock the boat, I'm a survivor." It did not help that Eldon had expected to be promoted into his boss's position, had been passed over, and consequently, harbored a great deal of resentment toward Margaret, who had been appointed executive vice president instead.

Margaret Mattson was two levels above Chuck in the corporate hierarchy (see Exhibit 1

for the organization chart) and Chuck met her only after he had taken up his position in New York. Unlike Eldon, Margaret was not satisfied with the Financial Institutions group or its performance. She had held Chuck's position open for a considerable length of time looking for the right person and was sure that Chuck was the person to carry out her "fix it" mandate.

In their very first face-to-face meeting, Margaret told Chuck that she was unsure if it had been the right decision to send Patrick Kinnard, one of the directors, from Montreal to New York. She was also critical of many of the staff that remained in Montreal and she wanted Chuck to fix the group by "getting rid of the weak staff." Margaret was sure that the group's current

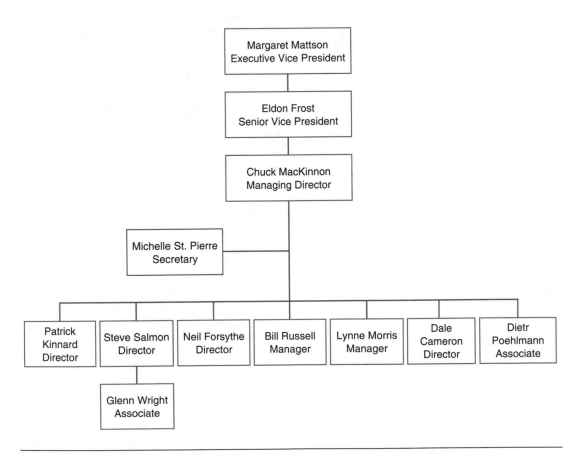

Exhibit 1   Financial Institutions Group Organization Chart

skills were not sufficient to meet the looming competitive challenges.

In their next meeting, Chuck convinced Margaret that there were also problems with the products the group had to offer, and that new ones were badly needed. "That clicked for her" when Chuck showed her the numbers on price concessions the group was making on traditional products and, from that moment on, Margaret fully supported Chuck in driving the group toward a new strategy. Unlike Eldon, Margaret had worked for another investment bank during the major downsizing at MBC. Possibly because of this, Chuck speculated, "she did not have the survivor mind set," and consequently, pushed hard for him to make major changes quickly.

Chuck informed both Eldon and Margaret of their conflicting expectations of him, but it appeared to have very little impact on either of his bosses. Eldon did tell Chuck that he and Margaret had a "you leave me alone, I'll leave you alone and we'll just work together but keep our distance as best we can" type of arrangement and implied that he would have to live with it. Chuck, himself, had seen that they were like "oil and water" and that they worked very hard not ever to be present in the same room. He wondered how he could possibly fulfill both mandates.

GETTING TO KNOW THE GROUP

When Chuck arrived in New York, his first order of business was to get to know his group (see Exhibit 2 for a profile of the group). He travelled to Los Angeles and Montreal, meeting members of his team and assessing their skills and prospects. In Los Angeles, he found a high-performing team of 50 under the deft leadership of Bruce Wilson. In Montreal, he discovered a group that felt that Patrick Kinnard, one of their number who had recently transferred to New York, "had cut a deal for himself and deserted them to get paid in U.S. dollars." Practically all of the Montreal people wanted to join Patrick in New York. Chuck knew that Patrick's parting words to the Montreal group were that their much desired relocation would happen.

Chuck was well aware that the financial institutions banking business required that banking professionals be within easy access of their customers, not a lengthy flight away. He decided that the Montreal group had to stay in Montreal. While the group struggled with the prospect of staying in Canada (and being paid in Canadian dollars), Chuck investigated means by which they could successfully operate as a team across

Name	Age	Years in Bank	Years in Position	PPR 1992	PPR 1993	PPR 1994
Chuck MacKinnon	39	3	1	EC	EC	QP
Patrick Kinnard	52	17	7	EC	EC	EC
Neil Forsythe	53	15	5	EC	EC	QP
Dale Cameron	40	18	1	EC	EC	QP
Glenn Wright	35	10	3	QP	QP	QP
Deitr Poehlmann	35	12	3	QP	QP	QP
Steve Salmon	50	20	7	QP	QP	QP
Lynne Morris	52	25	10	EC	EC	EC
Bill Russell	45	20	12	EC	EC	EC

Exhibit 2   A Profile of the Financial Institutions Group

PPR = Performance Planning and Review

EC = Exceptional Contribution

QP = Quality Performer

two countries and a continent. Technology and travel both offered solutions.

Travel was the easier of the two solutions. Chuck flew to Montreal on a varying schedule, never less than once a month, sometimes twice a week, to travel with his directors and senior relationship managers as they visited their clients. In an attempt to keep the lines of communication open, he augmented those personal visits with conference and groups calls. But, it was not enough; additional technology was required.

The Montreal group was not up to date technology wise. They didn't use e-mail or notebook computers in Canada. Chuck reflected, "possibly because of the technology lag, in Montreal they didn't see the vision" of a continent-spanning team. Chuck tried to correct the technology problem by supplying the Montreal group with notebook computers and cellular phones, primarily for use when they were travelling; but some members of the group could not, or would not, use them.

Chuck's frustration level grew. It took two days to track down one member of the group who was travelling in Europe when a client needed him; "nobody in Montreal even had an itinerary for him!" Why, he wondered, would they not use the scheduling package that he provided on their desk and laptop computers? Why did they view it as "big brother," or use it to check up on what Chuck was doing, instead of just acknowledging that it was merely a tool to make them accessible in times of need? Chuck felt that technology made it okay to have distant groups, while some of the group members said that it destroyed the camaraderie of face-to-face conversation. There was apparently not going to be a meeting of the minds.

Chuck had to admit that technology and travel could not furnish all of the answers to the group's problems. He discovered tremendous frictions within the group: Glenn Wright only worked with, and supported, Neil Forsyth, even though he was supposed to support the whole group; there was conflict between Steve Salmon, Neil and Glenn; and all of this was exacerbated when a demoted Patrick Kinnard moved to

New York and began to notice that Glenn was not supporting him either. The fact that Chuck himself was an unknown to the group, except for Dale Cameron and Patrick, added to the overall tension levels. Even though the "sales people got along with everybody and they were great," they were not enough to salvage the team.

Chuck knew that something had to be done to turn his disparate and geographically dispersed group into a team and he thought maybe skill-enhancing courses might be part of the answer. He enrolled the entire group in courses to improve organizational and sales skills and to introduce them to the use of technology in sales, figuring that if they went as a group and developed skills together, it would help to build camaraderie and team spirit. In keeping with that theme, in May, Chuck and the group attended a team-building and high performance team work course that, according to Chuck, went well.

People came out good friends. I thought there was commitment and I was positive about the whole thing.

Then, in July, Chuck hired the team-building course instructor to work as a consultant to the group.

THE STRATEGY

Chuck had another reason for providing the group members with a minimum of 10 training days per year, even though that number exceeded the average for the Bank. His first few months in New York and Montreal convinced him that the group's business strategy was hopelessly out-of-date with the needs of the financial institutions sector and that something had to change. When he arrived, the strategy had been very much cash management-driven, dealing mostly with cash letters and lock box type accounts. There were two problems with that strategy. First, with all the U.S. mergers, the group had lost business over time because their customers were taken over and they had not always been successful in gaining the acquirer's business. Second, the trend line in the cash management and lending business was downwards, and pricing pressures had been enormous. Even though volume had been increasing, prices were declining and the revenue line had been flat. Chuck knew that "if we had just stayed doing that, there would be no bonuses, no incentive, nothing. It would have been barely treading water . . . we needed to do something else."

Something else was a new strategy that involved expanding into other product lines such as Treasury, derivative products, stock transfer, lending and trust. The group had "never talked any of those other product lines to any U.S. financial institutions." Lack of familiarity bred resistance, even though Chuck worked hard to get and keep the group involved in designing and implementing the new strategy. His people, after all, knew their customers and presumably knew what their customers needed. In Chuck's words:

> That was part of the change that I was trying to get some of these people to deal with; to get up to speed with those products and go out and market them. And that was where I ran into resistance. They would say, why these products, what we're doing now is fine. Why change? And my feeling was that business was being commoditized and going to go away and that, in the long run, we were not going to be able to succeed with that.

He hoped by adding to their skill base and teaching them to perform as a team, their resistance to the new strategy would wither and die.

THE GROUP AS INDIVIDUALS

Neil Forsyth, Director

Located in Montreal, and in his mid-50s, Neil Forsyth was the first person to cause real friction for Chuck. He would say, "Why change, we cannot do this, I can't do it because I don't know how, I'm afraid, I don't see the need, I like the traditional thing and I'm good at it and it works." He was angry about the new strategy and kept agitating Chuck about it, making statements like, "You're nuts, it just won't work," while Chuck was trying to build a team. Although previously an exceptional performer, Neil received a quality contributor rating on his 1994 performance appraisal. While Neil believed that his performance ratings fell because of a personality conflict between himself and Chuck, Chuck noted that Neil's "ratings fell because he did not adopt the new strategy or provide that exceptional performance." Given the tension and disagreement between them, by late 1994, Chuck knew that he had to move Neil out of the group and he had started looking seriously for other opportunities for him within the Bank.

Glenn Wright, Associate

Also based in Montreal, during his first meeting with Chuck, Glenn told his new boss "what a great guy he was, how he was better than anyone else, and that he had been promised a directorship." Chuck, taking him at his word, promised to look into that directorship. What he discovered was that Glenn was not always delivering exceptional service. Indeed, Chuck was receiving mixed messages about Glenn's performance from Steve Salmon and Neil; evidently, Glenn had decided he would support Neil but not Steve. Chuck decided that he would not pursue the directorship for Glenn; in fact, he told Glenn that the only way to get promoted was through exceptional performance and that he had seen no sign of such performance.

Glenn felt that he could not deliver the expected exceptional performance in a strictly support role and asked Chuck to allow him to prove himself with his own clients. Trying to be fair, Chuck gave Glenn his own portfolio. Glenn liked having his own clients and did really well with some of them; others he alienated. According to Chuck, "if he needed you, you were his best buddy; if he did not need you, he ignored you; and if you pushed him, you were an !!!!!!!!!" Many of his client relationships were strained.

Glenn displayed very poor work habits and many Monday/Friday absences. Chuck started to get "a lot of heat" about Glenn from both Margaret and Eldon. Margaret, who had initially been critical of Glenn, became even more so after she saw him playing solitaire on his computer in the office. One day Eldon saw Glenn playing solitaire and called Chuck in wonderment, asking "how can an employee play solitaire right out in the open in the office?" Glenn, for his part, did not demonstrate that he wanted to work harder or support the new strategy. His attitude was, "I think you're wrong, I don't buy into any of this, I come in at nine and I'm leaving at 4:30." The chip on his shoulder just got larger and larger.

Deitr Poehlmann, Associate

Based in New York, Deitr's initial relationship with Chuck was a good one. Chuck saw from the beginning that, for some unknown reasons, Deitr was being "grossly underpaid" and undertook to make up a $20,000 annual shortfall over a period of time. As time went on, however, Chuck noted that "Deitr's work was spotty, sometimes okay and sometimes poor," particularly when it came to verbal and written communications in English. Deitr's first language was German, and that, to him, was sufficient reason not to do anything about his English. He believed people would make allowances for his language, even though Chuck spoke with him repeatedly on the matter and told him that they would not. At one point, Deitr went so far as to find an English-speaking trainer of operational staff to attest to his fluency in the English language.

Deitr also had "tremendous problems communicating internally; he would call people liars on e-mail and send copies of the e-mail to everyone, including their bosses" (see Exhibit 3). Such behavior created seemingly endless problems for Chuck, who was called upon time and again to smooth ruffled feathers of colleagues and clients who had been offended by Deitr's rather abrupt manner of communicating and by his tactless language. Chuck attempted to counsel Deitr on both his use of English and the English he used, but to no avail. Indeed, it seemed to have the

opposite effect; Deitr had, for many years, believed that the world was prejudiced against the Germans and eventually he directed those sentiments towards Chuck.

Dale Cameron, Director

Dale Cameron originally came from Corporate Bank International and started in the New York group following the 1992 merger between CBI and MBC. He had had a long standing and positive relationship with Chuck when the latter arrived in August 1993. Although Chuck did not push him, indeed, he let him slide because of more pressing issues with others, he did notice that Dale had problems with erratic work. Some of Dale's memos were totally unintelligible, while others were cogent and well written. Chuck suspected a drug or alcohol problem and suggested that Dale access the Employee Assistance Program, but Dale claimed that there was no problem. In retrospect, Chuck admitted that "I ended up protecting him a little bit, became a little co-dependent," and, in November 1994, he gave Dale a quality contribution rating on his performance appraisal, noting that Dale had both accepted, and attempted to implement, the new strategy.

Patrick Kinnard, Director

Patrick Kinnard was Chuck's predecessor, a very capable individual in the cash management business. He had developed some new product lines that were interesting and Eldon had moved him to New York from Montreal in the summer of 1993 to give him a fresh start in a new location after his demotion. Eldon publicly said that, in spite of the demotion, he thought Patrick was great at everything he did and he told Chuck that "Patrick's nose will be out of joint since you got his job, but he will come around." In the beginning, it seemed as if that might be true. Their early relationship was fine and, although Chuck had heard numerous stories about Patrick's serious drinking problem, he did not mention those stories to Patrick. Chuck had decided to reserve

From: Deitr Poehlmann
To: Chuck MacKinnon
Cc: Bob Grange; Joe Peoples; Stan Mantrop

Chuck,

Usually people that feel threatened, weak, try to hide their weaknesses, or try to ruin one's reputation will send e-mail as Joe did (the one below). I do not know that Joe has against me. I never create conference calls unless all parties know about it and agree to it.

I spoke with Bob Grange this morning. First, he still says that he was not aware of Cory's participation. Since this view is different from mine, I suggest that we call Cory and find out his view. Bob suggested (and I agreed) that we should not have our clients get involved in this. Bob and I decided that from now on, our phone conversations will not include third parties in order to avoid one's not knowing who else is on the phone. Bob also said that Boston Mutual's situation introduced to him is very clear.

I tried to call Joe but he is already in Hong Kong. I wanted to see what was so convoluted to him as, I hope, obviously you understood my e-mail. Obviously, Joe did not. Since it is so difficult to have this thing done with Joe, I thing we should just drop it and let Boston Mutual do its thing on its own (which they are as we speak).

From: Deitr Poehlmann
To: Chuck MacKinnon

Chuck, as we agreed and you asked me to do so, I am sending you this e-mail to friendly remind you that as of August 1, you were to consider giving me a merit increase in my salary. I hope that you will be generous and take into consideration all my contribution to growing revenue at International Portfolio. I hope that I am exceeding your expectations from working on reducing backlog, bringing new business, and cross-selling business to existing clients. I want to thank you for your prior recognition in the form of increases and bonus and hope that you see me as a productive member of your team. Also, as you know, my salary, in my view, is below average, although I must say that you kept your word to me about increasing it "over time" to higher level.

From: Steve Salmon
To: Chuck MacKinnon
Cc: Deitr Poehlmann

Yes, and I think we'll find Lansing were unhappy as to HOW we dialogued with them, and that also had an influence. While I'm sure it was misinterpreted, I'm told Deitr Poehlmann didn't come across very well in his conversations with them.

Exhibit 3   Deitr Poehlmann's Correspondence   *(Continued)*

From: Deitr Poehlmann
To: Chuck MacKinnon; Steve Salmon

Steve, it they told you that I am not surprised about the statement. There was only one person that I spoke at Lansing. She herself was rude, imposing and cancelled our (Chuck and myself) meeting with them day before we were to go to Atlanta. Their point was that we were "demanding" reciprocity business (custody) from them. I did what I was told by Chuck and Brett Davies. We did not extend the lines as they wanted and I am sorry if they did not like that. I have been dealing with them for the past 3 years without any problem until not all of their demands were met. At that point, I guess, I fell into disfavor. The only bad thing is that right now we are out of $40,000 + revenue.

Dear Merridith,

As you know, after closing USD account, Corporate Bank International still maintains Canadian Dollar account with your fine bank. With our ongoing process of reviewing all of our account relationships in an effort to process our business more efficiently and cost effectively, it has become apparent that we need to close the Canadian Dollar account that we maintain with you, as well. Therefore, we decided to close it effective May 15. The account by that time should have no balances left, however, should there be any money left on that day, please have it sent to:

Sincerely,

Deitr Poehlmann

Exhibit 3   Deitr Poehlmann's Correspondence

judgment and give Patrick a chance to prove otherwise.

Six months later, coinciding with the initiation of the new strategy, Patrick and Chuck's relationship started to deteriorate. Patrick had agreed to follow the new strategy, but felt that Chuck did not respect the traditional cash management business sufficiently. At one point, Patrick went to Eldon, complaining about the strategy and saying that they were heading for disaster. He even brought Dale along to say the same thing. Eldon's reaction was to call Chuck immediately, questioning him about what was going on in New York and demanding that they find a way to work together. Chuck's subsequent interviews with both Patrick and Dale got all of the issues out on the table and he did what could be done to address the doubts both men had about the new strategy.

Then, in the summer of 1994, Chuck received a call from Margaret inquiring about Patrick's random sick days; to her, the absences looked suspicious. Having had some experience with alcoholics and their habits and patterns, Chuck sat down with Patrick, asked him if he had a drinking problem and offered to work with him through the Alcoholics Anonymous steps. Patrick's response was that "he was dealing with it" (see Exhibit 4 for a synopsis of Patrick's absences). Chuck, who was not sure Patrick was dealing with it or that any alcoholic could deal with their alcoholism by *drinking moderately* or *keeping it under control,* suggested the Bank's Employee Assistance Program but Patrick did not take advantage of the offer. Chuck felt that he had done all that he could insofar as Patrick was concerned.

From: Eldon Frost
To: Patrick Kinnard

I am writing to register my concern on your performance on June 17 as reported to me and Margaret Mattson by Peter Delottinville, VP Employee/Industrial Relations, and as related to him by the two lawyers who spoke with you by phone on Friday June 17 on matters related to a criminal court case against the Bank and where your input was requested.

As advised to me your behavior was such that you were not making sense of the information provided you, nor were you able to answer the questions posed in a coherent and understandable manner. As a result, counsel for the Bank and for Elections Canada have had to prepare a list of questions for you to answer in written form.

In addition, I understand Margaret Mattson also spoke with you by phone the morning of Friday June 17, at approximately 10 a.m., and she was of the impression you had been on calls earlier that morning with Neil Forsythe and Bill Russell. In this regard I have been informed by Neil Forsythe that neither he nor Bill Russell called on customers with you that day and that in fact you advised them that morning that you were ill and could not attend the planned meetings.

Patrick, I am very much concerned with what happened on Friday as this is not the customary behavior expected of you.

In this regard your input on the above events would be appreciated so that we may work together to overcome whatever problems may exist. Eldon Frost.

Chuck MacKinnon's log of events:

12/9 Patrick at the last minute called in to take a vacation day.

1/23 Patrick arrived at 12:00 p.m. "Drove his brother-in-law to the airport."

4/26 Sick day.

6/12 Patrick arrived at 10:00 a.m., said a cab did not show up to take him to the train, so had to drive in.

7/7 Sick Day-back was out.

7/12 Sick Day-back was out.

9/1 Vacation day, family flight delayed in returning from holidays. Called Friday morning.

9/6 Sick day, called at 8:30 a.m. with the flu.

9/25 Had lunch with Patrick today to discuss some of the concerns that he has raised previously. At the same time we discussed some of the administrative problems he has had (the audit, problems with expense claims, not getting back to Redboard on time on information he needed for a board presentation, last minute absences and vacation days, etc.). I indicated that I did not think I should be put in a position of having to cover for him on these problems. I indicated that I thought they were a possible indication of the drinking problem we had previously discussed but Patrick indicated this was not the case. He said he was just sloppy on some things and tended to procrastinate but would work on cleaning this up in the future.

9/27 Sick Day, supposed to be in Montreal after calls in Pittsburgh the prior day, had the flu, was dizzy and sick to his stomach. Had dinner with PNC the night before.

Exhibit 4   Patrick Kinnard's Absences   *(Continued)*

9/28 Sick day, supposed to be in New York, had the flu.

9/28 Had conversation with Eldon this afternoon. Eldon was wondering where Patrick was on Wednesday as he had an appointment to see him. I told him he was sick and Eldon wondered if he was drinking again. I don't know whether Patrick was drinking on this occasion as I did not speak to him but this is not the first time that Patrick has missed a day in Montreal after travelling and having dinner with clients the night before. I did clarify for Eldon that I had had several conversations with Patrick as a friend about the drinking and cautioned him that he could not have any repetitions of past events. When Eldon heard that Patrick continues to drink (he regularly does so with and without clients although I have never seen him drunk again) and believes that he can handle it, he was very concerned as his deal with Ken is that there can be no drinking at all. If there is, their understanding is that Patrick will no longer be allowed to be in a client marketing position as his history in Montreal indicates he cannot control his drinking. Eldon referred to this as his "smoking gun."

Exhibit 4   Patrick Kinnard's Absences

THE 1994 CHRISTMAS PARTY

Thinking he could bring the group together and really cement the team spirit and acceptance of the new strategy that he thought was taking hold in the group, Chuck decided to hold the Christmas party in Montreal. He brought in all of the people from the New York office and some from the Los Angeles unit to join the festivities. The party was held in a fancy restaurant and they were seated out in the open. For a while, all went well, but as the evening advanced and people got progressively more "toasted," the illusion of camaraderie began to disintegrate.

The worst part came when group members rose to their feet and began to give speeches. Patrick and Glenn each gave 10-minute speeches putting down the new business direction, asking "where are we going with this strategy?" They also could not resist harping on the bitter relationships in the group. Bill Russell then gave a speech about how "we should all be getting along better." Chuck, who had been trying to sit near those individuals who had major issues, was both embarrassed, "everyone in the place was paying attention," and angry "at the group and at individuals, for rehashing old stuff. It had been a year and a half and they weren't suggesting anything new to replace what they didn't like."

Having had enough, Chuck decided it was time for the party to break up. Passing Lynne Morris on the way out of the restaurant, Chuck could see that she was as appalled as he was and as uncomprehending of what was going on. Although he only wanted to go to sleep, the evening was not over for Chuck. In order to stop Patrick from hitting on Michelle St. Pierre, his executive secretary, he bundled Dale and Patrick into a taxi and got them to the hotel bar. In the bar, Patrick first picked a fight with Dale, and, after Chuck broke up that fight, he picked a fight with Chuck. The whole miserable evening only ended, Chuck reflected, when he finally gave up and went up to bed.

The next day Patrick was nowhere to be seen. Chuck spoke with Bill Russell to see if he could make sense out of Bill's behavior the previous evening. Bill did not really remember making the speech about everyone working together as a team, but he was embarrassed and fully apologetic and vowed it would never happen again. Chuck, for his part, was able to overlook one slip from a stellar performer—it was, after all, Christmas—but he would not overlook another one.

As Chuck reflected on the previous evening's disaster, he found some things to be thankful for. His group was not completely dysfunctional.

The Functional Group

Steve Salmon, Director

Steve Salmon was based in Montreal. He was "a good guy, an average performer, one who would never be a superstar but he supported the strategy and did his best to implement it." He was very good at his job, well liked by his clients in a portfolio that he had handled for five years and he produced consistently good results. Steve was a "solid member of the team and a pleasure to work with. He is well liked by everyone on the team."

Lynne Morris, Manager

An exceptional performer and team player, Lynne was well liked and respected by clients and team members alike. She was a delightful individual who supported the new strategy, who had made the transition into new products fairly successfully, and "she was rewarded that way with big bonuses." Chuck counted on her for fielding calls on traditional cash management issues as well as for implementing the new strategy.

Bill Russell, Manager

Bill Russell was an exceptional performer who had increased his role in the identification of sales opportunities and was taking the necessary steps to close sales. Bill was a committed team member who supported the changes taking place, who willingly brought ideas and opinions to the table, who did a lot of cross-selling of products and who had made the transition to the new products well. Like Lynne Morris, Bill was a high performer and rewarded that way and, again like Lynne, Chuck counted on him for traditional cash management inquires and problems.

Bruce Wilson

A very high performer based in Los Angeles with 50 people reporting to him, Bruce Wilson managed a quality operation with a very thin staff that dealt with a wide range of responsibilities including systems and marketing. His service levels were high and his clients were both very loyal and supportive; his employee morale was high. Bruce emerged from the 1994 Christmas party saying, "Holy God, what the heck is going on here? Good luck to you!"

Chuck's Dilemma

The previous 18 months had not been easy for Chuck. He had always been an exceptional performer but had received only a "quality contributor" rating from Eldon on his 1994 performance appraisal. Although he had tried, he could not get Eldon to explain why he considered him only "quality" and what it would take to become "exceptional" again. Eldon had only suggested that maybe the problem with the group's dynamics was partly due to Chuck's management style. At his wit's end, Chuck thought maybe Eldon was right. Perhaps he "just did not get it." He thought, "This is it, I don't know what is going on around here, this isn't working" (see Exhibit 5 for an example of team conflict). But he did not have other avenues in the Bank to pursue. He had talked to people at CBI, but it was tough to get back in once you had left, and he had no network within MBC that he could tap. He felt stuck.

Chuck's growing self-doubts were reinforced by the messages he was getting from Margaret. Although he was convinced that he was pursuing the right business strategy, he wondered about his management style. Margaret's "fix it mandate" had changed; she openly wondered if Chuck's management style had been too severe, too hard. Chuck wondered if, and what, he could be doing better, if he had misunderstood the degree to which the bank was willing to change. "After all," he confessed, "when you have that many dysfunctionalities and a boss persistently saying everything is fine, the result is self-doubt."

From: Dale Cameron
To: Glenn Wright
Cc: Chuck MacKinnon

Thank you for your quick turnaround and I believe that your presentation was done well. I would add, however, that we should be careful about using words (in letters and our presentations) which tend to undermine the "relationship team" concept. Specifically and despite our clearly being more capable of answering their questions, it might have been nice to say that they could also call myself. Finally, I called Linda and Jennifer yesterday and asked for feedback. Had I known you had done so, we could have avoided the extra call and the potential of appearing that we are not coordinating with one another. I will, likewise, endeavor to do the same. I assume the reports and letters are in the centrepoint file, and will copy you on the ones for the other three visits.

From: Glenn Wright
To: Dale Cameron
Cc: Chuck MacKinnon

Dale, this is one relationship you should leave to me. I have an excellent rapport with them and I think we are starting to confuse them. They have also asked several times that the relationship be managed by me through Linda, Homer and now Jennifer, something Linda reiterated in the meeting, if you remember, and in subsequent conversations. In the end, through PPR, we will all share any rewards to be had.

Glenn

From: Dale Cameron
To: Glenn Wright
Cc: Chuck MacKinnon

I could care less about "rewards" and PPR, other than as it relates to doing the job we are expected to do in a fashion that places professionalism and client service first. For that matter, you can have 100 per cent of all the credit on anything that is done with this client. We should always do, within reason, what the client wants and as global R/M you are responsible. If you recall, I specifically said that in my intro. I do not ever remember hearing Linda say anything about this, it was never expressed that way to me by Mike or Linda on the intro call, and I would like to know what conversation you are referring to where Jennifer said this. She's your contact anyway. Finally, I haven't even heard about this request from you until today.

Chuck, your decision is needed and perhaps you should call Homer or Jennifer and ask them outright. In the meantime, as long as I am "responsible" for this specific entity, I expect to be kept appraised of what is being discussed, done and acted upon, as you would expect of me. I have done so and will continue to do so. For that matter, all other entities for which I have responsibility. Rewards—absolutely misses the point.

From: Chuck MacKinnon
To: Dale Cameron; Glenn Wright

P.S.   Sounds like there is some friction here. Let's talk about this on Monday between the three of us but the client's interests must be foremost.

Exhibit 5   Team Conflict

On top of the erosion of his self-confidence in his management style, Chuck was beginning to see himself as a co-dependent in protecting Patrick and Dale. He had helped both of them with their work, redone their work and covered for them by writing memos addressing what were major problems and making light of them. Had he been mistaken in his attempts to give everyone a fair chance to adjust to the new regime before taking action? Could some of the problems have been avoided if he had been, not softer, but tougher?

Then there was his personal life. He had been short-tempered with both his wife and children and had been feeling guilty about allowing his work stresses to spill over into his personal life. Normally, he had been adept in separating the two, but in this case, he had failed.

The day after the 1994 Christmas party found Chuck wondering what was going on. Should he be looking for work elsewhere? The messages from his boss and his boss's boss were clear: it might be his management style. Had he done something wrong? What could he, or anyone else, do to fix it now?

ELISE SMART

*Prepared by Jeffrey Gandz
and Elizabeth Spracklin*

Version: (A) 2003-03-06

Elise Smart looked over the performance assessment form that she had just completed on Darlene Ketchum. Clearly, it was going to come as a bit of a surprise to Ketchum, who had never received anything other than an "Excellent" overall rating in the last five years. Smart was also concerned that it might not be well received by her own vice-president, John Cheng, who had given Ketchum her previous two performance appraisals and who would probably not really want to deal with the conflict that might well ensue from this appraisal. Still, thought Smart, she had to call it the way she saw it, and over the last 12 months Ketchum's performance had fallen short of her expectations in her major assignment.

The performance management process at Millennium Insurance required Smart to first discuss the rating with Ketchum. She was pretty sure that Ketchum would expect an "Excellent" rating, whereas her own view was that Ketchum's performance deserved a lower "Needs Improvement" rating, two categories below. Following a discussion, Ketchum would be asked to agree to the rating and sign it. Then Smart would have to submit the performance assessment to Cheng, with or without Ketchum's agreement. He could,

if so inclined, either overrule her decision or convene a special review panel of other directors who would give both Smart and Ketchum an opportunity to defend their viewpoints before making a decision.

Smart realized that there was a more important issue than this particular performance appraisal. Whether or not she continued to lead this group over the next year or two, she felt that Ketchum's drop in performance level should be confronted and dealt with candidly. After all, when someone who had always been described as "Outstanding" stopped performing to that level, there must be a reason. And if that reason could not be identified and resolved, then further failures may result, to the detriment of both Ketchum and the company.

However, there were some unusual circumstances surrounding this appraisal. Ketchum's two goals had been very different in nature, and the one on which she had not performed well had involved a fairly complex and unstructured assignment, quite a "stretch" for Ketchum, given her background and experience. Also, Ketchum had taken a six-month maternity leave during the year, and although her goals had been adjusted to reflect this, she may have lost some focus on her work because of the leave and the responsibilities of a new family.

MILLENNIUM INSURANCE COMPANY

Millennium Insurance was a mid-sized insurance company with 10,000 employees and approximately 1.8 million customers. Most of its revenues came from various lines of insurance (life, property and casualty, health) as well as from a substantial mortgage business. It also had substantial numbers of employees involved in investment activities, trust and other related financial services. Although smaller than the giants in its industry, Millennium had no problem attracting the best and brightest employees in the industry and, especially in the information technology (IT) area, it was a preferred place to work. Young professionals from top schools were recruited and given challenging assignments as they built their early careers. They were given good mentoring and development programs and the opportunity to develop both technical and people management skills to high levels.

Millennium was organized into several business units to run its lines of business: life, health, property and casualty, mortgages, and others. These operated independently but relied on shared services for human resource management, IT and other support functions. In most cases, this worked well. However, when the centralized shared services departments did not respond quickly and competently to the business units' perceived needs, the complaints flew fast and furious and escalated quickly to the senior executive level.

ELISE SMART'S ASSIGNMENT

Elise Smart, 32, was a senior manager in the development group of the IT division where she had worked for over three years. She was hired as a high performer with a strong 10-year track record in the IT field. "If there's a problem area, Smart can probably sort it out" was her vice-president's opinion. She was technically strong as an IT professional, but above all, she had a reputation for being a good team leader, and her staff generally liked her no-nonsense approach to getting things done.

It was a time of considerable change in the organization of IT in the company. Many people in the line business divisions, from executives to lower-level analysts, were buying and using a variety of personal computers (PCs) and software packages. Many of these purchases were being done without advice from the central IT organization; there were numerous problems associated with PC set-up, connectivity to the backbone network, software incompatibilities and data security. When end-users contacted the IT department, they were not satisfied; the vast majority of the staff in IT were focused on mainframe computing and operational systems and knew little or nothing about PCs and the software that ran on them. This resulted in a litany of complaints from the line business units about the unresponsiveness and incompetence of IT. The small group within the development department of IT was overwhelmed with the volume of requests for assistance and the large variety of issues on which assistance was required.

The senior vice-president of IT was not happy about this situation since it affected the credibility of the whole IT function. He had designated funds and resources to promote successful adoption of PCs within the businesses and to isolate the problems caused by PCs across the IT organization. Smart and the other senior managers, along with their vice-president, had agreed to divide the roles as follows, and each put together their goals and objectives for the next year:

- PC Research and Development: a team of eight people was to check out new hardware and software and recommend standards, negotiate volume discounts from suppliers, and set up an order process to stimulate adoption and minimize integration issues.
- Knowledge Management: a second team of eight was to develop and maintain the advanced functions for knowledge management including

document handling, scheduling systems, and electronic work flow systems.

- End User Education and Support: a team of 12 was formed to launch a drop-in centre in the middle of the "business community"— where the business units were located—provide internal introductory training, handle the phone call support and assist users in the acquisition, installation and use of PCs and associated software and getting them networked. This was Smart's assignment.

In discussions with Cheng and the senior vice-president of IT, Smart recognized some ambivalence about creating this new drop-in centre. After all, there was already a well-developed and highly professional IT Helpline run by the operations department within the IT group. They had recently adopted a methodology of logging and analysing requests, ensuring that they provided timely response on a "24/7" basis, tracking the outcomes of advice given and all of the other things that good help-desks were supposed to do. The idea of creating a new, end-user oriented group—that appeared to do many of the same things but was dedicated to the PC-based, end-user community—did not sit well with some people.

When Smart took on her new role in December, she inherited a team that had already been assigned to end-user education and support and who had worked in the development group within IT. Most people on the team were discouraged and tired as they had been trying their best to answer calls from users with all kinds of problems—which were always urgent. There was no system for logging, analysing and tracking calls. Consequently, several staff could be going in different directions to solve the same underlying issue, and they were not really learning anything from each other.

In her typical manner, Smart soon started to get things organized. Within six months, her team of 12 was deployed in three ways:

- They manned and operated a "PC Help-Desk" accessible by telephone from any of the business units. Incoming calls were received at a central number, the requests were assigned to one of her team, and both calls and responses were tracked.
- They worked on projects generated from the user-groups such as analytical spreadsheets for investment professionals or PC notebook-based sales aids for the field representatives and brokers.
- They worked in a highly visible tech centre. This was physically located in the middle of the user community, rather than in the IT department. It was staffed on a shift basis by members of her team. As well as meeting "clients" who needed face-to-face help, the tech centre also carried products—PCs and software that could be ordered—and served as a location for hosting demonstrations and educational sessions.

PROGRESS

In spite of some early resistance to taking time to build an action plan, as opposed to just "doing it," the team quickly bought into the discipline of developing and following a project document, and began to enjoy working on their own tasks while still knowing what the other members of the team were doing. The tech centre took shape, and regular team meetings ensured that all their opinions and advice were considered and acted upon. The launch was a huge success—on schedule and a fun event. Responding to the steady stream of users with previously prepared and handy material enabled the team to move quickly into more interesting issues together. Users raved over the terrific customer service and the team took great pride in the professional approach.

Meanwhile, the PC support process was changed. Desks were set up in a small storage room dedicated to the PC support phone numbers, including phones with headsets. Logging was instituted and calls-in-process were marked on white boards for easy reference. Staff took turns on duty, choosing two-hour shifts. More difficult questions were reviewed as a team and assigned separately. All these changes gave users immediate access to a person rather than phone mail and gave the staff time at their desks uninterrupted by calls for their other work. Metrics were being gathered on all the activities, surprising the staff and enabling Smart to finally provide senior management with interim but regular, measurable results.

By mid-year, as planned, the team had accomplished quite a change in operation:

- A reduction in the questions relating to ordering equipment by providing a standard list of options.
- A reduction in the tedious explanatory questions by redirecting users to tips and frequently asked questions or to the introductory training courses provided on use of a PC, word processing and spreadsheets manipulation.
- Metrics on support calls from seven to eight months of data on the actual questions received.

Each team member in Smart's group split their time between giving personal consulting while on duty in the centre (run nine to five), answering and logging phone questions while on duty on support (two-hour shifts) and project work: assisting business groups with tougher problems; taking the lead on analysing common problems; overseeing the education scheduling; or marketing the tech centre services within the company.

A FUNDAMENTAL ISSUE

The establishment of this very visible PC support function had created a situation in which IT now had two separate help departments: one was the helpline run from within the operations group in IT; the other was the PC support group and its associated tech centre. One question posed by the senior executive even before the PC support group had been fully established was whether this was necessary and a good use of resources. Even while implementing the PC support group and tech centre concepts, Smart was given the task of developing a set of recommendations

as to how the whole help function should be handled in the future. Should there be two independent groups? Or should the help function be integrated as one unit, covering both operations and PC users? And, if the latter, how should it be done? Smart decided that this task—one of her three priority goals for the year—should be assigned to Darlene Ketchum.

DARLENE KETCHUM

Ketchum, 28, had worked in the end-user support group that Smart had inherited from the development department of IT when she had taken on this new role. A computer science graduate from a local university, Ketchum was well liked, extremely knowledgeable about PCs and related software and really seemed to like helping people, especially end-users who were neither knowledgeable about IT nor comfortable in dealing with technical issues. She was also pregnant and planned to take a maternity leave starting in February and returning in October.

Smart felt that it would be reasonable to assign Ketchum some duty time on the phones and tech centre but focus most of her effort towards the investigation and production of a recommendation on whether or not to merge PC support with the main IT helpline. Ketchum had been with the team doing both PC and e-mail support prior to her maternity leave so she was fluent in the kinds of problems users had and understood the importance of providing answers if possible. She was equally aware of the importance of managing their expectations—when they could expect an answer, so they can get back to work and know they will be contacted at a confirmed time period. What wasn't known was how the IT helpline would be working by then, and what the strengths and weaknesses would be of the two approaches—helpline and the PC support group with its tech centre.

In the prior year, Ketchum had just completed an assignment with a small, tightly knit team that very successfully launched document management across the company. The team had received a lot of recognition for good implementation, but Smart knew they had worked closely with the supplier of the document management system to produce and execute the launch plan, and she was not sure how capable Ketchum would be of working on an assignment independently.

But Ketchum was very enthusiastic and confident when she accepted the tasks in January. She gave the impression that she both understood the assignment and appreciated that she was being given the chance to deliver results. This project would clearly be her work to do in the time she had available and could potentially move her forward in consideration for promotion during the next 18 to 24 months. Ketchum left for maternity leave right after signing off on her objectives for the year.

OCTOBER

By the time Ketchum returned from her maternity leave, she was amazed at the changes and joined readily into the new structure. Smart gladly turned over leading the regular PC support staff meetings to Ketchum, since she believed that by chairing these meetings, Ketchum would be able to get a real sense of the value added by the PC support function and tech centre. Once she really knew what the PC support group was doing, Ketchum could look at what the helpline function was providing, and then decide whether and how the groups should be integrated.

The PC support team had already delivered beyond the targets set for the tech centre and training, but the capacity remained the same. Senior management was happy that the user community's response had completely turned around—and had in fact gone from complaining to congratulatory to quiet. As the senior management group began looking at budgets for the next year, the resources devoted to the three teams came under increased scrutiny, and Smart knew that cost-effectiveness was becoming more and more important for the coming year.

During several one-on-one meetings with Smart in October, Ketchum had communicated that she had scheduled meetings with the central IT helpline managers and staff to learn how they work. She had also begun to look at software packages to track and log calls, and she reported that the PC team meetings were going well. Unfortunately, at one-on-one meetings with other team members, Smart was hearing that Ketchum was using the meetings to secure "volunteers" to take on these tasks—and they of course didn't have time. When questioned, Ketchum defended her actions by saying that the team had identified issues and she was doing her job in addressing the issues with actions, and that they were working on the short-term resolutions while she worked on the longer term approach regarding PC support—her recommendations.

Ketchum backed off assigning work, but continued to be "busy" addressing the immediate issues from the team. Also, delays appeared in her own progress plans, because the helpline people had repeatedly cancelled her meetings due to various crises. Her preliminary assessments, all given in the form of verbal updates, leaned heavily towards the opinion that the calls were very different between the two groups and that the staff responding to the helpline calls did not currently have any PC knowledge, so redirecting users through them would clearly represent a delay in response. However, these meetings seemed to be long on opinions and feelings and rather short on facts.

Ketchum was suggesting that the PC support function should use automated call logging and escalation software that would greatly improve the overall provision of service for PC support. She wanted to proceed to look at options. Ketchum clearly felt frustrated that the helpline group did not yet see how they might share the new logging system they were implementing. Smart, for her part, encouraged Ketchum to stand back from the details of what systems should be used and instead focus on the bigger picture of whether and how to integrate the help function.

By the end of November, Ketchum had still not produced a position paper or set of recommendations, and she had continued to try to solicit help from the other team members to help her evaluate or develop a call-logging system.

PERFORMANCE ASSESSMENT AT MILLENNIUM INSURANCE

Millennium's culture demanded that qualitative operational goals be defined annually along with clear numbered priorities and evidence of completion required. At year end, employee performance evaluation, salary increases and bonuses were determined. Based on the achievement of these goals, employees were given an overall rating:

- Outstanding: Exceeding performance levels on all goals;
- Excellent: Meeting, but not exceeding, performance levels on all major goals, but not achieving some minor or less important goals;
- Needs Improvement: Not meeting objectives on one or more major goals;
- Unsatisfactory: Failing to meet performance objectives on most or all goals.

The "Outstanding" category was used in about 10 per cent of cases, as was the "Unsatisfactory" category. Most employees were rated as either "Excellent" or "Needs Improvement." Because the ratings applied to specific goals and levels of achievement of those goals, the system was thought by most people to be reasonably free of subjective assessments. However, since goals were negotiated between managers and those who reported to them, there was considerable variance in the extent to which they were "stretch" or easy to achieve.

THE PERFORMANCE ASSESSMENT

Smart had scheduled a performance review session with Ketchum some two weeks ahead and, as she put her thoughts together before the session, she was uncomfortable with her conclusions. Smart came back to the initial objectives for Ketchum, and had to conclude that while Ketchum had held up her part of on-call support, she had not technically delivered a consolidated recommendation that compared the approaches of the two support groups and defined possible options with pros and cons. With respect to herself, between the call profile data and the qualitative findings, Smart knew she could convey the situation to management successfully without an actual report from Ketchum, but it was going to take her time to do it.

Although clearly exceeding her main objectives, and likely meeting only the bare essentials on this objective, Smart realized that for herself, she would likely qualify for Excellent, but had to give up her hope of an Outstanding—and her hope for the extra bonus money. The difference in the two ratings was 25 per cent of base salary for Outstanding and 15 per cent for Excellent. Most of the rest of the team's objectives were heavily weighted on the main objectives and wouldn't be hurt—only Ketchum's were weighted heavily on the support alignment issue.

As she considered her decision, Smart was leaning toward a "Needs Improvement" rating for Ketchum. But she was far from confident in this. True, Ketchum had not completed her goal, but it was a difficult goal and quite unstructured. However, she had agreed to it when they had scoped it out in January. And, Smart wondered, what part had the maternity leave played in Ketchum's performance, and should that be taken into account? "Am I being too tough?" thought Smart. "And is it really worth the hassle of giving her such a low appraisal?"

MACINTOSH FINANCIAL: SEXUAL HARASSMENT (A)

*Prepared by Grace Kim under
the supervision of Professors
Joerg Dietz and Lyn Purdy*

Version: (A) 2001-05-23

In late July 2000, as Kelly Taylor, assistant supervisor of client services, was shutting down her computer to go home for the day, she received one last e-mail. It was from one of her client service representatives (CSRs), Brenda Matheson. Brenda's e-mail listed a number of examples of how she had been sexually harassed in the office, mostly by another CSR, Andy Crane.

Kelly sat there in utter surprise. She knew both Brenda and Andy well and was shocked that Andy would act inappropriately, but she also knew Brenda would not lie. Her team was the best-managed and top performing team in the entire department. Kelly wondered what had gone wrong.

COMPANY INFORMATION

Macintosh Financial, a wholly owned subsidiary of the U.S.-based company, Apple Financial, was the sixth largest asset-management company in Canada. Its headquarters were located in Toronto. Incorporated in 1951, Macintosh Financial had built a strong reputation for being conservative and dependable. Moreover, it had established itself as a pioneer in international investing.

Macintosh Financial specialized in domestic and international money management. It managed over 15 mutual funds including various small cap, blue chip, domestic and international equities, and offered a wide range of products including registered retirement savings plans (RRSP), registered educational savings plans (RESP), registered retirement income funds (RRIF), locked-in retirement accounts (LIRA), locked-in retirement income funds (LRIF) and life income funds (LIF).

Macintosh Financial sold its products through external investment advisors (IAs) and mutual fund brokers. The IAs were financial services professionals who provided a wide range of services to investors including the execution of trades, advice on which securities to buy or sell, advice on financial planning and tax shelters, and on new issues of stocks. Private customers could not purchase directly from Macintosh Financial headquarters, but for after-purchase questions and issues, they contacted Macintosh Financial's customer operations at headquarters.

MACINTOSH FINANCIAL'S CUSTOMER OPERATIONS

Macintosh Financial's customer operations had three departments: client services, account services and marketing.

The client services department was divided into four teams (see Exhibit 1) of 15 CSRs per team. A supervisor and an assistant supervisor led each team. Although the supervisors were officially responsible for managing their teams, they worked mostly on special projects assigned by the senior vice-president and, thus, had very little interaction with the CSRs. As a result, the assistant supervisors were actually in charge of managing the teams. The assistant supervisors worked directly with the CSRs, monitoring

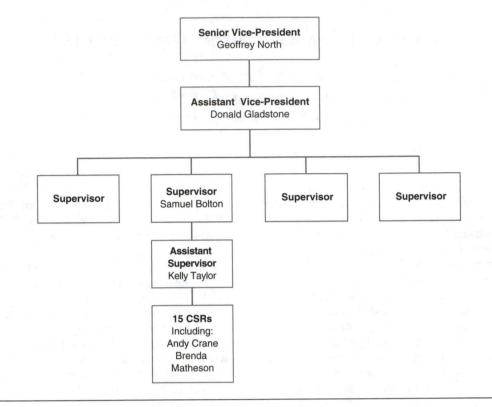

Exhibit 1   Department Chart—Client Services

their daily progress, answering their questions, solving their day-to-day problems and evaluating their performance on a monthly and yearly basis.

CSRs played an important role in the company, as they were the primary contact for brokers, IAs and private clients. They took all calls from the company's toll-free number. The receptionists also funnelled all other calls to the CSRs, who handled 90 per cent of these calls on their own. For example, they answered all questions dealing with specific client accounts, products and portfolio directions.

The account services department also had four teams of 15 to 60 account services representatives each. Their primary responsibility was to input data on all client transactions and to monitor client accounts. They did not take calls.

The sales department promoted Macintosh Financial's products through brochures, advertisements and special events. For example, sales managers made regular visits to brokerage offices. They also maintained contact with IAs, updating them on new products and the performance and direction of current products.

WORKING ENVIRONMENT IN THE CLIENT SERVICES DEPARTMENT

Macintosh Financial was known for giving young college and university graduates an opportunity to enter the financial services industry. With a strong and well-developed training program, Macintosh often hired these new graduates to start in the client services department.

The client services department had a great working environment—it was casual, easygoing, and many friendships had formed. The average age of the CSRs was 23. They generally had fun in the office and were socially active with one another outside the office. They would go for lunch, go for coffee, take their breaks together and, in the evenings and on weekends, they would go out too.

Thursday nights usually marked the beginning of the CSRs' after-work social activities. E-mails would begin to circulate Thursday morning detailing that night's activities. The plans usually included going to dinner and then to a dance club or a bar. On any given Thursday night, 10 to 15 CSRs would go out. The next morning, the same routine would begin again, inviting all CSRs to attend that night's outing.

Kelly liked to go out with the CSR group. On average, she would go out with the CSR group at least once every two weeks. She was social and got along well with almost everybody in the department.

Kelly Taylor and the New Team

Kelly Taylor, who was 27 years old, had been with the company for almost three years. She began at Macintosh Financial as a CSR shortly after graduation from university. After one year, she was promoted to assistant supervisor of client services. In January 2000, the assistant vice-president (AVP), Donald Gladstone, had decided to reorganize the department, giving Kelly and her supervisor, Samuel Bolton, an elite team of CSRs. The new team served only the high-net-worth IAs and, hence, took significantly fewer calls than the other teams. In addition, the team worked on special projects as well as special requests from the sales managers. The CSRs of Kelly's new team were the top performing people in the department, those who had proven that they deserved the interesting work.

Kelly knew the CSRs on her new team superficially, but had not worked with any of them before. Nonetheless, she did not anticipate any problems with them, as she was sure of her ability to manage the CSRs. The new team

included Andy Crane and Brenda Matheson. Andy had joined Macintosh Financial in September of 1998, and Brenda had joined in December of 1997.

Andy Crane sat in the cubicle next to Brenda (see Exhibit 2). Both participated in the social activities of the CSR department, attending Thursday and Friday night outings.

Unlawful Harassment Training

A month prior to Brenda's e-mail, Kelly had attended the company's unlawful harassment training and development program. The seminar was to help managers identify unlawful harassment and to outline a manager's responsibilities in harassment cases. The manual used in the seminar was the same one used by Macintosh's parent company, Apple Financial. Pages 19 to 22 of the manual, however, which would outline Macintosh's unlawful harassment policy, were missing. In the seminar, Kelly and the other managers learned that this policy had yet to be finalized. They also learned that the unlawful harassment seminars would first be given to managers and eventually rolled out to the staff, but that the time frame for staff members so far had not been determined.

THE CURRENT SITUATION

Assessing Brenda's E-mail

Kelly read the e-mail over and over again. She could not believe her eyes. She was not sure what she should do next. Brenda's e-mail recounted how men in the department had commented on how tight her sweaters were, how she should wear shorter skirts, and how they repeatedly asked her out, despite her refusals. At the end of the e-mail, Brenda named Andy as the primary person who was harassing her.

Kelly grabbed her manual. She remembered that as assistant supervisor, she was in a managerial position and was a responsible agent of the organization. She turned to the following passage:

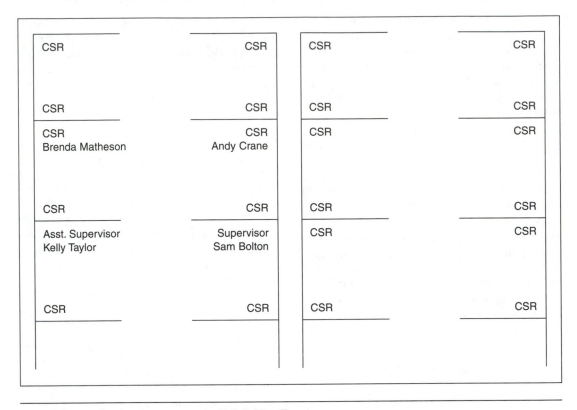

CSR	CSR	CSR	CSR
CSR	CSR	CSR	CSR
CSR Brenda Matheson	CSR Andy Crane	CSR	CSR
CSR	CSR	CSR	CSR
Asst. Supervisor Kelly Taylor	Supervisor Sam Bolton	CSR	CSR
CSR	CSR	CSR	CSR

Exhibit 2   Seating Arrangement in Kelly's New Team

Sexual harassment is a serious issue facing corporations and management alike. Both management and the employer can be held liable when sexual harassment occurs in the workplace. The question of liability depends on the circumstances surrounding each sexual harassment case.

Her manual told her that she needed to act, but it did not offer her any concrete suggestions on how to act. She was not sure exactly what to do next, but she knew she had to act fast.

She immediately forwarded the e-mail to her supervisor, Samuel Bolton, and to human resources (HR). She then called a meeting with her supervisor, her AVP, Donald Gladstone, and an HR representative.

Within 10 minutes, Kelly was in a meeting with Samuel Bolton and Linda Jones from HR. In this meeting, Samuel instructed Kelly to call a meeting with Brenda first thing next morning to discuss the situation. A representative from HR, Linda, would also be present at the meeting, while Samuel and the AVP would not attend. Linda had told Kelly that she would take care of the paper work, but that Kelly would have to run the meeting. Kelly was not sure what she was going to say or how she was going to lead the meeting—she had never done this before.

Meetings With Brenda and Andy

The next morning Kelly called a meeting with Brenda. Brenda was surprised to walk into the meeting room to find Kelly with Linda. Kelly asked Brenda to recount what she had written in her e-mail. Brenda said, "Working next to Andy, day to day, has become increasingly inhibiting and frustrating. I feel uncomfortable because of the way he looks at me and because of his comments to me."

She continued,

> Comments he would make repeatedly, despite me asking him to stop. Comments that were derogatory to women in general—too flirtatious and inappropriate for the office. Specific comments like, "Oh baby, what are you doing tonight? I wish I could get with you." And, "Who's got the keys to the *Beemer?*" comparing me to a BMW.

Kelly then asked, "How would you categorize your relationship with Andy? Friends? Working buddies? No relationship?"

Brenda emphatically replied, "We have no relationship."

"But didn't you hang out with Andy outside the office?" Kelly prompted.

"I don't go out with the other CSRs regularly—less than once a week. And I have never gone out socially with him—maybe once or twice we have been at the same bar with a whole crowd of people, but that's it," Brenda said.

At the end of the meeting, Kelly asked Brenda if she was comfortable finishing the rest of the work day sitting next to Andy. Brenda said she was fine and went back to her desk.

After Brenda's meeting, Kelly then called Andy into a meeting. Andy had no idea why he was being called into a meeting with Kelly and a representative from HR. Kelly told Andy that Brenda had approached her about being sexually harassed by him. It was apparent from the look of shock on his face that he could not believe that Brenda had made such an accusation. Kelly asked him to describe his working relationship with Brenda. "Brenda and I are really good friends. We always joke around, go out, enjoy ourselves and party," started Andy. "I know about her personal situation. And she knows about my personal relationships. We're close."

Kelly then asked, "Do you know why Brenda would file such a complaint against you?"

Andy replied, "We are used to cracking jokes—jokes of a sexual nature. It's the atmosphere in the workplace. I run the same sexual joke by her everyday. And like any other day, I ran it again yesterday. But then yesterday, she reacted defensively saying, 'Why do you want to know? You're always in my business!' But I pursued it—harped on it."

Andy sat there for a minute before continuing his thought, "I didn't take her seriously. I should have been smarter. I was at work. I should have caught on that Brenda was getting bothered by it."

He finished with,

> We are working buddies, but I would consider us friends because we talk a lot on borderline subjects like sex. And we have been out on numerous occasions as a group. When we first started to hang out, it was at least once a week. It is encouraged for the CSRs to be a close group, at least that's the way it seems with our regular get-togethers organized by the CSR department.

Kelly pushed him on this, "What do you mean?" Andy stated, "The situation at work is so open. You don't know when friendship starts and work stops or when friendship stops and work starts. Unfortunately, there are no clear lines at work."

What Next?

Kelly was not sure what she should do next. She did not think that Andy was intentionally harassing Brenda, but she needed to make sure that she did the right thing—for Brenda, for Andy and for Macintosh Financial.

She also thought about Andy's last words—"It is encouraged for the CSRs to be a close group." Was it that kind of mentality that led to the situation between Brenda and Andy?

She demanded from Andy that while he could stay in the office, he should avoid speaking to Brenda. She also told Andy that he would have 24 hours to think about the situation before being called back to meet with Kelly and Linda again.

3

TEAM MANAGEMENT

Most individuals working in organizations are part of a team—cross-functional team, product group, guiding coalition that is responsible for driving organizational change, or individuals who start up a small business. There are numerous reasons why organizations implement team-based structures. For example, Leigh Thompson (2004) mentions the following:

- To meet performance challenges that demand responsiveness, speed, and quality. The reorganization of GE, starting in the 1980s under the leadership of Jack Welch, is an example.
- To make organizational structures and processes seamless to customers. For example, WestJet Airlines has a strong customer service focus, and the airline uses teams to "get things done."
- To integrate people with specialized knowledge within units and across functions. Hewlett-Packard, for example, gets increased value from all pieces of the organization by bringing functional areas, suppliers, and customers together. Hewlett-Packard pursued this structure in an effort to gain viewpoints that would normally not be heard.
- To discover creative approaches to solve problems. Sometimes, one is too small a number to solve problems. The challenges that the crew of the *Apollo 13* faced are just one example.

In *The 17 Indisputable Laws of Teamwork,* John C. Maxwell (2001) writes that "the question is not, Will you participate in something that involves others? The question is, Will your involvement with others be successful?" (p. xi). Making teams effective is an important element of providing leadership. The focus on teams is appropriate also because the skills required to work effectively in teams have become necessary for hiring and promotion.

Organizations and their leaders have discovered numerous reasons some teams go straight to the top, whereas others derail. The seven cases presented in this module provide some answers to that question. The cases offer practical suggestions to better team performance. For example, what can team members do if the team is not performing at its potential? How can individuals maintain the momentum of the team as well as incorporate learning? The cases also offer thoughts as to how to design effective teams. What are the appropriate steps in setting up a team-based organization? The overall objective of the module is fourfold:

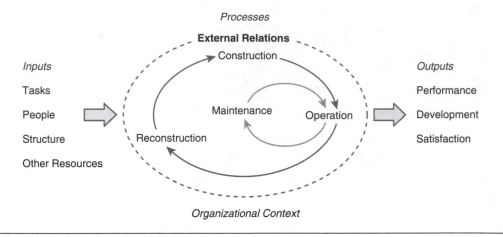

Figure 3.1   Model of Team Processes

- To understand the benefits of teams as well as potential problems of decision making in work teams
- To understand how effective teams form, develop, grow, and sometimes disintegrate
- To understand and develop competencies required for effective teamwork
- To provide insight into how to improve the effectiveness of students' own team efforts

The CORE model presented in Figure 3.1 can serve as a framework for analyzing the functioning and performance of the teams described in the cases. The model was developed by Fernando Olivera and Linda Argote (1999). The various components of the model are described next. It should be acknowledged that although there is some temporal ordering of the stages, the model allows for overlaps and feedback loops.

- Inputs

Team members need to have the physical, financial, technological, and human resources to be successful. If the team does not have the resources to attain its goals or accomplish the work, then it will not perform well. How are resources allocated? Structure refers to organizational or team structure. For example, it makes a difference for team process and potential outputs whether all team members are on-site or are dispersed across countries, states, or provinces. Team leaders also need to give thought to the disposition of potential team members. For example, what are the critical knowledge, skills, and abilities that team members must possess? What is the ideal size of the team? To what extent is the team autonomous or self-managing? Does the organizational context support the self-managing role of teams? These (and other) inputs tend to be necessary but not sufficient for success.

- Process

Team processes refer to team interaction. These include construction, operation, and reconstruction practices. Processes inform people about how teams do their work. Process can be managed.

- Construction practices

The group comes "into being." The following are examples of critical practices. Selecting members should be based on their skills, knowledge, and abilities or potential. Team members should think about establishing rules and sanctions of behavior. Taking a proactive approach is preferred over a reactive approach. What will team members do if others violate expectations? Common goals will need to be established, and team members need to commit to those goals. How can team leaders encourage members to sacrifice self-interest at the expense of focusing on the interests of the group? Team members begin to develop and share an understanding of team roles. Group norms begin to emerge; these norms guide subsequent behavior. Training is also critical at this stage, and technologies are implemented. In sum, team members create conditions for cohesiveness and positive performance norms; both contribute to team effectiveness.

- Operation practices

These are the activities of the group as it carries out its purpose. Examples include problem-solving and decision-making processes, conflict resolution, and task execution. The latter includes communication and coordination of activities of group members.

- Reconstruction practices

This means that teams learn through experience and from feedback; through learning or reflection, groups make changes that better the team. Reconstructing requires reflection. What is the team doing well? What works? What does not? Such reflection requires a team climate for open discussion. How does one create a climate that tolerates mistakes, and where it is okay to speak one's mind?

- Outputs

Outcomes are the result of the team's interaction. There are various outputs that are of interest: the "goodness" of team decisions, hard measures of actual team performance (e.g., sales revenue, number of new products developed, customer satisfaction, etc.), satisfaction with the team, and the desire to continue to work as a team.

- Organizational context and external relations

Teams are embedded in organizational context. The organization's systems, policies, and procedures need to support the team. All too often, however, teams are "launched in a vacuum" (and leaders give little or no thought to organizational design issues). For example, leaders need to give thought to the following question: How should we reward individuals operating under a team-based structure? One should be careful not to fall victim to one of Stephen's Kerr (1995) observations—in organizations, we hope for great teamwork, but we often reward individual-level behavior and performance. In sum, contextual variables can have a powerful effect on behavior, both at the individual and team levels. These variables must not be ignored in a team context. The more supportive the organizational context is of teams, the stronger the likelihood that teams will perform at high levels.

Several of the cases that are incorporated in this module address some of the classic errors or "sins of team building." Examples include mal-selection, or selection of team members based on personalities and personal acquaintances rather than needed skills; impatience, or the failure to allow time for teams to develop; aimlessness, or the failure to set clear expectations about teamwork or performance goals for the team; inhibited communication systems, or the failure to establish open communications and the absence of a climate that values differing opinions; competitive mania; and powerlessness, or the failure to build confidence and ensure accountability. The insights gained through working on the cases should be a first step in helping students to prevent the above (and other) errors in the future.

HAZELTON INTERNATIONAL

A consulting engineering firm, involved in a road construction project in Asia, is plagued with difficulties. The firm is working with the local government highway department on the project and has the status of adviser. Actual construction is done by the government department. The problems that the firm must contend with include technical problems, a budget process, differing objectives, and intercultural relations. Two years into the project, only 17 kilometers of the 245-kilometer highway were under construction. This case provides the background briefing for the in-basket exercise, "An International Project Manager's Day."

Assignment Questions

- Who are the stakeholders in this project, and what are their goals?
- What are the problems and their causes?

AN INTERNATIONAL PROJECT MANAGER'S DAY (A)

The newly appointed project manager of a highway project in Southeast Asia has a variety of issues to contend with all at once. The project is fully described in the Hazelton International case. The Hazelton case can serve as a briefing and must be done before this one. This case provides the company schedule and infrastructure information. Decisions need to be made regarding the items in the project manager's in-basket. These items are in the (B) case, which is included in the Instructor's Manual.

Assignment Question

- Detailed instructions for the exercise (individual, team) will be distributed by the instructor.

eProcure—The Project (A)

Two analysts have each been assigned to work on the conceptual and detail designs of two modules in a Web-based software solution. A week before the final design presentation, the analysts discover that their software designs are not integrated. The case focuses on the frustrations of one of the analysts and her concerns about the working relationship with the other analyst. They have had personal differences and are both prospects for early promotion. She considers how the project came to this point and how the situation might have been avoided. Supplement "eProcure—Finishing the Project (B)" discusses the analyst's strategies during the final week working on the design; supplement "eProcure—Conversation With Claire (C)" explores the analyst's decision to confront her coworker, and supplement "eProcure—End of the Design Team (D)" focuses on the outcomes for both analysts after the project is complete. These supplements are included in the Instructor's Manual.

Assignment Questions

- Could Sonya have done anything differently to prevent the situation with Claire?
- How should Sonya handle the fact that Claire lied during a meeting to their manager? Should she say anything to Molly? Should she say anything to Claire? If so, what should she say and when?
- Do you think the fact that both Claire and Sonya are being considered for early promotion is the cause of contention on the team, or is there more to the problem?
- What could Molly have done to prevent this situation on her team in the first place? What should she do now as the manager? Do you think she even recognizes the problem yet?
- What impacts do the issues presented in the case have for staffing on consulting projects?

SPAR APPLIED SYSTEMS (A)

The general manager must determine how to contend with a project overrun. The Avionics 2000 team had been working on their project for more than 2 years. In their presentation of the projected budget and schedule to the executives, the team identified a potential $1 million overspend to satisfy their contract with Phoenix Helicopter International. Their original budget was $3.5 million, of which $2.5 million was provided by the company. When Stephen Miller, general manager of Spar Applied Systems, questioned team members during the presentation about what had caused the overrun, he was amazed that the team was unable to respond. He adjourned the meeting, returned to his office, and contemplated what to do. Supplemental cases—"Spar Applied Systems: The Red Team Enters (B)" and "Spar Applied Systems: Aftermath . . . Business as Usual (C)"—follow the sequence of events (and are included in the Instructor's Manual).

Assignment Questions

- How do the current and historical structures fit with the overall strategy of the Applied Systems Group?
- What is your evaluation of the current structure of the Applied Systems Group?
- What led to the budget overrun of the Avionics 2000 team?
- What does Stephen Miller need to know before he makes a decision on the future of Avionics 2000?
- What are the pressures on Stephen Miller to resolve this budget problem?
- As Stephen Miller, what would you do? Be specific about the sequence and timing of action steps.

RICHARD IVEY SCHOOL OF BUSINESS—THE LEADER PROJECT (A) AND (B)

A student-run, not-for-profit program, Leading Education and Development in Emerging Regions (LEADER), sent teams of business students to teach Western business practices in the former Soviet Union. In preparation for the 3-week assignment at the end of the school term, the students were expected to participate in social events to build team spirit, as well as practical work, such as preparing teaching materials, making travel arrangements, and fund-raising. The program's annual budget was $110,000, and each team member was expected to provide a minimum of $250. Despite efforts to raise the needed funds, the program failed to reach its goal. As a result, team members were required to contribute $1,800, substantially more than originally anticipated. Some of the team members quit, expressing their dissatisfaction with the increased financial obligation. Other team members are boasting about the little time they spent working on the project. The once successful program is facing a dilemma. How can it sustain enthusiasm, raise the needed funds, and recruit members who are willing to work to ensure its success? The supplement "Richard Ivey School of Business—The LEADER Project—Kiev Site (B)" explores a personality conflict that begins when one team begins preparation for its trip. The problem escalates when the team is teaching in Kiev, Ukraine. One of the team members wonders what role she can play in resolving the situation that threatens the success of the teaching assignment.

Assignment Questions

- Is the LEADER Project a viable operation?
- As Kaitlyn, what recommendations can you make to the executive directors to change the LEADER Project to make it more effective in its purpose?
- What are the causes for the conflicts within the team?
- How should Kaitlyn approach Dennis and Beth?

ANTAR AUTOMOBILE COMPANY—PART I: THE AUTOMATION PROJECT

Rob Dander, a project manager in the Operational Research Department of an automobile assembly plant, must decide how he can most effectively redirect his team to meet management's deadline and design expectations. For 5 months, he had been supervising the work of three young company employees who were developing a simulated assembly line. However, because his current responsibilities left him in charge of four or five projects at a time, all in varying stages of completion, he had left his assistants to work together with very little intervention from him. None of the group members had ever dealt with the programming language that they were required to use. For two of the group members, this project was their first experience in creating computerized simulations. The group realized their progress was slow, but they attributed this to a number of "on-time" setbacks they had encountered in trying to acquaint themselves with the new language. As time passed, the group of assistants began to view the project as a personal battle and fought against the unforgiving computer, which monotonously rejected each program it was fed, sending the group back to the drawing board. The three soon lost their focus by trying to develop a model that had become far too cumbersome and uneconomical to complete their original assignment. Dander is now facing the pressure of an uncompleted project and an unnecessarily elaborate design.

Assignment Questions

- What sort of relationship (cohesive, neutral, hostile) do you think the group will build? Why?
- Will the group's output exceed, satisfy, or fall below Rob's expectations? Why?
- Will Mark Mancuso keep plant management (well, poorly) informed of the simulation's progress? Why?
- What will be the level of job satisfaction (high, medium, low) of the project assistants? Why?

THE LEO BURNETT COMPANY LTD.: VIRTUAL TEAM MANAGEMENT

Leo Burnett Company Ltd. is a global advertising agency. The company is working with one of its largest clients to launch a new line of hair care products into the Canadian and Taiwanese test markets in preparation for a global rollout. Normally, once a brand has been launched, it is customary for the global brand center to turn over the responsibility for the brand and future campaigns to the local market offices. In this case, however, the brand launch was not successful. Team communications and the team dynamics have broken down in recent months, and the relationships are strained. Further complicating matters are a number of client and agency staffing changes that could jeopardize the stability of the team and the agency-client relationship. The global account director must decide whether she should proceed with the expected decision to modify the global team structure to give one of the teams more autonomy or whether she should maintain greater centralized control over the team. She must recommend how to move forward with the brand and determine what changes in team structure or management are necessary.

Assignment Questions

- Assume the role of a Leo Burnett employee. (a) What is your everyday work environment like (assume this would normally involve face-to-face teams)? Specifically, consider how you would fill your day, what the office environment would be, what would determine your work priorities, and the nature of your relationship with your colleagues and your client(s). (b) How is this different from your role as part of the Forever Young virtual team?
- What are some of the difficulties that the Forever Young global advertising and communications team faced throughout the launch process? To what do you attribute these difficulties?
- As Janet Carmichael, do you now decentralize the team? Why or why not?

REFERENCES

Kerr, S. (1995). On the folly of rewarding A, while hoping for B. *Academy of Management Executive, 9*(1), 7–14.

Maxwell, J. C. (2001). *The 17 indisputable laws of teamwork: Embrace them and empower your team.* Nashville, TN: Thomas Nelson.

Olivera, F., & Argote, L. (1999). Organizational learning and CORE processes in new product development. In L. Thompson, J. Levine, & D. Messick (Eds.), *Shared cognition in organizations: The management of knowledge* (pp. 297–328). Hillsdale, NJ: Lawrence Erlbaum.

Thompson, L. (2004). *Making the team: A guide for managers.* Upper Saddle River, NJ: Prentice Hall.

HAZELTON INTERNATIONAL

Prepared by Henry W. Lane
and Lorna L. Wright

Version: (A) 2000-03-22

Dan Simpson, the incoming project manager of the Maralinga–Ladawan Highway Project, was both anxious and excited as he drove with John Anderson in their jeep up the rutted road to the river where they would wait for the ferry. John was the current manager and was taking Dan, his replacement, on a three-day site check of the project. During this trip John was also going to brief Dan on the history of the project and the problems he would encounter. Dan was anxious about the project because he had heard there were a number of messy problems, but was excited about the challenge of managing it.

Hazelton, a consulting engineering firm, was an adviser on the project and so far had little success in getting the client to heed its advice. After two years of operation, only 17 kilometres of the 245-kilometre highway were under construction.

BACKGROUND

Since 1965, Hazelton had successfully completed assignments in 46 countries across Africa, Asia, Europe, South and Central America, and the Caribbean region. A large proportion of the projects had been in Africa but the company was now turning attention to developing its Asian operations. Since the beginning, Hazelton had done only 10 projects in Asia—less than 10 per cent of all its projects.

Hazelton provided consulting services in transportation, housing and urban development, structural engineering, and municipal and environmental engineering to both government and corporate clients around the world. Specific services included technical and economic feasibility studies, financing, planning, architecture, preliminary and final engineering design, maintenance programming, construction supervision, project management and equipment procurement.

Projects ranged from extremely large (building an international airport) to very small, requiring the skill of only a single expert (advising on a housing project in Malaysia). The majority of these projects were funded by international lending agencies (ILAs) such as World Bank, African Development Bank and aid agencies like the U.S. Agency for International Development (USAID) and the Canadian International Development Agency (CIDA). The previous year Hazelton's worldwide annual fee volume exceeded US$40 million.

Hazelton staffed its overseas projects with senior members of its permanent staff. In addition, experts with international experience and capabilities in the applicable language were used whenever possible. Both these principles had been adhered to in the Maralinga-Ladawan Project.

MARALINGA-LADAWAN HIGHWAY PROJECT

Soronga was a nation of islands in the Pacific Ocean. This project required design and construction supervision services for a 245-kilometre highway along the western coast of the island of Tola from Maralinga in the north to Ladawan in the south (see Exhibit 1). Sections of the highway past Ladawan were being reconstructed by other firms funded by aid agencies from Japan and Australia.

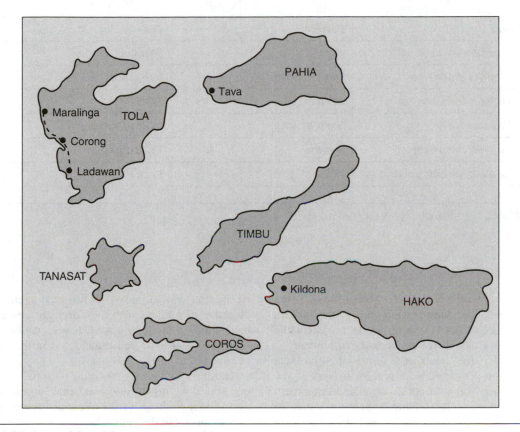

Exhibit 1   Map of Soronga (not to scale)

In addition to supervising the project, Hazelton was responsible for a major training program for Sorongan engineers, mechanics, operators, and administrative staff.

This was the fifth largest project ($1.6 million in fees) Hazelton had ever undertaken (see Exhibit 2). It was a joint venture with two other firms, Beauval Ltd. and McPherson Brothers International (MBI), whom Hazelton involved to strengthen its proposal. Hazelton acted as the lead firm on behalf of the consortium and assumed overall responsibility for the work. Over the life of the project, the three firms would send 22 expatriates, including highway designers, engineers, mechanics, and operators.

MBI was involved because it was a contractor and Hazelton felt it might need those types of skills when dealing with a "force account" project. Usually, Hazelton supervised the project and left the actual construction to experienced contractors. This project was different. Force account meant that the construction workers would be government employees who would not be experienced in construction work.

Beauval had been working in Asia for 17 years and had established a base of operations in Kildona. It had done several projects on the island of Hako, but this would be the first on the island of Tola. This local experience helped the proposal gain acceptance both in the eyes of the financing agency, and the client, the Sorongan Highway Department (SHD).

The financing agency provided a combination loan and grant for the project and played a

Project	Location	Fee
1. International airport	Africa	$4 million
2. Highway supervision	South America	$3.4 million
3. Highway feasibility	South America	$2.25 million
4. Highway design	South America	$2.25 million
5. Highway betterment	Soronga	$1.63 million
6. Secondary roads: graveling	Africa	$1.32 million

Exhibit 2   Hazelton's Six Largest Projects

significant role in the selection of the winning proposal. The grant portion paid for the salaries of the expatriates working on the project while the loan funds were for necessary equipment.

Under the contract's terms of reference, Hazelton personnel were sent as advisers on the techniques of road construction and equipment maintenance. The training component was to be the major part of the project with the actual construction being the training vehicle. The project was to last five years with Hazelton phasing out its experts in about four years. The Sorongans would be trained by that point to take over the project themselves. The training program would use formal classroom instruction and a system of counterparts. Each expatriate engineer or manager would have a counterpart Sorongan engineer or manager who worked closely with him in order for the expertise to be passed on. At the mechanic and operator levels, training programs would be set up involving both in-class instruction and on-the-job training.

SHD's responsibilities included providing counterpart staff, ensuring that there was housing built for the expatriates, and providing fuel and spare parts for the equipment that would be coming from Canada.

It was thought that a force account project—with government staff doing the work—would be the best way to marry the financial agency's objective of training with the Sorongan government's aim of building a road. It was one of the first times that SHD had found itself in the role of contractor.

Hazelton was in the position of supervising one arm of the organization on behalf of another arm. It was working for the client as a supervising engineer, but the client also ran the construction. Hazelton was in the middle.

In Soronga's development plans, this project was part of the emphasis on developing the transportation and communications sector. It was classed as a *betterment* project, meaning that Soronga did not want undue resources going toward a "perfect" road in engineering terms; merely one that was better than the present one and that would last. An important objective also was to provide employment in Tola and permit easier access to the rest of Soronga, because the province was a politically sensitive area and isolated from the rest of the country.

Tola

Tola was the most westerly island of the Sorongan archipelago. It was isolated from the rest of the country because of rough terrain and poor roads. It was a socially conservative province and fundamentalist in religion. The majority of Tolanese were very strict Moslems. The ulamas (Moslem religious leaders) played an important role in Tolanese society, perhaps more so than in any other part of Soronga.

Economically, the province lagged behind Hako, the main island. The economy was still dominated by labor-intensive agriculture. Large-scale industry was a very recent development with timbering providing the biggest share of exports. A liquefied natural gas plant and a cement factory were two new industries begun within the past two years.

From its earliest history, Tola had enjoyed a high degree of autonomy. In 1821, it signed a treaty with a European country guaranteeing its autonomy in commerce. This was revoked in 1871 when that European country signed a treaty with another European colonial power, recognizing the latter's sovereignty over the whole of Soronga. The Tolanese understood the implications of this treaty and tried to negotiate with their new master to retain Tola's autonomous standing. Neither side was willing to compromise, however, and in 1873 the European country declared war on Tola. This war continued for 50 years, and the fierce resistance of the Tolanese against colonization became a model for Soronga's own fight for independence later. Even after the Tolanese officially surrendered, this did not mean peace. Guerrilla warfare continued, led by the ulamas. With the advent of the Second World War and the arrival of the Japanese, resistance to the Europeans intensified. At the end of the war, the Japanese were expelled, and the European colonizers returned to Soronga, but not to Tola.

With the independence of Soronga, Tola theoretically formed part of the new nation, but in practice, it retained its regional social, economic, and political control. In 1961, however, the central government in Kildona dissolved the province of Tola and incorporated its territory into the region of West Pahia under a governor in Tava. Dissatisfaction with this move was so intense that the Tolanese proclaimed an independent Islamic Republic in 1963. This rebellion lasted until 1971, when the central government sought a political solution by giving Tola provincial status again. In 1977, Kildona granted special status to the province in the areas of religion, culture, and education.

Tola's long periods of turmoil had left their mark on the province and on its relations with the rest of the country. It was deeply suspicious of outsiders (particularly those from Hako, since that was the seat of the central government), strongly independent and fiercely proud of its heritage and ethnic identity. Although all Tolanese could speak Sorongan because that was *the* only language used in the schools, they preferred to use their native language, Tolanese, amongst themselves. The central government in Kildona had recently become concerned about giving the province priority in development projects to strengthen the ties between the province and the rest of the country.

PROGRESS OF THE PROJECT

The First Year

Negotiations on the project took longer than expected, and the project actually began almost a year after it was originally scheduled to start. Hazelton selected its personnel carefully. The project manager, Frank Kennedy, had been successful in a similar position in Central America. He had also successfully cleaned up a problem situation in Lesotho. In September, Frank and an administrator arrived in Soronga, followed a month later by the major design team, bringing the total expatriate contingent to 10 families. They spent a month learning the Sorongan language but had to stay in Kildona until December because there was no housing in Maralinga. The houses had not been finished; before they could be, an earthquake destroyed the complex. Eventually, housing was rented from Australian expatriates working for another company who were moving to a complex of their own.

Hazelton was anxious to begin work, but no Sorongan project manager had been specified, and the vehicles did not arrive until late December. When the vehicles did arrive, the fuel tanks were empty and there was no fuel available. Neither was there provision in SHD's budget to buy fuel nor lubricants that year. The project would have to wait until the new fiscal year began on April 1 to have money allotted to it. Meanwhile, it would be a fight for funds.

The Second Year

By the beginning of the year, the equipment was on site, but the Sorongan counterpart staff still were not. Hazelton had no control over SHD staff, since it had no line responsibility. When the SHD project manager finally arrived, he was reluctant to confront the staff. Senior SHD people on the project were Hakonese, whereas most of the people at the operator level were local Tolanese. There was not only the Hakonese-Tolanese strain but an unwillingness on the part of the senior staff to do anything that would stir up this politically volatile area.

Frank was having a difficult time. He was a construction man. There were 245 kilometres of road to build and nothing was being done. It galled him to have to report no progress month after month. If the construction could start, the training would quickly follow. On top of the project problems, Frank's wife was pregnant and had to stay in Singapore, where the medical facilities were better. His frustration increased, and he began confronting the Sorongan project manager, demanding action. His behavior became counter-productive and he had to be replaced. The person chosen as his replacement was John Anderson.

John Anderson

John Anderson was a civil engineer who had worked for Hazelton for 15 years. He had a wealth of international experience in countries as diverse as Thailand, Nigeria, Tanzania, and Kenya. He liked the overseas environment for a variety of reasons, not the least of which was the sense of adventure that went with working abroad. "You meet people who stand out from the average. You get interesting points of view."

Professionally, it was also an adventure. "You run across many different types of engineering and different ways of approaching it." This lent an air of excitement and interest to jobs that was lacking in domestic work. The challenge was greater, also, since one didn't have access to the same skills and tools as at home: as John said, "You have to make do."

Even though he enjoyed overseas work, John had returned to headquarters as office manager for Hazelton. His family was a major factor in this decision. As his two children reached high school age, it became increasingly important for them to be settled and to receive schooling that would allow them to enter university. John had no intention of going overseas in the near future; however, when it became evident that a new project manager was needed for Soronga, loyalty prompted him to respond without hesitation when the company called.

John had been the manager of a similar project in Nigeria where he had done a superlative job. He had a placid, easy-going temperament and a preference for operating by subtle suggestions rather than direct demands. Hazelton's top management felt that if anyone could make a success of this project, John could.

John's Perception of the Project

From the description of Maralinga in the original project document, John knew he would face problems from the beginning. However, when he arrived on site, it wasn't as bad as he'd expected. People were friendly, the housing was adequate, and there was access to an international school run by the Australians.

The work situation was different. The equipment that had come from Canada could not be used. Bridges to the construction sites had not been built and the existing ones could not support the weight of the machines. The bridge work should have been done before the road project started. Roads had to be widened to take the construction equipment, but no provisions had been made to expropriate the land needed. Instructions were that the road must remain within the existing right-of-way. Technically, SHD could lay claim to 15 metres, but they had to pay compensation for any crops lost, even though those crops were planted on state land. Because of these problems, the biggest pieces of machinery, such as the crusher plant, had to be taken apart and moved piece by piece. Stripping a machine down for transportation took time, money, and labor—all in short supply.

The budgeting process presented another problem. It was done on an annual basis rather than for the entire project period. It was also done in meticulous detail. Every litre of fuel and every nut and bolt had to be included. The budget was extremely inflexible, too. Money allocated for fuel could not be used for spare parts if the need arose.

When the project was initially planned, there was plenty of money, but with the collapse of oil prices, the Sorongan economy was hit hard and restrictions on all projects were quickly instituted. Budgets were cut in half. The money originally planned was no longer available for the project. Further problems arose because the project was a force account. The government bureaucracy could not react quickly, and in construction fast reactions were important. Revisions needed to be approved quickly, but by the time the government approved a change, it was often too late.

The training component of the project had more than its share of problems. Counterpart training was difficult because Sorongan managers would arbitrarily reassign people to other jobs. Other counterparts would leave for more lucrative jobs elsewhere. Among the mechanics, poor supervision compounded the problems. Those who showed initiative were not encouraged and the spark soon died.

John's Arrival on Site

John arrived in Soronga in March. SHD budgets were due soon after. This required a tremendous amount of negotiating. Expenses had to be identified specifically and in minute detail. By September, the process was completed, and the project finally, after more than a year, had funds to support it.

Shortly after John's arrival, the project was transferred from the maintenance section of SHD to the construction section. The Sorongan project manager changed and the parameters of the job began to change also.

SHD would not allow realignment of the road. To change the alignment would have meant getting property rights, which was an expensive, time-consuming process and inconsistent with a project that SHD saw as road improvement rather than road construction. This meant that half the design team had no work to do. Their roles had to be quickly changed. For example, the chief design engineer became costing, programming, and budgeting engineer.

The new SHD project manager was inexperienced in his post and concerned about saving money and staying within budget. Because of this, he was loath to hire more workers to run the machinery because the rainy season was coming and construction would slow down. The workers would have to be paid, but little work would be done. By October, with the rainy season in full swing, it was evident that the money allocated to the project was not going to be spent, and the project manager frantically began trying to increase activity. If this year's budget was not spent, it would be very difficult to get adequate funds for the next year. However, it was difficult to spend money in the last months because no preparatory work had been done. It took time to let tenders and hire trained staff.

The new SHD project manager was Hakonese, as was his predecessor. Neither understood the local Tolanese situation. Getting access to gravel and sand sites necessitated dealing with the local population, and this was not handled well, with the result that it took a long time to acquire land rights. The supervisors were also mainly Hakonese and could exercise little control over the workforce. Discipline was lax. Operators wouldn't begin doing any constructive work until 9:30 a.m. They would quit at 11:30 a.m. for a two-hour lunch and then finish for the day at 5:00 p.m. Drivers hauled material for private use during working hours. Fuel disappeared at an alarming rate. One morning when a water truck was inspected before being put into service, the Hazelton adviser discovered the water tank was full of fuel. No explanation as to how the fuel got there was forthcoming, and it soon vanished again.

Bridges were a problem. It had been almost two and one-half years since the original plans had been submitted, and SHD was now demanding changes. Substructures were not yet in place and the tenders had just been let. When they were finally received by midyear, SHD decided that Canadian steel was too expensive and they could do better elsewhere. The tendering process would have to be repeated, and SHD had not yet let the new tenders.

Although there was no real construction going on, training had begun. A training manager was on site, and the plan was to train the mechanics and equipment operators first. The entire program would consist of four phases. The first phase would involve 30 people for basic operator training. The second would take the best people from the first phase and train them further as mechanics. In the third phase, the best mechanics would train others. The fourth phase would upgrade skills previously learned. SHD cancelled the second phase of training because they considered it to be too costly and a waste of time. They wanted people to be physically working, not spending time in the classroom. Hazelton felt that both types of training were needed, and the cancellation raised difficulties with the financing agency, who considered the training needs paramount.

SHD, as a government agency, was not competitive with private companies in wages.

It was not only losing its best engineering people to better-paying jobs elsewhere, it could not attract qualified people at the lower levels. Its people, therefore, were inexperienced and had to be taught the basics of operating mechanical equipment. Ironically, equipment on the project was some of the most sophisticated available.

SHD was directing the construction, but there didn't seem to be any plan of attack. The SHD manager was rarely on site, and the crews suffered badly from a lack of direction. Time, materials, and people were being wasted because of this. Bits and pieces of work were being started at different points with no consideration given to identifying the critical areas.

In June, there was a push to get construction underway. There was a need to give the design people something to do and a desire to get the operators and mechanics moving, as well as the equipment, which had been sitting idle for several months. Finally, there was the natural desire to show the client some concrete results. Hazelton was losing the respect of the people around them. Most people were not aware that Hazelton was acting merely in an advisory capacity. The feeling was that they should be directing the operations. Since Hazelton was not taking charge, the company's competence was being questioned.

The rainy season was due to begin in September and would last until the end of December. This was always a period of slow progress because construction was impossible when it rained. Work had to be stopped every time it rained and frequently work that had been done before the rain had to be redone.

Besides the problem of no progress on construction, some of the expatriate staff were not doing the job they had been sent out to do. Because there was little design work, the design engineer was transformed into a costing and budgeting administrator. No bridges were being built, so the bridge engineer was idle. No training was being done, so the training manager was declared redundant and sent home.

It was difficult for Hazelton to fulfil even its advisory role because SHD personnel were not telling them what they were doing next. A communication gap was rapidly opening between SHD and Hazelton. Communication between SHD in Tola and SHD in Kildona was poor, also. It appeared that the Kildona headquarters was allowing the Tola one to sink or swim on its own. Little direction was forthcoming. It didn't seem as if SHD Kildona was allocating its best people to the project, either.

The one bright spot of the year was that the project was now under the construction section of SHD rather than the maintenance section, and, thus, they could understand the situation from a construction point of view. The feeling was that things would improve because now the people in headquarters at least understood what the field team was up against and what it was trying to accomplish.

The Third Year

At the beginning of the year, there was little to be seen for the previous year's work.

The Hazelton staff and their Sorongan counterparts worked out of a small two-storey building in the SHD office compound in Maralinga. The Sorongans occupied the top floor and Hazelton, the bottom. A field camp trailer site had been set up in Corong, the halfway point between Maralinga and Ladawan. The plan was to move construction out from this area in both directions.

John, his mechanic supervisor, and the bridge engineer made the five-hour trip out to the site at the beginning of each week, returning to Maralinga and their families at the end of the week. The second mechanic and his wife lived on-site, whereas the erstwhile design engineer,

now in charge of budgeting and administration, stayed primarily in the Maralinga office.

SHD was beginning to rethink its position on using force account labor. There were signs that in the next fiscal year it might hire a contractor to do the actual work because the force account was obviously not satisfactory. SHD also underwent another change in project manager. The third person to fill that position was due on-site in April but arrived the end of May. The new manager began making plans to move the Sorongan base of operations to Corong. The Hazelton expatriates, for family reasons, would remain based in Maralinga.

The project now also underwent its third status change. It was being given back to the maintenance section of SHD again. The budget process had to be started again. Hazelton, in its advisory role, tried to impress on the SHD staff the advantages of planning ahead and working out the details of the next year's work so that there would be funds in the budget to support it.

Construction had at last started, even though in a desultory fashion. However, Ramadan, the month of fasting for Moslems, was looming on the horizon and this would slow progress. This meant no eating, no drinking, and no smoking for Moslems between sun-up and sundown, which had obvious consequences for a worker's energy level. Productivity dropped during this period. This had not been a major problem the previous year because not much work was being done. Following Ramadan, there would be only two months to work at normal speed before construction would have to slow again for the rainy season.

John's briefing of Dan having been completed, they continued the site check. John wanted Dan to inspect the existing bridges as they arrived at them.

AN INTERNATIONAL PROJECT MANAGER'S DAY (A)

*Prepared by Lorna Wright under the
supervision of Professor Henry W. Lane*

Copyright © 1986, Ivey Management Services   Version: (A) 2000-03-23

SITUATION

The Maralinga-Ladawan Highway Project consists of 14 expatriate families and the Sorongan counterpart personnel. Half of the expatriates are engineers from Hazelton. The other expatriates are mechanics, engineers and other technical personnel from Beauval and MBI, the other two firms in the consortium. All expatriate personnel are under Hazelton's authority. This is the fifth largest project Hazelton has ever undertaken, with a fee of $1.63 million.

You arrived in Maralinga late on March 28 with your spouse. There was no chance for a briefing before you left. Head office had said John Anderson, the outgoing project manager, would fill you in on all you needed to know.[1] They had also arranged for you to meet people connected with the project in Kildona.

On March 29, you visited the project office briefly and met the accountant/administrative assistant, Tawi, the secretary, Julip, and the office messenger/driver, Satun. You then left immediately on a three-day site check of the 245-kilometre highway with John. Meanwhile, your spouse has started settling in and investigating job prospects in Maralinga.

On your trip you stopped at the field office in Corong. Chris Williams, second mechanic and his wife, Beth, were living there. Chris was out at the timber company site to get help in recovering a grader that had toppled over the side of a ravine the night before, so you weren't able to see him. However, you met his Sorongan counterpart and he advised you that everything was going well, although they could use more manpower.

You noted that Corong did not have any telephone facilities. The only communication link, a single side-band radio, had been unserviceable for the past few weeks. If you needed to contact Chris, it would involve a five-hour jeep ride to Corong to deliver the message.

You were able to see the haphazard way the work on the road was proceeding and witnessed the difficulty in finding appropriate gravel sites. Inspecting some of the bridges you had crossed made you shiver, too. Doing something about those would have to be a priority, before there was a fatality.

You returned to Maralinga on April 1 and met some of the staff and their families. Their comments made it clear that living conditions were less than ideal, the banking system make it difficult to get money transferred and converted into local currency (their salaries, paid in dollars, were deposited to their accounts at home), and the only school it was possible to send their children to was not appropriate for children who would have to return to the North American educational system.

That evening John left for another project on another continent. It is now Tuesday morning, April 2. This morning, while preparing breakfast with your spouse, the propane gas for your stove ran out. You have tried, unsuccessfully, on your way to work to get the gas cylinder filled, and have only now arrived at the office. It is 10 a.m. You have planned to have lunch with your spouse at noon and you are leaving for the airport at 2 p.m. for a week in Kildona to visit the Beauval office, the Sorongan Highway Department (SHD) people, and the International Aid Agency (IAA) representative for discussions concerning the history and future of this project (it takes about one-half hour to drive to the airport). This trip has been planned as part of your orientation to the job. Since the IAA representative and the senior man in the Beauval office were both leaving for other postings at the end of the month, this may be the only opportunity you will have to spend time with them.

On your arrival at the office, Julip tells you that Jim, one of the surveyors, and his wife, Joyce, are arriving at 10:30 a.m. to discuss Joyce's medical problems with you. This is the first opportunity you have had to get into your office and do some work. You have about 30 minutes to go through the contents of your in-basket and take whatever action you feel is appropriate.

INSTRUCTIONS

For the purpose of this exercise, you are to assume the position of Dan Simpson, the new project manager for the Maralinga-Ladawan Highway Project.

Please *write out* the action you choose on the Action Forms provided. Your action may include writing letters, memos, telexes, or making phone calls. You may want to have meetings with certain individuals or receive reports from the office staff.

For example, if you decide to make a phone call, write out the purpose and content of the call on the Action Form. If you decide to have a meeting with one of the office staff or another individual, make a note of the basic agenda of things to be discussed and the date and time of the meeting. You also need to think about establishing priorities for the various issues.

To help you think of the time dimension, a calendar follows (see Exhibit 1). Also, Maralinga is 12 hours ahead of Eastern Standard Time. An organizational chart also follows (see Exhibit 2).

NOTE

1. See Hazelton International Limited, 9A84C040.

Sunday	Monday	Tuesday	Wednesday	Thursday	Friday	Saturday
March 24	25	26	27	28 Arrival in Maralinga	29	30 Site check with John
31	April 1 ➤ Return	2 (Today)	3 — Visit to Kildona	4	5	6
7	8	9 ➤ Return to Maralinga	10	11	12	13
14	15	16	17	18	19	20
21	22	23	24	25	26	27
28	29	30	May 1	2	3	4

Exhibit 1   Calendar

Note: You are in a Moslem area. People do not work Friday afternoons. Saturday morning usually is a workday.

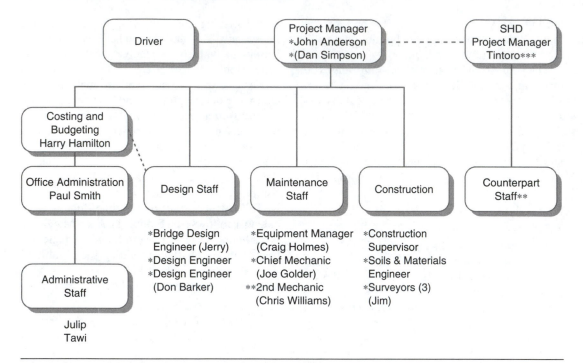

Exhibit 2   Organizational Chart

Notes:

* These people travel to Corong and other locations frequently.
** Stationed in Corong.
*** Located on the floor above Dan Simpson in the same building.
The 2 expatriates responsible for the training component had been sent home. The remaining 6 expatriates called for under the contract had not yet arrived in Soronga and the 2 construction supervisors recently requested by SHD would be in addition to these 6 people.

<u>Transportation Availability</u>: (1) PROJECT OWNED — a) 1 Land Rover for administrative use by HQ Staff, b) 1 car shared by all the families, c) most trucks are in Corong, however there usually are some around Maralinga (2) PUBLIC—a) peddle-cabs are available for short distances (like getting to work), b) local "taxis" are mini-van type vehicles which are usually very over-crowded and which expatriates usually avoid, c) there are a few flights to Kildona each week.

eProcure—The Project (A)

*Prepared by Monica Kumar under
the supervision of Professor Lyn Purdy*

Version: (A) 2002-12-09

Sonya Richardson, tired and frustrated, sat at her desk and stared at the design documents spread in front of her. She had just finished a design team meeting with her manager, Molly Berkson, and her fellow team member, Claire Bishop. Sonya and Claire had just presented Molly with the software designs they had been working on for the past three weeks. During the meeting, they realized that the modules that Claire and Sonya had designed weren't integrated.

Sonya was extremely frustrated with what had just happened. She had spent day and night for the past three weeks working on her designs and putting together all the necessary documentation for the designs to be passed to the technical development team. She had also been preparing for the final design presentation, which was only a week away. She and Claire were scheduled to present the final software designs to the co-founders of eProcure and to the Excel Consulting managing partner in charge of the project. This presentation was her opportunity to prove herself to the leadership and now she felt she had messed everything up. Sonya realized that she and Claire would have to work closely together for the next week and make their best attempt at fixing the designs, redoing all of the design documentation and putting together a final presentation. If only they had figured this out sooner.

COMPANY INFORMATION

Sonya, Claire and Molly all worked for Excel Consulting, a leading, global provider of management and technology services and solutions. With more than 35,000 employees, a global reach including over 55 offices in 20 countries, and serving mainly Fortune 100 and Fortune 500 companies, Excel was one of the world's largest and most reputable consulting firms.

Excel's primary focuses were delivering innovative solutions to clients and providing exceptional client service. Excel delivered its services and solutions by organizing its professionals into focused industry groups. This industry focus allowed the firm's professionals to develop a thorough understanding of the client's industry, business issues and applicable technologies to deliver tailored solutions to each client. Each professional was further aligned to a specific service function, such as strategy, process, human performance or technology. This alignment allowed an individual to develop specialized skills and knowledge in an area of expertise. The organizational structure encouraged a collaborative and team-based atmosphere. Most client teams included professionals from a similar industry focus, but from several different service function specialities.

Most Excel employees, however, displayed a variety of educational, cultural and geographical backgrounds, but most shared similar skills and attributes, including leadership, intelligence, innovation, integrity and dedication. Many professionals began their careers with Excel directly after completing an undergraduate degree; however, Excel hired experienced professionals as well. The career path at Excel generally made the following progression: analyst, consultant, manager, associate partner and partner. A new hire, directly after graduating with a university undergraduate degree, would begin as an analyst and then, typically after two years, would be promoted to consultant. After consultant, it would typically take another three years before a promotion to a manager position within the firm.

Along with its focus on client service, Excel also emphasized employee satisfaction. It conducted regular satisfaction surveys and had many corporate policies in place to help ensure work-life balance. These policies included flexible working hours and the assignment of professionals in the city of their home office to limit their travel. Partners and managers had the flexibility and discretion to implement these policies on their individual projects. In practice, most projects were unable to effectively implement these policies due to constrained project timelines and budgets. Balancing client service and employee satisfaction was a challenge at the firm and one that it shared with most consulting companies.

CLIENT AND PROJECT INFORMATION

eProcure, an Internet startup company based in Baltimore, Maryland, was founded by two former executives from a large diversified, multinational firm, who realized the critical need for a holistic sourcing/procurement solution. They founded eProcure in June 1999 to deliver a technology-based strategic sourcing solution for procuring goods and services. The Strategic eProcure (SeP) software that eProcure was building focused on providing purchasing professionals with the tools they needed to source and negotiate contracts with their suppliers online. The software incorporated the enabling technologies of online auctions, private bids and communication tools.

The vision of the eProcure solution was to allow purchasing professionals to electronically research, evaluate, plan and negotiate the lowest total cost for both direct and indirect goods and services. These goods and services could include both tactical and strategic buys within an organization. The SeP, Web-based software solution, was intended to enable buyers to analyse both internal purchasing and external industry data to determine and execute effective eNegotiation strategies. Those strategies could then be shared across the enterprise for repeat savings of money and time.

eProcure formed a strategic alliance with Excel Consulting in July 1999. Excel would contribute intellectual property in return for a percentage of equity ownership in eProcure. Excel had many years of experience in strategic sourcing through its numerous clients in a variety of industries. Currently strategic sourcing was a manual process. Excel would help clients research and analyse their internal and external data, and conduct negotiations with suppliers in order to procure goods and services in the most cost-efficient manner. These were long-term projects for Excel, typically ranging from three months to two years. Procurement and supply chain effectiveness was a very popular line of business for Excel as many large organizations had begun to shift their focus to operational cost savings. This partnership was seen as beneficial to both eProcure and Excel. eProcure needed Excel's experience and client base, and Excel was interested in getting more exposure to the booming startup industry.

In August 1999, a project team was formed in Baltimore, which included the eight eProcure employees and 20 Excel consultants from all over North America. The team's mandate was to work together to design and develop the SeP software solution. All members were distributed amongst several smaller teams, including process design, technical design and technical development/ infrastructure. Each of these teams included an Excel manager and several Excel consultants and/ or analysts. The eProcure employees would rotate among the different teams and help when and where they were needed. The entire project was overseen by George Fry, an Excel partner, along with William Sheppard and Steve Miller, the eProcure co-founders.

Sonya Richardson

Sonya was an analyst with Excel in the business process functional area, at the Toronto office. She began working with Excel in May 1998, right after graduating from the University of Western Ontario with an honors business administration degree from the Richard Ivey School of Business, The University of Western Ontario, London, Ontario, Canada.

Sonya had received a personal phone call from Molly, a supply chain manager from the Atlanta office, asking her to join the design team of the eProcure project. Sonya had just completed a strategic sourcing project for a financial institution in Toronto, and her manager from this project had recommended her to Molly as a valuable resource for the eProcure project. Sonya was interested in the supply chain line of business and was excited about working on her first out-of-town project. Sonya also was up for early promotion to consultant in December 1999; therefore, she wanted to ensure that she took a role that would give her the opportunities and exposure to prove herself worthy of an early advancement. After listening to the role description, Sonya was pleased with the prospects and immediately accepted the role.

The design team was managed by Molly, and consisted of Claire Bishop, Maria Hodge and Sonya. Claire and Maria were both analysts from the Atlanta office. Claire began working with

Excel at the same time as Sonya and therefore she was also being considered for early promotion in December. Maria was a new analyst who had only been at the firm for two months.

During their first meeting with Molly, both Sonya and Claire were informed that they were responsible for the conceptual and detail designs of the SeP product. Since a technical tool had never been developed for strategic sourcing, there were no previous projects or experiences they could rely on. As such, Sonya and Claire needed to research and analyse the manual process, and creatively design a technical solution for it. Molly had decided that the software would consist of four main modules: internal analysis, supplier analysis, strategy and eNegotiation. Sonya was responsible for designing the first two modules since she had hands-on experience with these parts of the process and Claire was responsible for the other two modules. Since Maria was new to the firm, she was there to support both Sonya and Claire by conducting research and putting final design documents together. They were told that they had three weeks to work on the designs. Upon completion, they would make a presentation to George Fry, William Sheppard and Steve Miller. Molly asked for weekly status reports to be completed by all team members. She would use these status reports to update the project timeline and to inform other Excel team members of her team's progress.

Molly Berkson

Molly was a senior manager with Excel in the supply chain line of business, at the Atlanta office. Molly had begun working with Excel in April 1993, after she graduated with an MBA from the University of Kansas.

Molly had been asked by George Fry to join the team in early August. She had worked on numerous strategic sourcing engagements throughout the firm and was considered an expert in the area. Due to her expertise, Molly had been assigned to lead the design efforts of the SeP software product. Her specific responsibilities involved managing all design efforts for the project, including managing a team of three professionals and ensuring project deadlines and deliverables were met. In addition, since Molly was one of only a few people with strategic sourcing knowledge, she was responsible for assisting all of the teams by answering any questions and helping people to understand specific strategic sourcing concepts.

Although Molly was excited about the prospects of working for an Internet startup company, she wasn't very excited about leading the design team. As a senior manager she was beginning to look for opportunities to increase her exposure to senior executives both inside and outside the firm. She hoped to be promoted to associate partner in a year or two. Leading the design team would be similar to many of her past management roles and therefore Molly was concerned that this role might hold her back from other opportunities. Since she had worked with George in the past, and he had asked her personally to join the team, Molly found it difficult to refuse the role.

THE DESIGN

Sonya and Claire began working on the designs immediately after their first meeting with Molly. Three weeks was a short period of time to complete all the research, and designs and documentation. With the added pressure of making a final presentation to the co-founders and the Excel partner, Sonya was even more eager to get a head start. She intended to work extremely hard over the next few weeks in order to come up with the most impressive designs. Sonya knew this project was her chance to prove herself and make a positive impression on Molly and, more importantly, on George.

Sonya had worked on a strategic sourcing project in the past and was familiar with the Excel methodology. She had also developed relationships with other supply chain managers in the Toronto office, so she was able to call them for reference materials and help with any questions. Sonya felt uncomfortable approaching Molly with too many questions for a variety of reasons: Molly always seemed busy or preoccupied; Molly was never very friendly or warm towards her and Sonya didn't want to leave the impression that she needed a lot of help and couldn't handle the task herself. Sonya spent a lot of time researching the first few steps of the process and worked day and night trying to come up with good ideas for the designs. She had developed a good relationship with Maria, the junior analyst on her team. Maria was very helpful in conducting any research and putting together the documentation that was necessary.

Sonya thought it was important that she work together with Claire on the designs in order to integrate them, but she found Claire to be very secretive about her designs and any progress she had made with them. Sonya knew that Claire would have to spend more time upfront understanding the process because she didn't have any previous experience with strategic sourcing. Sonya had offered Claire help if she had any questions about the process, but Claire only asked Molly any questions that she had. Although Sonya had tried to make several attempts to talk to and work with Claire on the designs, she had been unsuccessful.

Sonya felt that there was obvious tension on the team, but unfortunately, Claire had made no effort to get to know either Sonya or Maria. Sonya and Maria went for lunch together every day and whenever they asked Claire, she always responded that she was busy and went for lunch with Molly or with an eProcure employee instead. Maria found Claire difficult to deal with as well. In particular, Maria complained to Sonya that Claire treated her like her secretary, ordering her around to do research and to complete documents, instead of treating her as a colleague. Although Maria recognized that she was new to the firm, all three of them on the team were at the same analyst level.

Sonya had noticed that Claire and Molly had recently become very good friends. They often went to the gym together after work and met for coffee in the morning. This made Sonya feel very uncomfortable because she knew that both she and Claire were up for early promotion within a few months. Sonya had never been the type of person to get ahead purely because of relationships with people. Although she always got along with everyone on her team, she was usually quieter and really focused on producing quality work. She believed that hard work and initiative would get her ahead, and she hoped that Molly would appreciate this too.

RECENT EVENTS

Three weeks had passed and Molly had scheduled a team meeting to go over the designs before the final presentation at the end of the week. Both Claire and Sonya had sent their documentation to Molly a few days before the meeting. Molly had been unable to look at anything before the meeting, however, because she had been busy helping other teams on the project. Sonya and Claire were supposed to practice presenting their designs to Molly and Maria during the meeting.

Sonya presented her designs first, since she had designed the first two modules. Molly was impressed with all the work she had done and congratulated Sonya for her efforts. Claire presented next, but within 15 minutes of the presentation, Molly told her to stop and asked, "Why are the designs not integrated?"

Sonya wasn't sure how to respond. She didn't want to complain about Claire, but at the same time she didn't want it to seem like she had never thought about integrating the designs. As she was trying to think of a reasonable response to Molly's question, Claire immediately responded:

> I realized the importance of integration early on and talked about it to Sonya within the first few days. I have been trying to find time with Sonya to sit down to discuss how to integrate the designs as smoothly as possible; however Sonya has been very busy working on her own designs and documentation. Therefore, I have been working on my designs by getting ideas from the eProcure employees and other Excel personnel and have

been concentrating on putting together as many creative ideas as possible for the product. My designs are very flexible and I can easily work with Sonya to make sure they are integrated by the end of the week.

Sonya couldn't believe that Claire had completely lied, but she felt that she couldn't say anything about it to Molly, especially during the team meeting. Therefore, Sonya just responded that she had thought the same and had also been very busy working on her designs. She also assured Molly that integration would not be a problem.

Molly told them that she wished they had approached her earlier with any questions or concerns; however, she now just wanted to be sure that they could integrate the designs within the next few days. It was Monday and the final presentation was exactly a week away. Molly wanted to see all of the final integrated designs by the end of Thursday. She informed the team to cancel their flights home as they would be staying in Baltimore for the weekend to finish. Molly then asked Claire to finish her presentation. After the presentation, she brainstormed various ideas for Claire and Sonya and provided them with her feedback on the designs. She was generally happy, but Claire's section needed a lot more work. The eNegotiation module was probably one of the toughest to design and therefore Molly asked that the entire team spend a few hours together to brainstorm ideas for the design in order to help Claire.

The meeting lasted about six hours in total and Molly asked the team to get back to work and reconvene the next afternoon. She wanted to stay involved and make sure that she managed the rest of the week very closely. She was upset that the team had been unable to take the initiative to manage the design process on its own and she wondered why they had not been proactive in asking her questions and getting feedback during the process. She knew that she had been very busy lately helping other teams on the project, but she always thought of herself as accessible. The final presentation to the leadership would be a reflection on her as well; therefore, Molly wanted to ensure that her team was able to integrate the designs and complete all of the necessary documentation before Thursday.

NEXT STEPS

Sonya left the meeting feeling very frustrated. She had spent so many weeks working on her designs and now she had to spend the rest of the week working on the integration of the designs. This weekend was her best friend's birthday and she had planned the party weeks in advance. Now Sonya would have to call her and explain that she wasn't going to be there. Work was definitely different than she had expected.

There were numerous issues that were bothering Sonya. First, she was upset that the team was in this situation in the first place. She had tried to speak to Claire earlier, but that obviously didn't work. She wondered what else she could have done. She realized that she probably should have spoken to Molly earlier, but she was afraid of the perception Molly may have developed of her if she had. Molly may have thought that she wasn't able to handle the responsibility and Sonya didn't want to jeopardize any chance of an early promotion. Sonya also wondered what Molly could have done to have prevented this from happening.

In addition, Sonya was upset with the relationship she had with Claire. It was difficult when team members didn't get along and now that they had to work very closely together for the rest of the week, she was worried about the impact their personal relationship would have on the final designs. She wondered how much of her relationship with Claire had to do with personal differences and to what extent it was based on both of them being up for early promotion at the same time. She knew that there was a sense of competition between them as soon as they had met. They were both trying to impress Molly and the leadership so they could be promoted earlier. Could Excel and the eProcure leadership team have managed this better?

Sonya was definitely learning a lot from her first job out of Ivey. She realized that she needed to put these thoughts behind her right now and focus on the designs since she had a meeting with Molly the next afternoon. The first thing Sonya needed to do was to talk to Claire. She wondered if she should say anything to Claire about her comments in the meeting or just forget about them and focus on working on the designs. Sonya decided to make the first move and to talk to Claire immediately.

SPAR APPLIED SYSTEMS (A)

Prepared by Laura Erskine under the supervision of Professor Jane Howell

Version: (A) 2002-03-13

By late March 1996, the Avionics 2000 Team had been working on their project for more than two years. In their presentation of the projected budget and schedule to Applied Systems executives, the team identified a potential $1 million overspend in order to satisfy their contract with Phoenix Helicopter International. Their original budget was $3.5 million, of which $2.5 million was provided by the company. When Stephen Miller, General Manager of Spar Applied Systems, had questioned team members during the presentation about what had caused the overrun, he was amazed that the team was unable to respond. Stephen adjourned the meeting, returned to his office, and wondered what to do.

SPAR AEROSPACE LIMITED

Spar Aerospace Limited was Canada's premier space company and was a recognized leader in the space-based communications, robotics, informatics, aviation and defense industries. The company began in 1968, as a spin-off from de Havilland Aircraft, and was re-organized into four decentralized business segments over a period of two decades: Space; Communications; Aviation and Defense; and Informatics (see Exhibit 1).

The company employed approximately 2,500 people worldwide and approximately 60 per cent of Spar's sales originated outside Canada. Spar's expertise enabled Canada to become the third country in outer space and the company continued to innovate with achievements such as communications satellites, the Canadarm, and compression of digital communication signals.

SPAR APPLIED SYSTEMS

Spar's Aviation and Defense area featured two distinct businesses, one of which was Spar Applied Systems. Applied Systems Group (ASG) had been formed by a merger between Spar Defense Systems and the bankrupt Leigh Instruments Limited whose assets were acquired by Spar in 1990. ASG designed and supplied communication, flight safety, surveillance and navigation equipment to military organizations and commercial aviation customers around the world. It also offered advanced manufacturing services for complex electronic assemblies and systems. ASG operated out of two facilities in the Ottawa Valley: Kanata and Carleton Place; employed 340 people; and was the only non-unionized area of Spar.

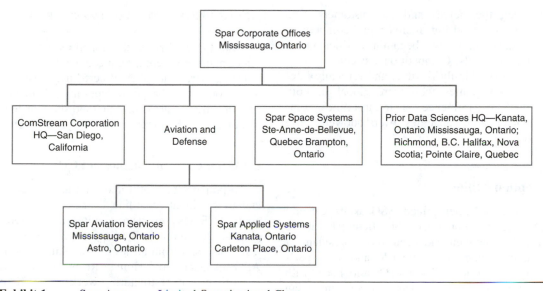

Exhibit 1   Spar Aerospace Limited Organizational Chart
Source: Company files.

The flight safety systems products included deployable emergency locator beacons, and flight data and cockpit voice recorders which collected, monitored, and analyzed aircraft flight information to assess equipment condition and improve flight safety procedures. Communications and intelligence products included integrated shipboard naval communications systems, ground-based aircraft navigation beacons, and infra-red surveillance systems. Advanced manufacturing incorporated the assembly of high quality, low volume, highly complex electronic assemblies and systems to meet stringent military and space specifications. Applied Systems' customers included Canada's Department of National Defense, the U.S. Navy and Coast Guard, Smith Industries, Hughes Aircraft Company, McDonnell Douglas Aerospace, Eastman Kodak and many others.

THE LEIGH ACQUISITION

By 1992, Spar Defense and Leigh Instruments had been successfully merged under the leadership of Jason Rigney, a consultant hired by Spar Aerospace. Jason's mandate had been to orchestrate the merger or, failing that outcome, to reorganize the work into the other Spar divisions because both Spar Defense and Leigh had been in serious financial difficulty prior to 1990. Leigh had declared bankruptcy and certain of its assets were sold to Spar Aerospace by the Receiver. Spar Defense was a fundamentally failing enterprise but it was protected financially through its relationship with Spar Aerospace. However, through Jason's leadership and his ability to put together the right mix of individuals and competencies, contracts were stabilized and Applied Systems began. By the time Stephen Miller replaced Jason Rigney as vice president and general manager of ASG in 1992, many of the contracts held by ASG were nearing completion and Stephen was faced with the necessity of generating new business.

In the narrow aerospace and defense markets, ASG was reliant on business decisions beyond its control. Commercial risk was being introduced to the aerospace industry and, for the first time, companies needed to balance the risk between themselves and the customers. The market was getting increasingly competitive and time to market was becoming a critical factor in winning bids. Competition was coming from larger-scale, highly flexible, and vertically integrated companies who were global in both strength and influence. Their capabilities, competencies and capacities overshadowed those at ASG.

Stephen Miller

Stephen Miller joined ASG as its General Manager in September 1992. Before his move to ASG, Stephen had been a vice-president of Marketing and Government Relations in Spar's Corporate Office in Toronto, Ontario. Faced with an organization ill-prepared to compete in an increasingly commercial marketplace, Stephen saw an urgent need to change. When Stephen joined ASG in the fall of 1992, the organization had a hierarchical structure (see Exhibit 2 for a partial organization chart); people had very precise position descriptions which directed all of their actions; and activities were directed at completing programs on a "cost-plus"[1] basis with limited regard for budgets and schedules. Stephen had three personal objectives. First, he wanted to change the culture at ASG so dramatically that any future successors would not be able to go back to the way things were in the fall of 1992. Second, he wanted the division to make money for more than six months in a row. Finally, he wanted a long-term strategy that would make sense in a global context and eliminate the short-term planning with which the company was familiar. These three objectives would drive every decision Stephen made. If successful, these objectives would increase both the flexibility and resiliency of the organization. Stephen also wanted to create a culture that fostered teamwork, open communication, accountability, and recognition of performance in a skilled, challenged workforce. He felt that the workforce was capable of greater achievements if properly managed and motivated.

ASG's Organizational Transformation

Organizational changes developed by a team of senior managers were introduced in stages over a four-year period and they affected many aspects of the company. Change was continuously occurring in different areas of ASG and the management team led by Stephen was not yet through.

i. Taking Care of Business (TCB)

To prepare the workforce for transformation and to get input regarding changes to various areas, TCB sessions were conducted in several phases. Beginning in January 1993, volunteer team members from all levels and skill areas of ASG responded to a Human Resources request to participate in restructuring workshops. These volunteers were empowered by ASG executives to operationalize the Strategic Plan; organize focus teams to study each area of the business; identify issues and actions that would dramatically impact growth; and recommend a new organizational structure that not only recognized core competencies but also introduced a new culture.

ii. Structure

When Stephen assumed the leadership of ASG in 1992, he found a company with multiple layers and organized around the programs underway at ASG. Each program was led by a program manager who maintained the budget, schedule, staffing, and task assignments of the project. Employees reported to the program manager who directed their tasks and evaluated their performance. The program manager assumed overall responsibility for the project and reported its progress to senior management and to the customer. By 1994, Stephen felt the leadership had the support and participation of a cross-section of employees to move ahead with a radically different organizational structure based on business processes. In order to capture people's attention, July 4, 1994, was the day the management team chose to "set off some fireworks"

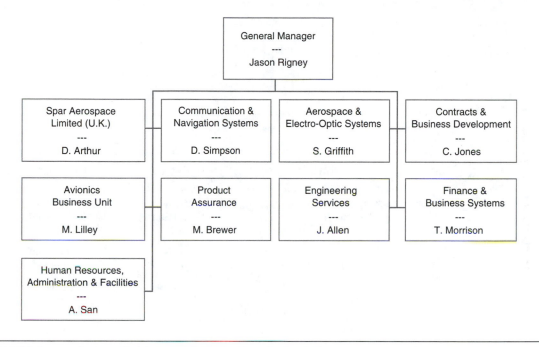

Exhibit 2   Spar Applied Systems Executive Organizational Chart

Source: Company files.

with the introduction of a new structure. As a result of these initiatives, the division's organizational chart was eliminated.

The new organizational structure was process-focused and was centered around skill clusters from which resources were drawn to create products (see Exhibit 3 for a graphical representation). Customer satisfaction was the primary goal and employees at all three stages of the process (Getting the Business, Performing the Business, and Supporting the Business) were brought closer to their customers. This allowed both greater communication and better understanding of customer requirements. People were identified as Leaders of the various skill clusters but their role was to coach and mentor, not manage, the people in their clusters. As job titles disappeared, so did position descriptions. The resulting ambiguity caused many people to be unsure of their ultimate responsibility and accountability. Few employees truly understood

their place in a structure where boundaries were often unclear.

iii. Integrated Program Teams (IPTs)

Another element in the change strategy was to encourage the development of project teams to deal directly with the customer for all business opportunities. Multidisciplinary IPTs were formed for projects in order to address issues quickly and resolve problems. They were responsible to both their customers and ASG for the successful realization of customer expectations.

An IPT was formed as soon as Marketing recognized a contract opportunity. Employees were drawn from different skill clusters based on the competencies required at the time. Each IPT worked with both the Market Development cluster and the Sales and Marketing clusters to estimate project requirements (scheduling, budgeting, and

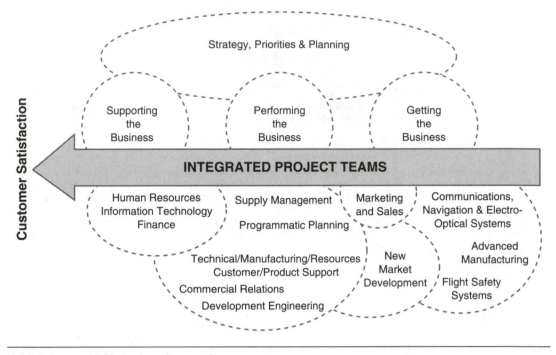

Exhibit 3   ASG's Business/Process Structure
Source: Company files.

personnel), to bid for new contracts, and to design and manufacture unique products.

Membership on an IPT was fluid because employees joined or departed from their teams according to their particular expertise and the stage of the project. Employees were frequently members of several IPTs at the same time. Team members represented a diagonal slice of levels and diverse competencies such as contract negotiation and creation; systems design; mechanical engineering; procurement; software engineering; qualification and testing; or manufacturing. Ideally, each team selected its own leader at the outset. Depending on the stage of the project (bidding, design, manufacturing), new leaders could be selected as required. Leadership skills, new to many employees, were offered through both formal training programs and practical experience.

In Stephen's vision, IPTs had responsibility for three kinds of business: repeat business, new business, and new product development.

Repeat business dealt with known products and processes so that the hours and materials required could be easily determined before a contract was signed and a due date imposed. New business usually included some front-end engineering to reconfigure existing technology. New product development, however, was the area in which IPTs were expected to shine. Once a contract was signed, the design would have to be created from scratch, move from engineering through testing and prototype, and finally into production. There were more risks to win business. Time in the marketplace was compressed and fixed price contracts had penalties for non-performance. By having everyone involved up front with the new IPT concept, management expected to reduce both the number and severity of errors throughout the process. Stephen recognized that not everyone supported or understood the IPT concept but he hoped that time and experience would validate the new idea.

As part of getting IPTs up and running smoothly, a comprehensive team skills development program was launched as part of RAPS (Real Achievers Pursuing Success). RAPS was created in the fall of 1994, by an outside consultant, to provide interpersonal training and soft skills development. Both management and employees felt that employee participation in the workshops was high. Stephen attributed this initial success to the involvement of the employees in creating the program but emphasized the need to get participation from more employees, especially engineers.

The organizational transformation had moved Applied Systems incredibly far in four years and most employees enthusiastically supported the changes. However, some employees left the organization, while others elected to stay but did not fully endorse the new systems and structures. The changes did not always occur in the way the leadership members had envisioned. The IPT was one of the concepts that was introduced with some rough spots along the way.

AVIONICS 2000

Because of the commitment to finding new business opportunities, R&D funding was dedicated to developing new products in the flight safety area—a philosophy endorsed and driven by Stephen, the General Manager. The Avionics 2000 project was identified as a prime business objective to pursue. Avionics 2000 integrated a deployable flight data recorder (FDR), cockpit voice recorder (CVR), and Emergency Locator Beacon (ELB) system. The technology (a very advanced version of a "black box") originated from a project for the F/A-18 fighter aircraft of the United States Navy. This technology offered unique survival and recovery capability and it was suitable for use on commercial and military helicopters with possible future use on commercial aircraft. The memory and beacon automatically deployed from the airframe in an emergency and tumbled away from the accident site. In the event that the accident took place over water, the system would float indefinitely. By combining the recorder and locator functions, installation, operation and maintenance costs would be reduced. The Avionics 2000 product would provide a cornerstone for the Flight Safety Systems business unit to grow over the next generation. Technologies developed and investments made would serve on other products in the future.

Avionics 2000 was a reincarnation of the black boxes that were created 25 years ago and the initial pressure came from within ASG to create an updated, more advanced and more integrated version for the military market. Late in 1993, ASG created a generic (R&D) project to develop technologies in six different areas related to the avionics business. They projected that these six critical components, called "nuggets," could be developed and eventually combined to produce a final product advanced enough to suit the needs of a changing market. In the same time frame, an opportunity was identified with Phoenix Helicopter International, a major European helicopter assembler, and in 1994 a verbal contract to proceed on the research was received.

The change from a program manager structure to IPTs, initiated by Stephen, created difficulties for the Avionics 2000 team (see Exhibit 4 for a timeline of organizational change and team development). As the nugget technologies were being developed and early discussions with Phoenix were taking place, the technical aspects of the project were led by Mike Ellis, a systems engineer, and supported by Jeff Haner who was providing mechanical engineering expertise. Mike maintained the customer relationship and grew very close to his engineering counterparts at Phoenix. He saw the program as his "baby" and he readily accommodated customer requests to keep the project alive and moving forward. He was highly committed and regularly worked overtime on the Avionics 2000 project. Mike directed the project and, working with Jeff and Phoenix Helicopter Internationals, evaluated technology and developed components for 18 months before a contract

Organizational Changes	Timeline	Avionics 2000 Development
Spar Defense and Leigh Instruments are merged to create Spar Applied Systems	1990	
Stephen Miller joins ASG as General Manager	Sept. 1992	
25 per cent reduction in workforce TCB Initiatives begin	Jan. 1993	
	Winter 1993–1994	R&D money designated for Avionics 2000; Mike Ellis is identified as the leader of the project
	Feb.– March 1994	Phoenix Helicopter is identified as a customer and a verbal contract to proceed is received
New process-driven structure	July 4, 1994	
IPTs and RAPS training are introduced	Fall 1994	
	April–Sept. 1995	Avionics 2000 Steering Team created
	Aug. 1995	Contract with Phoenix is signed
	Sept–Oct. 1995	New Avionics 2000 team members are added; co-leadership established (Mike Ellis and Hugh Greene)
	Jan. 1996	Symposium leads to scope changes
Jonathon Martin appointed CEO of Spar Aerospace Limited	March 1996	Mike presents the Avionics 2000 ETC to management

Exhibit 4   Parallel Development of the Organization and the Avionics 2000 Project

Source: Casewriter notes.

was formally signed in August 1995. During those 18 months, the project was continuously evolving. Its staffing, with the exception of Mike, was very ad hoc. The contract that was signed in August was based on a fixed price for a deliverable product.

THE AVIONICS 2000 STEERING TEAM

Since it was one of the first IPTs, management felt that a steering team of leadership members would be helpful. The role of the Steering Team was to act as an enabling body to focus on both development of the team and the issues introduced with the IPT concept. In an e-mail message during the summer of 1995, Stephen asked five leaders to form the Avionics 2000 Steering Team: Charles Hall represented the avionics business unit, Joe Rivers represented supply management and procurement, Duncan Pound represented finance, Sean Dunleavy represented engineering research and development, and Gord Johnson represented integrated resources and manufacturing. In January 1996, the integrated resources and manufacturing representation

Name	Title	Degree/ Designation	College/ University	Years @ SPAR	Years @ ASG	Came From . . .
CHARLES HALL	Leader, Avionics Business Unit	B.E.Sc. (mechanical) MBA	Canadian Military College U. of Western Ontario	1.5	1.5	Engineering Consulting
JOE RIVERS	Leader, Supply Management	Cert. Electronic Technologist, LIRM desig. (currently)	Algonquin College	2.4	2.4	Electronics
NEAL MCCORD	Leader, Finance	B.A.	McGill University	5.2	5.2	Telecommunications, Electronics
SEAN DUNLEAVY	Leader, Engineering— R&D	Eng. Master's PhD (currently)	McGill University Queens University	3.5	3.5	Telecommunications, Spar
GORD JOHNSON	Leader, Integrated Resources	H.B.A. (Fine Arts) MBA	University of Windsor Ottawa University	3.8	3.8	Telecommunications, Electronics
TODD MACDOUGALL	Leader, Integrated Resources	B.E.Sc. (electrical)	University of Edinburgh	5.1	5.1	Defence Electronics, Telecommunications, Government

Exhibit 5   AVIONICS 2000 Steering Team Membership and Profiles

Source: Casewriter interviews, company files.

changed to Todd MacDougall as a result of staff movement. The Steering Team was to act as a council to the Avionics 2000 team of Mike, Jeff, and their supporting players. The Avionics 2000 Steering Team met once in August to recognize and choose additional team members after the contract was signed and again once the overrun was announced.

THE AVIONICS 2000 INTEGRATED PROGRAM TEAM

Eighteen months following the development of the technology, in August 1995, the team signed a contract with Phoenix. ASG and the Steering Team wanted to include people from manufacturing in order to create a concurrent engineering team, and to add people from test engineering, procurement, and market development. Mike Ellis remained the leader of the IPT; however, Sean Dunleavy worried about the issue of programmatics. Since Sean knew that Mike resisted program management duties, Hugh Greene was selected by Sean and Gord as the manufacturing representative to act as a co-leader to take care of programmatics issues. Hugh had many years of experience and he was more willing to devote some time to managing the budget and schedule than was Mike, who was more interested in the systems design aspects. Jeff Haner continued his role of mechanical engineering while Michael Lekx became the official representative from Business Development. Edward Evans was responsible for electrical engineering and Claude Ste-Pierre had expertise in software development (see Exhibit 6 for profiles of the full team). The new IPT was directed by the Steering Team to develop a new Estimate to Complete (ETC) in August and again in November. However, the IPT was so busy meeting the deadlines agreed upon in the contract that they were not able to find the time to complete the ETC.

Mike had strong ties with Phoenix's engineers and was intimately familiar with the technology being developed for the Avionics 2000. It was difficult for him to give up some of his closeness to the project in order to make the new team members feel welcome. The genesis of the Avionics 2000 project had occurred before many of the organizational changes at ASG and many wished for the old way to resurface. The team experienced difficulty finding the time to participate in team skills training sessions. As well, planning and scheduling activities were challenging. To complete their project on time, most of the 20 to 25 engineers involved would have to work many hours of overtime each week. The engineers felt that taking time away from their design work was not adding value to the project. Without a program manager, the question of ultimate responsibility was not clear in many people's minds.

Because the Avionics 2000 was so different from any other product in existence, it did not meet any of the existing international regulations. It was clear that new regulations would have to be developed. A major change in scope occurred in January 1996 as a result of a symposium that included representatives from Spar Applied Systems, Phoenix Helicopter International, Transport Canada, CAA (Civil Aviation Authority—U.K.), FAA (Federal Aviation Authority—U.S.A.), and National Transportation Safety Board (U.S.A.). Standards and regulations agreed upon during the symposium almost tripled the standards being used by ASG engineers and resulted in a redesign of the project. The Avionics 2000 model had to withstand fire at 1,100 degrees Celsius for 30 minutes, maintain a beacon signal for 150 hours, and withstand a shock of such a grade that the testing facility had to be redesigned. All of these changes, like those introduced previously by Phoenix, were readily accommodated by Mike and the team without making equivalent changes to the existing budget and schedule.

THE ESTIMATE TO COMPLETE (ETC)

The Steering Team asked the Avionics 2000 team to prepare a new ETC when the contract was signed and again when the team was formalized, but several delays (including Christmas, the January symposium, deadlines for deliverables,

Name	Role	Degree/ Designation	College/ University	Years @ SPAR	Years With Team	Came From . . .
MIKE ELLIS	Systems Engineering	M.E.Sc. (electrical)	N/A*	3	3	Space
JEFF HANER	Systems Engineering	N/A	some college	5	3	Telecommunications, Space
TODD WOODCROFT	Leader, Commercial Services	N/A	N/A	8.8	1.5	Telecommunications, Government
MICHAEL LEKX	Business/Market Development, Strategic Planning	Engineering	Community College	6	1.5	Spar
CLAUDE STE-PIERRE	Software Development	B.E.Sc. (electrical)	University of Ottawa	1.5	1.4	Software Consulting
EDWARD EVANS	Electrical Engineering Systems Design	B.E.Sc.	Technical University (Nova Scotia)	2	1.5	Telecommunications, Spar
HUGH GREENE	Manufacturing— Configuration & Documentation Management, Bills of Material	RAF ground electronics training	N/A	5	0.5	Defence Electronics, Communications

Exhibit 6 AVIONICS 2000 Team Membership and Profiles

Source: Casewriter interviews, Company files.

*N/A = information not available

141

and lack of Steering Team pressure) had postponed the presentation until mid-March 1996. Mike Ellis continued his commitment to the project and he was the sole presenter from the Avionics 2000 team. The presentation to Stephen Miller, Sean Dunleavy, and other leaders included data which surprised most of the people present. The budget was close to being spent, production had not started, and Mike had not allowed for contingencies such as delays in material procurement and difficulties in the manufacturability of the design. Neither Mike nor any of the other team members present were able to explain the reasons for the overrun, a fact which was more alarming than the actual overrun. It became immediately apparent to Stephen and some of the other leaders at the presentation that the ETC needed more careful research because, if Mike's data were accurate, the project would need an additional $1 million from shareholders.

While Stephen sat listening to the presentation by the Avionics 2000 team, he knew that the second quarter forecast would have to be submitted to Corporate Headquarters within the next two weeks. In addition to projections of lower revenues, less impressive profit numbers, and overexpenditures in other areas, Stephen was now informed that a product on which the Flight Safety Services business unit had based their future would be over budget by close to $1 million. He had been promoting the product and the spin-off opportunities to other Spar divisions and the corporate office and he was worried about the impact of the presentation by Mike. Stephen was also hoping for acquisition funding to be released by Corporate Headquarters in order to achieve some of the growth goals set by ASG in their strategic plan. He needed R&D money on an annual basis to develop new products and new markets. Finally, as of April 1996, Jonathon Martin would be the new CEO of Spar Aerospace and Stephen was concerned that a program out of control would affect requests for extra shareholders' money.

Stephen wondered whether this project was worth continuing or not. If the answer to that was yes, should the team stay intact, should the leadership be changed, or should the team itself be changed in some fashion? Trying not to show his frustration, Stephen adjourned the meeting and said to the leadership members present, "I would like us to reconvene in an hour."

NOTE

1. Cost-plus contracts are structured such that the customer pays the costs of the supplier and adds a percentage or fee on top of the cost of the materials and labor. This differs from a fixed-price contract where the total value has been determined in advance and the profit margin for the supplier is determined by how closely they predict and stick to their costs.

RICHARD IVEY SCHOOL OF BUSINESS—THE LEADER PROJECT (A)

*Prepared by Krista Ewing under the
supervision of Professor Joerg Dietz*

Version: (A) 2003-10-02

On May 4, 2001, at Pearson International Airport in Toronto, Kaitlyn Johnston, along with two other members of her team, boarded a plane to Kiev in Ukraine. The team's three-week assignment was to teach Western business practices to Ukrainian students. The team was one of several sent by a not-for-profit, student-run initiative, called Leading Education and Development in Emerging Regions (LEADER), to the former Soviet Union (FSU). Kaitlyn thought that she should be excited, but she felt disillusioned. LEADER, located at the Richard Ivey School of Business (Ivey), The University of Western Ontario, in London, Ontario, Canada, experienced severe funding and morale problems. As a result, many members did not do their jobs and some jumped ship. Members had to pay $1,800 out of their own pockets to finance the foreign assignment, significantly more than the initially expected $250.

RICHARD IVEY SCHOOL OF BUSINESS

The *Financial Times,* the *Wall Street Journal* and *Business Week* ranked Ivey as the best MBA program in Canada and among the top 30 MBA programs worldwide. Ivey relied on the case method to fulfill its mission "to develop business leaders who think globally, act strategically and contribute to the societies in which they operate." With 74 faculty members and more than 1,400 students from more than 65 countries, Ivey offered HBA, MBA, Executive MBA and PhD programs.

Ivey prided itself on its global image. A recent article by Associate Dean Paul Beamish[1] listed the following statistics:

- One in seven students participates in an international exchange.
- 45 per cent of student client field projects involve international business issues.
- 43 per cent of students are landed immigrants or visa students.
- Faculty originate from the United States, Canada, the United Kingdom, Germany, France, Holland, New Zealand, Mexico, India and elsewhere.
- 31 per cent of Ivey cases have international (non-Canada/U.S.) content.
- Cases have been translated into German, Korean, Russian, Ukrainian and Spanish.

THE LEADER PROJECT

Overview

In 1990, Scott Hellofs and Paul Fitzgerald, two then-Ivey MBA students, founded LEADER. This student-run initiative annually sent 40 to 55 volunteers to the FSU to teach basic Western business practices to a diverse audience (students, executives, government officials and academics). Specifically, LEADER's objectives were:

1. To teach basic finance, marketing and general management skills to students, entrepreneurs, managers, joint venture partners and academics,

2. To provide an understanding of Western business practices in moving towards a global economy,

3. To enhance Canadian competitiveness by providing its members with experience in the cultural and business environments of emerging markets,

4. To develop its members' understanding of the economy, culture and competitive environment of rapidly developing markets, and to communicate this understanding to others in Canada, and

5. To act as ambassadors for Canada and Canadian business.

LEADER taught its classes in the FSU using cases. The case method required students to solve real-world business problems so that they learned business skills in an applied fashion. Since 1991, more than 400 LEADER members had taught more than 3,500 students in various parts of the FSU. In 2001, LEADER teams went to 11 sites in three former Soviet republics.

Exhibit 1 shows LEADER's organizational design. The top-management team (executive) consisted of two executive directors (EDs), who were second-year MBA students, two junior executive directors (JEDs), who were first-year students elected by their fellow members and the chairs of the divisional committees. These committees were fundraising, communications, finance, teacher training and recruitment, logistics and teaching materials. The executive met

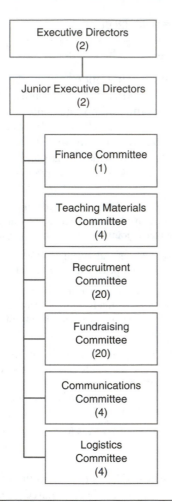

Exhibit 1 LEADER Organizational Structure

Source: LEADER Organizational Chart, 2001.

Note: There were 52 LEADER members in 2001. Because Kaitlyn Johnson served on two committees, the number of members adds up to 53. With the exception of the executive directors and the junior executive directors, each member also served on a teaching team.

weekly to co-ordinate LEADER's activities. LEADER members, who were not on the executive, participated on a committee. The committees met according to their needs. Each member, with the exception of the executive directors, was also on a teaching team.

The academic year, which ran from September to April, determined LEADER's business cycle and membership terms. Members were with LEADER for a maximum of two years (their term as students at Ivey). Recruitment and selection started in September, and the teams went on their foreign assignments in the academic summer break, usually in May. At a partner school's location in the FSU, each team taught a three-week course comprising three one-week modules (finance, marketing and general management), which culminated in a group business plan presentation. Most members completed two foreign teaching assignments: one after their first year at Ivey and one after their second year at Ivey.

Recruitment and Selection of LEADER Members, Sites and Teams

Each year in September, LEADER made presentations to first- and second-year MBA students and second-year HBA students. Moreover, interested students could attend informal LEADER functions to learn more about the program. In October, interested students applied, submitting a résumé and two to three short essays that described their potential contribution to LEADER. Annually, more than 100 students applied for the 20 to 25 available spots. The recruitment committee reviewed the applications and shortlisted 50 to 60 students for interviews. The interviewers, who were second-year LEADER members, held 30-minute interviews with each applicant, primarily asking several situational questions based on four competencies: teamwork, coaching, adaptability and ethics (see Exhibit 2 for the interview guide). After an interview, the interviewers rated the applicant on a scale ranging from "Do not Recommend" to "Highly Recommend." In early November, after completion of the interviews, the recruitment committee selected the new LEADER members on the basis of the interview ratings, whereby about 75 per cent of the selected applicants were first-year students to ensure the continuity of LEADER.

In January, the EDs and JEDs assigned the members to their teams and teaching locations in the FSU. Each teaching location required one team of four to eight students, depending on class size and number of classes to be taught. First, the EDs and JEDs picked the "site leader." The person chosen for this assignment was the liaison with the partner school prior to and during the teaching assignment at the assigned site. Moreover, the site leader was this site's team leader, which included the responsibilities of ensuring members' safety and effective team functioning (see Exhibit 3 for site leader responsibilities). Site leaders were typically second-year members, who were particularly involved with LEADER and who also served as chairs of divisional committees. Second, the EDs and JEDs assigned the other members to the site teams on basis of five criteria: (1) Second-year members' preferences for sites (second-year members had the right to pick their top five site choices), (2) Assignment of second-year members to sites different from their first-year sites; (3) Gender balance at each site; (4) First-year and second-year membership balance at each site and (5) Personality fit at each site with the intention to reduce the conflict potential.

LEADER Activities at Ivey

The vast majority of the work was completed prior to the foreign assignments. The activities included marketing, preparation of teaching materials, teacher training, determining logistics and securing financial resources.

The logistics committee co-ordinated the travel arrangements for the entire team, applied for the necessary entry visas, researched and documented emergency procedures for all the sites and wrote manuals for each site, which included helpful tips from site alumni. The committee required its members to commit approximately five hours per week for the months of January and February to complete the booking, then another four to five hours per week throughout April to co-ordinate any last-minute travel

changes, write, edit and publish the manuals, finalize hotel, train and air travel for all the members, and distribute tickets, passports and entry visas.

The recruitment committee was responsible for the development and planning of presentations to students and faculty to increase interest in LEADER, reviewing applicants' résumés and essays, scheduling and conducting interviews and ultimately selecting the 20 to 25 new LEADER members. It required its members to put in about four hours per week for a couple of months each fall.

The teacher training committee co-ordinated and conducted mock teaching sessions, provided cultural sensitivity training, taught basics of the Russian and Ukrainian languages and determined the curriculum to be taught in the FSU. It required its members to commit approximately three hours per week over a five-week period in January and February.

In addition, throughout the year, LEADER members, particularly those on the fundraising committee, tried to raise LEADER's annual budget of $110,000 (see Exhibit 4). The $110,000 budget translated into costs per member and the foreign assignment of approximately $2,500, consisting mostly of airfare, entry visas and teaching materials (the partner schools at each site provided accommodations and meals). In the past, the Canadian government through its Canadian International Development Agency (CIDA) had sponsored up to 50 per cent of LEADER's budget. With CIDA's change of focus away from the FSU to other emerging economies, CIDA stopped supporting LEADER. As a result, the fundraising committee required an intense ongoing commitment of three to five hours per week from its members throughout the year. For example, the fundraising committee organized a "Vodka Tasting" event, called corporations with operations in the FSU, approached LEADER and Ivey alumni for donations, applied for grants from foundations with an interest in the FSU and presented the LEADER Project as a charitable cause to many large multinational

(Text continues on page 149)

Candidates will be rated on three core competencies—Teamwork, Coaching and Adaptability—and on an Ethics question.** In answering the questions provided under each competency and in conjunction with the individual's résumé, evaluate the candidate's level of competency on a scale of 1 to 4, where 1 is a low rating and 4 is a high rating. Please read these descriptions carefully as they are critical to maintaining consistency in our selection criteria and in providing justification for selection decisions. Note each competency level builds on the description of the previous levels.

At the start of the interview, give a very brief outline of the project. Include a description of a team site, and the positions of site leader and ED. This is important information for the person to have in order to adequately answer the ethics question.

Suggested Format: 5 min—small talk
                          20 min—interview questions
                           5 min—candidate's questions

Interviewer: _____

Interviewee: _____

Section	Rating
Teamwork	
Coaching	
Adaptability	
TOTAL SCORE	
Ethics (Pass/Fail)	

Overall assessment of the interview:

_____

_____

_____

Highly
Recommend   Recommend   Not a Good Fit

[ ]   [ ]   [ ]

Exhibit 2   LEADER Interview Guide*   *(Continued)*

*In order to protect the integrity of the LEADER Project interview process, only one of the four competencies has been included, and questions/scenarios may have been slightly altered.

**A fail on the Ethics question will result automatically in an unsuccessful overall assessment.

Competency: Coaching

Looks like . . .

Level 1: effective communication and presentation skills; has a professional conduct and is mature—coaching is not about telling people what to do; it is about helping others to see what they need to do to become more successful

Level 2: all of the above; facilitates others' participation; reassures and encourages others after a setback; approachable

Level 3: all of the above; relevant work experiences that can be shared in the classroom; assesses abilities of the group and adapts course content to the appropriate level; gives positive and negative feedback in behavioural rather than personal terms

Level 4: all of the above; ability to influence others through the use of persuasive arguments and presentation skills

Questions:

Tell me about a time when you gave feedback to reinforce someone's ineffective performance.

_____

_____

_____

_____

_____

_____

_____

_____

Scenario: On the second day of teaching, after a brief lecture, you launch into the case, but to your dismay no one raises a hand. How would you handle the situation?

Notes:

Exhibit 2   LEADER Interview Guide*

Responsibilities of Site Leaders

The position of site leader is a critical factor to the success of the project. To be effective, the site leader must consider the following issues and begin the design of strategies and contingency plans immediately upon selection:

Operations and Timeline

Many norms and rules of behaviour among team members, partners and students will be established in the first week of the program. Final details may need to be settled or changes may occur with accommodations, transportation, materials, classrooms, teaching partners, translators, meals, cultural trips, visas, etc.

Safety

The site leader must ensure the safety of each LEADER participant on the team. A site leader can expect to deal with any of the following issues: bribery of private and public officials, robbery, the pervasive arm of the Mafia, illegal solicitation, abduction and, in a worst case scenario, widespread social unrest and potential evacuation of team members.

Other safety issues concern the health of the participants including viral and toxic contamination of food and water, injury due to accident, psychological and psychiatric instabilities, culture shock and other personal issues.

Partner Relationship

The relationship with the local partner is key to the site's success. This begins with initial selection of the partner, contact before arrival, first impressions upon arrival, meetings, idea development, problem solving during the stay and any followup required. We are in fact joint venturing with these partners and the foundation of that relationship is based on trust. Fortunately, several sites have a "history" of trust upon which to draw, while other sites will require that trust be developed this year.

Diplomacy

The site leader is responsible for the site team and the site team represents LEADER Project, the Richard Ivey School of Business and Canada. We will be judged whether we like it or not, on our behaviour both inside and outside the classroom. It is the role model behaviour of the site leader upon which our team members will base their behaviour.

Culture

The site leader has an opportunity to set the culture of the site environment. A site culture can be developed which combines professional demeanour with sensitivity to cultural differences, a desire to exchange and learn on both sides with the opportunity to meet and get to know our hosts personally, and respect for a long serious and rich history of the republics with a fun, upbeat, relaxed and positive attitude.

LEADER has tried to arrange cultural programs and lectures beforehand through the local partners. However, you may arrive on site and find that nothing has been set up. Site leaders should try to arrange with cultural programs, plant tours, company tours, political lectures, etc., throughout the program.

Current Opportunities

The site leader's role is to exploit as many opportunities as possible in developing the profile of the Project. This includes media exposure, contact with government, business and political officials, and contact with foreigners travelling in the area.

Exhibit 3   From LEADER Emergency Site Guide, 2001   *(Continued)*

Future Opportunities

There is an opportunity of project development with existing partners by planning for next year. It may include the development of new partners, as well.

Counselling

Many changes will occur to individuals over the course of our stay in the FSU. Some people will have no trouble adjusting, while others will have difficulty and need someone to hear them out, lend support and be a friend. Participants will be dealing with many issues such as culture shock, worry about future job prospects, worry about family, spouses, significant others, etc. . . . Site leaders will need to keep an eye out for these feelings and offer a sympathetic ear when needed.

A Sense of Perspective

The ideal site leaders will do their best in balancing these issues and others while keeping the overall project objectives in perspective.

Exhibit 3   From LEADER Emergency Site Guide, 2001

---

businesses. Simultaneously, LEADER lobbied Ivey officials for support. Charging the partner schools and their students was another option that LEADER considered. Moreover, members always had to provide a minimum of $250 out of their own pockets. Now, despite considerable effort, however, individual members had to top up their initial contribution of $250 to $1,800 to compensate for the lack of external funding.

Historically, in any given year, about two to four of LEADER's members did not return for their second year. This year, however, the attrition was higher, as about half of the returning members quit LEADER, largely blaming their dissatisfaction on the increased financial obligation. One first-year member also quit and others seriously considered it. The first-year member, who had quit, also had tried to convince other first-year members to quit based on the change in financial commitment. She said:

> In the information sessions the directors told us that we would only be required to give a deposit of $250 to show our commitment to the program. Now they are backtracking and telling us that they quoted a "best-case scenario," but that the balance

would come out of our own pockets. They misrepresented the situation, and I think that we should quit, en masse, showing our displeasure.

Overall, the morale of the group was very low, with few members attending the meetings of their committees.

The site leaders usually initiated site team activities, such as dinners and other site gatherings. Site alumni (members who had previously taught at the site) made presentations about the site's school and its community. LEADER did not co-ordinate these activities, leaving it up to the site leaders to decide their extent and contents. This year, the site leaders of some teams did not schedule any team activities.

THE FORMER SOVIET UNION (FSU)

In 2001, LEADER had sites in three countries that formerly belonged to the Soviet Republic: Russia, Ukraine and Belarus. In its entirety, the FSU countries comprised the majority of the land mass of Eastern Europe and Northwestern Asia. Many FSU countries were rich in mineral

Group	LEADER BUDGET Description	2001 Actual $ students	2002 Budget $ 45
REVENUE			
Fundraising	Corporate Donations	19,500	18,500
	Fundraising Events	6,649	31,000
	Alumni/Individual Donation	9,348	15,000
	Private Benefactor	25,000	
	MBA Association	10,000	
	Public Foundations	5,100	5,000
Student Contribution	Year 2000–2002	33,869	31,821
Other	Interest	821	100
	Previous Years Forwarded	—	
TOTAL REVENUE		110,287	101,421
	Difference	0	
EXPENSES			
Logistics			
	Visa Photos	810	800
	Flights @@$1,300.00	74,220	66,798
	Accommodation at Central Meeting Place	—	—
	Visas	10,505	12,195
	Emergency Site Funds	4,560	3,600
Recruiting	Introductory Dinner	957	950
	Mixer		700
Communications			—
	Report Covers	883	100
	Hats & Tees	1,250	1,300
	Web Site Development	52	500
	Video Camera		1,800
Treasurer	Quicken 2001 (to upgrade from Quicken '94)	—	−80
	Cheques/Web Charge	96	70
	Cheques/Stamps	37	50

Exhibit 4   LEADER Budget   *(Continued)*

Social	Executive Selection	160	200
	Site Olympics	648	700
	Meeting Snacks	26	30
Teaching Materials	Translation	560	600
	Teacher Training	41	50
	Site Bags & Teaching Materials	1,303	1,000
New	Carry Forward	5,000	—
	Board Formation		500
	Sub Total	**101,108**	**92,023**
Overhead-UWO Account			
		Approx	
	Case Printing and Duplicating (all in)	6,768	7,500
	Postage	27	300
	Supplies	—	100
	Telephone & Long Distance	0	300
	Telephone Equipment Rental $38/month	662	480
	Overhead	1,724	1,724
	Sub Total	**9,181**	**10,404**
TOTAL EXPENSES	**TOTAL**	**110,289**	**102,427**

Exhibit 4   LEADER Budget

Note: Numbers have been rounded to the nearest dollar value.

deposits and fossil fuels, but agriculture still constituted a significant portion of their economies. The economic and political development of the former FSU countries generally had been slow, as a strong communist sentiment still permeated all levels of government. North American oil companies had recently begun to form joint ventures in the FSU, whose oil and gas resources were alternatives to those of the politically instable Middle East.

Russia

With a population of 146 million, Russia was home to four LEADER sites in Omsk, Ekaterinburg, Nizhni Tagil (pronounced: nish'-nee tag-il') and Obninsk (pronounced: ob'-minsk). In the early years after the fall of communism in 1989 and the subsequent disintegration of the Soviet Republic, the Russian economy had been very unstable and only slowly developing. An unstable banking and monetary system, high crime rates, the dominance of mafia-type organizations in many parts of the country and government corruption contributed to this slow start. Since the 1998 Russian stock market crash, foreign investment had been sluggish, as these investments often depreciated rapidly. In the first six months of 2001, however, the economy showed marginal signs of stability. Russia's economy grew by five per cent, although the inflation rate was still at about 20 per cent. President Putin, elected in 2000, acknowledged the challenges Russia's economy faced and led a change initiative to overhaul it.

Belarus

In Belarus (which translates as White Russia), LEADER had two teaching sites in the city of Minsk. Throughout its history, Belarus, which had a population of 10.5 million, had been caught in the middle of political tug of wars, being at one time, or another a part of Russia, Poland, the Union of Soviet Socialist Republics, Romania, Lithuania, Hitler's Germany and independent. In 1944, Stalin's army liberated Belarus from Nazi rule. The destruction of the Second World War had left Belarus without an infrastructure, but under Stalin's rule a heaving manufacturing industry developed. In 1986, the Chernobyl disaster led to widespread nuclear contamination in Belarus, a fact that government only acknowledged three years later. Belarus gained independence in 1991 and reformed its constitution in 1996; however, President Lukashenki, elected in 1996, imposed a policy of "market socialism." In 1997, he halted privatization and re-imposed government-controlled price setting and foreign exchange controls. Belarus had very few foreign investments and its inflation of about 30 per cent was among the highest in the FSU countries.

Ukraine

Ukraine, which had a population of 49 million people, had three LEADER sites: Kiev (pronounced: either keev' or kee'-ev), Lviv (pronounced: le-veev') and Dnipropetrovsk (pronounced: de-nee'-pro pe'-trovsk). Ukraine had a historically strained relationship with Russia due to Russian rule for the majority of the previous two centuries and two Soviet-induced artificial famines that killed 8 million people. In many places, Ukrainian had replaced Russian as the official and only language. After Russia, Ukraine was economically the second largest FSU country. Having been known as the Soviet breadbasket, Ukraine's main industry remained agriculture. President Kuchma, who was elected in 1994, initiated substantial economic reforms and privatizations. Recent events, however, such as the earlier mentioned 1998 Russian stock market crash and the global recession had slowed economic improvements. Ukraine was still in arrears on wage and pension payments and the economy had been stagnant, while the inflation rate reached 20 per cent.

The LEADER Site in Kiev

Kiev was the capital of Ukraine. It had a population of three million people and was located more or less in the center of Ukraine. Despite near total destruction in the Second World War, the city had retained large portions of its pre-war appearance after decades of extensive restorations. Kiev was a very clean and manicured city. In May, lilacs and chestnut trees in full bloom decorated the streets, once leading former U.S.S.R. President Gorbachev to describe Kiev as "the city built in a garden." Kiev had wide boulevards and many parks that the citizens frequently used for picnics and other social gatherings. The sidewalks and streets, many of which were made of cobblestone, ran up and down very steep hills. The level of crime was generally low with the exception of the occasional pickpocket. New cars were only one sign of an improving standard of living.

LEADER had been in Kiev since 1993, when it partnered with the International Center of Privatization, Investment and Management. In 2001, the school, which was located in northwestern

Kiev, was a private institution that charged students approximately US$5,000 per year to attend an undergraduate degree program or an executive training program. The school's pro-rector was a Ukrainian-Canadian who earlier in his career had founded and led the MBA Program at the University of New Brunswick.

The school's facilities were in good condition. One large building was the school's home, which included several classrooms, a lecture theatre and two computer labs. The main computer lab held 25 computers with high-speed connections to the Internet, and the other (which was reserved for visiting dignitaries and business leaders) held five computers with Internet connections. The school also had a "Canadian Business Library," which housed many reference books on market-based business practices, GMAT preparation, Canadian maps, and Canadian university appli-cation forms for MBA and other programs. The equipment of the school included many ameni-ties such as photocopiers, whiteboards, overhead projectors and computer projectors.

LEADER had developed a strong relationship to the school. Students viewed the LEADER program as a valuable component of their degrees. In 2001, successful completion of the LEADER Project had become a requirement for graduation from the school's programs.

At the school, LEADER taught two classes with a total of 40 students, which required a team of four instructors. The day class of undergradu-ate business students ran from 9:00 a.m. through to 3:00 p.m. The evening class of 15 business executives ran from 6:00 p.m. to 9:00 p.m.

Kaitlyn Johnston

The 29-year-old Kaitlyn was a first-year LEADER member, who had just completed her first year in Ivey's MBA program. Prior to attending Ivey, she had received a Bachelor of Arts in psychology from The University of Western Ontario and, for five years, had worked for the Royal Bank of Canada in various man-agerial capacities. She had been married for two years, spending the weeks in London and the weekends usually with her husband in Toronto. She did not have a job lined up for the summer after the foreign assignment with LEADER.

Kaitlyn said about her involvement in LEADER:

It is a good fit with my previous experience. I have been on voluntary foreign assignments in South-east Asia and Central America with the Waterloo, Ontario-based International Development Agency named World Accord. LEADER allows me to con-tinue international philanthropic work in a differ-ent region. I can help LEADER in several ways. I am a friendly person who generally gets along with everybody, and I have the ability to smooth over explosive situations. These attributes will help me to build affiliation among team members. More-over, in the classroom I am comfortable speaking to a crowd.

As a member of the logistics committee, since November 2000, Kaitlyn had spent about five hours per week working on logistics. In addition, she had helped out with fundraising initiatives, including preparing and delivering presentations to her former employers, and writing letters to corporations in the FSU. Overall, Kaitlyn had dedicated between eight and 10 hours per week for LEADER-related activities.

CURRENT SITUATION

Walking on the gangway, Kaitlyn felt heavy-hearted. The excitement that she had felt when LEADER accepted her into the project had van-ished. Despite the concerted efforts of the fundraising committee, LEADER had been unsuccessful in raising any significant funds. Furthermore, the number of members, who, like Kaitlyn, were deeply committed to LEADER and had put in the work to get this year's teams underway, had shrunk to 15. Recent meetings of these core LEADER members had ended with discussions about how LEADER had to change if it was to survive. How could LEADER raise more money and recruit members, who carried their share of the load? What other alternatives might LEADER consider to achieve its objectives? How would LEADER's struggles affect the team on their foreign assignments?

Kaitlyn overheard her other two teammates, the site leader Dennis Graydon and Kevin Rae, joking about who had gotten away with the least amount of work on LEADER this year. Kaitlyn bristled at this attitude and became increasingly concerned that the next month would turn into a failure.

NOTE

1. Paul Beamish, "Think Global," *In Touch,* Winter 2002, pg. 23.

RICHARD IVEY SCHOOL OF BUSINESS—THE LEADER PROJECT—KIEV SITE (B)

Prepared by Krista Ewing under the supervision of Professor Joerg Dietz

Version: (A) 2003-10-02

On May 10, 2001, after five days of her three-week foreign assignment, Kaitlyn Johnston returned from a tour of the nightlife in Kiev, Ukraine. She was concerned that her team's leader, Dennis Graydon, had abruptly left the evening's tour. Subsequently, Kaitlyn had to repeatedly assure the local host (a student in their class) that Dennis' departure was not his fault. Kaitlyn, in fact, knew that Dennis had left because he was still angry with Beth Reese, another team member. When Kaitlyn had spoken to Beth, however, Beth responded that she did not know why Dennis would be upset with her. Kaitlyn pondered what had gone wrong between Dennis and Beth and how she could resolve the situation.

THE LEADER TEAM

In addition to Kaitlyn Johnston, the three other team members were Dennis Graydon, Kevin Rae and Beth Reese.

Dennis Graydon

Dennis Graydon, the site leader, was 27 years old and had just graduated from the MBA program at the Richard Ivey School of Business (Ivey), The University of Western Ontario, London, Ontario, Canada, on the Dean's List. Before entering Ivey, Dennis had graduated from the University of Toronto with a Bachelor of Arts in history. For three years, he had worked as an Air Canada flight attendant and for his family's small business. Upon returning from Kiev, he would marry at the end of June and join Accenture as a strategy consultant. Dennis viewed himself as a competitor, "who would not lose gracefully." His Ivey classmates viewed him as an opinionated and confident individual who was eager to debate.

Dennis was very vocal about his decision to join Leading Education and Development in Emerging Regions (LEADER): "I wanted to beef up my résumé. Participating in LEADER made me more attractive to the consulting firms, for which I wanted to work." Dennis was a "natural" teacher, who was very comfortable in front of a crowd and delivered the teaching material very clearly. Kaitlyn valued Dennis's teaching ability, but noted his lack of patience with team members.

Dennis, who was a member of LEADER's recruitment committee, boasted that he had only put in three hours in total for committee activities last fall, saying "the 'eager beavers' could do the recruiting without him."

Kevin Rae

The 32-year-old Kevin was also a recent graduate of the Ivey MBA program. Prior to entering Ivey, Kevin had graduated from the University of Alberta with a Bachelor of Arts in history and had spent five years as a manager with CP Hotels (now Fairmont Hotels). In Kiev, in addition to his LEADER duties, he studied for his certified financial analyst exams scheduled for mid-June. Upon returning from Kiev, Kevin would move to Toronto to join Royal Bank Dominion Securities in their mergers and acquisitions department.

Kevin had initially joined LEADER to have the opportunity to experience another culture. After having this experience in his first LEADER year, he said the following about this year's foreign assignment: "I am only returning because of my loyalty for one of the executive directors. Otherwise I would have dropped out of LEADER."

LEADER members valued Kevin's calm demeanor and quiet sense of humor. In the classroom, he generally was serious and formal, but showed a strong ability to assess situations, carefully position statements and suspend judgment. Kevin had been an active member of LEADER's teacher training committee, but did not participate in other LEADER activities.

Beth Reese

The 25-year-old Beth Reese had just finished her first year in Ivey's MBA program. Before attending Ivey, Beth had graduated from McGill University with a Bachelor of Science in chemical engineering and had worked three years for a Montreal-based manufacturing company that produced airplane parts. Upon returning from the FSU, Beth would join a marketing research company as a summer intern.

Beth told Kaitlyn about LEADER:

I am interested in LEADER because of the opportunity to spend time in the region where my parents originated and had to leave during World War II.

Beth and Kaitlyn had been in the same section during their first year at Ivey. They played squash weekly, worked on group assignments together and interacted at social gatherings. Beth was committed and intense in her studies throughout the year. Kaitlyn saw Beth as very independent, in fact, defiantly so. In previous interactions with Beth, Kaitlyn had difficulties reaching any kind of agreement because Beth tended to play the devil's advocate, stubbornly holding on to her positions.

Beth had been a member of LEADER's fundraising committee. She had worked very hard on the committee throughout the year, diligently following every possible lead for funds. She had not, however, participated in other functions with LEADER. In fact, her concern about LEADER's changing financial situation had caused her to consider seriously joining the crusade to drop out of LEADER, based on misrepresentation.

PRE-DEPARTURE OCCURRENCES

In early January 2001, the team members had learned about their site assignment. On February 6, 2001, Dennis organized the first team meeting at an on-campus restaurant. He saw the meeting as an opportunity to meet each other in an informal setting. At the meeting, Dennis said that although he was the site leader, LEADER was not his first priority and that he was not concerned with micro-managing the team because they were all adults, who did not need babysitting. He would schedule only one more meeting. Moreover, a Kiev alumnus was present and informed the team about the particularities of the site. The meeting took only about 30 minutes, but after the Kiev alumnus' presentation, each team member expressed excitement about the upcoming foreign assignment.

The next team meeting took place on March 19. Dennis scheduled this meeting for further team development and specifically to arrange the travel to Kiev and the teaching schedules. By e-mail, Dennis had suggested an off-campus site, but Beth ignored this suggestion, indicating her availability to meet on-campus. Dennis sent another e-mail reiterating that he wanted to go to an off-campus location and asked Kaitlyn to "break the tie." Kaitlyn sided with Dennis. Dennis, however, remained angry over the miscommunication with Beth.

At the meeting, Beth, to the surprise of her teammates, had her own agenda. While Dennis attempted to outline the items that needed to be resolved in the meeting, Beth asked the team to adjust its travel plans to accommodate her personal post-LEADER travel arrangements. She stated that she had reserved flights for herself that departed five hours after the flights already reserved for the Kiev team. If the rest of the team was not able to change its itineraries, Beth stated that she would travel alone to Kiev because this schedule allowed her to travel with her boyfriend after LEADER, while giving him the cheapest fare. Next, Beth requested a teaching schedule that allowed her to sightsee during the foreign assignment. Finally, Beth stated that her boyfriend might visit her in Kiev, which constituted a violation of LEADER policy. Dennis and Kaitlyn reacted with increasing agitation, shaking their heads in disbelief. Kevin remained calm and suggested that the team should try to accommodate Beth's boyfriend. Throughout the evening, the other team members tried to convince Beth of the merit of traveling as a team. In the end, the team agreed to accommodate Beth, if she needed to make alternate travel arrangements. Moreover, Beth would teach the day class throughout the project and Kaitlyn would teach the evening class. Dennis and Kevin opted to "flip for the teaching schedules" once they arrived in Kiev.

After the meeting, while Dennis gave Kaitlyn a ride home, he asked her: "How well do you know Beth?"

Kaitlyn responded by saying:

> I think I know her pretty well, but I must say that I was shocked by what happened tonight. It seemed that Beth wanted everything to benefit her and was not really interested in what would be fair to the rest of the team.

Dennis said: "I'm really trying to keep an open mind, but I can tell you that I will not be able to put up with this 'me' attitude for much longer."

Kaitlyn replied:

> She is on the fundraising team and I am sure that she is making a big deal about her travel plans now in order to make arrangements that will minimize the cost. I'm sure that once she is certain about her plans she will settle in and be more focused on the team.

On Friday, March 30, LEADER's annual "Site Olympics," organized by the LEADER executive, took place. The purpose of the Site Olympics was to create an opportunity for the teams to bond. Traditionally, each site team went for dinner first and then arrived in a team uniform for an evening of "mental Olympics." The event was a series of timed challenges including Trivial Pursuit, Pictionary and charades, which pitted one site team against another in a quest for the most wins. The day of the event, Dennis had still not arranged the team's participation, when Kaitlyn called him. Dennis said that he would go, but would not have time to meet before the event and would have to make it an early night. Moreover, Kevin would not be available. Kaitlyn considered discussing the team's situation with Dennis, but decided not to press the issue, as she did not know Dennis very well. Instead, she told him that it would be a good idea to attend, and asked if he could pick her and Beth up prior to the event. In the end, Dennis picked up Kaitlyn, but Beth decided that she would prefer to walk there alone. The team, without Kevin, participated in the event, but did not have uniforms. Dennis was continually irritated with Beth who kept wandering off, causing hold ups in the competition. Immediately after the event, Dennis wanted to leave, so in order to get a ride home, Kaitlyn left too. In the car, Dennis again commented on how easily Beth got to him. Kaitlyn thought if only Dennis and Beth got to know each other, they would get along fine. She felt that just by having conversations with Dennis, she got to know him better all the time.

ON-SITE DEVELOPMENTS

Arrival

On Sunday, May 6, after 12 hours of travel, Kaitlyn, Dennis, and Kevin arrived in Kiev. They waited three hours for Beth who arrived on a different flight. Kaitlyn had learned more about Dennis and Kevin during their travel and now felt significantly more comfortable with them as teammates.

After collecting Beth's luggage, the team headed to its quarters for the next three weeks on a bus sent by the host school. The accommodations, which were a 20-minute tram ride from the school, were modest, consisting of two rooms in opposite wings on one floor of a hotel. Each room had two small twin beds, a desk and a bathroom. Kaitlyn and Beth were in one room and Dennis and Kevin were in the other. There was neither refrigeration nor kitchen facilities available. The tap water was not drinkable and was rarely warm enough for showers. Kaitlyn wondered about the food supply, which was supplied by the partner school. It was picked up at noon daily at the school, with the entire weekend supply provided on Friday. Otherwise, the team had to visit local restaurants.

After a short rest, the team headed out together to explore their surroundings and to find a place to eat. Currency exchanges were not open and the team did not find a restaurant that accepted credit cards. Moreover, restaurants could not legally accept U.S. currency. After several hours of walking in the dark, the team finally stumbled upon a "bankomat," obtained local currency and went to a restaurant for dinner.

The Early Days

The next day, the team toured Kiev with the site hostess and, in the evening, prepared for the first day of classes. A coin toss meant that Dennis had to team up with Beth to teach the day class, and Kevin and Kaitlyn would teach in the evenings. Beth prepared on her own, whereas the rest of the team prepared together. Moreover, Beth prepared all cases, independent of whether she would teach them or not. She continued this habit throughout the assignment.

On May 8, the team taught for the first time. The team members considered their first day of teaching as a success and looked forward to the next day. In the evening, after the teaching preparation and dinner, Dennis and Kaitlyn played cards and Beth read a book, while Kevin rested in the other room to recover from the illness he contracted by brushing his teeth with tap water. Dennis, Kaitlyn and Beth chatted in a relaxed fashion about networks, but suddenly the conversation became loud, as Beth and Dennis engaged in a tense debate. Beth stated that a network served instrumental purposes, that she felt no obligation to reciprocate favors and that she did not worry about the long-term implications of her approach to networks. Dennis responded that her attitude toward networks was short-sighted. Over the course of an hour-long debate, Dennis showed his frustration, saying that Beth just could not be serious. Eventually, he also showed his anger, saying that Beth had to be out of her mind. Beth reacted by stating that Dennis, and also Kaitlyn, were ganging up on her. Kaitlyn finally asked Beth and Dennis to stop their debate, and mentioned that the next day's May Day celebrations required them to get up early.

On May 9, because of the May Day celebrations, there were no classes. Kevin stayed in bed all day, still recovering from his illness. Beth said that she also felt sick and did not want to go to the celebrations, so Dennis and Kaitlyn were the only ones to head out to the city for the parades.

On May 10, in the afternoon, while Kaitlyn sent e-mails from the partner school's computer lab, Dennis entered the room, his face bright red with fury. Kaitlyn asked Dennis if he wanted to talk things over, while having ice cream. As they exited the school, Dennis erupted in a tirade over Beth, ending with the words:

> You need to find a way to make sure that I don't snap! I have three more weeks of teaching with her and that seems like it will be way too long, right now.

At the ice cream stand, he told Kaitlyn, what had happened that morning between him and Beth:

> Can you believe it? On the tram ride in to the school this morning, she wanted to start another debate with me. I had a hard enough time to endure the thought of having to teach with her, and then this. So, I said that I was not interested in a conversation, which led to another angry exchange. One thing is clear for me: I will limit conversation with Beth to teaching-related issues.

Dennis concluded his conversation with Kaitlyn by reiterating that working with Beth would be very difficult and asked Kaitlyn to be a mediator.

Back at school, Kaitlyn tried to resume her e-mailing activities, but found herself recounting the discussion she just had with Dennis. He placed a lot of responsibility on her to bring the team back together. She decided to address the conflict later, and instead, left to meet Kevin to discuss the teaching plan for that evening.

THE TOUR OF KIEV'S NIGHTLIFE

After Kevin and Kaitlyn had finished teaching the evening class, the team went on an earlier scheduled tour of Kiev with a student as a host. About an hour into the evening, Dennis abruptly asked the host directions to the subway and left. For the remainder of the evening, Kaitlyn repeatedly reassured the host that Dennis's sudden departure was not his fault, and that he was neither boring nor offensive.

Kaitlyn was very disappointed about the way the evening had turned out. After her earlier conversation with Dennis, and on the basis of his behavior throughout the tour, it was evident to Kaitlyn that he had left because of Beth. She felt that the rift between Beth and Dennis had now started to impact the team's relationship with students. How could Beth and Dennis provide the students in the day class with a rich educational and cultural exchange, when they could not get along? What were the potential consequences for the relationship with the partner school?

As they returned home from the tour, Kaitlyn spoke to Beth:

> Are you aware that we have a problem? It does not bode well for us if problems in the team affect our relationship with the students. Look at our host: He is very upset and still does not understand why Dennis left.

Beth replied:

> Come on, Kaitlyn, that is the student's problem. Dennis probably had an upset stomach. We might have arguments, but I do not see how that affects our students.

Kaitlyn answered:

> Is that what you believe? You think that he left because he felt sick? Don't you realize that he left because he was not able to hide how upset he was with you?

Beth simply replied, "Why would he be upset with me?"

WHAT NEXT?

Kaitlyn was sitting on her bed. What had gone wrong in this team? Was it just a matter of personality conflict between Beth and Dennis? Was Dennis a good site leader? Was it Kaitlyn's responsibility to get more involved, or should she just allow the executive directors to smooth over the situation when they arrived on Saturday?

Antar Automobile Company[1]—Part I: The Automation Project

Prepared by Professors
Roy McLennan and Al Mikalachki

Version: (A) 2002-11-29

In early January, Rob Dander, a project manager in the Operational Research Department (ORD) of an automobile assembly plant, had been assigned the job of managing a computer project which would lead to the development of a more automated system. For five months he had been supervising the work of three young company employees who were developing a simulated assembly line. However, because Rob's current responsibilities left him in charge of four or five projects at a time, all in varying stages of completion, he had left his assistants to work together with very little intervention from him. As a result, by May he was facing the pressure of an uncompleted project and an unnecessarily elaborate design. As project manager, Rob had to decide quickly how he could most effectively redirect his assistants' energies so the team could meet management's deadline and design expectations.

Project Objectives

Senior management at Antar, an automobile manufacturing plant located in Southwestern Ontario, had recently decided to revamp their manufacturing process in a plan which included the installation of a robotics system that would complement a scaled-down version of the manually run assembly line. Antar's biggest task lay in determining the most effective locations for the robots along the line and the optimum number of robots to be utilized. This project was very important, because manufacturing costs had to be cut in order to keep pace with an extremely competitive market. Antar hoped that, when co-ordinated with its Just-In-Time inventory system, the new production line would give the company a financial advantage over its competitors.

Management decided to assign the task of simulating the new line to the ORD, a unit located in a separate departmental building a few miles from the plant. The ORD would run a full-scale simulation of the entire manufacturing process and determine the working requirements that would optimize production while lowering costs. A major concern of management was to establish a programme that would occupy minimal computer time and which could easily adapt to changing parameters and inputs. A secondary objective was to use the simulation to train operators on how to manipulate the new computer monitors which automation would bring. Management had a high interest in the way the project turned out.

Personnel

Rob Dander, a 40-year-old ORD project manager, had been an operational research (OR) specialist in the North American automobile industry for a number of years. When he undertook the latest Antar project, he decided that the simulation would use a new programming language called LATOC, which had not been used before in the Department.

Rob was assigned the services of three assistants: Susan Wright, Dan Vincent, and Mark Mancuso. These company employees, who had not met each other before, had obtained degrees from local universities in the Southwestern Ontario region. Susan, who was 23 and married, had worked in the ORD for a few months, and was interested in computer simulation. Before joining the staff at Antar, she had worked for another large automobile manufacturer in the region.

Dan Vincent, who was 22 and single, had joined Antar one year earlier, after completing his university degree. Dan had only been in the ORD for a few weeks, and his experience with computers was limited. He brought to the group the systems engineering skills that were important to the project. About the time the project began, he decided to return to school the following September to enter a PhD program, but he decided not to share his decision with his colleagues until he had received his acceptance into the program.

Mark Mancuso was 25 and married. His employment with Antar was into its third year, all spent at an operational level in the plant. At one time, he had unsuccessfully requested a transfer period in the ORD. He was now being released from his regular work-study duties for the duration of the manufacturing revamping project so he could provide basic data and expertise on assembling operations. During the initial stages of the decision to automate, Mark had taken part in an inconclusive study to determine the number of robots needed. He had no understanding of computers, and upon appointment to the task group was given instructions to provide a tight link between the project and plant management, essentially to keep management well informed on the simulation's progress. The plant still issued his salary, which was $1,000 higher than Dan's, and $2,000 higher than Susan's.

PROCEDURE

Normal OR procedure, when inexperienced assistants began work on a project, was for the project manager to provide a strong lead in constructing a rough model of the process under investigation. The manager would then hand the project over to assistants for refinement and conversion to a detailed expression in a computer language. However, Rob decided that this particular situation would be best served if the assistants were left to learn model building, in a computer language, on a trial and error basis. As each assistant reported for duty to Rob, he gave him or her a LATOC manual, and instructions to work through it and to build a working understanding of the language.

Susan was the first to acquaint herself with the new language, beginning her studies approximately two weeks prior to Mark's arrival. Dan joined two weeks later. After reporting to Rob for duty, Dan took his LATOC manual and disappeared immediately into a back room. He returned to the project room when Rob went to see him some days later.

Following an initial two-day briefing, Rob spent only a few moments each day with the assistants, usually calling them into his office twice a week for discussions. This routine, however, lasted only a few weeks, after which Rob left his assistants largely to their own devices, to build the simulation model for the assembly line, and express it in LATOC. He seemed confident in their ability to get the task done without considerable involvement on his part.

The assistants worked together, mostly in the same project room, until the middle of the year. Their room was simply furnished, containing about half a dozen chairs and desks. Three or four other members of the ORD shared the room with them. Two of these were women programmers working to prepare the compiler for LATOC, a task which would keep them in the room until mid-June. Periodically, Susan, Dan, and Mark made trips to another part of the building to test their programme on the ORD's computer.

For the most part, hours were from nine to five; however, there were very few rules, leaving project assistants relatively free to set their own work pace. ORD management had an informal policy of rewarding competent job performance on an individual basis by giving an annual increase in salary. Poor performance was penalized by withholding salary increments.

Working in the ORD involved a lot of running around. Project Managers were often away at company plants to discuss projects; the computer was routinely operated late in the night, sometimes early in the morning, and at times, around the clock. People who had worked together the previous night might not begin work until 10:00 a.m. or 11:00 a.m. the following morning.

Coffee breaks were taken on a non-scheduled basis, wherever personnel happened to be working. At lunchtime, all the project assistants, programmers and typists gathered to eat in one small lunchroom inside the building. The room was pleasant and could cater to approximately two dozen people. Project Managers had a small dining room of their own.

NOTE

1. Antar Automobile Company is a revision of the Chamberlain Steel Co. case written by Professor Roy McLennan.

THE LEO BURNETT COMPANY LTD.: VIRTUAL TEAM MANAGEMENT

Prepared by Elizabeth O'Neil under the supervision of Professors Joerg Dietz and Fernando Olivera

Version: (A) 2003-11-04

On July 2, 2001, Janet Carmichael, global account director for the Leo Burnett Company Ltd. (LB), United Kingdom, sat in her office wondering how to structure her global advertising team. The team was responsible for the introduction of a skin care product of one of LB's most important clients, Ontann Beauty Care (OBC). The product had launched in the Canadian and Taiwanese test markets earlier that year. Taiwanese sales and awareness levels for the product had been high but were low for the Canadian market. Typically, at this stage in the launch process, Carmichael would decentralize the communications management in each market, but the poor performance in the Canadian market left her with a difficult decision: should she maintain centralized control over the Canadian side of her team? In three days, she would leave for meetings at LB's Toronto, Canada, office, where the team would expect her decision.

THE LEO BURNETT COMPANY LTD. BACKGROUND

LB, which was founded in Chicago in 1935, was one of North America's premier advertising agencies. It had created numerous well-recognized North American brand icons, including The Marlboro Man, Kellogg's Tony the Tiger, and the Pillsbury Dough Boy.

By 1999, LB had expanded around the globe to include 93 offices in 83 markets. The company employed approximately 9,000 people, and worldwide revenues were approximately US$9 billion. In 2000, LB merged with two other

Traditional core agency services included:

Account Management

Account management worked in close partnership with planning, creative, media, production and the client to craft tightly focused advertising strategies, based on a deep understanding of the client's products, goals and competition, as well as insights into contemporary consumer behavior.

Creative Services

In most LB offices, creative was the largest department. Creatives focused its visual art and copywriting talents on turning strategic insights into advertising ideas. This department was a key part of each client's brand team and often interacted with both clients and clients' customers.

Planning

Planners conducted research to gain insights about the consumer and the marketplace. They also provided valuable input to the strategic and creative agency processes in the form of the implications raised by that research, specifically combining that learning with information about a given product, the social context in which it fit and the psychology of the people who used it.

Media

Starcom was the media division for LB's parent holding company. Its role was to identify the most influential and efficient media vehicles to deliver brand communications to the appropriate audience.

Production

Production staff brought creative ideas to life with the highest quality execution in television, cinema, radio, print, outdoor, direct, point of sale, interactive or any other medium.

In addition to these core services, most offices also offered expertise in more specialized services, including:

- B2B Technology Marketing
- Direct and Database Marketing
- Health-care Marketing
- Interactive Marketing
- Multicultural Marketing
- Public Relations
- Sales Promotion and Event Marketing

Exhibit 1   LB Agency Services

global agencies to form blcom3 (the actual company name), one of the largest advertising holding companies in the world, but each LB office retained the Leo Burnett company name.

LB Services and Products

As a full-service agency, LB offered the complete range of marketing and communications services and products (see Exhibits 1 and 2). The company's marketing philosophy was to build "brand belief." The idea driving this philosophy was that true loyalty went beyond mere buying behavior. LB defined "believers" as customers who demonstrated both a believing attitude and loyal purchase behavior. The company strove to convert buyers into believers by building lasting customer affinity for the brand.

One of the most important measures of an agency's success was the quality of the creative

Traditional Advertising Products

Television Broadcast Advertising—Usually 30-second (:30s) or 60-second (:60s) TV ads that ran during local or national television programming. This also included sponsoring specific programs, which usually consisted of a five-second announcement before or after the show, i.e., "This program is brought to you by . . ." accompanied by the visual of the sponsoring company's logo.

Radio Broadcast Advertising—Usually 15-, 20-, or 30-second (:15s, :20s, :30s) radio ads that were placed throughout local or national radio programming. Radio ads could include sponsoring specific programs, which usually consisted of a five-second announcement before or after the show, i.e. "This program brought to you by . . ."

Print Advertising—Included black and white and color print ads in local, national or trade newspapers, journals and magazines. Magazine ads could be single-page ads or double-page spreads (two pages facing each other).

Non-Traditional or "Below the Line" Advertising Products

Direct Marketing—Normally a series of mail-out items (letters, post cards, product samples, etc.) sent to a specifically targeted population(s) called "cells," e.g., companies might send promotional mail-outs to current customers, former customers who have not shopped with the company for a period or time, and new prospective customers—each of these groups would be considered a cell.

Digital or Interactive Marketing—Any marketing efforts that were delivered to the consumer online or by wireless networks (e.g., hand-held wireless devices). This could include Web site design and production, banner advertising and promotions on other Web sites, e-mail marketing, and internal corporate marketing tools such as customer relationship marketing or database building tools.

Collateral—Any piece of print material that was not strictly advertising, for instance brochures, annual reports, posters, flyers and in-store materials.

Promotions—Any marketing effort that included a time-limited offer or incentive to either purchase a product or offer personal data. Promotions could involve advertising, direct marketing, interactive marketing, product packaging and/or outdoor marketing.

Exhibit 2   LB Agency Products

---

product that was developed to connect brands to their end consumers. Each local office strove to produce outstanding creative advertising to break through the clutter of marketing messages that the general public was subjected to daily and truly reach the consumer in a memorable way. Award shows were held nationally and internationally to recognize this effort, one of the most prestigious being the annual festival in Cannes, France. With each award, individual employees (usually the art director and copy writer who had worked together to develop the ad) were recognized, as was the local agency office where they worked. These creative accolades were instrumental in helping an office win new client business. Even within the global

LB network, awards were given to the local offices that produced the most outstanding creative work.

LB Internal Team Structures

A multidisciplinary team serviced each brand. Each team had representatives from all core areas of the agency as well as members from the specialized services as appropriate for the brand. In most cases, team members had two sets of reporting lines.

First and formally, they directly reported to the supervisor of their home department (for example, account management). It was this formal supervisor who was responsible for conducting performance evaluations and assigning and managing an employee's workload.

Informally, the team members reported to a project team leader, the senior account services person, who usually was an account director or a vice-president of client services director. It was this team leader's responsibility to manage the project in question, ensure that the client was satisfied with project progress, and build and manage the overall relationship between the client and the agency. Employees on the project team would be responsible to this person for meeting project deadlines and managing their individual client relationships. This team leader would often provide input to a team member's performance evaluation, along with other agency colleagues (see Exhibit 3).

At any given time, an agency employee typically worked on two or three different brand teams, virtually all of them face-to-face teams servicing local clients.

LB Typical Office Environment

Most LB employees were young (in their 20s and 30s) and worked about 60 hours per week. Client needs and project deadlines dictated work priorities, and the volume of work often required late nights at the office. Agency office environments were often open-concept and social. Employees spent many hours each day up and about, discussing projects with colleagues and responding to client requests. The pace was fast and the general spirit was one of camaraderie; it was common for LB employees to socialize together after a late night at the office.

LB Toronto

LB's Toronto office was founded in 1952 to service the Canadian arms of the Chicago-based clients. It was LB's first expansion beyond Chicago. In 2001, it employed a staff of approximately 200 people and billings were approximately $200 million.

LB United Kingdom

LB acquired its London, United Kingdom, office in the mid-1970s as part of an expansion into Europe. By 2001, the office had grown to over 350 employees and billings were approximately $400 million. London was also the regional LB headquarters for all European, Middle Eastern and African offices.

LB'S RELATIONSHIP WITH ONTANN BEAUTY CARE

Ontann Beauty Care (OBC)

OBC was a leading global manufacturer of health and beauty care products. In the late 1990s, OBC made a strategic decision to centralize the global marketing of its brands and products, designating a global team to define the global strategy for a given brand and develop the core communication materials as templates for local markets to follow. Local offices were given the responsibility for adapting the global materials and developing local "below the line" (BTL) materials which would synergize with the global vision and creative templates. Below the line materials included direct marketing, in-store materials, digital marketing, public relations and promotions (that is, everything except strict advertising). In practice, on established brands with well-defined communication templates and strong local knowledge, some local markets (at least key regional markets) were awarded more opportunity to develop their own communication material. The global team, however, retained veto power to ensure all communications were building a consistent personality and look for the brand.

Each OBC global office had as many teams as it had brands. An OBC brand team usually consisted of the global category director, the brand manager and an assistant brand manager, plus a representative from each of the various departments: marketing technology, consumer, trade/distribution, PR, sales, product development, and production.

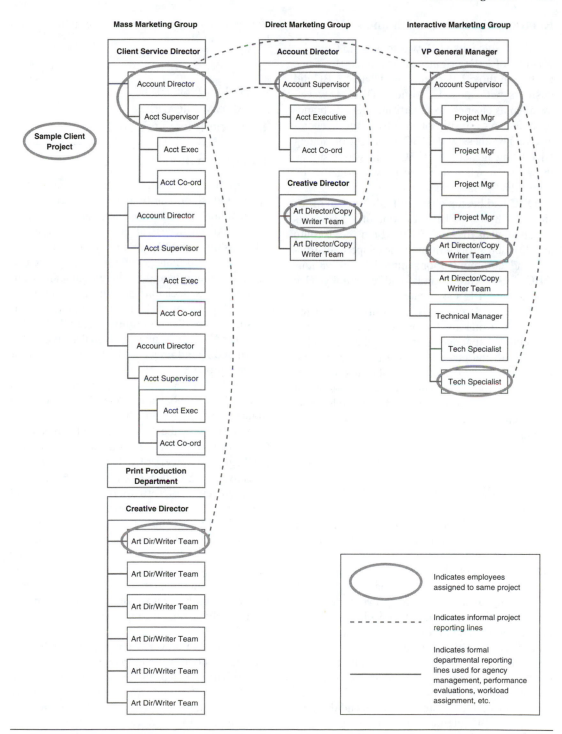

Mass Marketing Group

Client Service Director
- Account Director
  - Acct Supervisor
    - Acct Exec
    - Acct Co-ord
- Account Director
  - Acct Supervisor
    - Acct Exec
    - Acct Co-ord
- Account Director
  - Acct Supervisor
    - Acct Exec
    - Acct Co-ord

Print Production Department

Creative Director
- Art Dir/Writer Team
- Art Dir/Writer Team
- Art Dir/Writer Team
- Art Dir/Writer Team
- Art Dir/Writer Team
- Art Dir/Writer Team

Sample Client Project

Direct Marketing Group

Account Director
- Account Supervisor
  - Acct Executive
  - Acct Co-ord

Creative Director
- Art Director/Copy Writer Team
- Art Director/Copy Writer Team

Interactive Marketing Group

VP General Manager
- Account Supervisor
  - Project Mgr
  - Project Mgr
  - Project Mgr
  - Project Mgr
- Art Director/Copy Writer Team
- Art Director/Copy Writer Team
- Technical Manager
  - Tech Specialist
  - Tech Specialist

Indicates employees assigned to same project

- - - - - Indicates informal project reporting lines

———— Indicates formal departmental reporting lines used for agency management, performance evaluations, workload assignment, etc.

Exhibit 3   LB Agency Formal and Informal Reporting Lines

Relationship Between LB and OBC

OBC, which, like LB, was founded in Chicago, was one of LB's original clients. In 2001, as one of the top three LB clients worldwide, OBC did business with most LB offices. OBC, however, awarded its business to advertising agencies brand-by-brand. As a result, other advertising agencies also had business with OBC. Competition among advertising agencies for OBC business was strong, in particular when they had to work together on joint brand promotions.

OBC had been a client of LB's Toronto office since 1958 and of LB's London office since its acquisition in the mid-1970s. Both the Toronto and London offices initially developed advertising and communications materials for various OBC facial care brands and eventually also worked on OBC's skin care brands.

To better service OBC, LB also centralized its decision making for this client's brands and appointed expanded and strengthened global teams with the power to make global decisions. For its other clients, LB's global teams were significantly smaller, tending to consist simply of one very senior LB manager who shared learning from across the globe with a given client's senior management.

A NEW OBC BRAND: FOREVER YOUNG

In the fall of 1998, the OBC London office announced a new skin care line called "Forever Young." Product formulas were based on a newly patented process that addressed the needs of aging skin. For OBC, this brand presented an opportunity to address a new market segment: the rapidly growing population of people over the age of 50. The product line was more extensive than other OBC skin care brands. It also represented the company's first foray into premium priced skin care products. Product cost, on average, was double that of most other OBC brands, falling between drug store products and designer products. OBC intended Forever Young to be its next big global launch and awarded the Forever Young advertising and brand communications business to LB.

GLOBAL ADVERTISING AND COMMUNICATIONS TEAM FOR FOREVER YOUNG

Team Formation

For LB, a successful launch of this new product would significantly increase revenues and the likelihood of acquiring additional global OBC brands. An unsuccessful launch would risk the relationship with OBC that LB had built over so many years. LB management in Chicago decided that LB London would be the global team headquarters. This decision reflected the experience that the London office had in leading global business teams and the proximity to the OBC global team for Forever Young. It was also likely that the United Kingdom would be the test market for the new product.

In LB's London office, Janet Carmichael was assigned as brand team leader for the Forever Young product line effective January 1, 1999. Carmichael was the global account director for OBC. The 41-year-old Carmichael, a Canadian, had begun her career at LB Toronto as an account executive in 1985, after completing an MBA degree at the University of Toronto. In 1987, Carmichael moved to Europe, where she continued her career with LB. She became an account supervisor in Italy, an account director in Belgium, and finally a regional and global account director in Germany before taking on a global account director role on OBC brands in the United Kingdom in 1996. She was very familiar with OBC's business and had built excellent relationships with the OBC skin care client group.

LB's initial Forever Young brand team had six members who all were employees of the London office: Carmichael as the team leader, an account director, an account executive (she formally supervised these two employees), the agency's creative director, and two "creatives" (an art director and a copy writer). Carmichael outlined a project timetable (see Exhibit 4). The LB team worked with the OBC team on consumer research, market exploration, brand creative concepts (creative), packaging samples and global copy testing throughout North America and Europe. Carmichael viewed marketing a new product to a new consumer segment in a crowded category as challenging; however, after several months of testing, LB's Forever Young brand team developed a unique creative concept that was well received by OBC.

In the fall of 1999, OBC decided that the United Kingdom would be the lead market for another skin care product. Because North America was a priority for the Forever Young brand and Canada was "clean" (that is, OBC was not testing other products in Canada at that time), Canada became the new primary test market for Forever Young. In addition, Canadians' personal skin care habits and the distribution process for skin care products were more reflective of overall Western practices (i.e., the Western world) than were those in other potential test markets. Taiwan became the secondary test market for Asian consumers. These choices were consistent with OBC's interest in global brand validation.

In keeping with OBC's team structures, LB maintained the global brand team in London and, in January of 2000, formed satellite teams in Toronto, Canada, and Taipei, Taiwan, to manage material execution in their local markets. It was up to the LB Toronto and Taipei offices to determine their members in the Forever Young satellite teams. In Taipei, Cathy Lee, an account director who was particularly interested in the assignment, took the lead on local agency activities. In Toronto, Geoff Davids, an account supervisor from the direct marketing group, was assigned to lead the Toronto team. The global brand team and the two satellite teams now formed the LB side of the global advertising and communications team for Forever Young (see Exhibit 5).

Kick-Off Meeting

In February 2000, a face-to-face kick-off meeting took place in Toronto with the intent to bring all senior members of LB's and OBC's London, Toronto, and Taipei teams onto the same page regarding the new brand and the status of the launch process. One or two senior representatives from OBC London, Toronto, and Taipei participated in the meeting. From LB, the complete London team participated, along with Geoff Davids and a senior agency representative from the Toronto office, and Cathy Lee and a senior agency representative from the Taipei office. Carmichael and her U.K. team members shared their initial brand creative concepts, which had already garnered admiration throughout the LB network, and their knowledge about the product and target audience.

It was decided that Davids and Lee would serve as the main links to LB's London-based global brand team. Specifically, Davids and Lee reported to Annabel Forin, Carmichael's account director in the United Kingdom. Forin then reported to Carmichael and OBC's London team. Besides Forin, Carmichael's primary contacts would be Annabelle Manning, the global creative director at LB United Kingdom and Sarah Jones, OBC's global vice-president of skin care in London. All work produced by LB's satellite teams would require approval from LB's London team.

The Creative Assignments

The creative assignments for the Canadian and Taiwanese teams were slightly different from each other. Normally, the global team would produce a creative template for a brand (meaning the design of the advertising and communications materials), which would then be passed to the satellite teams to be adapted for the local market.

In the Taiwanese market, this would be the case. The Taiwanese LB team would be responsible for adapting the advertising materials, which would include re-filming the television ad to star an Asian actress, as well as retaking photos for the print ads, again, to demonstrate product benefits on Asian skin. The brand message (meaning the text in print ads and the vocal

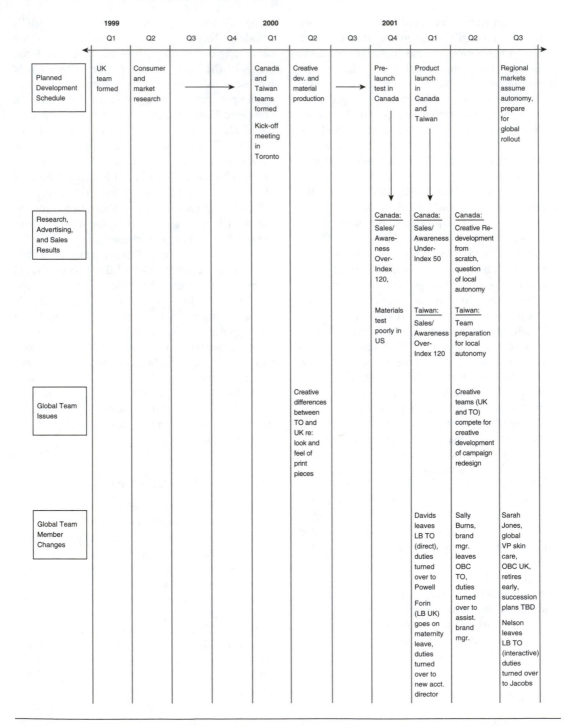

	1999				2000			2001			
	Q1	Q2	Q3	Q4	Q1	Q2	Q3	Q4	Q1	Q2	Q3
Planned Development Schedule	UK team formed	Consumer and market research			Canada and Taiwan teams formed Kick-off meeting in Toronto	Creative dev. and material production		Pre-launch test in Canada	Product launch in Canada and Taiwan		Regional markets assume autonomy, prepare for global rollout
Research, Advertising, and Sales Results								Canada: Sales/Aware-ness Over-Index 120, Materials test poorly in US	Canada: Sales/Awareness Under-Index 50 Taiwan: Sales/Awareness Over-Index 120	Canada: Creative Re-development from scratch, question of local autonomy Taiwan: Team preparation for local autonomy	
Global Team Issues						Creative differences between TO and UK re: look and feel of print pieces				Creative teams (UK and TO) compete for creative development of campaign redesign	
Global Team Member Changes									Davids leaves LB TO (direct), duties turned over to Powell Forin (LB UK) goes on maternity leave, duties turned over to new acct. director	Sally Burns, brand mgr. leaves OBC TO, duties turned over to assist. brand mgr.	Sarah Jones, global VP skin care, OBC UK, retires early, succession plans TBD Nelson leaves LB TO (interactive) duties turned over to Jacobs

Exhibit 4   Brand Development Chronology

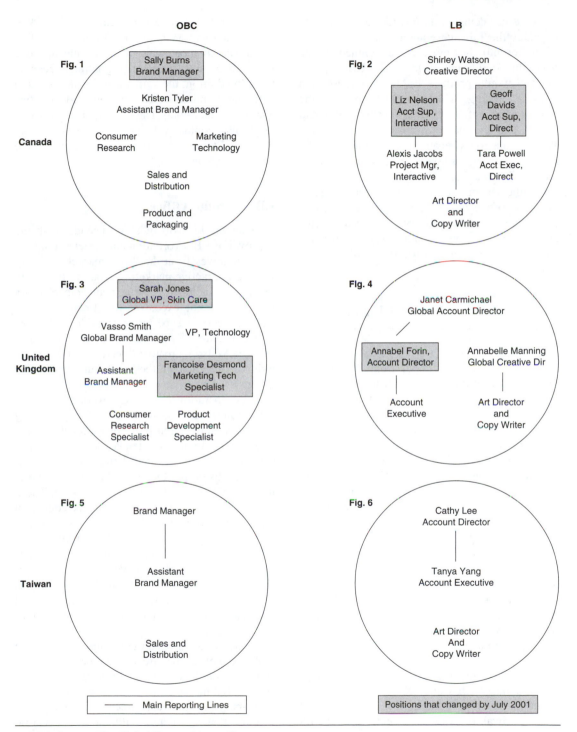

Exhibit 5   The Global Forever Young Team

message in television ads) would be adapted to appeal to the Taiwanese audience.

In Toronto, however, the assignment broke from this traditional format. The LB team in London would produce English television and print advertising, which would be used in the Canadian market. The LB team in Toronto would design and produce the direct marketing and Web site materials because the London office did not have strong in-house capabilities in these areas. While the Toronto office would have control of the design of these communication pieces, the U.K. office would require that certain elements be incorporated into the design (for example, specific photos and colors), in order for the pieces to be visually consistent with the print advertising.

EVENTS LEADING UP TO THE LAUNCH

LB's Taipei Office

After returning to Taipei from the kick-off meeting, Lee formed her local team, which consisted of an account executive (Tanya Yang) and a creative team (one art director and one copy writer). In co-operation with OBC's Taipei team, Lee and her team focused first on recreating the television ad. The ad followed the original creative idea developed in the United Kingdom but used a popular Taiwanese actress in the lead. The character differentiation was necessary to demonstrate the product's benefit to Asian skin because the original ad featured a blond, Caucasian actress as the lead. The team moved on to adapt the brand's print advertising and direct marketing pieces and developed a public relations campaign to meet local market needs. These communication elements were visually and strategically consistent with the television ad as they incorporated photos of the same Taiwanese actress.

Throughout this process, the Taipei team regularly updated LB's and OBC's London teams about its progress. Although all work required U.K. approval, the Taiwanese team worked with a significant amount of autonomy because of the cultural differences present in its market. Carmichael and Manning occasionally travelled to Taiwan to meet with the team and approve its creative work, which they generally received well. In addition, the Taipei team communicated with the London offices through videoconference calls and e-mail. The LB Taipei and Toronto teams had contact with each other only during the global team videoconference meetings, held every two months.

LB's Toronto Office

After the kick-off meeting, Davids, with the approval of LB's Toronto management, assigned representatives from the direct marketing group and the interactive marketing group to the brand team. This included account management (Tara Powell, account executive for direct; and Liz Nelson, account supervisor; and Alexis Jacobs, project manager for interactive) and creative staff (Shirley Watson, creative director; and one copy writer from each of the direct and interactive groups).

In co-operation with OBC's Toronto team, the LB Toronto team was responsible for developing a full communication plan for its local market. Along with running the television and print ads developed in the United Kingdom, the team would focus on producing the brand's below the line materials (i.e., direct mail, Web site). These communication elements served as the education pieces that supplemented the TV ad. Davids conducted an internal team debrief, outlining the information he had received at the kick-off meeting. From this, the team developed a communications plan that, in Carmichael's opinion, was "on-brief" (i.e., consistent with the original brand strategic direction) and included some very innovative thinking.

Next, the team began determining a creative look and feel for the direct mail pieces. The look and feel could be different from the television creative but had to be consistent across all of the paper-based (print ads, direct mail pieces and in-store materials) and online communication elements. The creatives in LB's Toronto team developed the direct marketing materials, and simultaneously the creatives in LB's U.K. team developed the print advertising. The two sides' creative work evolved in different directions, but each side hoped that the other would adapt their look and feel. Eventually, however, LB's Toronto team told its London counterpart to "figure it out," and they would follow London's lead. Communication between the two sides mostly flowed through Davids and Forin to Carmichael. Carmichael, however, had received a copy of the following e-mail from Watson to Davids:

> Geoff, as you know, it's always a challenge to work with someone else's art direction. I don't think the model that London chose is right for this market, and the photography we have to work with doesn't have as contemporary a feel as I would like.
>
> This would be easier if I could connect directly with Annabelle [Manning] but she's on the road so much of the time it's hard to catch her. We weren't asked for our opinion initially and, given the timing constraints at this point, we don't have much choice but to use what they've sent us, but could you please convey to Annabel [Forin] that in the future, if possible, we'd like to have the chance to input on the photography before it's taken? It will help us develop good direct mail creative.
>
> For now, though, I think we'll be able to do something with what they've sent us. Thanks.

There had been other challenges for LB's Toronto team. Davids described an incident that had occurred when his direct marketing team tried to present its creative concept to the team in the United Kingdom during a videoconference meeting:

> Our direct mail concept was a three-panel, folded piece. We sent two flat files to the United Kingdom via e-mail, which were to be cut out, pasted back-to-back [to form the front and back of the piece] and then folded into thirds. It took us *so* long to explain how to do that—somehow we just weren't getting through! Our colleagues in London cut and folded and pasted in different places, and what should have been a simple preliminary procedure took up 45 minutes of our one-hour videoconference meeting!

> By the time we actually got around to discussing the layout of the piece, everyone on the call was frustrated. That's never a good frame of mind to be in when reviewing and critiquing a new layout. It's too bad our clients were on that call as well.

A greater challenge came in September 2000, when the team was behind schedule in the development of the Web site after encountering difficulties with OBC's technology standards. The budgeting for the Web site development came out of the global budget, not the local budget. This meant that the members of LB's Toronto team who were responsible for the Web site development ("interactive marketing") received directions from OBC's London team. The budgeting for direct marketing, however, came out of the local budget, and the members of LB's Toronto team, who were responsible for the development of the direct marketing materials, dealt with OBC's Toronto team. The instructions from these two OBC teams were often inconsistent. Compounding matters, the two OBC client teams repeatedly requested changes of the Web and direct marketing materials, which made these materials even more different from each other and forced the LB Toronto team into extremely tight timeframes.

Carmichael learned about this sort of difficulty mostly through the direct supervisors of the team members. She frequently received calls from LB Toronto's Interactive Marketing Group and Direct Marketing Group senior managers. Carmichael repeatedly had to explain the basic project components to these senior managers and wished that the members of LB's Toronto team would just follow the team communications protocol and forward their concerns to Davids, who would then take up matters as necessary with the U.K. team.

CANADIAN PRE-LAUNCH TEST

Despite these challenges, LB's Toronto team produced the materials in time for the Canadian pre-launch test in October of 2000. The pre-launch test was a launch of the complete communications program (TV ad, newspaper inserts, distribution of trial packs, direct mail, and a Web site launch) in a market whose media could be completely isolated. A small town in the interior of British Columbia, Canada's most westerly province, met these conditions. In terms of product trial and product sales as a percentage of market share, the test indexed 120 against its objectives, which had a base index of 100. Subsequently, OBC and LB decided to move immediately into research to test the advertising in the U.S. market. The global OBC and LB teams worked with their Canadian counterparts to conduct this research, the results of which were very poor. As a result, OBC London required that LB's London and Toronto teams revise the advertising materials even before the Canadian launch.

national scale. The audience penetration in the small B.C. town, the pre-test site, was significantly greater than it was in the national launch. OBC decided that the results of the Canadian launch were below "action standards," meaning that OBC would not even consider a rollout into the U.S. market at the current time.

The tension levels on both LB's side and OBC's side of the Forever Young global advertising and communications team were high. LB's future business on the brand was in jeopardy. The OBC side was under tremendous pressure internally to improve brand trial and market share metrics and already planned to decentralize the local teams for the global product rollout. Despite numerous revisions to the advertising, it never tested well enough to convince OBC that a U.S. or European launch would be successful.

CANADIAN NATIONAL LAUNCH

The days before the launch were panic-filled, as LB's London and Toronto teams scrambled to revise the advertising. In February 2001, the campaign was launched in Canada with the following elements:

- One 30-second TV ad;
- One direct mail piece;
- The English Web site;
- Product samples available from the Web from direct mail piece, and from an in-store coupon;
- Specially designed in-store displays;
- Trial-sized package bundles (one week's worth);
- A public relations campaign; and
- Five print ads in national magazines.

Research following the national launch showed that the brand did not perform well among Canadian consumers. It indexed 50 against a base index of 100. Because of the success of the Canadian pre-launch test, OBC and LB were surprised. The Forever Young global advertising and communications team attributed the discrepancy between the pre-launch test and national launch, in part, to the fact that the pre-launch test conditions were not replicable on a

A DIFFERENT STORY IN ASIA

In Taiwan, the product launch was successful. Test results showed that the brand was indexing 120 per cent against brand objectives. Research also showed that Taiwanese consumers, in contrast to Canadian consumers, did not perceive some of the advertising elements as "violent." Moreover, in Taiwan, overall research scores in terms of "likeability" and "whether or not the advertising would inspire you to try the product" were higher, leading to higher sales. By June of 2001, the Taiwanese team was ready to take on more local-market responsibility and move into the post-launch phase of the advertising campaign. This phase would involve creating new ads to build on the initial success and grow sales in the market.

RECOVERY PLAN FOR CANADA

By June of 2001, LB needed to take drastic measures to develop a new Forever Young campaign in order to improve the brand's performance in the Canadian marketplace. Whereas, before the launch, there had been a clear division of responsibilities (with the United Kingdom developing the television and print advertising and Canada developing direct marketing, in-store and Web site communications), now the global LB team in London decided that it would be necessary to have all hands on deck. New creative teams from the mass advertising department in the Toronto office, as well as supplementary creative teams from the London office, were briefed to develop new campaign ideas. Each team had only three weeks to develop their new ideas, less than half of the eight weeks they would normally have, and the teams had to work independent of each other. The London and Toronto creative teams had to present their concepts to the entire global OBC and LB team at the same time. Subsequently, the results of market research would determine the winning creative concept. Squabbling between the offices began over which team would present first, which office received what compensation for the development, and whether or not overall remuneration packages were fair. Moreover, the communication between the account services members of LB's London and Toronto teams, which was the primary communication channel between the two agencies, became less frequent, less candid and more formal. The presentations took place on June 25, 2001, in Toronto. Watson, the creative director in Toronto, commented:

> This process has been exciting, but we're near the ends of our collective ropes now. We have a new mass advertising creative team [who specialized in TV ads] on the business in Toronto, and they're being expected to produce world-class creative results for a brand they've only heard about for the past few days. They don't—and couldn't possibly—have the same passion for the brand that the direct marketing creative team members have after working on it for so long. I'm having a hard time motivating them to work under these tight timelines.

> We're even more isolated now in Toronto. Our connection to the creative teams and the global creative director in London was distant at best, and now it's non-existent. And our relationship with the local OBC client feels very remote, too.

Still, we're moving forward with our work. We're trying to learn from the Taiwanese experience and are considering what success we would have with a nationally recognized actress starring in our television ads.

Evolution of the Forever Young Global Advertising and Communications Team

Personnel Changes

Between January and June of 2001, numerous personnel changes in the Forever Young global advertising and communications team occurred (see Exhibit 5). In LB's London office, Forin, the U.K. account director, had been replaced following her departure for maternity leave. In OBC's London office, Sarah Jones, the global vice-president for skin care, took early retirement without putting a succession plan in place. In LB's Toronto office, Davids, the Toronto brand team leader, had left the agency. Tara Powell, who had reported to Davids, took on his responsibilities, but she had not met most of the global team members. Liz Nelson, the account supervisor for interactive, left LB's Toronto office to return to school. Alexis Jacobs, who had managed the Web site development, took over her responsibilities. Powell and Jacobs did not have close relationships with their international counterparts. At OBC Toronto, Sally Burns, the local brand manager, who had been LB's main contact in the local market and had been with the brand since inception, left OBC. LB's and OBC's Taiwanese teams remained stable over time. Cathy Lee worked with a team that was nearly identical to her initial team.

Communications

Early on (between February and May 2000), Carmichael had orchestrated frequent face-to-face meetings to ensure clarity of communication and sufficient information sharing. In the following months, the team relied on videoconferences and phone calls, with visits back and forth between London and Toronto on occasion. Since early 2001, the team had relied increasingly on e-mails and telephone calls to communicate. In June 2001, Carmichael noted that the communication had become more formal, and she had lost the feeling of being part of a global team. She wondered if giving the LB's Toronto team more autonomy to develop the brand in their market would help the brand progress. Working together as a smaller team might improve the Toronto group's team dynamic as well. Carmichael was concerned that the current discord between LB's London and Toronto offices would negatively affect the relationship to OBC.

Budget Problems

The extra creative teams assigned to the redevelopment of the brand's television advertising and the unexpected changes to the Forever Young communication materials had meant that LB's costs to staff the project had been higher than originally estimated and higher than the revenues that had been negotiated with OBC. Since OBC did not want to pay more for its advertising than had been originally budgeted, LB faced tremendous internal pressure to finish the project as soon as possible. This situation created conflict between LB and OBC in the United Kingdom, who was responsible for negotiating LB's overall fees. Because all fees were paid to the global brand office (in this case, LB's London office) and then transferred to the local satellite teams, this situation also created conflict between LB's London and Toronto teams, who had both expended additional staff time to revise the advertising materials and wanted "fair" compensation.

What Next?

In three days, Carmichael had to leave for Toronto to sit in research sessions to test the recently presented new creative concepts. In the meetings that followed, she would present to the team her recommendation for how to move forward with the brand. Carmichael reviewed the brand events and team interaction of the past two years (see Exhibit 4) to determine the best global team structure for salvaging the Forever Young brand and maintaining the relationship between OBC and LB.

Carmichael felt torn in her loyalties. On the one hand, she was Canadian and knew LB's Toronto office well—she knew that LB's Toronto brand team worked hard, and she wished them every success. On the other hand, she had now worked in LB's London office for several years, and she had always liked the creative that the U.K. team had initially produced. If she maintained the current form of centralized control of the team, either creative concept might be chosen; however, if she decentralized team control, the Toronto team would almost certainly choose their own creative concept for the television ads. Since the creative direction chosen now would become the brand's advertising in most North American and European markets, it needed to be top calibre. Carmichael thought this posed a risk if the creative development was left to the new Toronto-based mass advertising creative team. It would be a shame to lose the U.K. team's original creative concept.

In making her decision on whether to decentralize the team, Carmichael considered the following:

1. Where was the knowledge necessary to create a competitive advantage for the brand in Canada? Would it be in the Canadian marketplace because they understood the market, or would it be in London because they had more in-depth knowledge of the brand?

2. Where was the client responsibility, and where should it be? Now that the London-based global vice-president of skin care was retiring, the client was considering creating a virtual global team to manage the brand, headquartered in the United States but composed of members of the original United Kingdom OBC team, in preparation for a U.S. launch. If the client team had

its headquarters in North America, should LB also structure its team this way?

3. If Carmichael decentralized the brand and gave the Toronto team greater autonomy, who would lead the brand in Toronto now that Davids had left the agency? How would the necessary knowledge be imparted to the new leader?

4. If they remained centralized, would the team make it through before it self-destructed? How much would this risk the client relationship? To what extent would it strain the already tight budget?

Carmichael had to make a decision that was best for the brand, LB and OBC.

4

CHANGE MANAGEMENT

Change is the only constant.

Change is occurring at an ever accelerating rate.

Some people change when they see the light; others change when they feel the heat.

The fact that most people have heard at least one variation of the above statements over the past few years only underlines the fact that organizations today must be able to change if they are to remain competitive and meet the changing needs of their customers. Executives, managers, and academics alike have spent considerable time planning change initiatives and determining which strategies are the most effective for facilitating change. However, the success rates for major organizational change initiatives have been dismal. This is not to say that there are not any success stories. For example, large organizational turnarounds have been recorded and held up as examples of leadership excellence. Most students of business have heard or read about Jack Welch's transformation of GE or Arthur Martinez's rescue of Sears, Roebuck from oblivion. Such stories, however, are fewer and harder to find than the cases of change mismanagement and subsequent organizational implosions.

The literature provides numerous reasons and frameworks for the poor track record of major organizational change efforts. A popular framework is the one developed by John Kotter (1996). He identified eight reasons why most transformation efforts fail:

- Not discussing the need for change
- Failing to create a powerful guiding coalition that communicates the need for change
- Underestimating the power of a specific, challenging vision and goals
- Under-communicating the vision to the various stakeholders
- Permitting obstacles to block the attainment of the vision
- Failing to create short-term wins that can generate enthusiasm and confidence
- Declaring the change effort a success too soon
- Neglecting to anchor the various changes in the corporate culture

A Comprehensive Change Model

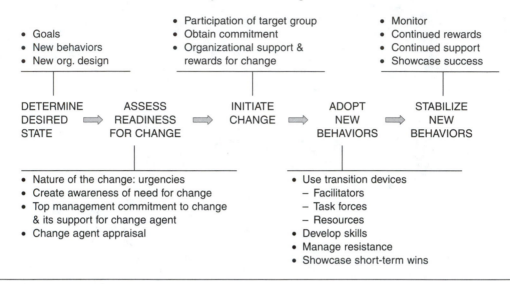

• Goals • New behaviors • New org. design	• Participation of target group • Obtain commitment • Organizational support & rewards for change	• Monitor • Continued rewards • Continued support • Showcase success	

DETERMINE DESIRED STATE ⇒ ASSESS READINESS FOR CHANGE ⇒ INITIATE CHANGE ⇒ ADOPT NEW BEHAVIORS ⇒ STABILIZE NEW BEHAVIORS

• Nature of the change: urgencies
• Create awareness of need for change
• Top management commitment to change
 & its support for change agent
• Change agent appraisal

• Use transition devices
 – Facilitators
 – Task forces
 – Resources
• Develop skills
• Manage resistance
• Showcase short-term wins

Figure 4.1   A Comprehensive Change Model

Together, these mistakes often lead to a host of negative consequences, including poor implementation of the change strategies and less-than-hoped-for results.

The challenge for organizational leaders is not to come up with good ideas or new business strategies that should help the organization to maneuver itself out of crisis-like situations or master the problems that it encountered. The challenge is converting ideas into action. There is, however, a shortage of leaders capable of translating the ideas into concrete action—a concerted, well-guided effort to lead organizational change. For example, Larry Bossidy and Ram Charan (2002), authors of *Execution: The Discipline of Getting Things Done,* wrote that "most often today the difference between a company and its competitor is the ability to execute . . . leaders placed too much emphasis on what some call high-level strategy, on intellectualizing and philosophizing, and not enough on implementation" (p. 5).

The organizational change framework depicted in Figure 4.1 serves as a guide to implement change. The framework offers the following "advantages." First, it is a straightforward model in the sense that organizational members can grasp the overall picture with relative ease. For example, the individual parts of the model can be used in sequence to manage the change effort. The model identifies steps that should be followed prior, during, and after the implementation of the change. Second, it suggests that multiple factors contribute to (un)successful implementation of ideas, strategies, or innovations and hence offers a multitude of options for "actionable intervention." Third, the model is open to revisions born of the user's experience (i.e., it allows for additional concepts to be incorporated). Fourth, it encourages organizational members to take a planned as opposed to an ad hoc approach to solving problems. Accomplishing change is a challenging exercise. Yet, taking a planned approach toward implementing change increases the likelihood that the problems and challenges involved are addressed in a proper manner. Fifth, the model incorporates elements of existing change models. It is also based on research. In sum, the organizational change framework is comprehensive.

The model is based on the following assumptions:

- The focus is on change that incorporates consensus, full participation, and negotiations as decision-making processes, which, in turn, minimize the use of power in a coercive sense.
- Those leading the change have adequate time for environmental scanning, defining problems, planning alternative courses of action, educating and training the people involved in the change, and implementing the various components that compose the actual change.
- Change involves a transition period during which individuals engage in "old" behaviors and routines while making an effort to learn the "new" behaviors. Discomfort in breaking with the old behavioral patterns tends to be the rule rather than exception but must be managed in an effective manner if the goals of the change effort are to be realized. Thus, it is as important to devote attention to the "during" and "after" stages of the organizational change framework as it is to spend adequate time on the "before" and "during" stages.

The various stages of the change model are explained next. Critical questions that change leaders and students ought to ask are indicated.

DESIRED END STATE

Determining the desired end state that an organization or department envisions is perhaps the most vital stage of the model because it affects the four stages that ensue. Examples of critical questions for those leading the change include the following:

- What are the organization's goals? What are its strategies? What are the characteristics (e.g., tasks, skills, and behaviors) that the organization will need to succeed?
- What is the department's vision for the organization? How can the department contribute to organizational excellence? What is the department's role now, and what would we like it to be? What should our agenda be? Our goals? What outcomes are we pursuing?
- What ideas, strategies, or practices could help the organization or department to best achieve its goals? Are our current structure, systems, tasks, and people aligned with the organization's strategies? How can our structure, systems, tasks, and people be better aligned with the organization's strategies?

Answers to the above questions should provide a clear and measurable direction for action that members of the organization or department leading the change effort can initiate. Setting challenging and measurable goals at both the micro and macro levels, as well as collecting feedback on goal progress, is important if change is to occur. Goals encourage action.

READINESS FOR CHANGE

Those responsible for planning and implementing the change must decide whether the desired end state and the proposed change goals are realistic. Thus, it is important to understand the factors that could block or support "new" behaviors and subsequent goal achievement. Important questions include the following:

a. Is top management sponsoring the change? Top management cannot be seen as divided, indifferent, or resistant in change efforts. Is top management seen as being 100% supportive of the new direction? Active management support in both words and actions is a requirement, though not a guarantee, for the successful implementation of change. There are several indicators of support for the proposed change.

- Does top management express visible commitment to the change (e.g., public communications stating the importance of the change and meetings with recipients of the change)? Does it communicate the problem the change is intended to resolve and the importance of solving the problem?
- Is top management willing to provide adequate time for the change effort as well as appropriate resources, including funds for training and materials?
- Does top management do all it can to move the change process forward? For example, is it prepared to alter existing structures or systems that might hamper change? Change agents should discuss these (and other) issues with top management prior to initiating action.

b. Is there a capable change agent? The person leading the change should have the skills and abilities (e.g., communication, planning, coaching, interpersonal skills, understanding team processes, and human resources—specific knowledge) for this role. In addition, the person needs to be seen as credible and, like top management, committed to the change.

c. What is the predisposition of the target group(s) to embrace the change? Are the recipients of change supportive, resistant, or neutral toward change? Leaders of change must learn to overcome resistance to change. For what reason(s) do people resist change? How can resistance be overcome? The outcome of these assessments will, to a large extent, drive the action plan. For example, if team members indicate resistance to coaching behaviors due to lack of self-confidence in providing constructive feedback to their colleagues, then skills training prior to the implementation of the change (e.g., implementing teams to get work done) might be required.

d. Does the situational context facilitate or hamper change? All too often, leaders of change fail to appreciate the importance of context. Change does not occur in a vacuum; instead, it is embedded in a situational context. The situational context can facilitate or hamper the change that is being pursued. For example, the past management of challenges such as management-labor relations tends to be an important determinant of the eventual outcome (failure or success) of the most recent change efforts. Another situational variable is timing. For example, the time might not be right for a particular change initiative if the organization is confronted with other, more pressing problems that warrant immediate attention. Thus, leaders of change have to evaluate the relative importance of the various problems that require an organizational response. Priorities need to be set.

INITIATE CHANGE

Change goals have been determined in the previous two stages. Prior to going into "action mode," it is important to assess whether the recipients of the change perceive a need for change. The likelihood that the new behaviors and desired routines will be valued and adopted is higher when the target group acknowledges the need for change. Two basic questions that need to be addressed are the following:

a. Is there a perceived need for change? Getting commitment to the change effort is facilitated when the need for change is visible or communicated in a compelling manner. For example, explaining the long-term costs of continuing with the status quo in plain language can signal a need for change. The need for change is more obvious when things unravel in particular departments (e.g., a dramatic drop in customer satisfaction in the marketing department) or when the organization as a whole is struggling (e.g., individuals complain that the rapid growth has a detrimental effect on the organization's culture). The challenge is how to convince people to commit to change when the immediate need for change is less obvious.

b. How can commitment to the change effort be obtained? A change goal without commitment to it will not have much effect on goal-directed behaviors and subsequent performance. Factors promoting goal commitment can be classified into two broad categories. The first category includes factors affecting the perceived appropriateness of attempting to reach for a particular goal. For example, as indicated earlier, it is important that top management is seen as being committed to the change. This will lead organizational members to believe that attaining the stated change goal is important. The second category includes factors affecting the perceived capabilities of those attempting to attain the change goal. For example, it could be useful to provide feedback on the change process as well as the outcomes of the change effort. Providing positive feedback is important because goal achievement, or making visible progress toward the change goal, tends to be motivating and helps build momentum for change.

A common source of resistance to change is the lack of participation or involvement on the part of the recipients of change. Leaders should consider involving recipients in the change process, if time permits. Participation can prove to be useful in obtaining commitment to change goals for several reasons.

- Participation alleviates fears of change on the part of the recipients. For example, it allows people to discuss how negatives of a change can be handled.
- Involving the recipients in defining the problem and its solutions contributes to their understanding of the problem and its consequences.
- Recipients can provide valuable information that can be used to formulate or reformulate both process and outcome goals of the change intervention that is implemented.
- Participation allows for opportunities to share and explore ideas together, which, in turn, fosters confidence and trust among the parties. Confidence and trust are often lacking in change interventions; both are requirements to make change happen.
- Participation fosters a sense of ownership of the change intervention; those who were involved will be more reluctant to critique and resist it.
- Participation signifies that management views its people as important and that their people have an important role in the change process.

ADOPTING NEW BEHAVIORS

Successful change involves the adoption of new behaviors. Behavior is, to a large extent, a function of the perception that the behavior leads to favorable and valued outcomes while at the same time minimizing negative outcomes. It is also a function of self-confidence to engage in a particular course of action. Hence, critical questions for leaders of change include the following:

a. What are the outcome expectancies of the new behaviors? If the costs incurred through the change appear larger than the positive outcomes associated with it, then there will not be a strong incentive to engage in the new or desired behaviors.

b. Do the recipients of change have the abilities to enact the new behaviors? Denial of the need for change as well as overt or covert resistance to the change effort will result if recipients sense they do not have the knowledge, skills, or resources to perform the desired behaviors. The more radical the proposed change and the greater the number of uncertainties regarding skills, responsibilities, and behaviors, the more resistance the change effort could engender. Thus, leaders of change need to find ways in which they can give the recipients of change the confidence to do the things they want them to do.

STABILIZING NEW BEHAVIORS

The last box in Figure 4.1 indicates that the new behaviors have to be stabilized. Long-lasting behavioral change and maintenance is pursued, not change that lasts weeks or a few months at best. It often does not take long for the recipients of change to revert to their previous behavioral patterns. Thus, the new behavior needs continuous reinforcement until it has become a routine.

For new behavior to be lasting, it must fit into the overall organizational design. Leaders therefore must ensure the alignment of the various components of the change intervention with the new organizational design.

Individuals will also be testing the new behavior; this can be reinforced through coaching behaviors as well as providing feedback on the effectiveness of the new behavior. Knowing that the behaviors being adopted are effective can provide both motivation and encouragement for those affected. Publicize when the expected benefits of the new behaviors are in the process of being realized. Showcasing success ("small wins") and celebrating milestones will increase confidence in, and commitment to, the change. Foster trust among those involved (e.g., top management, the change agent, and the recipients of change), increase confidence to demonstrate the required behaviors, and establish a culture that values change and rewards it. Providing both process and outcome information signals that those responsible for initiating and implementing the change, including top management, are sincere about managing the change process to the best extent possible.

There are 11 cases that focus on the challenges of change management. A brief description of each case is provided next, and specific assignment questions are suggested.

CUSHY ARMCHAIR

Cushy Armchair, based in Hong Kong, is a leader in the global armchair business, controlling fully autonomous business groups in 17 countries. Cabletronica has recently acquired the company and has sent one of its own senior personnel to restructure operations and integrate the company with another of its furniture divisions outside of the country. Acting as a consultant, the founder of Cushy is approached regarding a communication on a change in policy, but the new head of the company decides to use the parent company's standard method and now must manage with the results that change can have on a cross-cultural, multinational business.

Assignment Questions

- Why was Alison Sampson's directive ignored?
- Who would resist the change and why? How much power do they have?
- Who would support the change and why? How much power do they have?
- Outline an action plan for Alison Sampson at the end of the case.

CRAFTING A VISION AT DAIMLER-CHRYSLER

Chrysler and Daimler-Benz shareholders approved the largest corporate merger in history. After months of talks, the chairman of the German-based Daimler-Benz management board and the chairman and chief executive officer of the U.S.-based Chrysler Corporation were preparing for when the two companies would officially combine forces to create the fifth largest automobile company in the world. These two managers were officially charged with the responsibility of amalgamating two enterprises that were vastly different from each other. Chrysler was known for its efficient production and economically priced vehicles. Daimler-Benz sold only luxury vehicles, and its reputation was based on craftsmanship, quality, and safety. Chrysler executives were in the habit of limiting business expenses; Daimler-Benz executives were not. Between the two companies, there were huge discrepancies in cultures, market segments, product lines, salaries, and attitudes. Aware of the excitement of their investors and the concern of their critics, the two leaders are expected to forge and promote the vision on which Daimler-Chrysler will base its future.

Assignment Questions

- As CEO of the newly formed Daimler-Chrysler, you have decided to embark on a 2-week tour of all the key Daimler-Chrysler facilities in the world and to present a spirited speech on the new partnership. (a) What are the key elements of a persuasive speech? (b) What are the key factors you want to cover in your speech?
- Prepare before class a 10-minute speech that you would give to a gathering of the people at the key facilities.

ABB POLAND

The case provides students an opportunity to explore the constraints imposed by an organizational structure that, in most parts of the world, provides the company with significant benefits. However, in the context of Poland (and other former COMECON nations as well), the structure imposes a number of critical constraints. ABB is set up to operate as a multidomestic company—basically, a well-managed network of country-based organizations managed by local managers and competing in local markets. Historically, ABB has acquired well-managed companies it is able to integrate into its network relatively seamlessly. However, its recent acquisitions in Poland do not follow this pattern. They are not well managed, they require significant restructuring to reach world-class levels of productivity, and most of the managers in place lack the skills to get their companies to the world-class levels ABB expects. Yet, if ABB begins to send expatriate managers into the individual companies and firing what it regards to be the ineffective local managers, it risks jeopardizing future acquisitions. The recently appointed human resource director must consider his next step in promoting the much-needed restructuring of the companies they have acquired.

Assignment Questions

- What is the fundamental problem posed by ABB Elta for Artur Czynczyk?
- What specific problems need to be fixed within ABB Elta?
- How is Artur Czynczyk going to go about fixing these problems?
- Who should the change agents not be? Why?
- Who should the change agents be? What characteristics do they need to have?

CHINA-CANADA LEAN SWINE PROJECT—CHANGING LOCAL HABITS

David Wang, the enterprise development specialist with Agriteam Canada (Agriteam), is trying to determine how to increase business development at the Xiangzhou Feedmill (Feedmill) in Hebei, China. The Feedmill is a feed grain production facility that is being used as a test base for the China-Canada Lean Swine Project (the Project), a bilateral development effort between the Chinese and Canadian governments. After making an initial assessment of the operation, Wang has concluded that many of the difficulties he is facing are related to attitudes and behaviors associated with China's legacy of state planning. Therefore, he feels he needs to devise ways that will help the Feedmill's managers "undergo a profound reconceptualization of their roles and responsibilities in the workplace." Complicating matters is the fact that Wang is a native Chinese who has recently returned to China after spending about 8 years in Canada. Although he has some very impressive credentials, some of his compatriots feel that he is "out of touch" with the extraordinary changes that have taken place in China while he was away.

Assignment Questions

- What are the objectives of the China-Canada Lean Swine Project? Assess the economic environment in which the project is being implemented.
- What is your assessment of the Xiangzhou Feedmill operation? How "ready" are the managers to make the changes required to ensure the Project's success?
- As David Wang, which of the four alternatives would you select? Are there any other alternative solutions that David Wang should consider? Devise an action plan for the implementation of your decision.
- Is David Wang a suitable person for advocating change?

SALCO (CHINA)

Salco (China) is a global manufacturer of burners for hot-water boilers and industrial furnaces and ovens. The company has recently hired a new operations manager for its plant in China whose mandate is to improve the efficiency of the Beijing office, to eliminate Salco's Chinese distributors' poaching behavior, and to elevate Salco's brand equity in the Chinese market. Dahong Wong had a good track record, having succeeded in his previous jobs: as an analyst in a consulting firm and a star sales manager in a major manufacturing company. He was confident that he would be able to repeat his success at Salco. However, the initiative to eliminate distributors' poaching had failed, and Wong must determine why this initiative failed and prepare a report for senior management. He would have to justify his actions in front of Don Miller, Salco's Asia-Pacific area manager.

Assignment Questions

- As Wong, were you the right change agent at Salco (China)? Why or why not?
- As Wong, why did you not succeed in managing Miller, Pan, and the distributors? How do you evaluate your relationship to Yuan?
- Conduct a step-by-step analysis of Wong's "Distributor Restructuring Program." What was the desired end state? Why did the program not get off the ground?
- Should Wong cancel the meeting with the distributors after Miller's call? If so, why? As Wong, what should your plan be for the upcoming meeting with Miller? Why?

DELOITTE & TOUCHE: INTEGRATING ARTHUR ANDERSEN

In 2002, approximately 1,000 Arthur Andersen employees joined Deloitte & Touche, effectively creating the largest professional services organization in Canada. The combined entity employed 6,600 people and represented annual billings of more than $1 billion. A co-chair for the national integration team was faced with a huge challenge: to develop a company-wide plan to create support materials to aid the Deloitte staff in integrating the Andersen staff in the organization. The integration process was monitored through a monthly survey and would be used by the team to benchmark unit to unit over time and to take remedial action at specific stages if the integration goals were not attained. The most recent survey indicated that Deloitte employees felt that in the company's haste to finalize the deal with Andersen, it was forgetting about its own employees. Some within the Deloitte organization did not understand the amount of attention given to Andersen employees, whom they viewed as "damaged goods." The co-chair and integration team must determine the best way to deal with the feedback and the cultural differences that are surfacing.

Assignment Questions

- You just presented the new vision for the integrated organization, "Making a Difference Together." What will your next steps be, short term and long term? Please provide a rationale.
- Terry Noble identified cultural misalignment and subsequent conflict as a key risk factor that threatened to derail the success of the Deloitte-Andersen integration. What steps will you take to address the two different organizational cultures (see also Exhibit 4).
- Can "the Frenchman" and "the Englishman" Terry Noble is referring to work together, despite their individual cultures? What is your view? How will you deal with the constraints, as outlined at the end of the case, on your actions?
- Terry Noble and his team observed that there were numerous misperceptions regarding the Andersen people. In addition, the Pulse Survey data indicated some evidence of a backlash against the merger. You fear that these factors may negatively affect productivity. What actions will you initiate to minimize the effect of the misperceptions and backlash?

PETA's "Kentucky Fried Cruelty, Inc." Campaign

A year and a half after calling off their campaign against fast-food giant McDonald's, the vegan campaign coordinator of People for the Ethical Treatment of Animals (PETA) contacted Kentucky Fried Chicken (KFC) to warn them that they would be the next target. He pointed out in his letter that although many of KFC's competitors had convened advisory panels to help them investigate the welfare of animals raised and slaughtered for their businesses, KFC appeared completely uninterested in the issue. PETA would rather not engage KFC in a campaign, but if the company refused to put together an animal welfare panel and to begin to look into the issue of how to raise and slaughter their chickens more humanely, all the leaflets, action alerts, posters, billboards, T-shirts, and press releases PETA was now preparing would be dedicated to KFC and its cruel treatment of chickens. In January 2003, PETA, fed up with what it saw as KFC's lack of open communication, public misinformation, and outright stonewalling on change, announced a campaign against the company to the media in a news event replete with bloody descriptions of the cruelties of KFC's animal factories. Now it was time for Kentucky Fried Chicken to respond.

Assignment Questions

- How would you describe the relationship between PETA and KFC from April 2001 to August 2003? How did the two organizations communicate with one another? What specific messages were exchanged?
- How would you characterize PETA's "Kentucky Fried Cruelty, Inc." campaign? What tactics did the group use to put pressure on KFC? How effective were these tactics?
- How would you characterize KFC's response to the campaign? What tactics did the company use? How effective were these tactics?
- If you were David Novak, Cheryl Bachelder, or Jonathon Blum, how would you respond to PETA and other concerned stakeholders to ensure KFC's continued growth?

Maple Leaf Foods (A): Leading Six Sigma Change

Maple Leaf Foods is a leading global food-processing company with operations in Canada, the United States, Europe, and Asia. Under new management and with the desire to substantially upgrade the leadership capabilities throughout the firm, the chief executive officer and vice president of Six Sigma (an approach and methodology for eliminating defects in any process) embarks on a revolutionary change journey in this previously change-resistant multinational food business. The project has been rolled out to 3 of the 10 independent operating companies, and he must analyze the launch to determine whether it is on track and what can be done differently or better. The supplement "Maple Leaf Foods (B): Six Sigma in 2002" (included in the Instructor's Manual) follows the progress of the Six Sigma program a year later.

Assignment Questions

- Why would Maple Leaf Foods adopt Six Sigma? What did they want to achieve?
- What do you think about the way Maple Leaf Foods introduced Six Sigma? What grade would you give the management team for the way it implemented Six Sigma?
- Based on how things are going at Maple Leaf Foods, what opportunities and challenges do you see?

BLACK & DECKER-EASTERN HEMISPHERE AND THE ADP INITIATIVE (A)

The new president of Black & Decker-Eastern Hemisphere attempts to introduce a new performance appraisal and management development system. Black & Decker is a relatively weak player in the Eastern Hemisphere, and the president is convinced that he needs to significantly increase the number and quality of managers in the region. To assist in the development process, the president is considering introducing a U.S.-designed Appraisal Development Plan (ADP) in the region. ADP uses 360-degree feedback from peers, subordinates, and supervisors to assist employees in building managerial skills and in increasing personal accountability. Despite a successful track record for ADP in Black & Decker North America, members of the top-management team are concerned that ADP will be a failure in the Eastern Hemisphere. Local managers have raised serious questions about whether ADP will ever be accepted in the Eastern Hemisphere. They argue that the system faces huge barriers due to organizational cultural issues related to staffing, systems leadership, and structure. The president is flirting with disaster if he proceeds.

Assignment Questions

- Since arriving in Singapore, Lancaster has formulated several opinions about the health of the Eastern Hemisphere organization. What are his concerns both now and for the future?
- What problems does Lancaster want ADP to address?
- What concerns do Asian managers have about ADP? How substantive are these concerns?
- What action should Lancaster take: wait, go ahead with a hybrid, or full speed ahead with the U.S. version of ADP?

SANDALIAS FINAS DE CUERNAVACA, S.A.: TOTAL QUALITY MANAGEMENT (A)

John Kortright, the president and owner of Sandalias Finas De Cuernavaca, S.A., a small sandal factory, realized that if his company was to survive in the long run, the manufacturing operation would need to become more efficient. Relaxed tariff barriers had increased the level of foreign competition in the country, particularly in the footwear industry. The move to join the General Agreement on Tariffs and Trade (GATT) to strengthen the domestic economy had meant relaxed tariff barriers, allowing the freer flow of goods and services into Mexico. The result had been an increase in foreign-manufactured products, including sandals, that were priced competitively and were perceived by domestic consumers to be superior in quality. The North American Free Trade Agreement (NAFTA), which was looming on the horizon, would only make the situation worse from Kortright's point of view. He had recently attended a seminar on total quality management (TQM) sponsored by the local trade association. Despite the potential benefits of TQM and its record of past successes, Kortright was uncertain whether the Mexican employees would be able to implement TQM, a system that appeared to be based on different norms and values than those of Mexican workers.

Assignment Questions

- What are the major elements of total quality management (TQM)? Think in terms of the philosophy (values, beliefs), the processes that reflect these values in practice, the "tools" (systems, practices, structures) used in implementing TQM, and the skills required to work with the "tools" and in the process. What changes in roles and behaviors are required for workers and managers?

- How are the cultural assumptions on which TQM is based compatible or not compatible with Mexican culture?
- Assume that John Kortright has decided to implement a TQM program and that he has asked you for help. Put together an implementation plan for him that considers his immediate business needs and necessary changes in work structures and systems.

VICTORIA HOSPITAL REDESIGN INITIATIVE

The president and chief executive of a hospital is anticipating resistance to his newly formed vision for the hospital. The exact source and reasons for the resistance are not totally clear to him. Notwithstanding the difficulty of the change he would propose, he recognizes that the conventional hospital is no longer able to respond effectively to its demands with the resource constraints caused by government funding cutbacks. With varying degrees of support from the administration, doctors, nurses, and other professionals, he has to take action to get the proposed redesign plan back on track.

Assignment Questions

- As Dr. Frelick, what are the major problems facing you regarding your redesign plan? Be sure to include the major contributing factors to these problems.
- As Dr. Frelick, what would you do to deal with the major problems identified in the above analysis? Be specific (and realistic) about what you want to accomplish and why the action should result in meeting your objectives.

REFERENCES

Bossidy, L., & Charan, R. (2002). *Execution: The discipline of getting things done.* New York: Crown Business.

Kotter, J. (1996). *Leading change.* Boston: Harvard Business School Press.

CUSHY ARMCHAIR

Prepared by Professor Brian Golden

Copyright © 2001, Ivey Management Services

Version: (A) 2001-05-04

Cabletronica U.S. is a large, prosperous cable and wireless company based in upstate New York. In order to expand the scope of operations, it has recently targeted several strategically related industries in which to take a greater stake. Specifically, its research on changing demographic and cable viewing patterns concluded that reclining armchairs would be a growth business over the next 20 years. Cabletronica thus moved their minority investment position in Cushy Armchair (CA), based in Hong Kong, to a position of total equity and operating control. Cabletronica had just completed the acquisition of World-Furniture, also based in New York.

Cushy Armchair is a recognized leader in the global reclining chair business, with fully autonomous business groups in 17 countries. This decentralized model evolved as a result of the substantial communication and logistics challenges facing multinationals in 1962, the year it was founded. And since economies of scale had been inconsequential, while national market differences were substantial, this model had been sensible and had paid off handsomely. National differences could be seen, for example, in the U.S. division's recent introduction of reclining chairs that offered drink-holders and coolers built into the chair armrests. The Scandinavian market had introduced a "tingling fingers" massage chair, and although successful in that market, it was shown to have minimal attractiveness elsewhere. Other differences across the world included fabric preferences, as well as size requirements (to accommodate varying torso characteristics, as well as differing housing space constraints). Although historically a sleepy industry, the recliner industry is expected to heat up as a result of consolidation, new materials and technology, and shortening design cycles. In addition, competitors founded in the past few years have built global (centralized), rather than multidomestic (decentralized) businesses. This further enhances their potential cost and cycle-time advantages.

As part of Cabletronica's attempts to breathe new life into Cushy Armchair, the company dispatched Alison Sampson to take the helm of CA in Hong Kong, replacing the well-regarded founder, Frances Wong. Cabletronica's chief operating officer announced this appointment like all Cabletronica senior personnel changes, through a global e-mail message. Sampson's appointment was to begin March 14th, the busiest time of year as most of the businesses ramped up design and manufacturing for strong end-of-year holiday sales. Sampson's immediate goals were to reduce costs, speed product design and improve technology transfer. Specifically, production, design (fabric and style), sales and distribution (advertising), and procurement would be her focus in the short term. Sampson came to this with a successful background integrating numerous acquisitions for Cabletronica, mainly in the cable industry. She had risen through the finance ranks, and was looking forward to the challenge of moving into a manufacturing setting and working for the first time with line managers. Wong would serve as a consultant to Sampson for the next six months, in an effort to ensure a smooth transfer of control. Sampson, after careful examination of industry trends and competitor analysis, was keen to hit the ground running. After two weeks on the job, she drafted the following e-mail memorandum to the executives responsible for purchasing, sales and design in each of the 17 countries.

To: National Purchasing, Marketing, and Design Managers

From: Alison Sampson, C.A., M.B.A.

Date: April 1, 2000

As you know, our industry is changing dramatically, and although virtually all of our national business have been very successful these past years, that is going to change unless we change. I know you share my observations and concerns for the future of Cushy Armchair, and I trust that you will welcome these changes as I move to consolidate operations. We will begin with some small steps, all involving greater centralization in order to achieve economies of scale and scope. Specifically, from the first of next month onwards, I would like to request the following of all purchasing, marketing and design managers:

1. All purchasing managers should ensure that all chair glide-mechanisms, as well as fabric orders in excess of HK$35,000 be contracted through WorldFurniture's procurement division in New York.

2. Advertising campaigns will in the future be co-ordinated through New York, where we have an expert group of advertising specialists. Therefore, all interest in launching new advertising

campaigns should be cleared by our New York staff.

3. The New York staff should approve any substantial design and feature changes.

Though I haven't yet had the opportunity to meet with most of you, I look forward to doing so over the next three months to discuss the impact of these policy changes and the changes ahead.

A. Sampson, C.A., M.B.A.

Before sending this e-mail, Sampson asked Wong for his reaction. Wong suggested that e-mail was perhaps not the most effective way to deliver this message. While Sampson appreciated the advice, she felt e-mail was most expedient, given the urgency to change in time for next season's rush.

Two months later, in a casual conversation with the head of procurement for WorldFurniture, Sampson learned that no orders from any of Cushy Armchair's divisions had yet been received. It didn't take long for Sampson to learn that either all of her policy changes had been ignored *or* that no actions or decisions by purchasing, design or marketing had yet met the criteria set out by Sampson in her e-mail memo of April 1st.

CRAFTING A VISION AT DAIMLER-CHRYSLER[1]

Prepared by Nicole Nolan under the supervision of Professor Brian Golden

Version: (A) 2003-03-04

On September 18, 1998, Chrysler and Daimler-Benz shareholders approved the largest corporate merger in history. After months of talks, Jürgen E. Schrempp, chairman of the German-based Daimler-Benz management board, and Robert J. Eaton, chairman and chief executive officer (CEO) of the American-based Chrysler Corporation, were now preparing for November 17, 1998. This would be the historic day that Daimler-Chrysler would be born, and create the fifth largest automobile company in the world behind General Motors Corporation, Ford Motor Corporation, Toyota Motor Corporation and Volkswagen. Schrempp and Eaton were now charged with the responsibility of amalgamating two enterprises with very different cultures, market segments and product lines; they needed to forge a vision on which Daimler-Chrysler would base its future.

Chrysler Corporation, incorporated in 1925, was the third largest automobile manufacturer in the United States and was considered the most efficient in America, based on cars produced per employee. Chrysler was known for its economically priced minivans, pickup trucks and sport utility vehicles. Chrysler, however, was considered a regional car manufacturer, with nearly 90 per cent of its sales in North America and only one per cent of its sales in Europe.[2] In contrast, Ford and General Motors each had about 12 per cent of their sales in Europe.

Daimler-Benz, the oldest automaker in the world, ranked 14th in size among automakers worldwide. In contrast to Chrysler, Daimler-Benz sold only luxury automobiles and commercial vehicles. The Daimler-Benz reputation was based on craftsmanship, quality and safety. Daimler-Benz had 63 per cent of their sales in Europe, and 21 per cent of their sales in North America.[3]

To the investment community, the merger looked like a match made in heaven. Both the

North American and European markets were mature, thus making significant growth on their own for either firm very unlikely. Likewise, their product lines were complementary.[4] For instance, Chrysler lacked a luxury vehicle, and Daimler-Benz did not produce minivans or sport utility vehicles. Also, both the increased market power and economies due to the size of the merged firm were seen as critical.

Other observers, however, were less confident of the merger's likely success and whether this would be a "merger among equals" as Schrempp had indicated. Daimler-Benz employees were proud of the elite image and were concerned about having that tarnished by a "third string, mass market American firm." Chrysler employees voiced concerns about the "Germanization of America's No. 3 automaker." One senior Daimler-Chrysler executive had been quoted as saying:

> It is unthinkable for a Chrysler car to be built in a Mercedes-Benz factory, and for as long as I'm responsible for the Mercedes-Benz brand, only over my dead body will a Mercedes be built in a Chrysler factory.[5]

Shortly after the announcement, Chrysler's engineers released a Top 10 list of the ways in which Chrysler's corporate culture would change with a Daimler-Benz takeover. Beer in office vending machines and lederhosen on casual dress day were two suggestions offered by Chrysler designers.

Independent observers also noted the different business and national cultures of the two firms. One news account suggested the possibility of Daimler-Benz's button-downed managers possibly clashing with the more freewheeling culture of Chrysler. For example, Daimler-Benz employees referred to each other by their last names, for example as Mr. Schrempp instead of Jürgen. The Chrysler employees referred to each other by their given names.[6]

The two firms' strategies had also influenced their culture around spending. Daimler-Benz executives tended to fly first class and stay in luxury hotels. Chrysler executives travelled coach class and stayed in inexpensive hotels

to save money.[7] There were also substantial salary differences. Eaton earned US$9.8 million in the year before the merger. In contrast, the 10 members of the Daimler-Benz management board in total earned the equivalent of US$11 million that same year.[8] One reason for this discrepancy was that the Americans had bonus incentive programs and stock options, whereas the Germans did not.

Also, because Chrysler's cars tended to be in the US$20,000 range, and Daimler-Benz's in the US$80,000 range, Chrysler had long emphasized efficiency and economy in design and production. Daimler-Benz focused more on engineering excellence and luxury. Both partners, however, had developed substantial capabilities in terms of systems. For example, Chrysler's popular SCORE purchasing program had received national recognition. Daimler-Benz's TANDEM purchasing program, equally successful but very different, had received similar accolades at home.[9]

Middle managers at both firms were concerned. As one Chrysler manager, fearful of the significant overlap of support functions, commented to a local Detroit news reporter:

> We've all been waiting for the other shoe to drop. There's a fear of what will happen to salaried workers generally. If you look at other corporate mergers, what happens is, they axe middle management.

Stability and job security was not something Schrempp was known for. He had earned the reputation as the "Rambo of Europe" from his aggressive job slashing activities in the mid-1990s. For example, Schrempp had eliminated 11 of the 35 Daimler-Benz business units in a six-month period. In Germany, he was often referred to with the phrase "*Uber leichen gehen*" ("to walk over dead people"). The German tabloids called him "Neutron Jürgen" in reference to "Neutron Jack" Welch, who had aggressively downsized General Electric in the 1980s.[10]

One industry expert praised the merger in theory, but commented on U.S. national television that caution was called for. He reminded the audience that the *Titanic* was large and technologically advanced, but no longer with us—not unlike the 1980s merger of Ford's and Volkswagon's Brazilian and Argentinean operations (the now defunct Auto Latina). Aware of both the excitement among investors, and the concern of critics, Schrempp considered how he could best communicate the vision of the newly formed company.

NOTES

1. This case has been written on the basis of published sources only. Consequently, the interpretation and perspectives presented in this case are not necessarily those of Daimler-Chrysler or any of its employees.

2. www.daimlerchrysler.com *Daimler-Chrysler Special Reports: The Financial Picture*, September 2001.

3. www.daimlerchrysler.com *Daimler-Chrysler Special Reports: The Financial Picture*, September 2001.

4. www.daimlerchrysler.com *Daimler-Chrysler Special Reports: The Media Reaction*. Reprinted from David E. Cole and Michael S. Flynn. *The Detroit News* 6/26/98, September 2001.

5. Waller, David. *Wheels on fire: The amazing inside story of the Daimler-Chrysler merger*. Hodder & Stoughton. 2001. p. 243.

6. Ibid., pp. 253–254.

7. Vlasic, Bill and Bradley Stertz, *Taken for a ride: How Daimler-Benz drove off with Chrysler*. Harper Collins Publishers: New York. 2000, p.320.

8. Waller, David, p. 254.

9. Sorge, Marjorie. 1998. Daimler-Chrysler: How the two become one. *Automotive Industries*. October. http://www.ai-online.com, September 2001.

10. Vlasic, Bill and Bradley Stertz. pp. 129–130.

ABB POLAND

Prepared by Professors
Ann Frost and Marc Weinstein

Copyright © 1998, Ivey Management Services   Version: (A) 1998-11-24

INTRODUCTION

In May 1996, Artur Czynczyk,[1] the recently appointed human resource director for ABB Poland, pondered his next step in promoting the much needed restructuring of the companies acquired by ABB in Poland since 1990. At a meeting of ABB Poland's top management earlier that month, at corporate headquarters in Warsaw, he had reported his findings: the restructuring of operations within individual companies was stalled and the current personnel staff appeared incapable of facilitating the needed change process. Having had only limited success over the past two and a half years in facilitating change indirectly, Czynczyk needed a plan for what to do next.

ABB ORGANIZATIONAL STRUCTURE

ABB, a Swedish-Swiss multinational, entered the Polish market in 1990 with its acquisition of Zamech, a Polish manufacturer of turbines. ABB's entry was precipitated by the huge market potential in the former COMECON countries for infrastructure development. ABB's acquisitions in Poland stayed true to ABB's core businesses as the company acquired Polish companies in the power generation, power transmission and transportation fields (see Exhibit 1). By 1993, ABB was the third largest foreign investor in Poland after Fiat and International Paper. By 1996, ABB Poland had emerged as an important employer in the Polish economy, employing 7,500 people in

Year	Company Name	City	Major Product	1996 Employment
May 1990	ABB Zamech	Elblag	• Steam turbines, gas turbines • Service and retrofit of the complete turbine islands • Environmental protection systems (previously ABB Flakt Industry) • Pre-insulated district heating pipes • Gears and marine propellers • Casting steel and copper alloys • Service station turbochargers • Gas and oil equipment • Car industry robots	3,400
Oct 1990	ABB Dolmel	Wroclaw	• Turbogenerators • Industrial generators • Hydrogenerators for small hydro power plants	615
Oct 1990	ABB Dolmel Drives	Wroclaw	• Induction and synchronous motors • Marine generators • Generators for diesel-electric generating sets • DC winder motors for mines • Traction auxiliary machines • DC motor trams • Starters for induction slip-ring motors • Lifting magnets • Electromagnetic separators	603
April 1992	ABB Elta	Lódź	• Power transformers • Distribution transformers • High voltage (HV) switchgear • Insulation kits • Galvanizing services	932
Dec 1992	ABB Industrial Components	Warsaw	• Sale of products allocated within BA IIM, ILA and IAH as the core business • Network control & protection active in TNP BA	44
Oct 1993	ABB Instal	Wroclaw	• MV switchboards • LV switchboards MNS, KNS, INS • Complex performance of electric power engineering objects.	164
Jan 1994	ABB Centrum	Wroclaw	• Complete solutions for power plants and heating power plant control	69
March 1994	ABB Industry	Warsaw	• Production, engineering and sales of drives, rectifiers, excitation systems and instrumentation • Industrial control systems	117

Exhibit 1   ABB'S Acquisitions in Poland 1990 to 1997   *(Continued)*

Year	Company Name	City	Major Product	1996 Employment
June 1997	ABB Elbud	Kraków	• Construction, overhauling, upgrading and refurbishing of HV overhead lines, transformer substations and underground cable lines • Erection of steel-constructed masts • Assembly, testing and start-up of telemetry and remote control in HV, VHV substations	500
June 1997	ABB Elpar	Lódź	• MV switchgear • HV switchgear • Network control and protection equipment	230
Sept 1997	ABB Donako	Wroclaw	• Design and manufacturing of tools and process equipment, and steel sheet punching	171
Sept 1997	ABB Huta Katowice Service	Dabrawa Gornicza	• Service	100
Oct 1997	ABB Service	Legnica	• Service	200

Exhibit 1   ABB'S Acquisitions in Poland 1990 to 1997

13 companies located throughout the country (see Exhibit 2).

ABB Poland was organized using the same matrix structure that the company utilized throughout the rest of the world (see Exhibit 3). The basic matrix consisted of geographic regions and three product segments: power, transmission and distribution (T&D), and industry and building systems. Together these three segments comprised over 50 business areas (BAs). BA leaders operated as global optimizers and strategists for specific product lines such as power transformers or high voltage switchgears. Their role was to decide which factories made which products, what export markets each factory would serve, how factories should pool their expertise, and how research and development funds ought to be allocated for the benefit of the business world-wide. The BA leader also tracked talent. When a new plant manager for a particular business area was required anywhere in the world, then that BA leader was responsible for identifying an appropriate candidate from a shortlist of people that he or she maintained from the global operation.

Within national boundaries, ABB co-ordinated its activities through the use of country organizations (see Exhibit 4). Significant benefits to the component companies were derived on this basis. For example, the country organization could successfully recruit top people from the universities, build an efficient distribution and service network across product lines, circulate good people among local companies and maintain productive relations with top government officials. The country president also had responsibilities similar to those of a CEO of a large domestic firm: negotiating labor agreements, maintaining banking relationships and managing high-level contacts with customers.

The matrix organization produced clear benefits for ABB. ABB was a highly profitable company, leanly organized, and extremely responsive. However, to outsiders, ABB's organization structure appeared complex and difficult to manage. Percy Barnevik, the architect of ABB and its organizational structure, however, believed the organization was actually very simple for managers to operate within.

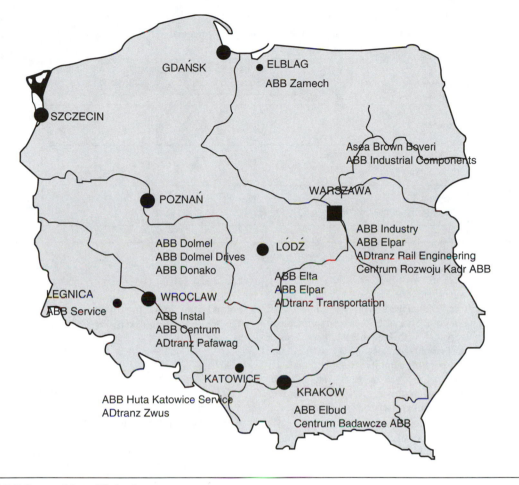

Exhibit 2   Map of Poland

The only way to structure a complex global organization is to make it as simple and local as possible. ABB is complicated from where I sit. But on the ground, where the real work gets done, all of our operations must function as closely as possible to stand-alone operations. Our managers need well-defined sets of responsibilities, clear accountability and maximum degrees of freedom to execute. I don't expect most of our people to have "global mindsets," to do things that hurt their business but are "good for ABB." That's not natural.[2]

Barnevik also stressed the importance of local accountability and autonomy.

ABB is a huge enterprise. But the work of most of our people is organized in small units with P&L responsibility and meaningful autonomy. Our operations are divided into nearly 1,200 companies with an average of 200 employees. These companies are divided into 4,500 profit centres with an average of 50 employees. . . . We are fervent believers in decentralization.[3]

Given the autonomy accorded to company presidents and the need for local "insiders," ABB shied away from the use of expatriate managers at the company level. Commenting on the need to have nationals managing their own companies Barnevik stated:

Region / Segment	Europe, Middle East, Africa	The Americas	Asia
	National Holding Companies (Finance, Human Resources, Legal Affairs Communications)		
Power			
Transmission & Distribution			
Industry & Building Systems			

Exhibit 3   ABB'S Matrix Structure

We can't have managers who are "un-French" managing in France because 95 per cent of them are dealing every day with French customers, French colleagues, French suppliers. That's why global managers also need humility. A global manager respects a formal German manager—Herr Doktor and all that—because that manager may be an outstanding performer in a German context.[4]

When they were used, expatriates usually filled corporate-level roles such as country presidents or segment managers.[5] In Poland, David Hunter, an American, was country manager from the founding of ABB Poland in 1990 until the end of 1996 when he was replaced by a Pole, Miroslaw Gryszka. In February 1996, Frank Duggan, a long-time ABB employee originally from Ireland, was appointed head of the Polish Transmission and Distribution (T&D) segment.

Entering the former eastern bloc for the first time, ABB (and Hunter and Duggan in turn) found conditions in the acquired companies far from the standards it was used to in western Europe. Many of the problems ABB management encountered were typified by the example of Elta, a manufacturer of transformers located in Lódź,[6] Poland. As part of the T&D segment, Elta fell under the responsibility of Frank Duggan. Arriving in Poland after spending several years with ABB in Thailand, he found what was in his words, "a bloody disaster."

ABB Elta—Historical Background

After a year of negotiation, ABB acquired 51 per cent of Elta Transformers and Traction Apparatus Factory (Elta) in April 1992. As was ABB's usual practice as a multidomestic firm, Elta entered into the ABB matrix system with its internal management structure intact and its existing managers in place. Located in Lódź, a city of about 850,000 inhabitants about an hour's driving time southwest of Warsaw, Elta was founded in 1925 to manufacture transformers for the Lódź power station. Nationalized in the wake of the imposition of Soviet-style socialism after World War II, by 1969, Elta was producing high voltage switchgear, power transformers and distribution transformers for both Poland and the then Soviet Union.

Because of its strategic importance in the Polish economy as a supplier of critical infrastructure materials, Elta was not a part of an industry association during the socialist period. Instead, company management reported directly to the Ministry of Industry. Following closely

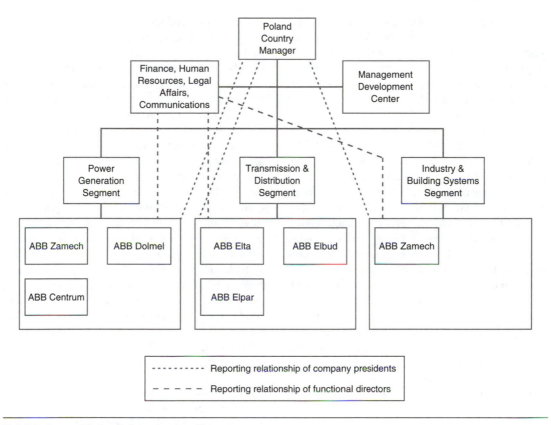

Exhibit 4   National Organization Chart

upon the Leninist principle of "dual power," all offices of the government were shadowed by parallel positions within the party. Administrative positions within the government were staffed by professional bureaucrats, who rose to power through party ranks. At the same time, the principle of "democratic centralism" required every party member to obey the orders of his superior. As a result, all power in the country flowed directly from the top. Similar structures reached down into the bureaucracy of Elta as well. Thus, Elta's factory-level party structures were well entrenched and employment, promotion and investment decisions at Elta were even more sensitive to political considerations than was usually the case in Polish enterprises.

Because Elta was a state-owned firm operating in a command economy, the central government set production targets, allocated contracts and set prices. Top management took its orders from the state ministry and relayed them down the organizational hierarchy. If unanticipated cost overruns occurred (and with the very crude accounting methods Elta had in place, this was common), they were simply funded by additional bank loans and allowed to accumulate on the books indefinitely.

Long before the Communists came to power in Poland, the working class was seen as a key element in Polish society. As early as 1918, workers were organizing into trade unions and forming worker councils to demand a role in determining wages, working conditions and limits on managerial authority. After the imposition of Communist rule, these worker councils were seen to be so consistent with the values of socialist organization that they were officially sanctioned by the new regime. Worker councils were empowered to negotiate wages, shape employment policies and to participate in workplace decision making. Even after the fall of Communism in 1989, state-owned firms retained their worker councils.

Consistent with the status of workers in a socialist economy, blue-collar workers at Elta earned 105 per cent of the average wage. Technical employees and engineers earned 98 per cent of the average and other support services earned about 90 per cent of the average. Top management's salaries were not much higher than blue-collar wages. Living in a socialist economy in which most necessities were provided or heavily subsidized by the state (housing, medical care, education, day care, vacations, recreation activities) and in which consumer goods were scarce, wage increases only led to an increase in the oversupply of money. While both engineers and blue-collar workers tended to be very skilled, both groups were highly alienated and lacked independent initiative. Over the years, they had been socialized to defer decisions to others.

ABB Elta—Production

ABB Elta was made up of six separately managed divisions: power transformers, distribution transformers, high voltage switchgear, insulation component production, galvanizing and engineering. The first three divisions produced final products, while the latter three were support divisions. The insulation component production division produced the insulation kits used in the two types of transformers. All insulation kits were produced by hand. The galvanizing division was responsible for the zinc coating of small metal parts used in the production of the transformers and switchgear to prevent rusting and corrosion. Each part was galvanized by hand-dipping in liquid zinc. Finally, the engineering centre provided engineering expertise including design and troubleshooting to Elta as a whole.

The main production area within Elta, where the insulation kits, switchgear, and both types of transformers were produced, had been thoroughly modernized after ABB's acquisition of the facility. This plant was bright, clean, and the floor area relatively uncluttered. However, other parts of the Elta facility remained as they had been for 40 or more years. The paint shop, where all transformer casings were painted before final assembly, was dark, covered with decades of grime, cluttered, fume-filled and lagged considerably behind Western health and safety standards. Men painted with hand-held spray guns, often immersed up to their knees in paint, and without eye or breathing protection. Although masks were available, they were so uncomfortable and they distorted the painters' vision so badly few wore them. Despite these conditions, especially in contrast to the refurbished main production site, most people saw there being no alternative way to set up the painting facility to overcome these drawbacks.

The organization of production, even in the modernized plant at ABB Elta, was similarly underdeveloped. Power transformers are enormous pieces of equipment standing approximately 15 feet high, 12 feet long and six feet wide. Distribution transformers look like a scaled down version of power transformers with dimensions of approximately five feet high, six feet long, and three feet wide. Each transformer was individually built. Production was highly labor intensive from the stacking of pre-cut metal pieces to produce the core, to the addition of insulation, to the welding of the housing. Work in process was managed very inefficiently with semifinished transformers or enormous pieces of transformers having to be moved multiple times. There was no integration of design and manufacturing. Mistakes in design were often only discovered upon final testing, which then necessitated a laborious deconstruction of the transformer to correct the problem before its consequent rebuilding.

However, despite ranking near the bottom of the list of ABB's 26 power transformer plants in terms of productivity, Elta's product was price competitive at the time of its acquisition by ABB due to comparatively low wages. Where western European or North American workers in a comparable ABB facility might earn up to US$2,500 per month in wages, Elta's Polish workers earned only about US$350. But, Polish wages were rising and were expected to reach Western levels relatively soon. Productivity had to improve markedly if Elta was to survive.

ABB Elta—Human Resource Management

Historically, employees at Elta were assigned to jobs on an almost random basis with little thought as to the needs of the job or the skills and abilities of the employee. Recruitment and selection processes were simple: applicants who showed up to be hired when there was an opening were hired. Performance appraisal was little more than a yearly ritual in which managers gave their subordinates high ratings and filed the results with the personnel department. These ratings were rarely shared with subordinates and were never used as a development tool. There were also no well-thought-out plans for employee training or career development. The compensation system in place was equally unsophisticated. Blue- and white-collar employees alike were paid salaries, dispensed in cheque or cash on a weekly basis. As stated earlier, wages were highly compressed with top management earning only slightly more than the average blue-collar worker. The human resource system in place created a number of problems for Elta as it struggled to restructure.

Elta's personnel department was typical of that found throughout the Polish economy. An internal ABB study found that Elta's 104-person personnel staff (for the most part long-tenured female employees), was consumed entirely by administrative work including the tracking of absenteeism, tardiness, disciplinary problems and pay administration. Without computerization, these were tedious and laborious tasks. The rest of the time was taken up by myriad other duties including monitoring and enforcing employment laws, reporting company statistics to government offices, organizing workers' holiday excursions and undertaking special projects such as restructuring the employee cafeteria.

After years of significant growth in the post-war period, Elta's employment levels peaked at over 3,000 in the early 1980s, making it one of Lódź's largest and most prominent employers. During the 1980s, however, Elta experienced a number of years of low demand as a result of the deterioration of the Russian economy. As demand from the former Soviet bloc declined precipitously, many Elta employees left the company to find work elsewhere. After its acquisition by ABB in 1992, and on the heels of several years of losses as the Polish economy went through economic shock therapy after 1990, Elta needed to successfully restructure to be able to compete successfully in the deregulated economy. Elta continued to downsize, laying off people in order of reverse seniority. By 1996, employment stood at about 940.

THE NEED TO RESTRUCTURE

When Frank Duggan arrived to head up the T&D segment for Poland in early 1996, he found conditions in Elta appalling, even when compared to his most recent posting in Thailand. He immediately recognized change had to occur and to occur quickly if the Polish companies were to survive. If the management of the companies did not improve dramatically and quickly, ABB Poland would find itself holding a set of uncompetitive companies as their one source of competitive advantage—low wages—was eroded, as wage levels rose to Western levels. (See Exhibit 5 for a summary of ABB Elta's financial performance.) Although an engineer by training himself, Duggan was stunned by the attitudes of the managers and technical personnel he found within his segment's companies. Duggan recounted:

	1992	1993	1994	1995	1996
Revenues (thousand $)	21,997	34,023	39,416	45,266	62,887
Net Profit (Loss) (thousand $)	1,876	1,329	1,606	136	747
Employment	1,911	1,303	1,190	932	951

Exhibit 5   ABB Elta Financial Performance 1992 to 1996

Quite frankly, our managers think empowerment is a load of crap. A survey we did a few months ago told us that. The same survey told us that workers don't want to be empowered either. Basically, the technical people here focus on the technology, not the people. But, come on, people are the only thing we have to differentiate ourselves with. This is old technology. Anybody can buy it. What we have here is nothing different from anybody else.

Elta's condition was not unusual in the companies that ABB was acquiring during the first half of the 1990s in Poland. Observing these conditions, David Hunter, the country manager for Poland, recognized the need for significant restructuring. He knew, however, that it would have to be driven from inside the companies and that it would likely entail a considerable amount of time and resources. His first course of action was to set up an external training organization to which company managers could be sent to develop a number of critical skills needed in the new environment. Not only would managers within the ABB Poland companies require knowledge related to the operation of a market economy and modern business practices, but they would also require English language skills, the language of ABB. To help in this endeavor, Hunter contracted with a consultant to locate an appropriate director for the training centre he envisioned.

The consultant found Artur Czynczyk. Studying for a doctorate in sociology and lecturing at the University of Warsaw in 1989, the then 28-year-old Czynczyk found plenty of consulting opportunities to supplement his meager university salary after the fall of Communism. It was in his role of advising clients on labor-management relations and organizational restructuring, that Czynczyk came to the attention of the consultant hired by Hunter in early 1993.

The Management Development Center (MDC) opened in May 1993 with a threefold purpose: to aid in the development of ABB employees and to facilitate the restructuring of ABB companies; to integrate the various acquired companies in Poland into a country-based organization; and to integrate the ABB Poland organization into the larger ABB global network. Having understood the lack of knowledge in several critical areas—finance, marketing and sales, and human resource management, in particular—Czynczyk and his staff had set about to develop and deliver training to managers of ABB Poland to help them "get up to speed" and begin to proactively change their organizations. Between 1993 and 1996, MDC trained more than 3,000 people during more than 600 program days.

After two and a half years, it became clear that the MDC-developed training was not having a significant effect upon organizational performance. Only a few managers, from any particular organization or area in an organization, came to MDC at a given time. Company presidents perceived MDC as a "corporate" organization designed to achieve "corporate" goals such as integration about which the individual companies cared very little. More importantly, many middle ranking managers faced significant constraints in applying their newfound knowledge in their organizations after their training and were frustrated by their inability to utilize skills newly acquired at MDC training sessions. Eventually, Hunter concluded that additional steps were needed. In late 1995, Hunter asked Czynczyk to move to corporate headquarters as human resource director of ABB Poland. In January 1996, Czynczyk assumed this new position overseeing the human resource management of ABB Poland's 7,500 employees.

Czynczyk realized the stakes involved in restructuring ABB Poland's companies. He also had the experience of operating the MDC behind him and the knowledge of what was needed inside the individual companies. He realized he needed to have access directly into the companies if he was to create the kinds of changes that were required to successfully restructure the companies of ABB Poland. He wondered what he would do and who he would use to lead the change.

NOTES

1. Pronounced "Chinchick."
2. Taylor, W. 1991. "The Logic of Global Business: An Interview with ABB's Percy Barnevik." *Harvard Business Review*, March–April, pp. 90–105.
3. Ibid.
4. Ibid.
5. In Poland, segment managers played a more important role in guiding company policy than did the BA leaders.
6. Pronounced "Woodge" (where the "oo" sounds like the "oo" in wood).

CHINA-CANADA LEAN SWINE PROJECT—CHANGING LOCAL HABITS

Prepared by Tom Gleave under the supervision of Professor Joe DiStefano

Version: (A) 1999-07-07

In November 1995, David Wang, enterprise development specialist with Agriteam Canada, was trying to determine how he could infuse positive and sustainable change at the Xiangzhou Feedmill in Hebei, China. The Feedmill was associated with one of three sites previously selected as test bases for the China-Canada Lean Swine Project (the Project), a cooperative development effort initiated by, and ultimately accountable to, the Chinese and Canadian governments. Wang, a native Chinese who had recently returned "home" after spending several years in Canada, was responsible for enterprise development at the three Project sites. In the short time he had been with Agriteam Canada, he had acquainted himself with the managers and operations at the sites and, subsequently, determined that his most urgent priority lay with the Xiangzhou Feedmill, particularly its approach to sales and market development. After analyzing the situation more closely, Wang had concluded that many of the difficulties he faced were due to attitudes and behaviors that had become entrenched during China's legacy of state

planning. In summarizing the challenge before him, he stated:

> It is clear that one of the most important things we need to do is to educate the Feedmill's management and staff about the Project's objectives, to have them "buy in" to these objectives, and to seek ways to achieve these objectives. This will require these people to undergo a profound reconceptualization of their roles and responsibilities in the workplace. I can sense what will be especially problematic is that they now must ensure that profitability targets are achieved. This is a major departure from the mindset that has existed in so many of China's state enterprises, including the Xiangzhou Feedmill.

CHINA'S ECONOMIC REFORMS AND THE SWINE INDUSTRY

In 1978, China introduced the first in a series of sweeping reforms designed to increase the country's overall development by transforming the country's centrally planned economy into one that was responsive to market forces. Previously, China's state sector was governed by central planners who issued specific quotas for goods which enterprises were obligated to produce, regardless of whether or not supply equalled demand. This left many state-owned enterprises (SOE) insolvent and having to continually ask for bank loans in order to keep the operations open. In what became a fundamental shift in China's economic model, the ruling Communist Party began the reform process by allowing farmers to sell their excess production on the open market provided that their specific quota obligations had been met. The success of these reforms encouraged the government to expand the process to most other sectors in the economy. The result was that, from 1980 to 1995, China experienced an average annual economic growth rate of about 10 per cent. Despite this unprecedented growth, it still faced the daunting challenge of having to feed 20 per cent of the world's population with only seven per cent of the arable land. Therefore, the efficient use of land and feed grains (for livestock production) became a national priority. Accordingly, the Chinese government began to seek viable methods for achieving higher feed conversion ratios (FCR) within its livestock industries, including the swine industry.[1] Increased efficiency in the swine industry was especially critical since China was already the world's largest producer and consumer of pork.

Pork production in China came from three main sources—backyard farmers, specialized pig households (SPH) and commercial farms. Backyard farmers were mostly subsistence farmers who typically raised fewer than five pigs per year, yet collectively produced over 75 per cent of all swine in China. Backyard farm production was slow since most pigs were given "green" (vegetable matter) diets instead of more expensive and efficient commercial feeds. This meant that these pigs required 10 to 12 months of feeding before they reached their average market weight of 100 kilograms, thus yielding a FCR of 5.0.

In contrast, China's SPH and commercial farms had comparatively more disposable income and were, therefore, much more active in using different breeding techniques and feeding programs in the development of their swine. As a consequence, they were able to get their swine to market much more quickly than the backyard farmers. SPH were mainly family-owned businesses that raised over 20 head per year. The use of cross-breeding and commercial feeds allowed SPH to raise their pigs in an average of six to eight months, in turn yielding a FCR of about 4.5. Commercial farms were the most sophisticated players in the industry and enjoyed the benefits of scale economies. Therefore, they were able to make significant investments in genetic breeding techniques and nutritional development programs, as well as food quality and animal disease control measures. The result was that these farms were able to raise their pigs in an average of six to seven months and achieve an average FCR of 3.5.

One of the most notable characteristics of traditional Chinese pigs was the high level of fat content present at the time of slaughter. The lean meat yielded from most Chinese pigs was typically 45 to 50 per cent of the body weight, while most North American and European breeds provided a 60 to 65 per cent lean meat yield. In the late 1980s, the Chinese government began to recognize that the swine industry's FCRs were inefficient, and therefore, it began to solicit international support for the establishment of lean swine industry in China. On the domestic side, the Ministry of Agriculture encouraged the industry's development by offering subsidies to designated counties and farms that produced leaner swine based on fat content targets and improved herd genetics. By 1995, a lean swine industry had been established in many parts of China with the support of various foreign interests, although the level of industry development was still small in comparison to traditional swine farming. Lean swine accounted for about 15 per cent of all swine produced in China, most of which were raised by commercial farms in the south for consumption in China's major cities and for export to Hong Kong.

AGRITEAM CANADA AND THE
CHINA-CANADA LEAN SWINE PROJECT

Agriteam Canada (Agriteam) was a profit-oriented, international development consulting company based in Calgary, Alberta. It delivered a range of services to international financial institutions, governments and private sector projects throughout the developing world. The company was usually involved in all phases of a project's life cycle, including preparation, appraisal, implementation, monitoring and evaluation. Agriteam prided itself on consistently being able to achieve its primary objective, namely the delivery of sustainable benefits to project constituents while recognizing the need to accommodate local customs and conditions.

In 1993, Agriteam won a contract issued by the Canadian International Development Agency (CIDA) to help manage the China-Canada Lean Swine Project, a bilateral initiative co-sponsored by the Chinese and Canadian governments. The objective of the Project was to help China further develop its lean swine industry by transferring and disseminating Canadian knowledge about lean swine genetics, as well as requisite technologies and feeding programs, to China. In addition, the Project was expected to demonstrate that viable swine breeding farms and their associated feed-mill operations could make the transition from being SOEs reliant on public-sector funding to competitive, self-sustaining businesses.

The principal Canadian players involved in the Project were CIDA and Agriteam. CIDA was responsible for managing almost 90 per cent of Canada's overseas development assistance programs. To this end, CIDA contracted with Agriteam to help manage the Project. The main Chinese organizations involved were the Ministry of Foreign Trade and Economic Cooperation, the Ministry of Agriculture, and the Animal Husbandry Bureaus in the three respective municipalities and/or counties where the Project's test bases were established.

The first phase of the Project began with the Chinese and Canadian partners working together to select three swine farms (among China's 24 nationally designated commercial swine breeding centres) as test bases for the Project.[2] It was at these farms that so-called "nucleus" herds of Canadian Landrace and Yorkshire swine were eventually established. Each Animal Husbandry Bureau then opened a Project Site Office (PSO) which was used to coordinate activities among the local farming and feedmill operations, the Ministry of Agriculture and Agriteam. Once the PSOs were established, six key people from each test site were provided with one year of intensive English training before being sent to Canada where they were trained in specific areas of responsibility. Agriteam believed that, after spending several months in Canada, the Chinese staff would be technically prepared to handle the demands of their positions and that their English would be sufficient to communicate with their Canadian counterparts.

In late 1994, Dr. Brian Bedard, a Canadian veterinarian, established Agriteam's Project Management Office in Beijing. Its primary functions were to coordinate the Canadian activities among the three Project sites, as well as provide centralized support to four long-term technical advisors (LTTAs) who were hired by Agriteam over the ensuing months. Each LTTA assumed a specific technical area of responsibility for all three Project sites, and all were stationed in the field. In May 1995, David Wang was hired as Agriteam's LTTA in charge of economics and enterprise development. His mandate included market development and planning, sales program design and training, as well as information gathering and dissemination. His credentials included two graduate degrees from the University of Saskatchewan (located in the heart of Canada's prairie farming region)—an M.Sc. in agricultural science, and an MBA. After signing on with Agriteam, Wang chose to be posted at the Xiangzhou Site because it was near his wife's hometown. The other LTTA stationed at the Xiangzhou Site was Dr. Mary Pierce. Dr. Pierce brought over 20 years of Canadian veterinarian experience to the Project. Her main area of responsibility was in overseeing pig production, including monitoring the nucleus swine herd's health and controlling the spread of disease.

Agriteam's two other LTTAs were Dr. Mark Davis, a Canadian swine nutritionist, and Heather Watkins, a Canadian swine production specialist. Davis was responsible for developing appropriate nutrition and dietary health programs that would ensure that the three nucleus herds (and their progeny) developed normally and healthily. Watkins was responsible for developing production management programs at the three breeding farms. Davis also served as Agriteam's Site Manager at the Neijiang Project Site, while Watkins also served as the Site Manager at Jinhua. Each of the LTTAs received an expatriate compensation package that included a salary equivalent to what they could expect in Canada, an overseas housing allowance, and four weeks annual vacation. In characterizing the working relationship among the four LTTAs and Dr. Bedard, David Wang offered the following remarks:

> Despite the vast distances that often separate us, we still have a very team-oriented spirit. We willingly and openly discuss our ideas with each other, particularly on issues that are very problematic. Even though our discussions often take place on the phone, I still believe that everyone is very accessible. If we do run into a problem which requires one or more of us to travel, there is usually no difficulty or debate. The reception we get at the Project sites is generally warm and friendly, although the Chinese are still a little bit cautious about us. We are still considered "outsiders," but are seen as credible technical experts in our respective fields.

> One of the reasons why we work so well together is because we implicitly trust each others' opinions and decisions. Part of this comes from having vastly different job responsibilities and vastly different skills. And because we spend at least two weeks every quarter travelling to each other's sites, we have had the opportunity to get to know each other quite well, both personally and professionally. This obviously provides us with a high level of comfort in dealing with each other. This also

lends itself well to group decision making. To be sure, even though we each have specific responsibilities, we willingly and openly encourage the input of all Project team members on many issues. After all, the ideas from five or six people are certainly better than one.

In September 1995, "nucleus" herds of the Canadian pig breeds were established at the farming operations of each test site. The partners were expected to work together to ensure that the herds became scientifically sound in terms of genetic pedigree, climatic adjustment and disease control. After these factors were verified, the progeny of the herds could then be sold to other breeders. Once each site could demonstrate that it had established smooth-running pig production and feedmill operations, as well as a strong potential for independent profitability, Phase Two of the Project could begin. This phase would involve replicating the three "model" operations at other commercial farms and feedmills throughout China, as well as attempting to influence Chinese agriculture policy at the national level.

THE YUTIAN PROJECT SITE

The Xiangzhou Project Site was located in Xiangzhou County, one of China's prime agricultural growing regions.[3] The Site's facilities were owned by the Xiangzhou County Animal Husbandry Bureau (XAHB), which reported to the Ministry of Agriculture. The main facilities included in the Project were a newly constructed pig breeding farm, which came equipped with a veterinarian laboratory, and a renovated feedmill. The breeding farm (the Farm) was located 25 kilometres outside of the town of Xiangzhou (population 70,000) and about 200 kilometres from both Beijing and Tianjin, two of the country's largest cities. After it became part of the Project, the Farm switched its focus to breeding Canadian Yorkshire and Landrace pigs. The Feedmill, which was located five kilometres from town, originally operated three businesses under one umbrella company—a feed production facility which produced mainly swine and poultry feeds, a chicken farm, and a plastics recycling plant. In 1995, management moved to focus solely on animal feed production.

To ensure that Xiangzhou's nucleus herd was raised in proper conditions, the Ministry of Agriculture funded the building of several new barns prior to the pigs' arrival. The Ministry also recognized the need to fund a major renovation of the Feedmill for two main reasons. First, in order to ensure maximum production efficiencies, the Canadian pigs required specific feeds that had yet to be produced in China. Therefore, by renovating the Feedmill, the Xiangzhou Project Site would become self-sufficient. In addition, it would also be able to directly supply local farmers who decided to raise the Canadian lean swine breeds. Second, China's Feedmill industry had become very competitive in recent years with the nation's annual livestock feed production growing from two million tonnes in 1980 to 50 million tonnes in 1995. During this period, many producers had made major improvements in their production systems, in turn permitting the manufacture of more diversified and scientifically sound feeds. Thus, the renovation was considered necessary in order for the Feedmill to be competitive in an increasingly market-driven economy. After the renovation was complete, the Feedmill's capacity grew from 6,000 to 10,000 tonnes of feeds per year. Since only 360 tonnes of feed per year were needed to raise the Farm's Canadian swine, most of the excess capacity was expected be used to produce various other swine and poultry feeds, which could then be sold on the open market. The 1995 production level was running at about 2,400 tonnes per year, 60 per cent of which was chicken feed and the remainder pig feed. The Feedmill received an average price of 2,000 Rmb. per tonne for its pig feeds and 1,800 Rmb. per tonne for its chicken feeds. The average net profit margin for both types was five per cent of the selling price. Breakeven sales volume was estimated to be 3,000 tonnes per year assuming the current sales mix. Wang believed that "with

the right people, systems and support, the Feedmill could easily sell all of its capacity in the local market." Wang's reasoning was that there was only one other local feedmill which was inherently inferior to the Xiangzhou Feedmill, and that most of the local demand, including 20,000 tonnes of pig feed alone, was supplied by operations as far away as Beijing. Given the XAHB had a strong presence in the county, Wang believed that the Feedmill had the potential of garnering over 50 per cent local market share.

In addition to the renovations made at the pig farm and the Feedmill, existing space at the XAHB office was converted into a classroom in order to serve as a management training centre. The classroom came equipped with an overhead projector, television and VCR, and was suitable for facilitating both management and customer education seminars.

The Feedmill operation was divided into four departments: production, sales and marketing, accounting and quality control. The person in charge of the long-term planning and overall financial responsibility was Mr. Zhang, a director with the XAHB. Mr. Zhang began his 35-year career with the XAHB as a clerk. In keeping with the common practice of many Chinese government institutions, he had advanced through the management ranks at the XAHB largely because of his years of service at the Bureau. He was due to retire in three years at the age of 55.

Reporting directly to Mr. Zhang was Mr. Liu, the Feedmill's manager and resident animal nutritionist. He came to the XAHB in 1985 after graduating from Hebei Agricultural University with a highly regarded animal science degree. The first several years of his career were spent at the local office of the XAHB where he was engaged in what David Wang described as "daily administration—meaning pushing a lot of paper." In 1989, he was transferred to the Feedmill where he assumed the quality control manager's position, as well as the title of deputy manager. Since he was considered a key figure in the operation, Liu was sent to Canada where he worked in a feedmill for five months in order to learn about Canadian animal nutrition techniques. He returned to Xiangzhou in November 1994 to assume responsibility for the nutritional quality of the Feedmill's products. Two months later, he was promoted to general manager by Mr. Zhang, after the previous general manager retired. Therefore, in addition to his nutrition management duties, which included the supervision of one laboratory assistant, Liu became responsible for day-to-day operating and financial management issues. In describing his feelings about his promotion, he stated:

> I just wanted to cry . . . I didn't want the job at all because I knew we would not be able to meet our monthly payroll obligations. We had 3,000 Rmb. in cash-on-hand, an outstanding bank loan of 800,000 Rmb. and all three operations were consistently losing money, including a 300,000 Rmb. loss at the animal feed production plant over the past year. The thing that really bothered me was I knew the workers would expect their salaries on time, even if the plants were idle and they were not working. This is what is meant by the term "iron rice bowl"—the State is expected to look after its workers, in good times and bad.

Reporting directly to Liu was Mr. Chen, the Feedmill's deputy manager who was in charge of enterprise development. He was responsible for establishing and developing a network of sales dealers, ensuring that farmers and dealers received timely delivery of orders and managing outstanding accounts receivable. He was also expected to gather relevant information that could be used in the development of the Feedmill's marketing programs. Chen was a university-educated economist who, like Liu, had also begun his career with the XAHB as a clerk in 1987. He was later transferred to the Feedmill after it was selected as a Project test site, where he assumed supervisory responsibility for two sales representatives. The representatives were each assigned specific sales territories that were approximately equal in terms of geographic size and the number of resident farmers. Soon after he was transferred to the Feedmill, Chen was sent to Canada

(along with Liu), where he was trained in sales and marketing by Canadian feedmill sales representatives. During this time, he also studied English.

The production manager, Mr. Ding, was responsible for scheduling and supervising production, ensuring that the equipment was performing properly and storing raw materials and finished products. The 45-year-old ex-soldier had no agriculture industry experience before coming to the Feedmill two years previously, after he retired from the army. The Feedmill's accounting department consisted of one accountant and a cashier. The two individuals, who reported directly to the XAHB accounting department, were responsible for handling daily cash transactions and bookkeeping.

In March 1995, Mr. Liu decided that focused management at the Feedmill was necessary, if it was going to become operationally self-sufficient. He, therefore, began to restructure Xiangzhou's operations. To this end, he found an external party who agreed to lease the chicken farm for a "rent" of 7,000 Rmb. per year. He also closed down the plastics plant and transferred the affected employees to the Feedmill. Given the financial situation, he was unable to raise any more funds from the bank. Therefore, he issued an edict to all employees stating that, if they wanted to continue working, they would each need to loan the Feedmill 2,000 Rmb., for which interest would be paid at the end of the year. All but one of the 30 employees complied within the three-day deadline decreed by Liu. The one employee who was unable to raise the 2,000 Rmb. was so distraught over the prospect of losing his job that he threatened Liu that he would continue coming to Liu's house in search of food and shelter. This led Liu to ask Mr. Zhang to transfer the employee to another XAHB operation. This also gave Liu the opportunity to persuade Zhang to approve a 100,000 Rmb. loan from the XAHB to the Feedmill based on the commitment demonstrated by the remaining employees.

With 160,000 Rmb. in available working capital, Mr. Liu believed that he was now in a position where he could make the necessary changes to ensure that the Feedmill produced high quality-low cost feeds. Some of the first measures he took were designed to rectify the quality control issues that had plagued the operation in the past. As the resident animal nutritionist, Liu was intimately aware that the Feedmill lacked a properly equipped and functioning quality control laboratory. This, coupled with the fact that the Feedmill often could not afford to buy high-quality ingredients for its production, had resulted in serious quality control issues. For example, it was widely believed, although never formally proven, that the Feedmill's poor quality feeds had contributed to the deaths of many chickens raised by several local farmers. The Canadian partners acknowledged the gravity of the situation and agreed to fully fund the construction of a new quality control feed analysis laboratory, as well as provide extensive training to Liu and his junior staff. This meant that Liu could expend the bulk of working capital on other items, such as a basic management information system and high quality ingredients. All of the efforts were designed at regaining the confidence of the local farmers.

DAVID'S OBSERVATIONS

David Wang's first mandate with Agriteam was to familiarize himself with the three Project sites. After spending several months surveying the sites and their surrounding market conditions, he concluded that the Xiangzhou Feedmill required the most attention. His assessment was based on his belief that the managers' attitudes and behaviors were resistant to the objectives of the Project. In particular, Wang was concerned that Xiangzhou's managers were impeding the development of a business that was capable of independently succeeding in an increasingly market-driven economy. These problems were manifested in the management's attitudes towards sales and market development. In trying to determine how to proceed, Wang drafted profiles of the three key

managers responsible for the Feedmill's overall performance and market development. He based these profiles on personal observations and discussions he had with the three managers, as well as discussions he had had with other employees. These profiles were as follows:

Mr. Zhang (director—XAHB) typifies the senior level managers found in many State enterprises throughout China. He has worked for the same institution his whole life, and this employer has taken care of all of his basic needs. From the time he was hired as a clerk almost 35 years ago, the Bureau has provided him and his family with housing, medical care services and basic education. As his years of service grew, he was increasingly able to use his "guanxi" (close personal relationships) to help him obtain positions of greater responsibility. I think this is one of the main reasons why he treats all of the Farm and Feedmill employees as if they are members of his extended family.

In terms of his willingness to endorse the Project's efforts, Mr. Zhang has been very stubborn. His basic rationale is that "the Canadian pig is good, but it should adapt to China's climate and the Chinese way of living." I think that this is just an excuse to avoid making any further effort in improving the efficiency of the Farm or the Feedmill. What we have been trying to do is to get people to change their management styles and systems to become more market-oriented. But Mr. Zhang believes that "if the Canadians want something done, they should do it or pay for it." This is so typical of the thinking in China's government institutions—nobody wants to take responsibility for anything and everybody wants to rely on others for money and ideas. Needless to say, trying to effect change through Mr. Zhang is going to be very difficult.

Mr. Liu is an interesting study. He has a very solid education and good technical exposure, but is lacking sufficient management experience. The thing that I find most troubling is that, even though he is only in his early 30s and he has been to Canada, he still has some of the old state enterprise mentality. As a consequence, he is often conservative and resistant to new ideas. He seems unwilling to take responsibility for any legitimate management decisions that need to be made. In fact, when it comes to decision making, he sees only risk and no reward. However, he does try to demonstrate leadership to others when they are not doing their jobs. For example, there are times when trucks come in that require unloading, but none of the workers is willing to help out or they are off sleeping somewhere. This prompts Mr. Liu to unload the trucks himself, even though he is the most senior manager on-site. I think he runs into this problem because many of the workers have been lulled into a false sense of security about their future. They think that the "Gongchandong" (Communist Party) will look after them, even if the Feedmill continues to operate at a chronic deficit. What they fail to realize is that the government is showing signs that it will not be able to support inefficient enterprises forever, and it is only a matter of time before many state workers will need to look after themselves.

Mr. Chen's approach to enterprise development has given me real cause for concern. Despite his training in Canada, he has not created any sales or marketing systems at all. Instead, he continues to run the sales department like a shipping department. This is because he believes it is okay for him and the two sales representatives to sit around and wait for farmers to come to them for sales. The only time they seem to go out is at the end of each month to collect any outstanding receivables. This is clearly unlike the training Chen received in Canada, where the feedmill sales people spend most of their time calling on dealers and farmers. I have urged Chen and the two sales reps not to waste time and to go out and sell, but they simply respond by saying "you have been away a long time—you don't know China anymore." What they say is true in the sense that a lot has changed in China since I first left. But many of the changes are more in line with Western style economics, so I do not feel that I am at a serious disadvantage. Something tells me that this is just an excuse to cover up some strained relations between Chen and Liu. I really don't know what is going on, but I detect some definite tension between the two, and I do not feel that it is my position to be intruding into their personal relationship. The difficulty is that their relationship is affecting business performance.

Another reason why sales levels are unacceptable could be related to the sales team's compensation package. As is typical in most state enterprises, the salespeople have no incentive to go out and sell. Regardless of whether they sell or not, each person is paid 300 Rmb. per month, and they each receive free housing, medical services and education for themselves and their families. Even Mr. Chen is paid only a little more than the two others, and he is given no incentive to see them perform. Salespeople are entitled to a travel allowance of 4 Rmb. for each day that they go out in the field, but they are expected to use their own motorcycles, so the stipend often does not cover the cost.

POSSIBLE SOLUTIONS

In exploring his various options for achieving a more market-driven approach to sales and marketing, David Wang identified four possible solutions:

1. encourage Mr. Liu and Mr. Chen to undertake further management training;

2. urge Mr. Liu to change the sales department's compensation systems;

3. have both managers visit other successful feedmill facilities in southeastern China;

4. encourage Mr. Zhang to consider re-assigning Mr. Liu or Mr. Chen.

Management Training

In considering the management training option, Wang realized that Beijing Agriculture University periodically held two-week seminars related to feedmill management. The curriculum involved technical elements related to production, nutrition and quality control systems, as well as general ideas about selling livestock feeds in China, and cost 1,400 Rmb. per person. By undergoing a comprehensive training program together, instead of separate specialized training regimes (like in Canada), Wang was hoping that both managers would gain a better appreciation of each other's responsibilities and mutual interests. Although Wang was convinced that the training in Canada was very solid from a technical point of view, he was concerned that it lacked some sensitivity towards certain Chinese realities. For example, in China a much greater emphasis was placed upon relationship building, to the point where business associates often needed to spend several months getting to know each other before they formalized any business partnership. This custom had a clear impact on customer development, particularly with local grain dealers. In addition, the ability to service accounts and ensure timely delivery of feeds was much more chaotic in China due to the country's general state of underdevelopment. For instance, much like the sales staff at other feedmills, Xiangzhou's sales representatives (and Mr. Chen) were expected to use either their own pedal bicycles or rural public buses to visit farmers and feed dealers within their territories.[4] In the event that orders were placed with the representatives, it usually took two to three days before they were filled because the Feedmill only had one delivery truck.

Wang did have some reservations about the program in Beijing. First, he was concerned that with both Liu and Chen gone for about two weeks, nobody would be left who could adequately manage the operation. Although Mr. Ding (production manager) would still be in town, his health had become increasingly problematic to the point where he was often unable to come to work. In addition, given Ding's limited feedmill management experience, Wang was also concerned that Ding did not have the basic skills required to manage the operation, particularly if any pressing issue should arise. Second, Wang was also concerned that the sales and marketing training in Beijing might not be very creative in its approach, because of its reliance on marketing and sales theory instead of practical hands-on training. His concern was that this might prevent the managers from thinking about different ways in which they could generate greater sales.

Change the Compensation System

In discussing the possibility of changing the compensation system of the sales department to one that was more incentive-based, Wang found Liu to be quite receptive. In fact, Liu proposed that Chen and the two sales representatives receive 70 per cent of their current salary as their monthly base salary, and that up to 30 per cent more of their current salary would be based on confirmed sales orders. Under this scenario, Liu suggested that each sales representative would receive 5 Rmb. for every tonne of feed sold. Therefore, if a sales representative sold 18 tonnes of feed in one month, he would receive compensation equivalent to his previous salary based upon a 210 Rmb. starting salary, plus a "bonus" of 90 Rmb. Liu also proposed that a penalty, in the form of a salary deduction, be levied on any sales representative who did not show up for work more than three days per month. However, he was unsure what level of penalty would be suitable.

The major concern that Wang had with Liu's proposal was that it did not provide the employees with enough incentive to sell more than 18 tonnes of feed each month, since these people were already accustomed to a lifestyle based on a salary of about 300 Rmb. per month. Furthermore, if all four sales people each sold 18 tonnes per month, it would only amount to 864 tonnes per year, far below the 3,000 tonnes needed to breakeven. Therefore, in response, Wang proposed that the entire sales department move to a system which would see their base salary become 50 per cent of their current monthly wage, along with an unlimited bonus based on 15 to 20 Rmb. for each tonne sold. Wang felt that this was tenable because the current average profit margin was 90 Rmb. and 100 Rmb., respectively, for each tonne of chicken and pig feed sold. He also suggested that Liu and Chen work together to hire more salespeople so that greater coverage of the surrounding markets could be achieved, and to consider buying new motorcycles, which could be purchased for about 7,500 Rmb. In rationalizing his proposal, Wang suggested that "the salespeople need greater incentive to get out of the office. At the same time, we could broaden our scope beyond Xiangzhou to other neighboring counties." The proposal that Wang laid forth was met with a great deal of resistance by both Liu and Chen which, Wang speculated, was "because it was too risky and too expensive for them." This led him to wonder if there was a compromise solution that would satisfy the managers' concerns, as well as ensure that sales would grow sufficiently to see the Feedmill become profitable within the next 12 to 18 months.

Study Tour of Other Facilities

Another option that Wang was considering was asking the Feedmill's managers to accompany him on a tour of several feedmill and farming operations in the southeast province of Zhejiang for a period of 10 days to two weeks. In providing a rationale for this option, Wang stated:

> Zhejiang is another world compared to Xiangzhou. The environment there is much more entrepreneurial and aggressive, and it does not take much convincing for people to want to develop markets. I think this is because the southeast has traditionally been one of the more entrepreneurial regions in China. The feedmills that I have seen in Zhejiang are nothing special in terms of physical resources—what separates them from us is management attitudes. I met one 26-year-old who is running a state-owned feedmill with facilities that are inferior to our own—but he made two million Rmb. last year—and he is confined by the same state restrictions as Xiangzhou. If our managers could witness how these other Chinese are succeeding under similar conditions, I think that they may be inspired to learn more about new management systems and approaches.

Wang acknowledged that a trip to Zhejiang was not without its risks. This was largely because

of the wide cultural, language and historical differences between the regions. These differences had led to widely held, but little discussed, suspicions and mistrust between the Chinese who lived near Beijing and those who lived in the south and southeast of China. These suspicions translated into the northern Chinese often feeling that their southern compatriots placed too high a value on making money, while the southerners often felt that northerners lacked energy and were not very creative.

Another concern that Wang had was the cost—part of which the XAHB would have to bear. Even if Wang drove the managers to the region in an Agriteam van, the total cost for modest accommodations and meals, as well as entertainment expenses and gifts for the hosts, would be at least 5,000 Rmb. Given the financial predicament of the Feedmill, Liu might have a hard time justifying such intangible expenses.

Lobby to Re-Assign Liu or Chen

The final option that Wang was considering was whether or not he should approach Mr. Zhang to have Mr. Liu or Mr. Chen reassigned internally, or possibly transferred to another XAHB operation. Wang felt that several arguments could be made for and against the re-assignment of either manager; however, he also expected to meet some strong resistance from Zhang, particularly if what he recommended meant that the XAHB would need to absorb greater financial costs.

In the case of Liu, Wang felt that it would be in the Feedmill's best interest to have Liu dedicated solely to nutrition management and quality control instead of having to also assume the general manager's responsibilities. Given that Liu had received specialized training in Canada, and given that the Feedmill still suffered from quality control problems, Wang believed that this would be a "natural fit." Wang realized that Liu had not felt comfortable about his recent promotion to general manager, and therefore a re-assignment might make him feel more comfortable. Furthermore, such a re-assignment might also ease the tension between Liu and Chen since there would no longer be a direct reporting relationship between the two men. On the other hand, Wang also recognized that "face" was very important in Chinese society, and that any move which appeared to be a demotion would likely be viewed as a "loss of face" for Liu. Another factor was that within the XAHB there was no obvious successor to Liu who had both feedmill management experience and sufficient English language skills to be able to effectively work with the Agriteam's unilingual LTTAs.

In the case of Mr. Chen, Wang felt that a demotion to sales representative, or transfer to another XAHB facility, might serve as a "wake up call" that the Project's participants were serious about sales and market development. In examining a possible demotion, Wang still needed to be wary of the "face" issue. He also recognized that such a move would not put Chen and Liu on an equal level in terms of managerial responsibility, which was possibly the root of the tension between the two men. What made the re-assignment or transfer more compelling, however, was that Wang had identified a Mr. Xu as a possible successor to Chen as the manager of enterprise development. Mr. Xu was currently working in the XAHB's Project Site Office helping to coordinate the Project's activities, as well as acting as the Site's interpreter. He had previously been sent to Canada at the same time as Liu and Chen. His studies there were largely focused on English proficiency, although he did have some general exposure to swine farming and feedmill management. Over the past several months, Wang had established a good rapport with Xu and he was comfortable that Xu understood and embraced the Project's objectives. The question that remained, however, was how the other employees would respond, particularly the other sales representatives, to a change that was brought about by Wang. He knew that he was still widely perceived to be an "outsider" at Xiangzhou.

DECIDING WHAT TO DO

In trying to create a more market-driven approach to sales and marketing at the Xiangzhou Feedmill, David Wang identified four possible solutions he believed would be effective—although he was still unsure about which option would have the most positive impact. At the same time, he realized that other options existed that he still had not thought about and, for this reason, he was open to any reasonable suggestions. Regardless of how he proceeded, Wang knew that he needed to be very clear about what actions he was recommending and why, if he was to have any hope of making the Xiangzhou Feedmill a Project success story.

NOTES

1. Feed conversion efficiency ratios were common productivity measures used in the livestock industry. The ratio was calculated by dividing the total quantity of feed that an animal consumes in its life by the weight of the animal at the time of slaughter. Therefore, if a pig consumed five kilograms of feed for every kilogram of body weight, its feed conversion ratio (FCR) would be 5.

2. The three farms were "Neijiang" in China's Southwest province of Sichuan, "Jinhua" in the eastern province of Zhejiang and "Xiangzhou" in Hebei, the province surrounding Beijing. See Exhibit 1—Project Organization Chart.

3. Xiangzhou County was about 1,500 square kilometres (30 km x 50 km) in area and was home to about 650,000 residents, most of whom lived on an estimated 150,000 farming households. About 60 per cent of these households were backyard pig farms, with 30 per cent dedicated to backyard chicken farming. The remaining 10 per cent belonged to larger volume pig (i.e., SPHs) and chicken farmers.

4. The sales staff were permitted to use the Feedmill's only motorcycle, unless it was already reserved for other purposes.

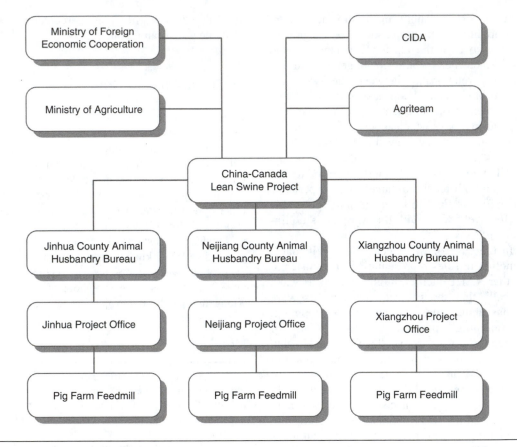

Exhibit 1   China-Canada Lean Swine Project Organization Chart

SALCO (CHINA)

*Prepared by Alan Yang under the
supervision of Professor Joerg Dietz*

Version: (A) 2003-08-19

On Wednesday, November 18, 1998, Dahong Wong, China operations manager of Salco, a globally operating manufacturer of burners, received a call from Don Miller, Asia Pacific area manager at Salco's headquarters in London, England:

Dahong, I just asked for change, not for a revolution. Don't take a machine gun and shoot at everybody. The situation is getting out of hand. We need to meet, when I come to Beijing next Monday.

Miller had hired Wong three and a half months earlier with the mandates of increasing brand equity in China, optimizing channel performance and improving the efficiency of Salco's Beijing office. Wong admittedly felt that he had not made much progress, but he did not understand why. What should he report to Miller in the upcoming meeting?

DAHONG WONG'S CAREER (1990–1998)

After his graduation from Beijing University with a bachelor's degree in business administration in

1990, the then-22-year-old Wong started working as a project manager in the Beijing office of Watson Consulting, an international consulting firm (see Exhibit 1). The office mostly produced customized reports about China for foreign companies. Wong recalled that, after about six months, he felt overqualified, once he had brought his English up to par and had learned the basic frameworks for writing reports. He also viewed himself more as a people person than as an analyst.

In 1992, Wong left Watson Consulting for Denver Pneumatic, a U.S.-based manufacturer, as a sales engineer. As the first staff member of the electric tool division in the company's Beijing office, his task was to sell electric tools

Dahong Wong	
Professional Experience	
Sales Manager, Denver Pneumatic, Beijing, China	**1992–1998**
• Promoted from a sales engineer to senior sales engineer and to sales manager in 18 months. • Developed and led a top-performing sales and support team of 10+ to develop new business and deliver superior value-added services, achieving the highest customer satisfaction. • Built mutual trust and positive working relationship with customers to generate $20 million sales revenues annually, exceeding sales quota by over 30 per cent in four consecutive years and achieving highest level of sales target fulfilment in the whole company.	
Consultant, Watson Consulting, Beijing, China	**1990–1992**
• Conducted market research and presented insightful recommendations on sales and marketing to IKEA and Tetra-Pak; these recommendations were made part of their China marketing strategies. • Organized and conducted feasibility study that led to the successful setup of Sino-Sweden Dairy Training Center, the first foreign-invested project done in China after June 4, 1989, and the Tiananmen Square Massacre.	
Education	
Beijing University, Beijing, China Bachelor of Business Administration	**1986–1990**
Achievements and Interests	
• 1st Prize in a nationwide spontaneous speech contest on free trade • Chief editor of the student magazine *HORIZON*	**1990** **1989–1990**

Exhibit 1   Résumé

to industrial clients and to develop the division. Peter Yu, his supervisor recounted:

> Wong is a born salesman. He has a great business sense and is very convincing. He knows how to approach an issue, when to compromise and what to achieve in a deal. Customers enjoy his personal and humorous style. He also travels like a bee. He always has many leads, talks with many customers, and as a result, he brings in a lot of orders. Customers trust him. Wong also is a "parrot." When he started, he knew very little about technical stuff, but he mimicked other colleagues and customers. Now he sounds like an expert, discussing complex technical issues with grey-haired customers.

By 1994, Wong had been promoted to senior sales engineer and then to sales manager. In 1996, Wong managed a team of six sales engineers, three technical support engineers and one secretary. Wong described the situation:

> My fast promotion to sales manager was nearly unprecedented in the company's history. People used the phrase "riding a helicopter" to describe my career at Denver Pneumatic. I know they were jealous. So what? My performance spoke for itself. I could always "fix" the tough customers, but they could not. Most importantly, Yu backed me up strongly. As a result, I enjoyed great respect from my staff for four reasons: First of all, I recruited those guys. I knew them. They were selected to suit both my personal style and the job requirements. Second, I was here first; I'm like a founder of this office. If you know more stories both about internal politics and customer demands, you have more power. Third, I trained them. They learned a lot from me. Fourth, I could nail down the "tough deals." When you are able to accomplish supposedly impossible missions, your subordinates have no choice but to bow to your legend. How would they ever dare to even imagine "climbing up over my head"?[1]

SALCO

Industry and Company Background

Burners were electromechanical appliances that were designed to regulate combustion applications. Most burners were components of hot-water boilers. They were also used in absorption chillers, industrial furnaces and ovens, ceramic kilns and car painting booths. In recent years, the traditional markets for burners in Europe and the United States had become saturated. But emerging markets in Asia, the Middle East and parts of Africa were growing rapidly.

Salco, founded in the early 1900s in England, was a leading European manufacturer in the heating ventilation and air conditioner industry in Europe. In 1997, Salco built burners in the domestic (201,000 units), commercial (35,000 units), and industrial (1,400 units) segments. Most burners were exported. Robert Johnson, director of the commercial department, commented:

> With a 70 per cent export rate, we are one of the largest burner exporters in the world. We are very strong in Europe, but we are now building a global customer portfolio to diversify our export business. China is the most important emerging market, and I believe that soon it will be the single largest burner market worldwide. Currently, I'm satisfied with our growth there.

Salco China

After entering the Chinese market in 1995, Salco established a Beijing office to support its distributors—initially only Longli Trading Company (Longli), and, starting in 1996, Everest Company Ltd. (Everest) and Kenergy Mechanical Engineering Company (Kenergy)—with marketing-related information and technical support. Salco had exclusive contracts with these distributors, forcing them to carry only Salco burners. The distributors were expected to carry and offer the complete line of Salco burners. As a rule of thumb, the prices for domestic burners ranged between Rmb2,000 to Rmb5,000; for commercial burners Rmb5,000 to Rmb20,000 and for industrial Rmb20,000 and up. The gross margin for all types was roughly between 10 per cent and 15 per cent.

Moreover, each distributor had an assigned territory (see Exhibit 2). Sales in other territories were not allowed. According to the contract, the distributors had three major responsibilities.

Distributor	Province
Longli	Guangdong, Guangxi, Yunnan, Hunan, Jiangxi, Hubei, Fujian, Hongkong, Sichuan, Tibet, Hainan
Everest	Shanghai, Jiangsu, Zhejiang, Shandong, Henan, Anhui
Kenergy	Beijing, Tianjin, Liaoning, Jilin, Heilongjiang, Inner Mongolia, Shanxi, Shaanxi, Hebei

Exhibit 2   Assigned Territories in China

First, they were responsible for the funding of purchases, minimizing the financial risks for Salco. After placing an order with Salco, they had to open a letter of credit through their banks with Salco's bank. That way, the distributors had to purchase the burners from Salco, and their opening banks needed to effect the payment once Salco had dispatched the ordered burners. Second, the distributors were responsible for arranging local transportation and for keeping a "sufficient inventory" at their cost. Third, the distributors had sales and service functions, which included maintenance checks and repairs.

The Distributors

Wei Lam had established Longli as a family business in Guangzhou in 1995 with the sole purpose of selling Salco burners. As Salco's first Chinese distributor, Longli covered 10 southern provinces of China and Hong Kong. Miller had chosen Longli as a distributor because of his long-standing relationship with Lam and because of Lam's deep knowledge of burners and the burner market. Although Longli sold 3,458 domestic, 568 commercial and 52 industrial burners in 1997, it had a reputation among customers for being consistently out of stock.

Everest was a large Chinese trading firm headquartered in Hong Kong. It had subsidiaries in all major cities including Beijing, Shanghai and Guangzhou. Everest had a small but rich territory—the five most developed provinces in China and Shanghai. In 1996, Miller had chosen Everest because it had strong guanxi (connections and networks) in the greater Shanghai area and a strong financial base. Everest's business with Salco burners had taken off immediately. In 1997, it sold 3,075 domestic, 433 commercial and 48 industrial burners.

Concurrently with Everest, Miller had also selected Kenergy, a subsidiary of a state-owned research institute in Beijing, as a distributor. The company had been going through the privatization process since 1996 and, therefore, its management team, which would own it after the privatization, was highly committed to growing the business. Its territory covered that vast area of eight northern provinces and Beijing. Kenergy, which previously had distributed Korean-made burners, had a large customer base and a strong technical sales team. Kenergy's customers were highly satisfied with the after-sales service and technical support, but some customers complained of Kenergy's higher prices relative to those of the other two distributors. In 1997, Kenergy sold 4,354 domestic, 876 commercial and 33 industrial burners.

Despite the territorial arrangements, some customers, mainly those for commercial and industrial burners, checked the prices with all three distributors, in part because a customer's assigned distributor had frequently run out of stock. In addition, all major players in the Chinese burner market knew each other, and Salco was, as competitors and customers acknowledged, the "black horse" among burner manufacturers.

SALCO'S BEIJING OFFICE

In 1998, Salco's Beijing office had three staff members: Don Miller, Jun Yuan and Lilly Pan. Miller, who constantly travelled between the United Kingdom and China as well as other Asian countries, recruited Wong in June 1998 as Salco's China marketing manager, effective August 1, 1998. Wong's responsibilities were to increase brand equity in China, optimize channel performance and improve the efficiency of the office. He was also to be in charge of office operations.

Wong did not find it easy to leave Denver Pneumatic, but he finally chose to "wash his hand in a gold basin."[2] Wong said he sensed that it would be hard to make further career progress without a change. He also noted:

> Moving to Salco was associated with a 50 per cent pay raise. I got the opportunity to learn channel management. It did not matter to me that it had little to do with direct sales. I thought that either way I would deal mostly with people. I "had seen all kinds of birds in the forest"[3]—bosses, subordinates and customers—for so many years. It would be easy for me to survive the three-month probation period.

Don Miller

As the Asia Pacific area manager, the 38-year-old Miller had offices in London, England, and Beijing. He had been in charge of building the Beijing office, and, although he was its chief representative, he was in the office only every one or two months for a few days. When he was in the office, he was typically quiet but friendly, saying that he enjoyed the distance of the Beijing office to the headquarters in London, that "place of gossip and politics." Occasionally, he complained that Salco kept him too busy to have a family and at the same time did not promote him fast enough. Wong began to feel that Miller was waiting for a promotion or an outside job offer.

Jun Yuan

The 29-year old Yuan had a master's degree in science (with a specialization in thermo engineering) from one of China's top universities, where he had held the important position of vice-president of the student body. He had joined Salco two years ago after quitting his job in a state-owned design institute because, as he put it, he did not want to be an engineer. He was the technical manager of the office with the responsibility of providing technical training and counselling to distributors and customers. This responsibility included decision-making authority over compensations to distributors for "epidemic burner defects": a distributor was able to get compensation anywhere from several thousand RMB to several hundred thousand, once approved by Yuan, who had a budget equivalent to two per cent of the year's revenue (revenue in 1998 was US$6.3 million).

Yuan always wore a pair of thick, black-framed glasses that reduced his eyeballs to small black points; he talked at a slow pace. He frequently talked about the large market potential for burners and related products in China and marvelled about the entrepreneurial achievements of his former classmates, who already had made "millions of U.S. dollars." Yuan worked hard and was always the first one to arrive at the office each morning.

Lilly Pan

Having previously worked for three years as a secretary and receptionist in the local offices of multinational companies, the 25-year old Pan was the first local staff member in the Beijing office. She was deeply involved in the process of setting up Salco's Beijing office under Miller's leadership. Pan felt pride in her role and Miller occasionally referred to her as "the co-founder." When Miller first introduced Pan to Wong, he also called her "his most favorite secretary," causing Pan and Miller to smile. Her responsibility was to be the liaison with headquarters. Her main task was the scheduling of deliveries from England: it was largely up to her to determine which distributor's order should be dispatched first, especially during rush seasons when burners were in high demand. She also managed the office's everyday funds.

Pan always started the work day by doing her make-up. At work, she often complained about her lack of time "for her pet doggie Albert, daddy and mommy." She also frequently screamed at janitors, the property manager and employees in other offices.

WONG'S FIRST THREE MONTHS AT SALCO

First Week of August

Wong started working for Salco on Monday, August 3, 1998. After his first day at work, he felt disappointed about the size of his new work environment: "Only 200 square metres and two subordinates," he noted. At the same time, he found this encouraging because, as he said, "With my experience of managing about a dozen people, this office should be a small piece of cake." Wong, Pan and Yuan had lunch together on Wong's first day, which gave Wong a positive first impression of Pan and Yuan. At the end of his first week, Wong noted:

> Yuan and Pan really are great people to work with. Pan is outspoken. She is very communicative in English and Chinese. She really knows how to talk. She also seems to be an independent person who enjoys her lifestyle with her memberships at a couple of beauty salons and fitness clubs. And she is emotional about her work, showing her great commitment to the office. She described with great passion how she helped Miller set up the office, but also almost burst into tears when talking about the distributors, who were "not polite enough" to her. It seemed that she expected me "to teach these arrogant distributors a good lesson."

> Yuan shows great respect for me. He always addresses me as "Manager Wong" rather than "Dahong" or "Mr. Wong." I feel flattered to be treated like this by someone who was the vice-president of the student body at one of China's most prestigious universities. He always works very long hours, saying that this is the advantage of being a single man, who does not have to rush home to cook. Yuan also is so confident and mature, and he has promised to spare no effort to

support me in my mandates. He also told me that my experience is strong enough to deal with the distributors, and he dismissed my concern about a lack of knowledge about burners with a wave and smile, saying that "the manager does not need to have such small dirty skills." He would handle that stuff. Gee, what else could you expect from a good subordinate like Yuan?

Last Three Weeks in August

During in the second week of August, Pan began to arrive one or two hours late to the office each day. Wong thought that her late arrivals resulted from extended parties and dinners. One day, Pan showed up at the office at lunch time. When Wong questioned her during lunch, Pan responded angrily in a loud voice:

I don't have your good luck of sitting in the office from nine to five. If you wish, I'm willing to switch my job with yours. You go dealing with the red tape in the customs and tax offices, and I'll sit in the air-conditioned office, making phone calls. Dahong, you should pay more attention to the distributors, not me and Yuan.

Meanwhile, Yuan ate his lunch and read the day's "Beijing Youth Daily," not reacting to Pan's outburst. Wong was confused by Yuan's behavior, but did not mention it. Moreover, within one week Wong received two faxes from the shipping department at Salco's London headquarters with complaints about: (1) the infrequent responses by the Beijing office, and (2) the large number of mistakes in the shipping information provided by the Beijing office. When Wong spoke to Pan about the faxes, she shrugged and said that "they made mistakes too."

Towards the end of August, Wong planned to visit the distributors. For one of the flights to the distributors, Yuan made about a dozen calls to help Wong find a ticket. Eventually, Wong had the one-week trip scheduled starting August 24. On August 20, when Wong asked Pan to confirm the flights and book hotels for him, she replied that she was not his secretary and that the office did not have the funds to pay for the trip. Wong

was shocked. A secretary at Denver Pneumatic would have never given such a response. Wasn't he supposed to be in charge of office operations? Now he wondered exactly what that meant. He took it for granted that it included control over the office funds, but this had never been formally defined. And didn't Pan know that he was in charge? Did she legitimately think that she had the authority over the office's account? Because Miller was on vacation until September 1, Wong could not get in touch with him. Wong felt that he had no choice but to call the distributors one by one to cancel the trip. Yuan said that he felt sorry for Wong and that it was not just that Wong did not have control over the funds. Tied to the office, Wong continued to spend most of his time reading files to better understand the situation with the distributors. Frequently, he also called the distributors to discuss issues. On the basis of Yuan's sympathy and earlier help in organizing the trip, Wong started to consider Yuan as an ally. He began to confide in Yuan when problems with the distributors, Pan or Miller came up.

First Two Weeks in September

On September 1, Wong contacted Miller, who immediately instructed Pan to release the funds for Wong's business trips. Yet, the funding issue left a bad aftertaste with Wong, who decided that he would raise his concerns in a one-on-one meeting with Miller during Miller's next visit to Beijing in mid-September. From September 8 to 12, Wong finally visited the three distributors in Beijing, Shanghai and Guangzhou.

Wong had mixed reactions to his visits with the distributors. Each distributor seemed to respect him and Salco. The distributors were always very kind to Wong, and they always stressed that they would never want to lose Salco's business. However, they also gave him conflicting information on many issues. Wong had learned from the files that each distributor had engaged in cross-territory poaching, i.e., selling burners in a district that was assigned to another distributor. In a consistent fashion, each distributor always accused the other two of violating the contract first and appeared to be a victim. Another source of confusion was that Pan and Yuan continued to describe the distributors as "rogues and villains" with very low moral standards, who needed to be ruled with an "iron-wrist," but it appeared to Wong that the distributors treated Pan and Yuan with silk gloves. Whenever Wong tried to argue with Pan and Yuan over the distributors, they raised numerous examples to prove Wong's judgment wrong. Wong occasionally was suspicious about Pan and Yuan, but he could not understand why they should try to mislead him about the distributors. On the basis of the examples that his colleagues provided, he felt that they also had a point with their negative assessments of the distributors.

Second Two Weeks in September

On September 15, Miller arrived in the office. Yuan and Pan were excited to see Miller, and Miller made faces when Pan was touching his fresh-cut hair. Yuan gave Miller Chinese herbs believed to enhance a man's potency. Miller noted that he did not need them, but still accepted the gift. Wong thought Miller looked tanned and energetic after his vacation, but also felt Miller's smile at him was a bit forced.

During his one-on-one meeting with Miller, Wong raised his problems in the office. To achieve his mandate of improving its efficiency, he needed more authority within the office, particularly access to funds and the authority to hire and fire staff. He also needed a laptop computer and a cell phone. Miller replied:

> Dahong, the issue of power is a non-issue. As the China operation manager, you have the highest salary in this office and the greatest power. Your colleagues and distributors all know that, and you have authority and access to the office funds. Note, however, that hiring and firing is not the way to run this office. To abuse power is more harmful than not to have it. See, I will not fire you because last month you arrived late in the office three times. And don't worry; I will get you a laptop and a cell phone soon.

Wong felt a chill in his bones, when he heard Miller's response and did not know how to respond. Obviously, Miller had a spy in the office.[4] Wong continued by sharing his opinion about the distributors with Miller, saying that, while they had engaged in contract breaches, overall, the distributors appeared to value Salco's business. Miller's response was that Wong should not jump to conclusions just because the distributors treated him nicely. He asked why Wong would want to be on their side and concluded by saying that clarifying the situation with the distributors was exactly the job for which he had hired him.

Month of October

One morning early in October, Wong found a laptop and a cell phone on his desk. On the same day, Pan also got a cell phone. On another morning, Wong found part of an unsent fax on the fax machine signed by Yuan. It was a synopsis of a business plan for distributing air heaters in China for a European company. When asked by Wong about the fax, Yuan immediately turned pale, explaining that he was "simply helping a friend to send a fax." He said he would not use the office fax machine for his own purposes again.

During the month of October, Wong continued to collect information on the distributors. As he had suspected earlier, cross-territory poaching was the most serious problem. When one distributor sold burners to customers in another distributor's territory, the discount for the customer typically exceeded the 25 per cent limit stipulated in the distributor agreement. The harmed distributor would retaliate by offering even lower prices to "steal" customers in the territory of the infringing distributor. The cross-poaching had several negative consequences for Salco. First, it drove down the prices for Salco burners, which, as Wong thought, harmed Salco's brand equity. Second, customers who had bought their burners from the "wrong" distributor typically did not receive satisfactory after-sales maintenance services. Third, as a result, Salco began to lose its "dark horse" image in the burner market.

Wong found out that Everest accused Wei Lam and his company of "having fired the first shot." Lam, however, argued that he had been the only Chinese distributor in 1995 and that if he sold in other territories, he sold only to his old customers. Lam found that selling to old customers was entirely acceptable, whereas the poaching by Everest and Kenergy was "sheer stealing." Wong commented:

> On the surface, poaching is the result of an "it is okay to feed your cows on your neighbor's grassland" mentality. The issue, however, is more complex. Typically, the distributor who sells the burner also sells the spare parts. The margin on these spare parts is 15 per cent to 20 per cent higher than it is on the burners. If the distributors have a larger base of sold and installed burners, they also have more sales of spares. The problem is compounded by the lack of respect that the distributors have for the contracts. Salco forced these contracts onto the distributors, not understanding that they do not care. In addition, Salco currently uses only three distributors in a country of 1.2 billion people. Inevitably, there are coverage deficits, which customers exploit.

> On top of that, you have to understand that in this new economy, most Chinese entrepreneurs are very concerned about the longevity of their endeavors. Change happens very quickly, leading people to believe that making a quick buck is the right strategy. In that sense, the behavior of the distributors is entirely understandable. On the other hand, if this behavior becomes the new code for society as a whole, then China will face serious economic problems because of a lack of trust. This lack of trust, in turn, leads to higher transaction costs. Unfortunately, as of today, the quick-buck attitude has already spread like a virus. You can hear it everywhere: "use your power as much as possible today before it expires," "planning your business can never catch up with changing your business," and "distant water won't help put out a nearby fire." The incentive systems in many organizations also reflect the short-term mentality: in all likelihood, the distributors' salespersons are paid on the basis of their monthly, quarterly or annual sales, totally disregarding the long-term consequences and indirect costs associated with achieving these sales targets. Of course, the quick-buck attitude comes along with decaying business ethics.

Wong also viewed the distributors' chronic lack of inventory as a problem:

> Inventory requires funding, but the distributors argue that they are short on working capital and cannot afford a large inventory. I believe, however, that the cause of the lack of inventory is the absence of mechanisms for forecasting demand and subsequently fine-tuning the inventory. The folks at headquarters have already repeatedly complained that the Beijing office has "too many rush orders" and "great volatility in its orders." I don't think it's a big deal for our office to build a forecasting model. We would need, however, the co-operation from the distributors. They would have to provide their monthly and seasonal forecasts to us, but they are not doing their homework. They just complain.

The distributors had raised other issues to Wong. Kenergy complained about the lack of training on Salco burners and about frequently less-than-competitive prices; Longli asked for more support in the funding of orders; and Everest found that Salco was not fair on the issue of compensating for epidemic defects.

Month of November

By early November, Wong finished a first draft of a distributor restructuring program (DRP). His analysis had made him aware of the complexity of the situation, but he felt that his mandate of improving channel performance forced him to come up with a quick solution. According to his draft, effective January 1, 1999, distributors would be punished with a one per cent increase in price on their next order if they sold a burner outsider their territory. Moreover, distributors would have to disclose all customer information to Salco, and they would have to provide seasonal sales forecasts, which they had to adjust on a monthly basis. A deviation of larger than 10 per cent in sales volume from the forecast would be punished with a price increase on subsequent orders.

For Wong, this first draft was only a starting point. He found it almost a bit too aggressive and asked for Yuan's opinion. Yuan was very excited at the draft, but said that it was not tough enough. He suggested that Salco keep a "deposit for fines" of US$5,000 from each distributor that a distributor would lose upon violation of a rule. He also asked Wong to include a punishment for "stock-outs" (lack of inventory) in the DRP. Wong accepted these suggestions. Wong also asked Yuan whether he should get Miller's feedback on the DRP. Yuan reminded him what Miller had said in their meeting in September, namely that dealing with the distributors was exactly what he had been hired to do. Subsequently, Wong decided to proceed without consulting Miller, thinking that a successfully implemented initiative would be a great way to impress Miller. Moreover, his three-month probationary period had now passed, and he could not wait for the rabbit to die so that he could catch it.[5] He scheduled a meeting with the distributors for November 18, 1998, in Shanghai to announce the DRP.

On November 18, 1998, all three distributors and Wong gathered in a meeting room of the Hilton Hotel in Shanghai for a full-day meeting. Wong hoped for a positive meeting, noting that the Chinese pronunciation of the number 1118 was "must, must, must, be fortunate." In the morning, Wong and the distributors went through the sales budget for the current year and then proceeded to discuss next year's sales budget. At the beginning of the afternoon session, Wong gave a presentation of the DRP. Bin Kong, an alumnus of the very prestigious Yuan Jun University and general manager of Kenergy, said:

> Mr. Wong, allow me to be direct. Your proposals are fundamentally wrong. We are not your enemy, but your friend. Why should Salco treat us this way? The iron fact is that we have worked hard for Salco and have been so successful. You make a good salary because of us. Without us, you could drink only north-west wind.[6] Get real! We are not beggars, and we can distribute burners for somebody else. I see no reason for passing on customer information to you. You are like a dog who tries to catch mice.[7] How could you convince me that you do not use our information for your own purposes?

Wei Lam from Longli said:

> Manager Wong, how old are you? Thirty years? OK. I forgive you because you are still young. I was far more naïve than you when I was your age. The Cultural Revolution is over; the era of "reporting to Chairman Mao from morning till night"[8] is over. What's the use of these hectic reports? Do you really think they work? Life is short, do something useful, OK?

Sheng Xu, sales manager for Everest, noted:

> Dahong, I appreciate your effort to bring order to Salco's China business. We know that you need performance to justify your salary, but you just can't do things that way. Cross-territory poaching is a problem, but not a serious problem. Everybody has that problem. Our working capital is tight enough; why should I deposit another US$5,000? You have been with Salco for only three months. It's too short a time for you to understand the business. We distributors are much easier to deal with than some people around you. We have been able to fulfil the budget year after year. Don't be too demanding on us. We have problems, as have you. Crows everywhere are equally black after all. There is no perfect company, right?

As Wong listened, he could feel his face reddening in anger and embarrassment. He stopped the meeting and said he would schedule a second meeting soon.

What Next?

Miller called Wong in the late afternoon in his hotel room. The phone call prompted Wong to review his performance in the past three months. He felt as if he was riding on a tiger's back— difficult to pull back. He knew he would be in for a tough meeting with Miller next week. What had gone wrong? Was his analysis flawed? Was his plan flawed? What should he have done to avoid this disaster? Whom could he trust? Wong suddenly recalled Mao's famous motto: "Who is our enemy, who is our friend; this is the most essential question for any revolution."

NOTES

1. Chinese metaphor: to outperform one's boss, take his/her position and to flourish.

2. Chinese metaphor: chose a completely new career path.

3. Chinese metaphor: had a lot of experience in dealing with different types of people.

4. Sun Tze's *Art of War* has a chapter that highlights the use of spies as a winning strategy (Chapter 13).

5. Chinese metaphor: The chance of catching a rabbit that died is very slim. Instead of waiting, one must act to get things done.

6. Chinese metaphor: to have nothing to eat and drink.

7. Chinese metaphor: describes a person who is too inquisitive and cares about things that are none of his/her business (dogs can catch mice, but catching mice is the business of cats).

8. This was a slogan during China's "Cultural Revolution."

DELOITTE & TOUCHE: INTEGRATING ARTHUR ANDERSEN

Prepared by Ken Mark under the supervision of Professor Gerard Seijts

Copyright © 2003, Ivey Management Services   Version: (A) 2004-01-15

INTRODUCTION

It was a rainy September morning. Terry Noble, the Toronto Group Managing Partner for Deloitte & Touche (Deloitte), stretched his back and contemplated the results of the most recent "Pulse Survey" that were just presented to him.

Noble co-chaired the national integration team that was faced with a huge challenge: to develop a company-wide plan to create support materials to aid the Deloitte people in integrating more than 1,000 Arthur Andersen (Andersen) people into their 5,600 person strong organization. Noble's team monitored the integration process through a monthly Pulse Survey, which would allow the team to benchmark unit to unit over time, and to take remedial action if, at specific stages, the integration goals were not attained.

The data that Noble just had seen did not come as a total surprise. In fact, he and the Deloitte senior management team were feeling a certain degree of backlash from a number of people in their own organization. Some Deloitte employees, it seemed, feared that Deloitte management, in its haste to consummate this new deal and welcome Andersen, was forgetting about its own employees. There was an attitude among some employees within Deloitte, the larger organization, that people coming from Andersen were "damaged goods" and that these people should be grateful that they had found a good home. Comments such as "Damn the torpedoes and let's get on with business," and "It's our way or the highway . . . after all, we acquired the Andersen business" began to surface. The cultural issues were showing up in day-to-day behavior. Noble mulled over how he might best address this issue. Should he address it at all? For example, he did not yet know whether the opinions voiced came from a few vocal employees, or if others in the Deloitte organization shared their sentiment. The integration issues were rather complicated because, at the outset, the integration message was interpreted by some as "a merger of two equals."

The Integration

On June 3, 2002, across Canada, approximately 1,000 Andersen people (700 professional staff, 200 support staff and 70 partners) would join Deloitte, effectively creating the country's largest professional services organization. The large majority of these people would be located in Toronto. Noble estimated that the value of Andersen annual billings brought to Deloitte was between Cdn$100 million and Cdn$180 million. If the integration were somehow mismanaged, annual billings would be around Cdn$90 million or even less. However, if the integration were successful, the number would be closer to the Cdn$180 million mark. The combined entity would employ 6,600 people in total, representing annual billings of approximately Cdn$1.1 billion.

A welcome breakfast involving 1,300 people was planned to kick off the integration at the Metro Toronto Convention Centre, followed by a series of introductory speeches. Colin Taylor, Deloitte's chief executive and managing partner, stated:

> Now we're integrating the Andersen people and clients into Deloitte with the same energy, enthusiasm and speed that we brought to closing the transaction. We have a lot of work ahead of us and our goal is to make this transition absolutely seamless for our clients and as smooth as possible for our people.

At Deloitte, "Making a Difference Together" was the vision for the integrated organization that expressed the combined company's commitment to its clients and each other. It also expressed the belief that the integration with Andersen would strengthen existing capabilities. Deloitte included these words in a new logo created to highlight all integration communications. The logo symbolized Deloitte's conviction that, as the number one professional services firm in Canada, it will be even stronger and more successful in the marketplace (see Exhibit 1).

Exhibit 1   Deloitte's New Logo for the Integrated Organization

Source: Company files.

Deloitte & Touche

Deloitte in Canada was part of a worldwide group named Deloitte Touche Tohmatsu. Deloitte Touche Tohmatsu was a Swiss Verein, an association, and each of its national practices was a separate and independent legal entity.

In Canada, Deloitte had 2001 revenues of Cdn$895 million and 5,600 people (including 515 partners). Its main services were four-fold. Assurance and Advisory services provided attest services (financial audits of organizations, rendering an independent opinion). Financial Advisory services included investigative services directed at solving business crime and reorganization services to allow managers to regain control amid organizational crisis—essentially crisis management services. In addition, this group facilitated public offerings of stock or debt, mergers and acquisitions, and performed due diligence work for clients. Consulting-type services were offered to help clients develop and enhance their business strategies. Tax services supported personal and corporate filings as well as advised clients on how to achieve tax savings. Deloitte had offices in all major cities across Canada. The four services listed above were offered in each of these offices.

ANDERSEN

Andersen Worldwide SC, a Swiss Societe Co-operative, was a co-ordinating entity for its autonomous member firms that had agreed to co-operate in the market with a common brand, philosophy, and technologies and practice methods. Thus, each Andersen Worldwide member firm, including Andersen in the United States and Andersen in Canada, had its own governance and capital structure. There were Andersen consultants serving clients in 390 locations around the world.

In 1960, Andersen established its Canadian practice with 26 people. Prior to 2002, it was considered the smallest of the five largest accounting firms in Canada with 1,300 people. At the time of the integration in 2002, Andersen had sized itself down to approximately 970 employees. The firm serviced clients across the country from seven offices located in Vancouver, Calgary, Winnipeg, Mississauga, Toronto, Ottawa and Montreal. It offered services that were very similar to those offered by Deloitte.

Noble was impressed with the Andersen organization in Canada, stating:

> We knew that Andersen had the best litigation record of any professional services firm in Canada. We admired and envied Andersen. At Deloitte, we would often hold Andersen practices up as the industry benchmark, including their tools, skills, marketing, and knowledge management capabilities. Their link to a global network of consultants with expertise in a multitude of areas, and which could be accessed at any given time, was unparalleled.

THE EVENTS THAT LED UP TO THE INTEGRATION

In 1999, Enron had been the seventh largest U.S. company (based on reported revenues). For the last 10 years, it had evolved from a regional natural gas provider to, among other things, a trader of natural gas, electricity and other commodities, with retail operations in energy and other products. In 1998, Enron was number 73 on Fortune's annual list of "100 Best Companies to Work For."

Andersen U.S. provided Enron with internal audit services as well as serving as Enron's external auditor. Although Andersen's international branches were legally separate from Andersen U.S., the Andersen name became a huge liability as a result of the Enron scandal. Andersen U.S. faced a felony charge of obstruction of justice, accused of trying to block a Securities and Exchange Commission (SEC) investigation into Enron's financial disclosures by destroying documents related to the accounting firm's audits.

In statements released to the media, Andersen stated that the action taken against its firm by the U.S. Department of Justice was "both factually and legally baseless." Nevertheless, the damage had been done and the company faced a crisis from which it would not recover.

Enron's collapse and allegations of illegal activity by Andersen created debate around auditor independence and scope of services. Criminal indictment of Andersen U.S. created a negative impact on the accounting profession. One of the questions that persisted in the public arena was whether an accounting firm could objectively perform an audit when it also made millions of dollars providing other services to the same client. Audit firms refuted that an audit could be enhanced by the extra knowledge the firm gained through its consulting arm.

The collapse of Enron and the court of public opinion effectively destroyed the Andersen brand in a few months. In accepting Andersen professionals, some Deloitte managers were concerned that the Enron fallout might carry over to the Deloitte brand.

THE INTEGRATION TALKS

Although it was thought that rival accounting firms—either KPMG or Ernst & Young—already had a deal to acquire Andersen, Deloitte's senior management team was pleasantly surprised when it found out that Andersen's U.S. tax practice had urged Andersen Canada to talk to Deloitte. In the United States, Andersen's tax practice had aligned with its Deloitte counterpart. In the first week of April 2002, Andersen Canada contacted Deloitte to begin integration talks.

On Friday, April 12, 2002, Deloitte completed a memorandum of agreement with Andersen Canada to integrate its practice with Deloitte. This transaction was subject to a due diligence review, partner approvals by both firms and regulatory approval. Because of its size, the transaction was subject to regulatory review by the Competition Bureau under Canada's Competition Act. Noble stated:

> The run-up to the integration has been a disaster for Andersen. Despite their Canadian client base and staff remaining loyal, their phones were not ringing. Even when they were the frontrunner for new business, potential clients would almost always shy away from them. The day-to-day press surrounding Andersen was very negative.

Andersen had been negotiating with KPMG and the media was speculating that a deal was imminent. Deloitte took a less public profile, avoiding speculation. Because both sides moved rapidly, the transaction was completed in six weeks. Closing the transaction quickly was critical because a lengthy process increased the risk that a major client and a significant number of talented professionals would be lost.

Alan Booth, director of National Human Resources with Deloitte, explained that the detailed negotiations on people and other critical integration issues proved very challenging due to various reasons, including:

1. Strict limitations on contact between Deloitte and Andersen to permit regulatory review;

2. Imminent systems loss at Andersen set to occur when it would withdraw from Andersen worldwide;

3. Numerous rumors that fed anxiety among people in both organizations; and

4. Co-ordination of messages to people from Deloitte and Andersen was greatly affected by the necessary contact limitations.

On Friday, May 31, 2002, at 5:00 p.m. Pacific Daylight Time, Andersen Canada "went dark." All its systems including phones, e-mail, and personal computers (PCs) were disconnected from the worldwide Andersen network. This signaled the beginning of the actual integration of the former Andersen people into the Deloitte organization.

THE NATIONAL INTEGRATION TEAM

A national integration team consisting of 12 individuals was formed to lead the integration. The team was co-chaired by Terry Noble, who had trained as a chartered accountant with Andersen in Canada, and Russ Robertson, Andersen's managing partner. Colin Taylor, Deloitte's chief executive, knew that both men had been classmates at the Western Business School undergraduate program at The University of Western Ontario, London, Canada, in the 1960s, and thus knew each other. Equal numbers of Deloitte and Andersen personnel were represented on the team. An effort was made to ensure that key people from both sides were involved, in order to guide the integration challenge. For example, heads of functions, integrating officers from the five Deloitte offices, and several "thought leaders" were part of the team.

The main goals of the integration team were to put together a company-wide plan for integration and to create support materials (e.g., "A Primer on Organizational Grieving") to aid the Deloitte people in integrating their new colleagues into their organization. Geographic and functional leaders were to execute the plan with support from national functions such as human resources (HR), information technology (IT) and finance. For example, HR was, to a large extent, responsible for communicating the Deloitte policies, as well as explaining administrative items, such as compensation, the incentive plan, pensions and benefits, and promotion policies. The IT department was responsible for issues such as a seamless transition of e-mail, telephone systems and computer applications. There were significant differences in the IT systems between the two companies. However, by the end of Monday, June 3, 2002, almost all new Deloitte people had their PCs reconfigured to the Deloitte systems, a new phone number, a connection to the network and new business cards to give to their clients.

The national integration team would monitor the integration process through an Internet-based Pulse Survey, which would allow the team to benchmark unit to unit over time, and to take immediate remedial action if in the various stages the integration goals were not attained. The Pulse Survey was conducted every month with a random sample of people from both organizations. For example, among other things, people were asked:

1. How they felt the integration was proceeding overall;

2. If they were kept informed about the personal impact integration would have on them;

3. Whether they perceived fair treatment;

4. Whether their ability to do their jobs was maintained or increased;

5. If they felt that client service levels were being maintained or improved; and

6. If they intended to remain with Deloitte one year into the future.

Participants in the survey were also given the opportunity to provide open comments on how they felt the integration was progressing, or any other message they wanted to communicate in confidence. All offices received detailed feedback on all of the questions that were incorporated in the survey. The questions that were part of the Pulse Survey are listed in Exhibit 2.

Once every two weeks, the managing partners of each of the five Deloitte offices would convene for a conference call to share updates and ideas, some of which resulted from the Pulse Survey. Best practices were identified, and integrating officers were encouraged to implement these practices across offices. Last, the integration team would present status updates to Deloitte's executive committee and board of directors.

Commenting on the Deloitte and Andersen integration, in November of 2002, Noble stated:

Integration is easier said than done. It takes at least three to five years. There is often a strong tendency on the part of those leading the change efforts to declare victory too soon. Early on we need to outline the present and future state of our organization. Cultures do not change that quickly. We do not want a situation where the integration unravels and turns into a bad business deal because we did not manage the process, people, systems, and business fundamentals in a proper fashion.

One thousand Andersen professionals are joining us and not one of them had chosen to be part of our organization. The integration is like an arranged marriage and we have to find common ground. The Andersen people probably have a fear that they will be taken over and their identity and sense of value will be lost. I'm sure that they are not prepared to let that happen.

There are workplace productivity issues that we will have to manage. At first, the Andersen people will be busy getting used to their new titles, new surroundings, and new colleagues. Many people will be concerned with "me" issues: my office, my promotion, my salary, my computer, my role and responsibilities, and so forth. While they have all that to sort through, our job is to figure out how to mitigate the productivity drop. A significant drop in our productivity could tie up the organization for years.

Of course, we want to be able to retain all of our clients—particularly those that are brought in by Andersen. We want our new clients to be proud of their association with Deloitte and confident in the ability of the combined entity to deliver quality and excellent service. Our combined client base needs to be convinced that Deloitte will not be affected by the aftershocks of the Andersen events in the U.S. We cannot afford to slip on our client service delivery. Otherwise there would not be enough work for our people.

RISKS IDENTIFIED BY THE INTEGRATION TEAM

As Noble saw it, the real challenge for the Deloitte and Andersen organizations was to

No.	Questions
1.	Overall, the integration is going well.
2.	The firm is committed to making the integration as smooth as possible for our people.
3.	I am being kept informed about how the integration will affect me.
4.	I am being treated fairly during the integration.
5.	My ability to do my job effectively has been maintained or improved as a result of the integration.
6.	I am confident dealing with client questions about the integration.
7.	Client service levels have been maintained or improved as a result of the integration.
8.	My clients are feeling positive about the integration.
9.	I intend to be with D&T one year from now.
	Overall score.

Exhibit 2   Pulse Survey Questions

move beyond the integrated HR and IT systems toward a unified, market-leading organization. The actual successes achieved in the marketplace would hold the combined entities together. For example, financial success served as glue and, as Noble observed, would all but ensure that partners felt they had shared in the success of the transaction. Essential to the long-term success of the integration, therefore, was that individuals would see (or feel in their pocket) that investing significant resources in the transaction, time and money, was indeed worth it. Noble believed that the Andersen people would be blamed if the combined organization missed the financial targets that it intended to achieve. Such scapegoating would detract from the integration efforts.

Noble identified the top three risk factors that threatened to derail the success of the integration: cultural misalignment and subsequent conflict, insufficient integration and lack of organizational synergies. Exhibits 3 and 4 describe the method and results of the cultural assessment

that was conducted in July 2002 to determine the differences between the Deloitte and Andersen cultures.

The results of the assessment revealed how each organization viewed itself, the "other" organization and the challenges of the integration. The cultural gaps between members of the two organizations identified critical organizational issues that required special attention from the national integration team. It was quite clear that people from Deloitte and Andersen were different from an organizational culture point of view.

Noble elaborated:

The Andersen organization is being told that they will join a new organization. They would not have volunteered to integrate with us if not for the crisis that occurred in the U.S. Will they be enthusiastic about the integration? Some of them may be. However, others may not completely understand why we do things in a certain way here at Deloitte. Addressing the differences between the two cultures was essential to successfully guiding the integration.

228

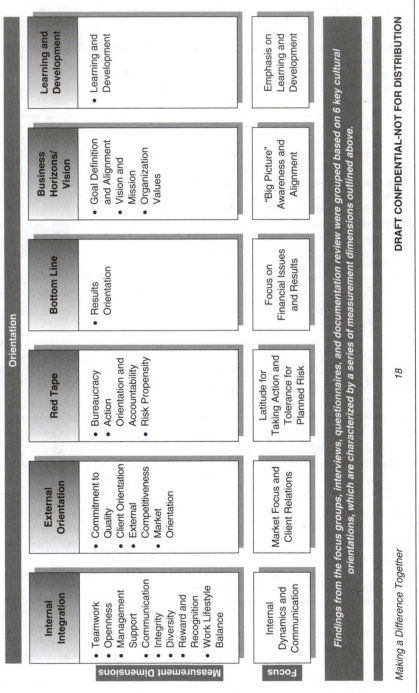

Deloitte &
Touche

Methodology/Framework

Orientation

	Internal Integration	External Orientation	Red Tape	Bottom Line	Business Horizons/ Vision	Learning and Development
Measurement Dimensions	• Teamwork • Openness • Management Support • Communication • Integrity • Diversity • Reward and Recognition • Work Lifestyle Balance	• Commitment to Quality • Client Orientation • External Competitiveness • Market Orientation	• Bureaucracy • Action Orientation and Accountability • Risk Propensity	• Results Orientation	• Goal Definition and Alignment • Vision and Mission • Organization Values	• Learning and Development
Focus	Internal Dynamics and Communication	Market Focus and Client Relations	Latitude for Taking Action and Tolerance for Planned Risk	Focus on Financial Issues and Results	"Big Picture" Awareness and Alignment	Emphasis on Learning and Development

Findings from the focus groups, interviews, questionnaires, and documentation review were grouped based on 6 key cultural orientations, which are characterized by a series of measurement dimensions outlined above.

Making a Difference Together   18   DRAFT CONFIDENTIAL–NOT FOR DISTRIBUTION

Exhibit 3   Methodology Used to Test Cultural Alignment Between Deloitte and Andersen

Source: Company files.

Deloitte & Touche

Overall Assessment

CULTURAL SYNERGIES

Dimension	Degree of Alignment
Commitment to Quality	⊕
Client Orientation	⊕
Teamwork	⊕
Communication	⊕
Openness	⊕
Integrity	⊕
External Competitiveness	⊕
Results Orientation	⊕
Risk Propensity	⊕
Vision and Mission	⊕

CULTURAL GAPS

Dimension	Degree of Alignment
Bureaucracy	⊕
Market Orientation	⊕
Diversity	⊕
Action Orientation and Accountability	⊕
Learning and Development	⊕
Reward and Recognition	⊕
Organizational Values	⊕
Work Lifestyle Balance	⊕
Management Support	⊕
Goal Definition and Alignment	⊕

Legend: Degree of Cultural Alignment

Low	⊕ ⊕ ⊕ ⊕ ⊕	High

Ten areas were identified as having either a moderate or low degree of cultural alignment. The remaining ten areas revealed a relatively high degree of cultural alignment.

Making a Difference Together 19 **DRAFT CONFIDENTIAL-NOT FOR DISTRIBUTION**

Exhibit 4   Results of Cultural Assessment

Source: Company files.

The great payoff will be, that if we do this right, and utilize the talent of Andersen employees, we will not only become the best professional services firm, but also the largest in the country.

Ultimately, this is a talent play for us. We've got the best 1,000 people coming into our organization fully trained. We have to figure out how we can get their commitment to us and to serve our clients. We want the Andersen people to be proud of their new organization.

We will lose people, but we want to lose them for the right reasons. People may have goals or values that are different from the ones espoused at Deloitte. However, we don't want to lose people because of poor interpersonal treatment.

THE SEPTEMBER MEETING

The data from the Pulse Survey (the third since June of 2002) that Noble had received earlier in the morning confirmed, at least to some extent, what he had been hearing through the grapevine. The data suggested that a number of Deloitte employees feared that Deloitte management, in its haste to consummate the deal with Andersen and welcome the new employees, was forgetting about its own people. Some elements within the Deloitte organization did not understand the amount of attention given to the Andersen people, whom they viewed as "damaged goods." Comments indicating that it was time for all people involved in the integration to "get on with business and focus on the market" began to surface.

However, Noble was not certain of the number of individuals that shared such views. Were these the concerns of a few vocal people? Or did these individuals voice what many others in the Deloitte organization were thinking? Clearly, this was not the kind of feedback he was hoping for. The results from the Pulse Survey led Noble to contemplate how he and his colleagues from the integration team could best deal with the cultural differences in the short term. In his words:

> There is the naive view that a new culture will be formed with relative ease. I doubt it. Cultures involve deep-seated beliefs. For example, at Andersen, there had always been a strong drive to focus on the clients' needs above everything else. In contrast, at Deloitte, while acknowledging the importance of commitment to quality and the client's needs, there was also a focus on employee issues.

> A Frenchman and an Englishman will always retain their culture. But they can learn to work together to achieve a common goal. Or can they really?

> It takes a lot of effort and patience to help new behaviors and practices grow deep roots.

In Noble's mind, this was a complex issue to manage. Furthermore, there were a number of situational constraints on actions that could be undertaken to address the issue. For example, Noble and his integration team had to contend with the fact that people were constantly on-site at the client's business. How then should managers work to resolve tensions that might arise between the two cultures? Moreover, taking the people from the two organizations to an off-site location to deal with the issue of cultural differences would certainly affect billable hours. Were we prepared to do that? On the other hand, addressing these and other issues in a timely and proper fashion could make the difference between being a good organization versus being a great organization. True integration would be hard to achieve without the knowledge, skill and, above all, the commitment of the Deloitte people. It was 10:29 a.m., and Noble got up to go to the meeting with the integration team.

PETA's "Kentucky Fried Cruelty, Inc." Campaign

Prepared by Professors
Gerard Seijts and Michael Sider

Version: (A) 2004-03-29

September 2000 was a very good month for McDonald's: on September 6, 2000, People for the Ethical Treatment of Animals (PETA), the world's largest animal welfare activist group, announced a one-year moratorium on its McDonald's campaign. For six years, PETA had been demanding, very publicly, that the world's best-known burger chain dramatically improve its treatment of the chickens, cows and pigs raised and slaughtered for its restaurants.

The animals McDonald's called "food," PETA claimed, were grossly abused. If dogs and cats received similar treatment, those responsible would be subject to legal action. PETA's views had been prominently exposed in *The Washington Post* by reporter Daniel Zwerdling, who had also appeared on National Public Radio's "All Things Considered" and "Talk of the Nation" to discuss PETA's campaign. A prominent British lawsuit by PETA against McDonald's, threatening letters to Jack Greenberg, McDonald's chief executive officer, verbal attacks at shareholder meetings, and a plethora of bloody parodies of McDonald's most prized marketing ideas—"Unhappy Meals" passed to children outside McDonald's restaurants colorfully illustrating how McDonald's chickens live their entire lives crammed five to a cage in cages the size of a desk drawer; media-friendly "Cruelty to Go" advertisements showing bloody cows' heads above captions asking "Do you want fries with that?" (see Exhibit 1)—had brought McDonald's to its knees: the company agreed in August 2000 to some of PETA's demands, and PETA, hoping to encourage further compromises, backed off.

Encouraged by its success, PETA set its sights on other major restaurant companies, all of which, PETA claimed, made their profits from the pain and suffering of fellow creatures. Kentucky Fried Chicken (KFC), and its parent company, Yum! Brands, Inc. (Yum), was one of the next companies targeted.

Yum! Brands Inc.

Yum, headquartered in Louisville, Kentucky, was the world's largest quick-service restaurant company. It had nearly 33,000 restaurants around the world in more than 100 countries. Yum operated KFC, Pizza Hut, Taco Bell, A&W All American Food (A&W) and Long John Silver's. The company had been an independently publicly owned company since October 7, 1997, when it spun off from the Pepsi-Cola Company (PepsiCo), who owned and franchised the KFC, Pizza Hut and Taco Bell brands. In 2002, the company changed its name to Yum from Tricon Global Restaurants to reflect its expanding portfolio of brands and its ticker symbol (YUM) on the New York Stock Exchange (NYSE).

KFC, Pizza Hut, Taco Bell and Long John Silver's were global leaders in their respective restaurant categories. Yum's global system sales totaled more than US$24 billion in 2002. The chairman of the board, CEO and president of Yum, David C. Novak, had served in this position since January 2001. Novak previously worked for KFC, Pizza Hut and Pepsi-Co. He held a bachelor's degree in journalism from the University of Missouri.

Yum's Vision and Founding Truths

Yum dedicated itself to putting a smile on the faces of its customers throughout the world. It wanted its restaurants to offer customers food that made them want to return, and service that put them first. The company believed a smiling customer had lifelong loyalty to the brand, and thus trained its employees throughout the world to be fanatically devoted to customer service. Employees were trained to respond to customers, rather than just listening to them, and to show they cared for them. In order to empower its employees, Yum made the general managers of each of its restaurants their most important leaders. In turn, general managers ran their restaurants as if they were their own—indeed, as if they were Yum's only restaurant. Yum looked to each restaurant for the operational discipline and marketing innovation that bespoke this sense of devoted ownership.

KFC Corporation[1]

KFC, based in Louisville, Kentucky, sold fried chicken all over the world. It had a 45 per cent market share of the fast-food chicken business. It tailored its chickens to customers' increasingly diverse tastes, offering original recipe, an extra-crispy version of the original for those who liked their chicken well-fried; chicken strips

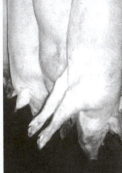

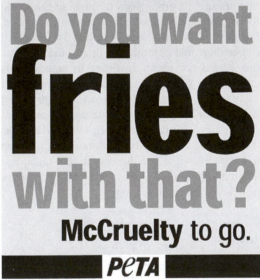

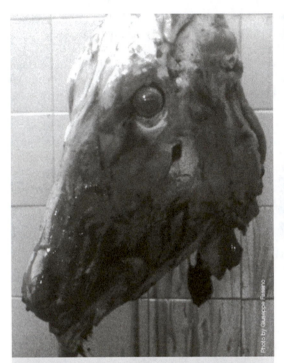

McCruelty to go.

In 1997, McDonald's was found "culpably responsible" for cruelty to animals in a court of law. Despite appeals to the company, McDonald's has failed to take even one tangible step to reduce animal suffering.

Here are just three examples, among many, of McDonald's indifference to animal suffering:

■ **Chickens raised for McDonald's** are crammed into crowded, filthy warehouses with less space per bird than a standard sheet of paper. This overcrowding causes disease, suffocation, and heart attacks.

■ **Some breeding pigs raised for McDonald's** live their entire lives in cement stalls, unable to turn around, lie in a comfortable position, or nuzzle their babies.

■ **U.S. federal standards for slaughter** say that all animals should be fully stunned before their throats are slit, but McDonald's has no mechanism in place to penalize slaughterhouses that consistently skin and dismember conscious animals.

McMisery
In 1997, the British High Court found McDonald's responsible for cruelty to animals. What has McDonald's done in response? **Nothing.**

WHAT YOU CAN DO TO HELP:
■ Please write to McDonald's and urge the company to take steps to lessen the suffering of the animals killed for its restaurants.
Jack Greenberg, CEO
McDonald's Corporation
1 Kroc Dr.
Oak Brook, IL 60523

■ Go vegetarian! Call **1-888-VEG-FOOD** for a free vegetarian starter pack, and check out **www.MeatStinks.com** for more information on PETA's negotiations with McDonald's and on this campaign.

Do you want fries with that?
McCruelty to go.
PeTA

PeTA PEOPLE FOR THE ETHICAL TREATMENT OF ANIMALS
501 FRONT ST., NORFOLK, VA 23510 • 757-622-PETA
www.peta-online.org

Exhibit 1   PETA Advertisement
Source: Company files.

(the long, boneless chicken "tenders" well-liked by children); and, most recently, "popcorn" chicken, small, popcorn-sized balls of fried, boneless chicken served in a bucket to resemble movie-theatre popcorn. Hungry—and health-conscious— patrons could purchase salads, beans, mashed potatoes and other side dishes to accompany their chicken entrees.

KFC's founder, Colonel Harland Sanders, born September 9, 1890, actively began franchising his chicken business in 1955, at the age of 65. He took his fried chicken recipe to restaurant owners, and, on a handshake, they agreed to pay him a nickel for every fried chicken they sold. By 1964, he had more than 600 franchised outlets for his chicken in the United States and Canada. In 1966, KFC went public. It was listed on the NYSE in 1969. KFC was taken over by Heublein Inc. for US$285 million in 1971 and became a subsidiary of RJ Reynolds Industries Inc. in 1982. PepsiCo bought KFC from RJ Reynolds in 1986 for US$840 million.

KFC served more than a billion chicken dinners annually, and had more than 11,000 outlets in more than 80 countries around the world. At the end of 2002, it operated 5,472 outlets in the United States. KFC served more than eight million customers each day. In the United States alone, 26 million people per week visited a KFC restaurant.

People for the Ethical Treatment of Animals[2]

PETA, an international non-profit organization based in Norfolk, Virginia, was founded in 1980 by Ingrid Newkirk, its current president, and Alex Pacheco. PETA had branch offices in San Francisco, Boston, New York and Washington, D.C. PETA had people working from their homes or rented office space in many cities. It had international offices in London, Stuttgart, New Delhi and Hong Kong.

PETA, the largest animal rights organization in the world, operated under the single principle that animals are not ours to eat, wear, experiment on or use for entertainment. PETA educated

policy-makers and the public about animal abuse and promoted an understanding of the right of all animals to be treated with respect. It also worked through undercover investigations, research, animal rescue, legislation, special events, the involvement of celebrities, consumer boycotts and direct action. PETA focused its attention on the four areas in which the largest numbers of animals suffer the most intensely for the longest periods of time: in factory farms, in laboratories, in the fur trade and in the entertainment industry.

The International Grassroots Campaign Department was responsible for co-ordination among the various local and international offices to facilitate grassroots activism. Local offices, however, had considerable autonomy in initiating actions that served the welfare of animals. PETA was funded almost exclusively by the contributions of its 750,000 members; it received no government support. Contributions in the fiscal year 2001/2002 totaled US$16,443,110.[3] The annual membership fee was US$15, but members were free to contribute more. PETA received uniformly high ratings from charity watchdog groups for spending less than 25 per cent of its budget on administration and fund-raising (e.g., most employees earned less than US$25,000 a year).

A significant number of PETA's staff members—about 150—were vegetarian or refrained from use of animal-derived food or products altogether. Being a vegetarian or vegan, however, was not a condition for employment or membership. Nevertheless, no animal products were allowed in PETA buildings. Most PETA members were young to middle-aged people with a high school or college degree. Anybody who was interested in animal rights and welfare was welcome to join PETA.

PETA had earned a reputation for its strong commitment to its goals and its bold pressure tactics. PETA had been responsible for numerous accomplishments:

- PETA uncovered the abuse of animals in experiments in 1981, launching the precedent-setting Silver Spring Monkeys case. PETA's actions resulted in the first arrest and conviction of an animal experimenter in the United States on charges of cruelty to animals, the first confiscation of abused laboratory animals and the first U.S. Supreme Court decision for animals in laboratories.

- PETA's undercover investigation of a huge contract testing laboratory in Philadelphia and PETA's subsequent campaign led to Benetton's permanent ban on animal tests—a first for a major cosmetics company. Other leading companies, such as Avon, Revlon and Estée Lauder, followed suit. Gillette announced a moratorium on animal tests after PETA's 10-year campaign. In 2004, PETA listed more than 550 cosmetics companies that do not test products on animals.

- PETA was able to convince General Motors Corporation not to conduct crash tests on pigs and ferrets.

- PETA released undercover photographs and videotapes showing ducks being violently force-fed on a foie gras farm in New York, resulting in the first ever police raid on a U.S. factory farm. Since this action, many airlines and restaurants dropped foie gras from their menus.

- In another precedent-setting case, a California furrier was charged with cruelty after a PETA investigator filmed him electrocuting chin-chillas by clipping wires to the animals' genitals. The American Veterinary Medical Association denounced the killing method, saying it causes animals to experience a heart attack while fully conscious. In another undercover exposé, PETA videotaped a fur rancher injecting minks with weed killer, causing them to die in agony. Both farms ended these killing methods.

- GAP Inc. agreed to stop using leather from India and China after PETA members protested in its stores. J. Crew, Liz Claiborne, Clarks and Florsheim also agreed to stop selling Indian and Chinese leather. PETA persuaded 40 other companies, including Nike, Reebok and DaimlerChrysler, to place a moratorium on the purchase of leather from India, where, they claimed, animals were transported in bone-breaking conditions and skinned alive.

- PETA convinced Mobil, Texaco, Pennzoil, Shell and other oil companies to cover their exhaust stacks after showing how millions of birds and bats became trapped in the shafts and were burned alive.

- Following PETA's five-month "Murder King" campaign, Burger King announced that it was taking action to ease the suffering of the animals raised and slaughtered for its restaurants. The company responded by conducting un-announced inspections of its slaughterhouses, requiring that hens be given greater space in cages and stopping the purchase of hens from suppliers who starve the birds to shock their bodies into another laying.[4]

Indeed, PETA has had a profound effect on the manner in which multi-billion-dollar corporations treat animals. In 1995, *The Washington Post*[5] concluded that because of PETA "labs have closed. . . . Many designers have stopped using fur. . . . Rules, laws have changed. . . ." *The Virginian-Pilot*[6] stated that PETA "has cajoled, bullied and embarrassed world-famous fashion designers, research hospitals and medical schools into changing their policies. . . ." The *Globe and Mail*,[7] in 2003, wrote:

> fur coats, once the most tangible signs of one's success, were virtually outlawed through PETA's small acts of terrorism . . . and an enormously successful ad campaign that featured models and actors declaring that they would rather go naked than wear fur. . . .

Many of PETA's actions were aggressive and had a touch of sensationalism. Said PETA's Michael McGraw:[8]

> We sort of operate here under the observation that we're living in a tabloid age. Things have to be sensational and flamboyant to get attention. We really play into that.

Attracting media attention was the job of PETA's campaigns department—it had one of the largest staffs at the organization's headquarters. Media coverage translated into donations, volunteers and clout. PETA's media savoir faire had contributed to a large extent to its success. However, a number of people found some of the actions PETA initiated to be provocative and even offensive, and it is questionable whether these actions created goodwill with the general public. For example, in 2000, Rudolph Giuliani, mayor of New York, announced that he would end his campaign for the U.S. Senate because he had been diagnosed with prostate cancer. PETA then put up billboards depicting Giuliani with a milk moustache over the caption, "Got Prostate Cancer?" The message was based on research suggesting that dairy products may be linked to the disease. Newkirk made no apologies to those who found the advertisement insensitive or cruel. In her own words:[9]

> It didn't occur to me that this was hurtful to a man like Giuliani, who is, like is in a way, a press slut. . . . He's out there all the time, just doing what he needs to do to further his agenda.

> I believe we should be—and I say that at staff meetings—a lean, mean fighting machine. This is not a rest home for people who just have warm feelings about animals.

PETA's take-no-prisoners strategies have angered a growing group of people. For example, J.P. Goodwin, founder of the Coalition to Abolish the Fur Trade, lashed out at PETA, charging that its "goofy stunts" are turning people off and obscuring the movement's core issue—animal suffering.[10]

PETA, KFC AND THE POULTRY INDUSTRY[11]

The poultry industry in the United States was one of the most successful sectors in agriculture. Chicken consumption surpassed beef consumption in 1992; it had already surpassed the consumption of pork in 1985. The poultry industry had enjoyed a remarkable period of growth for at least two reasons. First, health-conscious Americans were eating more chicken. Second, chicken meat was economical relative to competing food items. For 2003, consumption of chicken in the United States was estimated at about 81 pounds per person.

In 2004, more than 90 per cent of all chickens raised for human consumption in the United States had been produced by independent farmers working under contract with integrated chicken production and processing companies. Most of the other 10 per cent were company-owned farms. KFC purchased its chickens from 18 different suppliers who collectively operated 52 farms around the United States: contacts with suppliers included a specified amount of chickens at an agreed upon price. Suppliers or growers thus avoided market risk. These suppliers were independent and controlled their own operations (e.g., housing facilities, utilities, labor and other operating expenses, such as repairs and maintenance). KFC had little or no formal authority to dictate to the suppliers how they conducted their business (e.g., how to raise or transport chickens). Similarly, KFC did not own or operate any processing facilities (see Exhibit 2).

The National Chicken Council (NCC), based in Washington DC, was the national, non-profit trade association representing the U.S. chicken industry. The NCC promoted and protected the interests of the chicken industry and represented the industry before Congress and federal agencies. NCC member companies included chicken producers and processors, distributors and allied industry firms that accounted for approximately 95 per cent of the chickens produced in the United States. The NCC argued that:

> Assuring the physical well-being of chickens being raised and housed is a high priority of today's broiler industry. It is vital to the success of companies because top-quality food can be produced only from top-quality birds that have been treated properly. Carefully formulated feed, plenty of clean water, adequate room to grow, professional veterinary attention, and proper handling are all important to flock management and the production of high-quality food products.

But, to PETA, the industry guidelines were baggy and imprecise. The NCC's acceptance of weak evaluative terms, such as "adequate" and "proper" allowed too much room within the industry for abuse of poultry. Relying on scientific studies by poultry experts, such as Dr. Ian

The commercial chicken industry has become a sophisticated and efficient vertically integrated industry. Through the process of vertical integration, chicken processors and members of the allied industry, who provide products and services to the poultry industry, work together to produce the high quality, nutritious products consumers have come to expect.

A typical vertically integrated broiler (or meat-type chicken) company today consists of several production stages combined under one company in an efficient operation. The following is a brief description of the various stages in the production of chicken products.

Primary Breeder Company—Development and reproduction of strains of chicken that meet the requirements of chicken producer/processing companies are the responsibility of Primary Breeder Companies (PBCs). These companies maintain diverse populations of chickens that are used for breeding purposes. Often beginning with selected lines, also referred to as the pedigree lines, chickens are multiplied over several generations to achieve desirable characteristics such as abundant white meat and efficient feed conversion. Breeder chicks with the appropriate mix of desirable characteristics are then sold to integrated chicken firms.

Feed Mill—Chicken companies own feed mills that convert raw materials such as corn, soybean meal, vitamins and minerals into finished feed according to very specific formulas developed by poultry nutritionists. Over the course of 6 to 7 weeks required to grow broiler chicks to market weight, the feed given to the birds is formulated into 4 or 5 different phases to meet the changing nutritional requirements of the birds as they grow.

Breeder Farm—Often breeder farms are operated by contract growers who raise the breeder chicks to adult birds. Breeding hens and roosters are kept under tight biosecurity on breeder farms to produce fertile hatching eggs for the integrated company. The offspring of breeder parents will then be raised to become broilers for the market.

Hatchery—A hatchery is a specialized facility designed to hatch fertile eggs received from breeder farms. Fertile eggs are placed in incubators and carefully monitored to ensure that correct temperature and humidity levels are maintained throughout the entire incubation period. Eggs are automatically turned in the incubators hourly to keep the embryo from sticking to the shell. Towards the end of incubation, the eggs are placed in hatching trays where the chicks hatch out by pecking their way through the large end of the egg. The chicks are inoculated against disease either while they are still in the egg on the eighteenth day of incubation or shortly after hatching.

Growout—The newly hatched chicks are transported to growout farms where independent farmers raise them to market weight under contract with the company. The company provides the chicks, feed, and any necessary pharmaceuticals; the farmer provides the growout house, water, bedding ("litter"), electricity, and his own management skill. In a few cases, the broiler company owns and manages its own growout houses, but the contract arrangement is more typical.

The chickens' diet consists of feed made mainly from corn and soybeans. Feed may contain compounds that prevent disease and promote growth of the animal by improving its intestinal flora. Feed does not, however, include any hormones or steroids. Under regulations of the Food and Drug Administration, no hormones or steroids are allowed to be given to chickens, and none are used in U.S. chicken production. Pharmaceuticals approved for animal use by the Food and Drug Administration are used to treat outbreaks of illness if they occur; if medication is used, there is a withdrawal period before slaughter. The chickens reach market weight of approximately five pounds in six or seven weeks and are collected to be taken to the processing plant.

Processing Plant—At the plant, chickens are stunned unconscious by a low-voltage electrical charge and are then humanely killed. The feathers, feet and head are removed and internal organs pulled for inspection by USDA. Inspectors look for signs of poultry disease and for manufacturing defects, such as broken wings. After inspection, the carcasses are immersed in ice-cold water to reduce their temperature to 40 degrees Fahrenheit to inhibit bacterial growth. After chilling, whole chickens are packed for distribution or cut into parts.

Exhibit 2   Production Processing in the Vertically Integrated Chicken Industry   *(Continued)*

Processing plants operate under Hazard Analysis and Critical Control Points (HACCP) principles to reduce potential hazards from microbiological, chemical and physical sources. Plants also operate under USDA Pathogen Reduction rules to improve the microbiological quality of the product. Some plants are on a system in which plant employees conduct sorting of processed chickens for defects under USDA oversight.

Further Processing—Further processing plants are specialized operations or plants that receive whole chicken or cut-up parts and perform a variety of further processing steps, such as cooking, breading, or marinating.

Transportation and Marketing—Chicken products are transported in refrigerated trucks from processing and further processing facilities to market outlets such as supermarkets, foodservice operations, distributors and other market channels to reach domestic and overseas customers.

Whether the product is a whole bird, cut-up parts, or a further-processed item, the industry continually seeks to produce products that meet changing consumer demands. Vertical integration within the poultry industry gives producers greater control over the production of quality products that successfully meet consumer wants and needs in an attractive, timely, and efficient manner.

Exhibit 2   Production Processing in the Vertically Integrated Chicken Industry

Source: National Chicken Council Web site.

Duncan from the University of Guelph and Dr. Temple Grandin from Colorado State University, PETA had come up with a list of very precise and measurable improvements it wanted to see implemented as industry standards, and, until the industry made these changes, PETA would continue to attack its practices.

And so, in the words of Dan Shannon, co-ordinator of PETA's campaign against KFC, stonewalled by an industry that refused to take its demands seriously, PETA "turned to consumers and instituted a broad-based public pressure campaign to bring about changes." KFC was the target of this campaign, because this company was responsible, in PETA's eyes, for particularly egregious cruelty to chickens:

> KFC's chickens are denied everything they would like to do and are grotesquely abused, as well. Each year, more than 700 million KFC chickens are consumed worldwide. Before the chickens are slaughtered, they are crammed by the tens of thousands into filthy warehouses, with no access to fresh air or sunlight. Many don't even make it into the KFC bucket because they die prematurely from dehydration, respiratory diseases, bacterial infections, crippled legs, heart attacks, and other serious ailments. They are given three times as many antibiotics as cattle or human beings in this country, so

that they will grow as quickly as possible and be able to survive the horrible conditions that might otherwise kill them. When the birds are sent to slaughter, their throats are cut, and they are often run through scalding hot water (for feather removal) while they are fully conscious.

> We support any action that will help reduce animal suffering, even those that can't save animals' lives, but "only" make the way they are treated a bit less miserable or make their deaths less cruel. We don't stop there, of course—our goal is the abolition of the meat industry, but we certainly won't pass up the chance to make improvements for animals simply because it's not all we'd hope for.

Around the same time, PETA began to put pressure on the NCC to adopt a list of quantifiable animal welfare recommendations or make public any list of such animal welfare recommendations that it already provided to its members.

A Shot Across the Bow

On April 25, 2001, a year and a half after calling off its campaign against McDonald's, PETA's Bruce Friedrich, vegan campaign Coordinator, wrote to Cheryl Bachelder, president and chief concept officer of KFC, U.S.A., Mark Cosby, chief operating officer (COO) of KFC, U.S.A., and David Novak, Yum's CEO, to warn them that PETA was "looking ahead to [its] next target"— KFC (see Exhibit 3). In his letter Friedrich pointed out that while many of KFC's competitors had convened advisory panels to help them investigate the welfare of animals raised and slaughtered for their businesses, KFC appeared completely uninterested in the issue. PETA, Friedrich wrote, would rather not engage KFC in a campaign, but if the company refused to put together an animal welfare panel and begin to look into the issue of how to raise and slaughter their chickens more humanely, all the leaflets, action alerts, posters,

---

April 25, 2001

Cheryl Bachelder, President & Chief Concept Officer
KFC, U.S.A.

Dear Ms. Bachelder:

I am writing on behalf of People for the Ethical Treatment of Animals (PETA) and our more than 700,000 members and supporters.

I am sure you are aware of PETA's successful campaign to convince McDonald's to improve the welfare of many of the animals killed for its restaurants (read all about it at McCruelty.com), and our present campaign to compel Burger King to follow suit (www.MurderKing.com). This latter campaign has already resulted in hundreds of demonstrations, including events in all 50 states and more than a dozen other countries. We have people leafleting weekly or monthly in more than 100 cities across the country.

I'm writing to ask why KFC, even as McDonald's, Burger King, and Wendy's convene animal welfare panels to discuss animal abuse, and even as McDonald's and Wendy's are auditing slaughterhouses and making animal welfare improvements, does nothing at all? I am happy to put you in touch with the consultants who are assisting these other corporations, should you wish that to happen.

As you must know, chickens raised for your restaurants lead lives of unmitigated misery, from their births to their violent deaths. As just two examples, chickens now grow 6-to-7 times as quickly as they would naturally, but their hearts, lungs, and legs cannot keep up, so they frequently suffer lung collapse, heart failure, and crippling and painful leg deformities. At slaughterhouses, many chickens are literally boiled alive as they reach the scalding tank used for hair removal while still fully conscious. Will KFC, as McDonald's and Burger King have, convene an animal welfare panel to address issues of particular animal suffering and how to abate it? And will KFC, as McDonald's has, work on the issues of chicken catching and slaughterhouse cruelty?

Business and agricultural consultants tell us that Burger King will be forced to capitulate in the not-to-distant future. In anticipation, we are looking ahead to our next target (for leaflets, action alerts, posters, billboards, T-shirts, articles, and so on). We have no desire to engage KFC if there is action on the part of the company. I am happy to discuss what KFC & Tricon can do in this regard. I hope to hear from you soon. Please call me any time at 757-622-7382.

Sincerely,

Bruce G. Friedrich
PETA

cc: Mark Cosby, Chief Operating Officer, KFC, USA
David C. Novak, CEO, Tricon Global Restaurants

Exhibit 3

billboards, T-shirts and media releases PETA was now preparing would be dedicated to KFC and its cruel treatment of chickens. After all, Friedrich wrote, "chickens raised for your restaurants lead lives of unmitigated misery, from their births to their violent deaths." They "now grow 6-to-7 times as quickly as they would naturally, but their hearts, lungs, and legs cannot keep up, so they frequently suffer lung collapse, heart failure, and crippling and painful leg deformities." At the slaughterhouse, "many chickens are literally boiled alive as they reach the scalding tank used for hair removal while still fully conscious." It wasn't hard to see the threat in Friedrich's letter underneath the politely measured prose: convene an animal welfare panel, involve PETA in its decisions or we'll expose the blood and guts of your dirty business to the people who eat in your restaurants.

Friedrich's letter drew a quick response. On May 24, 2001, Jonathan Blum, senior vice-president of public affairs, met with Friedrich to discuss PETA's concerns. Blum told Friedrich that he believed in being "honest, down-to-earth, easily approachable, and easy to reach," and said that Tricon wanted to maintain an open dialogue with PETA on the issue of animal welfare. He also let Friedrich know that Tricon had contacted Dr. Temple Grandin, head of both McDonald's and Burger King's animal welfare panels, and would meet with her the week of June 11 to discuss who would be best to sit on a Yum animal welfare panel. Grandin, he said, would also review Yum's present animal welfare guidelines, even though the company already included an animal welfare component in all its contracts with its suppliers. Blum said that Yum realized its present guidelines were not good enough and wanted to "raise the bar" for animal welfare in the poultry industry. He also promised to keep PETA informed about the company's progress on this issue at every stage in its development. For his part, Friedrich let Blum know that if the company honored its commitments, PETA would not launch a campaign against it. As Blum left the meeting, Friedrich gave him some reading material: a scientific report on the animal welfare concerns of electrical stunning of chickens.[12]

Over the next three months, Friedrich and Blum spent several hours on the phone discussing the composition of Yum's intended animal welfare panel. Friedrich was allowed to suggest the names of several poultry scientists whom he believed could provide Yum with an objective view of its current animal welfare guidelines and give unbiased advice to the company in its creation of future guidelines. He also asked Blum again that PETA be allowed to sit on the panel, or, at the least, to attend some of their meetings, but received no commitment from Blum on this matter. However, communication between the two representatives was cordial and productive.

Blum continued to tell Friedrich that Tricon "believe[s] in open communication," saying in one e-mail "while I can't tell you we'll always agree . . . we'll always listen and discuss." Friedrich was cautiously optimistic. By August, he by and large approved of the people the company had on its panel, including Dr. Ian Duncan, along with several poultry experts unattached to the industry, but he was concerned that time was beginning to fly, and wanted the new panel to meet as soon as possible. Still, both men were happy enough with the company's progress that Friedrich was content to turn all media enquiries about KFC's animal welfare problems over to Blum, and Blum, for his part, agreed to talk to the media about these issues.

Blum's casual and friendly mid-August e-mail to Friedrich suggested the beginning of a mutually beneficial relationship:

> Thanks for the update, Bruce. Hope you're having a good summer. It's OK for [the press] to contact me. I'll also be calling [PETA] today as our invitations went out two weeks ago to the council and we're waiting on their response. We think they'll accept, and I'll let [you] know who (sic) we invited. Also, we're scheduling the first meeting in September. So, all's moving in the right direction.

Indeed, in early September, Blum's invitations to prospective panel members having been accepted and Yum's new animal welfare panel having been constituted, Blum invited Friedrich and PETA's lead scientist, Dr. Steven Gross, to suggest animal welfare proposals to the panel, allowing PETA the input for which Friedrich had been asking for several months. Friedrich and Gross jumped at the chance, sending Blum a lengthy report requesting major changes to KFC's treatment of its poultry, including:

- Replacing current chicken-killing methods with gas killing,
- Installing cameras to enforce humane standards in all slaughterhouses,
- Implementing mechanized rather than manual chicken catching prior to transportation, avoiding the broken leg bones that commonly occur when chickens are caught and thrown by hand into packing crates,
- Providing chickens with more room in which to grow, exercise and engage in their natural activities (such as perching and seeking out shade),
- Stopping forced rapid growth and use of drugs for non-therapeutic purposes; feeding chickens an analgestic drug to reduce the pain,

- Phasing out the use of the wire cages that destroy chickens' feet, and
- Establishing effective, objective audits of its breeding and killing facilities, audits accompanied by real penalties for failure.

Over the next six weeks, though, PETA heard little from KFC, despite several requests to hear about the panel's response to their requested changes. On October 30, Friedrich faxed Blum a letter expressing his concern that Tricon had "stopped updating PETA on [its] progress." Friedrich reminded Blum that Blum said "when we met and in subsequent conversations that [he] wanted to work with [PETA] and that Dr. Grandin and the others on [the] panel would brief [PETA] as to progress." Friedrich also reminded Blum that, since that assurance, PETA had not criticized the company in the media and had even directed media the company's way "with a positive nod." The same day, Blum sent Friedrich the following response (see Exhibit 4 for the full letter):

From: Blum, Jonathan
Sent: Tuesday, October 30, 2001 10:23 AM
To: "Bruce Friedrich"
Cc: "Steve Gross (E-mail)"; "Joy Mench (E-mail)"; "Ian Duncan (E-mail)"; "Adele Douglass\(Business Fax\)"

Subject: RE: Wondering what happened . . .

Bruce,

Thank you for your letter. Our advisory council is in the process of doing its due diligence. They are reviewing and discussing policies, external recommendations (including PETA's) and industry practices and proposals. They are working toward a year-end goal of proposing new guidelines for KFC with regards to poultry welfare. Once a recommendation has been proposed to KFC's senior management, it will be reviewed, discussed and then next steps will be determined. That may include adoption of the proposal in sum or part depending on the specifics of the proposal, ease of implementation by suppliers and importantly, cost implications. We will certainly let you know of any decision taken, or any questions about your recommendations. In the meantime, I thank you for your ongoing interest.

Sincerely,

Jonathan Blum

Exhibit 4   Blum's October 30 E-mail to Friedrich

Source: PETA Web site. Accessed September 15, 2003.

Thank you for your letter. Our advisory council is in the process of doing its due diligence. They are reviewing and discussing policies, external recommendations (including PETA's) and industry practices and proposals. They are working toward a year-end goal of proposing new guidelines for KFC with regards to poultry welfare. Once a recommendation has been proposed to KFC's senior management, it will be reviewed, discussed, and then next steps will be determined. That may include adoption of the proposal in sum or part. . . . We will certainly let you know of any decisions taken. . . . In the meantime, I thank you for your ongoing interest.

Later, PETA was to post this e-mail on its Web site with the following caption: "Yum! informs PETA that its animal welfare panel is still only having discussions and holding meetings and is not making any changes in the way animals are treated."

Skirmishes

In PETA's eyes, Yum accomplished nothing in the next year-and-a-half. Friedrich wrote to or phoned Blum regularly, emphasizing at every turn his dissatisfaction with being excluded from the advisory panel and his frustration at the lack of information from KFC about the panel's discussions. KFC (usually Blum) continued to reply to all of Friedrich's communications, but insisted that they couldn't share specifics with PETA. In July 2002, Blum wrote to Friedrich to tell him that new guidelines were in place, audits had been held, and "all suppliers passed this self-audit." Friedrich responded by asking for the evidence, and stating "we're not convinced that anything you've done has helped a single animal." As the summer came to an end, and KFC refused to share the specifics of its new guidelines and the evidence to support its claims of a successful audit, Friedrich began to use the word "fraud" to describe what PETA saw as KFC's ongoing attempt to misinform PETA, the media and the public about its attempts to "raise the bar" for animal welfare.

For its part, KFC thought it was still acting in the spirit of "open and honest communication." It had posted its new guidelines very visibly on its Web site, where, it insisted, "we only deal with suppliers who maintain the very highest standards and share our commitment to animal welfare."[13] "Birds," the guidelines stated, "have to be clean and healthy when arriving for slaughter." Suppliers can't use growth hormones, and "must have clean chicken houses with appropriate space and proper ventilation." The company, it said, provides incentives to its catching crews not to harm birds when catching, and transport and holding of birds "have to be humane." In addition, in the slaughterhouses, all birds have to be killed quickly and without pain. As for PETA's specific requests, on January 7, 2003, KFC issued a news release stating that its animal welfare council had reviewed PETA's recommendations for change (e.g., gas killing, mechanized transport and more space for its chickens to grow in) "and determined that the majority of them are impractical and not based on sound science" (see Exhibit 5).

Open Warfare

On January 6, 2003, however, PETA, fed up with what it saw as KFC's lack of open communication, public misinformation and outright stonewalling on change had already announced a campaign against the company to the media in a news event replete with bloody descriptions of the cruelties of KFC's animal factories and a "Kentucky Fried Cruelty" video that supported its claims. PETA told the press:[14]

In May of 2001, Jonathan Blum, senior vice president of Yum! Brands, KFC's parent company, told a PETA representative face-to-face that KFC already had a comprehensive animal welfare program but that it planned to "raise the bar" on animal welfare. Yet he could not point to a single standard, and 21 months later, KFC standards are still sorely lacking. The company has formed an animal welfare advisory board and touted its progress, but the board hardly ever meets, and KFC

KFC Denies PETA Claims

Company Cites Established, Comprehensive Animal Welfare Program Including Strict Enforcement, Animal Welfare Advisory Council and Unannounced Audits

LOUISVILLE, Ky. (January 7, 2003)—KFC Corporation dismissed allegations made by PETA today, stating that KFC has an established and (sic) comprehensive Animal Welfare Program. KFC has developed and implemented specific, quantifiable guidelines for the treatment of chickens by its suppliers at processing facilities. The Company has engaged outside experts to conduct regular unannounced audits at its poultry suppliers to ensure full compliance with KFC's Animal Welfare Policy. Failure to comply with these guidelines could result in KFC's termination of a supplier's contract and relationship with KFC. The guidelines were developed in consultation with KFC's Animal Welfare Advisory Council which consists of leading scientists and academics in the field of animal welfare.

"KFC is committed to the well-being and humane treatment of broiler chickens," said Dr. Joanne Plichta, Vice President, Research and Development, KFC Corporation. "Our Animal Welfare Council has established a set of quantifiable guidelines that have been implemented in our supplier processing facilities. The experts on our council have also reviewed several PETA proposals and determined that the majority of them are impractical and not based on sound science," Dr. Plichta added. The Council will continue to review proposals from outside groups and provide KFC with an independent perspective on each.

Under the guidance of Dr. Temple Grandin, one of the world's foremost experts in the field of animal welfare, KFC is conducting unannounced audits to ensure that its suppliers are complying with guidelines. "KFC and its Animal Welfare Council have established very specific, quantifiable broiler processing facility guidelines," said Dr. Temple Grandin. "I am working closely with KFC as it implements its audit program to ensure supplier compliance with those guidelines," added Dr. Grandin.

"KFC's Animal Welfare Advisory Council contains some of the leading experts in the field," said Adele Douglass, Executive Director, Farm Animal Services, American Humane Association. "That Council has helped KFC develop sound, science-based guidelines for poultry processing facilities, and I'm pleased that KFC is using Dr. Grandin to conduct its audit program to ensure compliance," Douglass said.

"In our view, KFC, through its Animal Welfare Advisory Council, has been an industry leader in establishing specific, enforceable poultry welfare criteria for our processing facilities," said Dr. Ellis Brunton of Tyson Foods. "They have also been instrumental in developing effective and reasonable farm-level welfare guidelines for the poultry industry," Dr. Brunton stated.

In addition to its own initiatives, KFC is helping to spearhead the current effort by the National Council of Chain Restaurants, the Food Marketing Institute, and the major supplier trade associations, to develop industry-wide, comprehensive guidelines for the humane treatment of beef, pork and poultry on farms. Our expectation is that these industry-wide guidelines will be completed in February.

"We also believe it is important to develop farm-level welfare guidelines that are consistent across the industry. We will continue to work with our welfare council as well as through the NCCR and FMI process to accomplish this goal," said Dr. Plichta.

"KFC has been instrumental in helping initiate and lead the process we are now engaged in to develop comprehensive, industry-wide guidelines for farm animals" said Terrie Dort, President of the National Council of Chain Restaurants.

KFC's Animal Welfare Council is comprised of: Dr. Temple Grandin, Colorado State University; Dr. Joy Mench, Director of the Center for Animal Welfare, University of California (Davis); Dr. Ian Duncan, Dept. of Animal & Poultry Science, University of Guelph, Ontario; Adele Douglass, Executive Director, Farm Animal Services, American Humane Association; Dr. Bruce Webster, The University of Georgia; Dr. Ellis Brunton, Senior Vice President of Science & Regulatory Affairs, Tyson Foods and Jim Ayers, Director of Research & Quality Assurance, Goldkist, Inc.

KFC Corporation, based in Louisville, Ky., is the world's most popular chicken restaurant chain specializing in Original Recipe®, Extra Crispy™, Colonel's Crispy Strips® chicken and Popcorn Chicken with home-style sides and freshly made chicken sandwiches. Since its founding by Colonel Harland Sanders in 1952, KFC has been serving customers delicious, already-prepared complete family meals at affordable prices. There are over 11,000 KFC outlets in more than 80 countries and territories around the world serving some 8 million customers each day. KFC Corporation is a subsidiary of Yum! Brands, Inc., Louisville, Ky.

Exhibit 5   News Release

Source: KFC News Release, January 7, 2003. Accessed on KFC Web site, September 15, 2003.

refuses to implement or even discuss the array of reforms that its members have supported. Furthermore, KFC has completely ignored PETA's detailed list of sorely needed animal welfare improvements, preferring instead to take baby steps on the issue of chicken slaughter, while doing nothing at all to decrease the abuse of chickens on farms or during transportation.

PETA called on consumers worldwide to campaign against KFC, and said it would give away hundreds of thousands of the leaflets, posters and stickers that journalists had already received in their media packs to activists around the world. The campaign, they announced, would be international, with massive efforts planned throughout the world, "wherever there are KFC stores and people who care about cruelty to animals."

And efforts there were. It took PETA only two weeks to get in contact with Jason Alexander of Seinfeld fame, KFC's popular spokesperson, whose amusing pitches for the company's chicken had entertained millions worldwide (two of his ads had been voted among the top 20 ads of 2002 by a renowned advertising industry newspaper). In May 2003, Alexander met with PETA President Ingrid Newkirk to discuss PETA's concerns, and, according to PETA, told her "I am your ally." PETA leaked its meeting with Alexander to *The Washington Post*, which discovered that Alexander's contract was not to be renewed by KFC. Even though Alexander insisted the parting of ways was friendly, PETA was reported by the *Post* as saying that Alexander "either fell on his sword for the birds or got fired because he stood up for chicken rights." His statement about his amicable relations with KFC during his departure was, PETA insisted, typically Seinfeldian, "a classic non-denial denial." KFC and Alexander's agent remained mum throughout the affair, telling the *Post* they would send written statements and nothing more. By July 2003, PETA had the high-profile support of Canadian Ryan Gosling (*The Believer, Murder by Numbers*), singer Chrissie Hynde of *The Pretenders*, who was arrested along with Newkirk in a protest at a Paris KFC,

and, most notably, Sir Paul McCartney, who signed an open letter to David Novak published in the *Louisville Courier-Journal*, the largest newspaper in Yum's hometown.

In addition to its celebrity campaign, PETA sent letters to Yum! Brand companies worldwide, asking them to investigate the issue of animal welfare in the company's factories worldwide. PETA enlisted the support of animal right's groups in other countries (for example, in Canada, The Canadian Coalition for Farm Animals and The Animal Alliance of Canada) to put pressure on the brand. They called Bachelder at her home, where Bachelder's daughter was able to listen surreptitiously to the conversation, and began to write to Novak at his home address. Novak began to travel with bodyguards, but even still was unable to stop German animal rights activists from dousing him in fake blood and real chicken feathers at the opening of Yum's first A&W in Hanover in June of 2003. "KFC stands for cruelty in our book," Friedrich told the media. "There is so much blood on this chicken-killer's hands, a little more on his business suit won't hurt." PETA took legal action, pressing the Food Safety and Inspection Service to investigate reports of animal cruelty in factories that supplied KFC with chickens, and filing a lawsuit in the California Superior Court accusing KFC of false advertising.

In August 2003, when KFC was in the process of revamping its ads in the wake of parting with Alexander, PETA sent letters to two advertising agencies urging them to withdraw from the bidding for KFC's advertising account. In the letters sent to Foote, Cone & Belding and BBDO, PETA stated that:

> . . . the negative publicity that KFC generates would reflect poorly on your firm. Accepting an account to promote a company as abusive as KFC would be the moral equivalent of accepting an account to promote a bus company that required African Americans to sit in the back. Accepting an immoral account would invite people of conscience to protest against your agency and its officers. . . . There are plenty of advertising dollars to

be made with ethical, humane companies that do not share KFC's reputation, and we hope that you will pursue business opportunities elsewhere.

KFC and the NCC in turn attacked PETA. For example, Richard Lobb, spokesperson for the NCC said that:[15]

PETA's objective is not to improve animal welfare but to eliminate meat, poultry and other food of animal origin altogether from the human diet. They desire a totally vegan society and will say or do anything to achieve this objective. PETA even approves of the use of violence.

Central to KFC's response was an attempt to discredit PETA's claims, especially the veracity of the damaging "Kentucky Fried Cruelty" video PETA had first aired on January 6, and which, by now, was a popular designation for visitors to PETA's anti-KFC Web site:[16]

PETA is attempting to mislead the public with an outdated and questionable video on chicken production . . . the beak-trimming machine shown in the PETA video is a "Lyons" model used about 30 years ago. The system shown is no longer in common use in our industry. . . . PETA's attempt to portray this outdated method as today's standard practice is false and misleading. . . . PETA's campaign must be seen in light of its willingness to bend or totally ignore the truth in pursuit of its objectives. . . .

PETA's spokespeople Friedrich and Shannon insisted that the video was shot within "the last year and a half." Said Shannon:

Doing things that are dishonest would not make for effective campaigning . . . trust in us may be lost . . . the media may decide not to give us additional exposure. . . .

Finally, in August of 2003, PETA dispatched a team of three activists to Louisville, the site of KFC's headquarters and the home of Bachelder and Novak, to build support for its campaign against KFC. The purpose of the activists or envoys was to visit Bachelder's and Novak's neighbors, as well as churches, schools and other local institutions with which KFC executives were affiliated, in an effort to build support for the campaign in KFC's own backyard.

As the activists descended on suburban Louisville's elite, Friedrich wrote a letter to Novak suggesting a meeting to work on the road to progress and talk about peace. Friedrich told Novak he had "the power to make a real and reasonable difference in the lives and deaths of a truly unimaginable number of animals." He insisted that PETA was not "expecting KFC to make monumental changes overnight," but simply asking for a pledge that you will make the changes, do so in a meaningful way and on a reasonable time frame, and make all the changes transparent and verifiable." Blum, not Novak, responded, and his response was short and unambiguous:

In light of the fact that PETA has initiated litigation against us, we do not believe further meetings would be productive. As you know, we have had a number of meetings, conversations and written correspondence with your organization in the past and listened carefully to your concerns . . . we are implementing animal welfare guiding principles that we believe are comprehensive at both the processing and farm levels. (see Exhibit 6)

Meanwhile, in the United Kingdom, the *Sunday Mirror* ran pictures of distressed and dying chickens in the cramped sheds of KFC Europe's leading supplier under the caption "No One Does Chicken Like KFC." Said the undercover journalist: "I have investigated animal welfare for many years, but this easily ranks amongst some of the worst cruelty I have seen."

NOTES

1. www.kfc.com, September 15, 2003.
2. PETA provides detailed information on all of its past and ongoing activities at www.peta.org., September 15, 2003.
3. Annual Report 2002.
4. After laying eggs for about one year, commercial laying hens start to become unresponsive to the

Jonathan D. Blum
Senior Vice President, Public Affairs

August 20, 2003

Yum! Brands, Inc.
1441 Gardiner Lane
Louisville, KY 40213
Tel: 502874 8825
Fax 502 874 8315

VIA FAX: 757-622-0457

Mr. Bruce Friedrich
Director of Vegan Outreach
PETA
501 Front Street
Norfolk, VA 23510

Dear Mr. Friedrich,

Thank you for your letter to David Novak, which was referred to me as I oversee our company's animal welfare initiative.

In light of the fact that PETA has initiated litigation against us, we do not believe further meetings would be productive. As you know, we have had a number of meetings, conversations and written correspondence with your organization in the past and listened carefully to your concerns.

Yum! Brands is the owner of restaurants and does not own, raise or transport animals. Nonetheless, we are implementing animal welfare guiding principles that we believe are comprehensive at both the processing and farm levels. We are also monitoring our suppliers on an ongoing basis to determine whether they are using humane procedures for handling the animals they provide to us. In fact, to further demonstrate our ongoing commitment to animal welfare, we have recently appointed Dr. Al Baroudi as Chief Officer of Scientific, Health and Regulatory Affairs. Dr. Baroudi and others from our company recently spent nearly three days with Dr. Temple Grandin training our auditors on farm level guidelines, augmenting their prior training on supplier processing guidelines.

We will continue to review our progress in this area. Thank you again for your interest in this matter.

Sincerely.

Jonathan D. Blum

Exhibit 6   Blum's Fax to Friedrich

artificial light that keeps them laying for extended hours, egg production starts to fall and eggshell quality decreases. The bird's skeleton has been depleted of calcium. If hens were then exposed to short days, say of eight hours, they would gradually go out of reproductive condition and then would molt naturally. However, natural molting is a slow process, and there would be a wide range of times within a flock of hens to complete the molt. Currently, the poultry industry is not prepared to accept this extended loss of production. At about 74 weeks of age, therefore, hens are sent to slaughter as "spent laying hens" (in Canada) or are "force-molted" (in the United States) to speed up the molting process and get the hens back into reproductive condition for a second and sometimes third laying year. Forced molting programs usually involve withholding feed for 10 to 14 days and simultaneously reducing day length. Forced molting shortens the period of non-production to about eight weeks but results in a huge increase in stress and suffering. For more information, see Ian Duncan, "Welfare Issues in the Poultry Industry," *Journal of Applied Animal Welfare Science*," 2001, pp. 207-221.

5. Lorraine Adams, "What is PETA's Beef?" *The Washington Post*, May 28, 1995, F-01.

6. Bill Sizemore, "PETA: Lean and Mean Norfolk-Based Group's Zeal Pushes the Envelope Too Far for Some," *The Virginian-Pilot*, December 3, 2000, A-1.

7. Lynn Crosbie, "PETA Has to Rethink its Own Ethics," *The Globe and Mail*, January 18, 2003, R-2.

8. "PETA's PR: Controversy, 'Yes,' Compromise, 'No.,'" *PR News*, April 1, 1996, Vol. 52 Iss. 14.

9. Bill Sizemore, PETA: "Lean and Mean Norfolk-Based Group's Zeal Pushes the Envelope Too Far for Some." *The Virginian-Pilot*, December 3, 2000.

10. Ibid.

11. www.nationalchickencouncil.com., September 15, 2003.

12. Chickens in most North American slaughterhouses are hung by their legs from shackles on an assembly line, their heads dragged through an electrified trough that is meant to render them unconscious before their necks are cut by rotating blades and their bodies dropped into vats of boiling water to remove their feathers. Some chickens raise their heads from the electrical bath before they are stunned, permitting them to go fully conscious to the blade and sometimes, if they twist away from the blade, to the boiling water itself.

13. www.kfc.com/about/animalwelfare.htm, September 15, 2003.

14. Excerpt taken from PETA's KFC News Conference Presentation, January 6, 2003. Accessed via PETA's Web site, September 15, 2003.

15. "PETA Attempts to Mislead Public with Outdated Video on Chicken Production," KFC News Release, January 7, 2003.

16. Ibid.

Maple Leaf Foods (A): Leading Six Sigma Change

Prepared by Ken Mark under the supervision of Professor Brian Golden

      Version: (A) 2003-03-19

It was the spring of 2001 and Bruce Miyashita, vice-president (VP) Six Sigma of Maple Leaf Foods, was reflecting on Maple Leaf's Six Sigma experiences to date. A year after its launch, Six Sigma had been rolled out to three of the 10 Independent Operating Companies (IOCs) at Toronto-based Maple Leaf Foods (MLF). It was a project that was off the ground but was not yet completed. Several questions were going through Miyashita's head: "What was and was not working?" "What should we have done differently?" "Have we pushed the program hard enough and fast enough?" "Should we be satisfied?"

OVERVIEW OF MAPLE LEAF FOODS

MLF was a leading, global food processing company, based in Toronto, Canada. Employing more than 12,000 people at operations across Canada, the United States, Europe and Asia, the Maple Leaf brand had been introduced more than 100 years ago. Currently known as Maple Leaf Foods, the company was the result of a merger of Maple Leaf Mills Limited and Canada Packers, the most recent of numerous transformations during the company's history. Among its 11 IOCs were Maple Leaf Pork, Maple Leaf

Poultry, Canada Bread, Maple Leaf Consumer Foods, Shur-Gain and Landmark.

Its present incarnation was incorporated in 1990, and began operations in 1995 under the control of the McCain Capital Corporation and the Ontario Teachers' Pension Plan Board. MLF common shares traded on the Toronto Stock Exchange under the symbol "MFI." In 2000, MLF reported sales of about Cdn$4 billion, up from Cdn$3.5 billion in 1999. Net earnings were Cdn$90 million, down from Cdn$147 million in 1999. This drop in earnings was expected, due to increasing hog prices and the startup costs of MLF's new Brandon plant, the largest pork processing plant in Canada. MLF was expecting to report healthy profits by the second quarter of 2001.

From leadership and human resource decisions, to relations with customers, to market-entry decisions, MLF prided itself as being guided by six fundamental values:

- Do what's right
- Be performance driven
- Have a bias for action
- Continuously improve
- Be externally focused
- Dare to be transparent

At the strategic level, MLF was driven by its seven core strategic principles:

- Build High Performance Leadership
- Focus on Markets and Categories Where We Can Lead
- Develop Brand Equity
- Offer the Best Quality Products
- Be the Lowest Cost Producer
- Execute With Precision and Continuous Improvement
- Think Global

THE INTRODUCTION OF SIX SIGMA

Six Sigma was a disciplined, data-driven approach and methodology for eliminating defects in any process. The name "Six Sigma" was also a metric referring to the achievement of only 3.4 defective parts per million. The fundamental objective of the Six Sigma methodology was the implementation of a measurements-based strategy that focused on process improvement and variation reduction through the application of Six Sigma improvement projects. This was accomplished through the use of two Six Sigma sub-methodologies: define, measure, analyse, improve, control (DMAIC) and define, measure, analyse, design, verify (DMADV). The Six Sigma DMAIC process was an improvement system for existing processes falling below specification and looking for incremental improvement. The Six Sigma DMADV process was an improvement system used to develop new processes or products at Six Sigma quality levels.

MLF embraced Six Sigma as the essential discipline to achieve and maintain what was known internally as the "Leadership Edge." The term "Leadership Edge" at MLF signified two things: competitive edge through leadership, and the competitive edge of its leaders.

Michael McCain, the 42-year-old president and chief executive officer (CEO), believed that the personal success of the employees was highly integrated with the continuous success of the business. This belief led MLF to establish an array of processes to support the internal development of leaders. MLF used these processes to aim the spotlight on values, accomplishments, potential and goals. Thus, senior management worked with employees to plan specific development actions to ensure the employees' continued growth and progression as business leaders. McCain explained:

> When we created MLF, our predecessor companies had a history of continuous improvement—it was an improved version of TQM (Total Quality Management). I wanted to build a culture around continuous improvement, but in 1995, we agreed that the organization needed to be ready to accept part of this process. This reorganization included restructuring and stabilization, which were huge issues in terms of management changes, etc. We used that period to consider what foundation to build.

We decided to go with continuous improvement in some form, recognizing that this was a journey, not a one-off program. For me, it was almost a personal life decision because the leader of a business can only champion a small set of things. And two of the central pieces in MLF I was championing were Six Sigma and Leadership Edge.

Our values and principles define the type of people and the culture in which they work. And Six Sigma defines the way they work—having a tight linkage between leadership and culture.

What makes our situation different from others is that I am a CEO who is not just here for a short time. We're owner-operators and Six Sigma has been endorsed by our board of directors[1]. This is not just another job for us and we're going to be here long-term.

THE FIVE DIMENSIONS OF SIX SIGMA

Philosophy

At MLF, the Six Sigma philosophy—doing the right things right—meant quantitatively understanding and consistently meeting critical customer needs with minimal waste throughout the entire value chain. This was tied to MFL's core values, and was an approach to be applied to all business and to every kind of business process. In the manufacturing area, for example, one Six Sigma project addressed customer complaints by reducing defects incurred while processing bacon. Another project decreased the work needed to clean chicken thighs that had gone through the deboning machine. In the service area, a project was initiated to improve the office communications with Japanese customers.

Metric

The sigma metric (which measured variation relative to customer expectations) helped MLF to quantify quality, to benchmark every one of its products and processes, and to establish measurable stretch goals. As the capability of business process increased (as measured through the sigma metric), costs decreased, cycle time was reduced and customer satisfaction increased.

The difference between 99 per cent effectiveness and almost 100 per cent effectiveness can be illustrated as follows:

Ninety-nine per cent is roughly 3.8 sigma. A 3.8 sigma or 99 per cent capability is like going without electricity for seven hours per month, while Six Sigma is seven seconds per month without electricity.

Miyashita regularly recounted this imagery in his communication efforts to make the Six Sigma metric tangible to employees.

Methodology

Six Sigma provided a common problem-solving framework and language that would help MLF to design processes from the very beginning, improving existing processes to allow them to achieve their full performance potential. This standardized approach would help MLF to better share knowledge across businesses, sites and functions (see Exhibit 1).

Tools

Six Sigma utilized and integrated a broad range of tools—from statistical tools, such as the design of experiments and hypothesis testing, to process design tools, such as group-facilitation techniques. MLF's approach was to build a practical Six Sigma toolbox that provided a set of useful tools from various disciplines and to continuously support its people through training and coaching.

People

McCain and his leadership team recognized that the philosophy, metrics, methodology and tools would all be of little value in the absence of employees willing and able to implement the Six Sigma program. With this in mind, MLF invested

Excerpted from "The Vision and Philosophy of Six Sigma," a training document intended to introduce Maple Leaf Foods employees to Six Sigma.

WHAT IS THE SCIENTIFIC METHOD?

1. Formulating the question
2. Generating hypotheses
3. Experimenting
4. Deriving conclusions

You choose a question or problem that can be formulated in terms of hypothesis that can be tested. Tests done to check hypothesis are called experiments. To design a suitable experiment, you must make an educated guess about the things that affect the system you want to investigate. These are called variables. This requires thought, information gathering, and a study of the available facts relating to your problem. As you do experiments, you will record data that measures the effects of variables. Using this data you can calculate results. Results are presented in the form of tables or graphs. These results will show you trends related to how the variables affect the system you are working with. Based on these trends, you can draw conclusions about the hypothesis you originally made.

Exhibit 1   Scientific Method

Source: "The Vision and Philosophy of Six Sigma," August 24, 1999.

considerably in its human resources. Among other things, McCain invested in a highly professional group of human resource professionals who spearheaded a continuous program of senior and middle management development (e.g., the Leadership Academy), regular and effective performance reviews and coaching, a meaningful performance-based compensation schedule and a new program of "top-grading" based on the experiences of other world-class organizations.

BRUCE MIYASHITA
BRINGS SIX SIGMA TO MLF

Miyashita, age 39, had a BSc in mathematics and history, and an MBA from the Richard Ivey School of Business. He started his career at IBM, worked as a consultant for nine years with McKinsey & Company and most recently had been VP of Six Sigma at Bombardier, a leading aircraft manufacturer. Miyashita offered:

Six Sigma has gained popularity since 1996, primarily because of General Electric, although Six Sigma's successes have been well documented at other firms, such as Motorola and Allied-Signal. McCain has followed the career of Jack Welch, GE's CEO, saying that Six Sigma was the tool he wanted to introduce at MLF. But he did not have the internal resources to do that.

At the same time, a friend of mine, who became president of Canada Bread, convinced me to speak with McCain about Six Sigma. McCain knew about Six Sigma and was willing to go through the pain of implementation. I thought it would form a good partnership. He understood that I had to be an advocate and provide guidance, but I did not want Six Sigma to be seen as "Bruce's thing."

McCain believed that I had the temperament to lead it and to find ways to let line management accept it as their idea. I was sensitive to the fact that their previous quality person inflated the earlier program's success, took credit for it and irritated people. I don't want to have Six Sigma associated with me.

I want it to be such that if I were hit by a meteor, it could go on. Everyone is replaceable. As we continue to implement Six Sigma and get more managers involved, the principles of Six Sigma will be more deeply ingrained into our cultural fabric in every quarter. Soon, Six Sigma will be second nature to us.

McCain and Miyashita believed that there was value in the Six Sigma name, from an internal marketing standpoint. They had initially thought of giving Six Sigma a more neutral name, such as "continuous quality." However, they felt that there were too many ambiguous or negative connotations associated with that name. Canada Packers had previously implemented Crosby, a quality program, with mixed results. Both men, not wanting to associate Six Sigma with Crosby, had to disassociate Six Sigma from past quality efforts. They felt that the Six Sigma name was strange enough to spark curiosity. Once asked, it could then be explained what Six Sigma was and how it was unique.

According to Miyashita, Six Sigma had several attractive qualities. First, it combined the best from the various quality efforts from the past 20 years. Next, there was a greater emphasis on statistical tools. Last, the version to be implemented at MLF was very broad and included other tools besides Statistical Process Control (SPC), such as process engineering and change management. Six Sigma recognized that success came from managing the "socio-technical" system—the interaction of technology and social systems at MLF.

In sourcing the Six Sigma toolkit, Miyashita explained that MLF did not have to "reinvent the wheel" because Michael O'Hara of the Six Sigma Academy had defined it already. Instead, Miyashita spent considerable time assembling and customizing Six Sigma training material, while at the same time interest in Six Sigma was growing at MLF. Rather than riding the growing wave of interest, however, one of Miyashita's first decisions was to recommend that Six Sigma be delayed.

IMPLEMENTING SIX SIGMA

With little fanfare, an announcement letter in July 1999 stated that Miyashita had joined MLF senior management as "vice-president, Six Sigma," a newly created position. It was again unceremoniously mentioned in a company town hall meeting. No other actions were taken during the next six months. McCain and Miyashita believed that if Six Sigma had been announced and defined immediately, there would not have been enough substance to their program. Thus, they first concentrated on building the infrastructure for what would be a monumental change. As an added benefit to the delay, Miyashita noticed that curiosity about Six Sigma—and what it was and would be—was growing.

To further enhance the initial attraction and mystery of Six Sigma, and to attach a value to it, Miyashita elected to limit distribution of binders explaining the purpose of Six Sigma. These manuals included "Why Six Sigma?" "The Vision and Philosophy of Six Sigma" and "Roles and Training in Six Sigma." Miyashita explained that, of course, if employees requested information, it would be provided. Thus, implementation was deliberately slow.

From McCain's perspective, and based on previous experiences (including some failures) with new initiatives, any change initiative would encounter resistance. He believed that the difference between a flavor-of-the-month program and something MLF did for the long term was determined by how MLF responded to resistance. McCain explained:

We have a readiness assessment process[2] that estimates our IOCs' readiness for Six Sigma. There were tons of naysayers at the beginning, but this is typical of any significant change initiative. I imagine that for any given population faced with change, 20 per cent will be active supporters, 20 per cent will be active objectors and 60 per cent will be passive resisters. My job is to work hard to convert the 60 per cent passive resisters.

First, we created a vision for Six Sigma, and then we demonstrated personal involvement—I went and learned what master black belts do. I was there at every green belt class spending time training people. This was done to emphasize how important Six Sigma is to MLF. We communicate Six Sigma victories by announcing them companywide. This further underscores the value that Six Sigma brings and will continue to bring to MLF. If we keep this up, Six Sigma will be built into the fiber of the firm.

All this hard work takes the 60 per cent of passive resistors and shrinks that number. People know that we're committing resources. On a parallel track, if some people do not eventually buy in, they'd better get their résumés on the street. If you don't get on the train, it's going to leave the station without you. We will remove people before we change the process. We will help you, hold you by your hand, but at the end of the day, you may have to find something else. Six Sigma is so important to MLF that we cannot let stubborn resistance to change stand in our way.

Miyashita explained that the first training session did not occur until January 2000, a full six months after his appointment. Although MLF could have started with Six Sigma shortly after Miyashita's arrival, both he and McCain wanted to think through how and when they would start. They decided not to rush the implementation, starting with just two of the 11 Independent Operations Companies (IOCs).

This was done because many IOCs simply were not ready. For instance, the Pork IOC was still getting its plant in Brandon, Manitoba, up and running. The Consumer Foods IOC was recovering from a very disruptive strike and had some significant restructuring ahead. As Miyashita put it, "there was firefighting in various forms."

Also, Miyashita knew considerable internal selling was necessary to make the case for Six Sigma, particularly after earlier quality programs had come and gone. Miyashita relied, in part, on sharing the experiences of other leading companies. For example, the internal publication "The Vision and Philosophy of Six Sigma" described the benefit to Motorola from moving from Three to Six Sigma—an improvement in bottom-line profitability of between 10 per cent and 20 per cent. In the same publication, Mazda's and Ford's transmission production processes were compared. Though both companies built identical transmissions (Mazda is owned by Ford), Mazda was able to achieve a level of 11 sigma on key characteristics, compared to Ford's 4.3 sigma. Mazda not only did not require more expensive capital equipment, but also had transmissions with warranty costs that were 10 times less that those of the Ford transmissions, demonstrating that higher quality could be achieved at lower costs. These examples were a few among many that were recorded in internal MLF publications and frequently communicated in presentations by Miyashita and others. In addition, Miyashita spent considerable time debunking the myths of Six Sigma (see Exhibit 2).

The internal selling campaign took six months before Six Sigma was formally rolled out in the first two IOCs. When it was launched, each Six Sigma "champion" would be paired with each IOC president. This was to ensure that the program remained top-of-mind and sufficiently resourced; champions did not have formal authority to force a program to completion. Thus, although Six Sigma implementation was ultimately the IOC president's responsibility, the champion could be counted upon to provide guidance, support and expertise—none of the IOC presidents could devote 100 per cent of their time to Six Sigma.

Structural changes within the IOCs were essential for Six Sigma success. Six Sigma champions, who themselves take black belt training, would be seconded to the Six Sigma effort, and would act as collaborators with management in project identification, integration, co-ordination, and change management. The full-time black belt's role was in coaching of the managers, performing diagnostics to help in identifying projects, leading projects, educating employees about the particular tools used and their relevance to the project, and analysing and interpreting results. An equally important role, after educating about the meaning of data, was to ensure that this information was reaching the right team members. Post-project, black belts would ensure a control plan was in place and continued to operate. Plant employees who assisted black belts would be given permission by their supervisors to participate in projects, forming temporary cross-functional improvement teams that would disband once the results were collected and analysed.

Six Sigma Is Just for Manufacturing

Six Sigma is appropriate for any business process, whether it's a factory making something out of metal, transforming something (like turning pulp into paper), or processing something like poultry or pork, or whether it's a paper factory, that is, a factory that processes documents or forms.

Sigma Quality Costs Too Much

The old belief in industry was that Four Sigma was the optimum quality level. To improve beyond Four Sigma was unprofitable because, the thinking went, the cost of detecting and fixing defects rose faster than the benefits. This is true if you reduce defects through inspection. If, on the other hand, you use tools to prevent defects through better process setup, operation and product/process design, the cost of reducing defects is more than offset by the benefits. Also, as defects become rarer and rarer, a company can radically change how it does business. People can be redeployed to do value-added work rather than fighting fires or finding and fixing defects.

Ninety-Nine Per Cent Is Good Enough

Ninety-nine per cent is roughly 3.8 sigma. A 3.8 sigma or 99 per cent capability is like going without electricity for seven hours per month, while Six Sigma is seven seconds a month without electricity.

About Product Quality

Six Sigma is focused on the quality of processes and understanding what root causes affect the ability of business processes to work consistently. Six Sigma is not about inspection or rework. While Six Sigma is concerned about the end results of a process, the focus of Six Sigma is, first, to ensure we precisely quantify the customer's needs, and second, to improve the ability of business processes to consistently deliver the required results with a minimum of waste. When we focus only on product or service quality, we tend to have a mindset of inspection. When we focus on the process, we take on a mindset of defect prevention.

About Product Quality—Part 2

The Six Sigma focus on process quality is important because you can have a situation where the end product has no defects, but there is a huge "hidden" factory to find and fix defects. The goal is to have no defects in the end product without the hidden factory.

It's Just TQM

TQM or Total Quality Management has many positive aspects. But as implemented by the vast majority of organizations, it suffers from three things that the Six Sigma approach, as described here, avoids. First, most organizations approached TQM and "quality" as primarily an issue of people's attitudes. While this is important, it ignores the need to demonstrate real bottom-line financial results. Money is the reason we do Six Sigma. Defect elimination is how we make the money. Second, most TQM efforts, despite the rhetoric of management, was something delegated down. Quality was of concern to the "technical people or the workforce." The Six Sigma philosophy is that while we must achieve buy-in at all levels of the company, direction and ownership must flow from the top. Third, while TQM uses some statistical and other advanced tools, the Six Sigma toolkit embraces a wider spectrum of tools, ranging from the basic to the advanced.

About Technical Stuff

While statistics and other improvement tools are important to Six Sigma, at least 80 per cent of the challenge of Six Sigma is about change and leadership. Continually striving for Six Sigma performance in an organization presents enormous change challenges. Entire ways of thinking about the business are questioned. People who have vested interests in the status quo are threatened. People must learn new things and assume new roles.

Exhibit 2   Six Sigma Misconceptions   *(Continued)*

Better metrics reveals gaps we never saw before. In short, truly pursuing Six Sigma unleashes tremendous forces, and unless the management of a company takes on the task of leading Six Sigma, not just managing it, the result will be some money-saving projects, but not a sustained competitive and strategic improvement.

People Have to Be Perfect

A Six Sigma level of performance is 99.9997 per cent right. How is it possible to have this level of performance in businesses that are people intensive? Maybe this is possible with an automated assembly line, but not when a lot of human beings are involved. First, Six Sigma focuses on the process, not the personalities. It says: let's better understand how this process works. Let's use various tools and techniques to eliminate or make it very difficult for defects to occur, even when a lot of people are involved, by better process design and set-up. Second, the Six Sigma methodology spends a lot of time making sure we understand what is truly critical to the customer and translating those needs to something we can quantify. Many times a process is making defects because of the way we interpreted the customers' needs. Often, we misinterpret the needs, assume we know what they are, don't update the specifications, or react to one person's idea of what the needs are, rather than understanding what others are saying. In short, a "defect" might not really be a defect, depending on how well the customer's needs are defined. Third, with the use of various tools, we can often achieve high sigma performance by making processes robust to the variability of inputs and environmental factors.

Just Cost Reduction

Six Sigma is focused on bottom-line results. But these results don't come just from direct cost savings from less inspection, rework and scrap. They can come from reducing cycle times and, therefore, helping to reduce the raw material and work-in-progress inventories, which cost us money. It can come from the reduction of warranty and other customer claims. It also comes from market share benefits of better product and service quality that enhances our brand.

By systematically driving down defects throughout the business system, Six Sigma helps improve not only costs, but also cycle time, and, therefore, working and fixed capital requirements. Fewer defects means less rework, scrap or down-graded product. It also frees up capacity, often reducing the need for capital expansion. Fewer defects reduce the number of inspections. The reduction of defects in the system reduces the quantity of escaping defects, defects that make it through inspections. These defects drive repair, claims and warranty costs. They also hurt customer satisfaction.

Longer cycle times hurt our ability to consistently meet delivery requirements. Increased costs make it harder for us to profitably compete on lower costs. Lower product and service quality hurts our costs as well as our brand.

"Doing Some Projects"

While it's understood that Six Sigma requires buy-in from all levels, and that senior management must let others take the initiative, the fact remains that if the executives and senior management of a company view Six Sigma as low priority for their time and attention, Six Sigma will languish and achieve only a fraction of its full bottom-line potential. When practices, policies and behaviors are questioned as they are questioned by Six Sigma, there can be no gap between the philosophy of Six Sigma and the actions of senior management, otherwise Six Sigma will be just another flavor-of-the-month program.

Six Sigma Is a Program

Six Sigma is definitely not a program. Programs begin and end. While the start-up of a Six Sigma effort does require resources to get it going, the end state of Six Sigma is a never-ending performance mindset. The goal is to move from Six Sigma as a new concept to "this is the way we do things around here."

Exhibit 2   Six Sigma Misconceptions
Source: Company files.

THE BLACK BELT PROGRAM

The resources and manuals developed by Miyashita included detailed descriptions of each of the Six Sigma roles, and the skills and attributes necessary to perform them (see Exhibit 3). Project leaders, called black belts, were seconded full-time to the Six Sigma program and ventured within the various IOCs to diagnose, improve and design processes. These individuals had to request permission from their individual IOC managements to apply as black belts. Initially, participation in the black belt program was fully voluntary. Maple Leaf's management wanted to encourage interested individuals to step forward and apply for black belt training.[3] Other personnel could attend a five-day "green belt" education course that provided both awareness in Six Sigma and a grounding in some basic tools.

The ideal black belts were smart, mature people intrigued by processes, with, on average, five to six years of work experience at MLF or another organization. This afforded them a realistic view of work situations and allowed the candidates to not be too frustrated by initial inertia. They had to be "people persons" since they served as consultants to line managers and teams, lacking formal authority to implement programs. As another attribute, McCain and Miyashita wanted level-headed people with no ego problems. These black belt trainees had to be confident in their abilities and had to be able to share project successes.

Miyashita and technical consultants began schooling green belts and by July 2000, the first class of black belts was five months old. Miyashita noticed that although the program had sufficient numbers of interested trainees, it was not drawing the appropriate numbers of women. He explained:

> We've had significant problems attracting women. My pet theory is that all things being equal, women make better black belts. One common stereotype for men recounts that men do not like to look at road maps. We need black belts to be very good at networking and getting coaching. The vast majority of coaching comes from me right now and I notice that some people are very eager to learn.

> I think guys feel bad asking what they perceive as "silly" questions.

Over the next few months, however, the number of external candidates (including a substantial portion of women), had grown, as MLF was able to use the profile of its Six Sigma program to attract new candidates.

Black belts signed up for 25 days of training and a minimum of two years in that role—there was no limit on maximum length. MLF had 16 black belts currently, targeting to add at least 24 to 34 new black belts per year. Miyashita aimed to produce 120 to 150 black belts by 2003. It cost MLF approximately Cdn$140,000 to train each black belt, including salary and training costs. He thought that they would perform between 1.5 to 2.0 projects per year, saving MLF at least Cdn$100,000 per project annually.

Miyashita noted that at his previous role at Bombardier, the attrition rate for black belts was 18 per cent. In reality, if the numbers of people lured away to other companies was subtracted, the attrition rate was only four per cent.

INITIAL CHALLENGES AND PRE-EMPTIVE MEASURES

Early on in the process, Miyashita was aware that many employees were wondering how Six Sigma would affect their lives on a day-to-day basis, and also over the long term. In anticipation of this possible reaction, Miyashita crafted a message that identified the benefits to employees (and not just MLF) from Six Sigma. The benefits he often spoke of included the following:

- I'll be more marketable internally and externally because of the training I've received
- I'll have time for training
- I'll have time to make improvements
- There'll be less firefighting
- I'll understand other parts of the business better
- I'll have power over numbers
- I'll be focusing on the process that creates a product or service; I'll see more of the whole process
- Defects or problems will be things to learn from

Profile Summary	Who?	What Do They Do?	How Many?
Executive Group	• Business unit executives; also known as "quality council" in some companies	• Approve Six Sigma policy • Set goals • Commit resources; select BBs • Own the results • Create the vision of Six Sigma • Approve projects	• Executive group as a whole
Six Sigma Champion	• Champion is an executive or senior manager who provides day-to-day implementation leadership • Experienced line executive who knows the business and is respected	• Change agent • Link between vision and strategy of Six Sigma • Formulate Six Sigma policy with corporate • Help define projects • Help select Black Belts • Set up business unit infrastructure (e.g., project tracking) • Co-ordinate deployment in business unit	• One full-time executive per business unit
Business Unit Core Team	• Led by Six Sigma champion • Reps from line management and support functions (HR, Finance, IT) (part time) • Black Belts	• Help formulate Six Sigma policy • Co-ordinate their functions' support of Six Sigma	• One core team for each major business unit, e.g., where you have a president, and/or one at a corporate level • Part-time
Process Owners	• The person responsible for all aspects of a process' performance • The process owner might also be the project owner	• Measure process performance • Improve process performance through such actions as application of Six Sigma methodology and tools in a project • Ensure improvements are implemented and sustained	• All managers own one or more processes • Processes exist in levels or tiers
Project Champion (Sponsor)	• The person responsible for all aspects of a project's success • The project owner might also be the process owner or champion	• Ensure the right resources are on the team/available to the team • Ensure project is implemented • Provide day-to-day support • Ensure process owner is on-board	• Each project has one accountable Project Owner (no committees!)

Exhibit 3   Six Sigma Roles and Responsibilities   *(Continued)*

Profile Summary	Who?	What Do They Do?	How Many?

All employees	• Any employee from the president to the most recent new hire	• Walk the talk of Six Sigma philosophy and principles in their job
		  − What and how they measure things
		  − Supporting project teams
		  − Helping to sustain the improvements
		• Help others understand the goals and methods of Six Sigma
		• Apply Six Sigma training in their area, e.g., might receive Black Belt or Green Belt training and apply on their job
			• Whole organization

Project Team Members	• Salary and/or hourly employees • Work in the process, understand the process, or understand the customer • Could include customer and/or suppliers	• Identify the root causes of the problem and find solutions • Implement the change with the process owner • People from the process to sustain the gains	• Most projects have anywhere from three to 10 people—it depends on the project • Most are part-time; some might be full-time for a few days of weeks—depends
Black Belts (BBs)	• Full-time project team leaders	• Lead project teams through the Six Sigma methodology to solve the program defined in the project charter • Provide problem solving/analytical support to the organization • Train project team members • Work closely with the project owner to ensure implementation	• Typically one or two Black Belts per 100 employees, often more as justified by the payback (this is in addition to people who receive Black Belt training and apply on-the-job)
Master Black Belts (MBBs)	• Experts in tools and methods of Six Sigma • Full-time coaches and trainers • Have gone through Black Belt training • Strong teaching/communication skills • Long term career path	• Provide coaching and training to the organization (technical and change management) • Provide regular (e.g., weekly) technical advice to Black Belts and the project teams • Participate on core team to create Six Sigma infrastructure, e.g., project database, training curriculum	• Usually one MBB per 20 to 30 BBs, depending on factors such as geography

Exhibit 3   Six Sigma Roles and Responsibilities

Source: Company files.

McCain also recounted some initial resistance to Six Sigma:

> People would say: "I don't like it, and I won't do it" "If I put my head down long enough, this too will pass." Yes, if someone else owned MLF, perhaps that would be the case. But this is not so—people should realize that we're here for the long term. Six Sigma is championed by the board of directors and shareholders, and is the fundamental way that we're doing things.
>
> In 1998, I told them that we would be starting a program in a year. Six months later, I reminded them that July 1999 would see the kickoff of an improvement process. Even when we announced Six Sigma, half the people in the room thought that I was crazy.
>
> They said, "3.4 defective parts per million is impossible." People who say that have not gone through the program[4]. They also said "Six Sigma only applies to metal benders—in food, we have natural causes that are God-given and we can't control them."

In addition, some plant managers were embarrassed that Six Sigma was able to diagnose quality problems that had been previously undetected. Other managers were not pleased that they were not seen as the "heroes"—that a green belt or black belt was necessary to help them improve their own business. Miyashita lamented that this was an indication that Six Sigma was not implemented as well as possible. One of the objectives of the change management training was to stress the importance of sharing success.

An anticipated issue was low statistical literacy among employees, delaying black belts at the preproject level. To counteract this, the black belts were trained to educate employees as necessary, in the course of project design and implementation. Relevant statistical terms would then be put in context and explained to the employees. A frequent example was the need for black belts to explain the requirement to monitor variance from the mean, rather than relying solely on the mean.

Another concern was MLF's bias to action—a core value. MLF faced a long history of "shoot first, ask questions later." With Six Sigma, employees had to do research prior to prescribing solutions. Thus, this cultural bias to action was seen as an impediment to Six Sigma. The challenge was how to get people to value "looking before leaping."

In addition, succession planning was a constant issue. As one manager in the International IOC commented:

> If someone moves from green to black belt, we need to backfill that person in the IOC. There can be fallout since the new person (replacing the new black belt) needs to be able to step in and fill the gap. It might take some time for them to be able to do that, and if a bottleneck is created because of the time to get up to speed, Six Sigma gets blamed. We weren't given any additional resources when we lost the IOC member to his black belt role, so Six Sigma can actually make my life harder, not easier.

It was ironic then that many newly minted black belts and green belts, full of excitement about the new skill sets they had developed, had no immediate post-training projects on which to work. According to one manager, "Some people were trained 14 months ago, and if these are concepts that you don't deal with every day and were new to begin with, I don't know how helpful they will be." In other cases, the projects were perceived as make-work projects just so a new green belt could "tick off the box and say they completed a project." Over time, as interest in Six Sigma began to build, it was expected that the supply and demand of important projects would reach an equilibrium.

Finally, Six Sigma was not, strictly speaking, necessary for MLF's success; MLF had performed well without Six Sigma. Thus, a challenge for McCain and Miyashita was to create dissatisfaction with the status quo. It was one thing to espouse the MLF value of continual improvement; it was another to create the impetus for change (with the risk of failure) when business was good (and rewards were tied to performance). To address this challenge, Miyashita's "Why Six Sigma?" publication and the presentations provided numerous examples of well-performing companies (e.g., GE, Motorola, Mazda) that were able to markedly improve performance through Six Sigma.

THE FIRST PROJECT AT POULTRY

Located at the Toronto facility, already considered to be the benchmark plant in MLF, the first Six

Sigma project involved deboning chicken thighs. Jim Long, black belt at Poultry was in charge of this "boneless chicken thigh process." Employees had been spending an inordinate amount of time performing inspections and compensating for machines that were not producing optimal output. At the start, six out of every 10 thighs to arrive at the trim table still had excess skin or bone that had not been removed by the equipment. A design experiment was created and carried out, resulting in an increase of 15 per cent to 16 per cent in the output per employee, per hour.

Brock Furlong, president of Poultry, one of the first three IOCs selected for Six Sigma implementation, explained that there were initial challenges. First, there was the issue of being first—he did not have anyone to turn to for implementation plans. There were no benchmarks to go by, as Poultry was a unique IOC in the Food Division. There were also no detailed process outlines or maps and this hampered the division's ability to implement the first projects quickly.

Cultural issues also came into play because decision-making at Poultry had been top-down. But Six Sigma calls for implementation at the ground level. Part of that previous culture of top-down decision-making had a strong bottom-line focus, and Six Sigma was a significant investment in time, energy and resources at the lower and middle levels. Furlong concluded, "Many people in our IOC were sitting back and saying 'Prove it.'"

THE BACON PLANT

For months, Maple Leaf Food's bacon plant, located in Manitoba, had been receiving a high number of customer complaints because of defective products. Its unionized workforce was constantly reminded by plant supervisors that bacon yield had to improve, leading to a high degree of frustration during work hours. In addition, because they were not achieving their bacon yield numbers, employees were not receiving performance bonuses.

Louann Hulsman, black belt trainee at MLF Consumer Foods, recounted her initial project experience:

> Consumer complaints about bacon had started to climb in 1999 (prior to Miyashita's arrival) and we had to go in and try to fix the issues at our bacon plant. We inspected-out the defects so that the products coming out were of higher quality. But that increased the cost of production to the plant. We found a bottleneck in the flow, and the result was that we had created a holding spot for work-in-progress. This became a scheduling nightmare for a while, and we were looking for a solution.

> As soon as Six Sigma resources were available, we grabbed them, pulled them in and said, "Let's go!" Some employees even said, "I don't understand what you want me to do, but if you're telling me that it will reduce my frustration, improve my processes, then let's go." The employees gave us 120 per cent support, to the point that we were fully staffed with volunteers to schedule experiments and monitor results. We had sign-up sheets and people were signing up for two to three steps each!

> Originally, we were at about 3,000 defects per million, and now we're at 1,400 defects per million. Complaints have come down from 50 per million pieces to less than 20 per million. But that came at a cost—we could not make our standard yield of product per pound of raw material. Then we found factors and levels that could increase first grade yield by another 10 per cent.

> Fundamentally, the people did not want to come to work to make bad finished products and have supervisors yelling at them. It worked and the team at North Battleford is amazing. There was someone in the plant almost 24 hours a day and all the people on the floor were interested in the project, giving us suggestions and moral support.

> When we first started, we figured that poor quality of raw materials was the source of the problem. But we've made improvements without changing raw material quality, increasing our first grade yields. The line workers could really see the difference. They'd say, "We want this kind of bacon because this is the best." In my mind, the projects are working when people on the job notice the difference.

LONG-TERM MANAGEMENT COMMITMENT

McCain recounted:

> Most people can tell if the CEO is championing the project. I tell people that I am the champion for it.

In my opinion, Bruce Miyashita has executed Six Sigma brilliantly—he overcame such objections as "we're doing so many things besides Six Sigma," getting people to cough up their best people for black belt training.

We've got to be committed to this as a five- to 10-year process. It is a cultural revolution. And people might not fundamentally appreciate what it takes to embark on that. There will be people deselected because they don't buy in. We did three IOCs in our first year. Our management informed everybody that we were not mandating when they jumped on the train—if they did not feel ready, they did not have to do that immediately. But it's not a question of if, it's when.

For the first 18 months, we started with more Six Sigma resources than demand. But now we've got more demand than resources. We've told people that unless they are at the top of their game, Six Sigma will not work. You will only get it if you're good. And, it matters—25 per cent of an IOC president's short-term bonus is based on Six Sigma implementation.

We've told them how well the three IOCs are doing. We've spread the stories of initial success. We've got tangible victories, but if the baseball game analogy could be used, we're in the first inning of a nine-inning game.

Miyashita was also doing his part to publicize Six Sigma to MLF management. In addition to the work he performed with the black belts, he was a regular speaker on the Leadership Edge Foundations Program (which trained the top 500 MLF managers). This program, designed and delivered by a leading business school, provided another opportunity for McCain and Miyashita to stress the importance of Six Sigma and to broadcast ongoing successes.

THE FUTURE

As demand for Six Sigma resources outstripped supply, Miyashita wanted Six Sigma documents available online and the new black belts shouldering more of the training load. In addition, he wanted the program institutionalized with a more robust project tracking system. Also, he wanted to train or

hire a couple dozen more black belts in order to achieve critical mass for Six Sigma resources. Last, he wanted to promote a black belt to master black belt. He knew that McCain's commitment was vital. Miyashita concluded:

McCain is preaching it. Given the limitations of a CEO's time, he does enough. He'll go to the shop floor and ask "What's the sigma of that hog?" That flaws people, because he *really* expects you to give him the answer. McCain understands this stuff and, along with me, preaches it every day.

The jury is out as to whether this will be successful. But honestly, only time will tell. What can I do to increase the odds of success? If you think about it, the odds are stacked against us. Many companies have tried and failed. Within MLF, if we do not resolve all the tiny issues as soon as they arise, we also run the risk of failure.

Are we being aggressive enough? We know that we have a thin bench of players, but are we pushing hard enough, being disruptive enough? Maybe we should've launched the IOCs all at once, instead of going in with our contained approach. It's a legitimate question. Some of it is irreversible and we'll have to deal with what we have done. I agree with McCain that we're in the first inning of a nine-inning ball game . . . in a 162 game season.

NOTES

1. Family members owned approximately one-third of MLF's equity. McCain's father, Wallace McCain, was chairman of MLF and McCain's brother, Scott McCain, was the president of the agribusiness IOCs.

2. McCain believed that an IOC had to achieve stability before Six Sigma could be of any use. He stressed that if an IOC were involved with "putting out fires"—in a state of flux—attempting to implement Six Sigma would certainly be an exercise in failure. He stated, "Unless you're at the top of your game, Six Sigma will not work."

3. "Master black belt" is the industry term for the people who train and coach the black belts.

4. McCain elaborated that Six Sigma was not a goal but a philosophy of constant improvement. He invited dissenters to improve their processes to the point of diminishing returns, stating that if that level of quality could be achieved across the company, Maple Leaf Foods would be peerless.

BLACK & DECKER-EASTERN HEMISPHERE AND THE **ADP** INITIATIVE (A)

Prepared by Professors
Allen Morrison and Stewart Black

Version: (A) 2004-08-18

In late April 1996, Bill Lancaster, president of Black & Decker-Eastern Hemisphere, faced a difficult decision. Should he accept a new performance appraisal and management development system presented to him by Anita Lim, manager of Human Resources, or should he introduce a U.S.-designed Appraisal Development Plan (ADP) throughout the Eastern Hemisphere? ADP had been launched in the U.S. a few years earlier and Lancaster, who had recently arrived in Singapore, had been very impressed with its impact on management development. A key feature of ADP in Lancaster's mind was a 360° performance instrument which provided each employee with feedback from subordinates, peers and supervisors.

Before moving forward with ADP in the Eastern Hemisphere, Lancaster had asked for feedback from a number of local managers. Several expressed concern that 360° feedback might not work in Asia. To counter these concerns, Lim had proposed a modified version of ADP that included many of the features that Lancaster believed in and wanted to see, but lacked the 360° feedback element that he thought had been critical in ADP's success in the U.S. Lancaster was torn. On the one hand, he believed strongly in ADP and had seen it change the management and culture of Black & Decker in the U.S. On the other hand, he knew that 360° feedback might not be universally embraced because of cultural differences.

BLACK & DECKER CORPORATION

Black & Decker was founded in 1910 by Duncan Black and Alonzo Decker who invested $1,200 to start a company that manufactured industrial machinery. In 1914, the partners patented a drill with a pistol grip and trigger switch that revolutionized the power tool industry. By 1918, the partners had opened representative offices in Canada, England, Russia, Australia and Japan. Seventy-eight years later, Black & Decker had sales offices in 109 countries and was the world's largest producer of power tools, electric lawn and garden tools, and related accessories. By 1996, Black & Decker's sales had reached $4.9 billion, net income was $229.6 million, and the company employed just over 29,000 people. Headquartered in Towson, Maryland (just outside Baltimore), Black & Decker was noted for its stable of well known brands including DeWalt™ and Black & Decker power tools, Dustbuster™ portable vacuums, Kwikset™ (locks and security hardware), Price Pfister™ (faucets), Emhart (glass and fasteners), and Black & Decker brand household products (irons, mixers, food processors, coffee makers, toasters, and toaster ovens). Under the direction of Nolan Archibald, Black & Decker's Chairman, President and CEO since 1986, recognition of the company's brand had grown to such an extent that in a survey of 6,000 brands in the early 1990s, Black & Decker was ranked seventh in the U.S. and nineteenth in Europe.

Despite major successes in North America and Europe, Black & Decker continued to face challenges in Asia and Latin America. By the early 1990s, senior corporate executives began to refocus efforts on strengthening the company's position in these emerging markets. Lancaster explained the situation in the early 1990s:

During the early 1990s, there was a separate North American Group [located at corporate HQ in

Towson] and a separate European Group [located in London]. Everything else was part of the International Group [located at corporate HQ in Towson]. At the time, International was thought of as mostly an opportunistic, export business. In Asia, we had a small team in Singapore on the Black & Decker payroll and that was it for the entire region. Not surprisingly, whereas Black & Decker was number one in market share in the U.S., we were a weak number five in Asia.

In 1993, there was a major reorganization of Black & Decker's operations. The International Group was split into Latin America, and the Eastern Hemisphere. Latin America's headquarters was moved to Miami; Eastern Hemisphere's headquarters was moved to Singapore. The territory covered by the Eastern Hemisphere office included the Middle East, Africa, India, Pakistan, and all of Asia-Pacific including China, Japan, Korea, the Philippines, Indonesia, Malaysia, Thailand, Singapore, Australia, and New Zealand.

Both the Eastern Hemisphere and Latin America offices reported to Black & Decker's Worldwide Power Tools Group. In the Eastern Hemisphere, about 70 per cent of sales were power tools or accessories. The remainder of sales included such products as small appliances, fasteners, and security hardware. Power Tools was Black & Decker's largest single business and represented the "spiritual heart" of the company. Reporting through the Power Tools organization was viewed as an effective way of avoiding the duplication of infrastructure that would be necessary if multiple business unit headquarters were established in the Eastern Hemisphere.

BILL LANCASTER APPOINTED AS PRESIDENT OF EASTERN HEMISPHERE

In October 1995, Bill Lancaster was appointed President of Black & Decker Eastern Hemisphere. Although new to Singapore, Lancaster had held senior administrative positions for Black & Decker in Australia from 1988 to 1990. From 1990 to 1995, he was Vice President Marketing and Sales, Professional Products for the North American Power Tools group.

Lancaster worked closely with Jim Barker, Executive Vice President and President of Worldwide Power Tools. Under Barker's lead, the two undertook extensive market research in the early 1990s on the professional-industrial power tool segments. DeWalt had been purchased by Black & Decker in the 1970s and was known for large stationary tools, including radial arm saws. Recognizing the potential of the professional-industrial and professional-tradesmen segments, DeWalt was repositioned as Black & Decker's answer for these markets. An entirely new line of professional quality power tools was launched with a bold and innovative marketing strategy. DeWalt tools were yellow in color (a symbol of safety often found on job sites) and were introduced to potential buyers at construction sites. A fleet of yellow DeWalt vans was set up, and "events" were staged at major construction sites. The events included product demonstrations and free give-aways (T-shirts, hats, etc.). By putting the tools in the hands of professionals, it was believed they would experience first-hand the quality, durability and innovative features of the DeWalt product line. The strategy was a huge success. DeWalt sales in North America went from essentially nothing to $300 million in a little over two years. In October 1995, Lancaster was promoted to run the Eastern Hemisphere.

By the time Lancaster arrived in Singapore, Black & Decker had either spent or had committed to spend nearly $80 million to set up its Singapore headquarters and build new factories in Singapore, India and China. In early 1996, the Eastern Hemisphere had nearly 1,000 employees. Growth plans called for employment to increase significantly by 2001, of which a large percentage would be new managers.

LANCASTER'S INITIAL IMPRESSIONS

When Lancaster first arrived in Singapore, he spent a lot of time talking to employees throughout the organization. He started with members of the Eastern Hemisphere's Management Advisory Council (MAC). The MAC was composed of Lancaster's direct reports—eight vice presidents or directors, seven of whom were expatriates.

He also spent considerable time talking to rank and file employees throughout the Eastern Hemisphere organization. He summarized his conclusions:

> I found that there was a major disparity in the management styles of people here. Some had styles that emphasized employee empowerment. Others were of the old authoritarian school. Some, quite frankly, were bad managers.
>
> I also ran into a lot of people who had been doing the same jobs for five or more years. They didn't seem to be growing or developing. About 70 per cent of management and supervisory jobs were being filled by outsiders. Something wasn't right about this. We weren't growing our own people and needed to do something about it.
>
> Finally, I felt uncomfortable with the existing management assessment and development system and thought that it needed to be changed. Managers were using a MBO-type system that had been replaced in the U.S. some time ago.

Management Appraisal and Development

ADP was first introduced in the U.S. in 1992 as a replacement for the company's Management by Objective (MBO) plan. Under the previous MBO program, superiors would meet individually with each subordinate to discuss the subordinate's performance and jointly establish clear and comprehensive objectives for the subordinate for the coming year. During the review session, criteria would also be set for assessing the subordinate's progress on the agreed-upon objectives and a schedule for follow-up meeting(s) would be set. Managers were encouraged to have at least one interim meeting with subordinates during the year to review progress and provide coaching.

MBO systems were widely used by Western businesses. During the late 1980s, for example, it was estimated that slightly less than half of the *Fortune 500* companies were using MBO-type systems. Yet, despite their widespread use, not everyone was happy with the results. Bill Lancaster commented on his U.S. experience with Black & Decker's MBO system:

> It had some good components. But it didn't seek input from others in the organization. This is important because as a boss, I was only seeing my subordinates doing their job maybe 10 per cent of the time. Either I was gone or they were gone. I would see reports, maybe hear a few things in terms of their performance, but that's about it.
>
> Under the MBO system, I used to dread having to give performance reviews. In many cases, I wouldn't have a lot to say. If someone wasn't making their numbers, I often wouldn't really know why. So I would make up a list of suggestions. It probably wasn't very helpful, but it was the only feedback I could give. Sometimes the sessions got contentious. People would argue against my assessment saying that I didn't know enough about what they were doing to form an accurate opinion. Maybe they were right.

Casey Chan, Singapore-based Senior Brand Manager for Black & Decker Eastern Hemisphere, shared some additional insights into the MBO system:

> A MBO system has the advantage of making you be responsible to your boss. He knows you best and best understands the business objectives. Unfortunately, if you don't get along with your boss, your reviews might be bad. But it also goes the other way. If you are friends with your boss, you might get great reviews. It can be difficult to make the system objective.

The Appraisal Development Plan

In the U.S., ADP included six major steps. *First*, the appraising manager requested input from between three and six of the employee's peers (see Exhibit 1 for a sample of the form they receive). *Second*, the appraising manager requested input from between three and six of the employee's subordinates (see Exhibit 2 for a sample of the form they receive). *Third*, the appraising manager asked the employee to perform and submit a self-review. The self-review included a document covering the employee's background, past year's performance, job function and other feedback (see Exhibit 3) as well as a nearly blank form for each employee to summarize his/her objectives and accomplishments

Name of employee to be assessed: _____

Period under review: From _____ To _____ (DD/MM/YY)

Please answer the following questions as objectively as possible with reference to the above employee's performance under the review period.

    i. What do you see as this person's key contributions over the period under review (as applies to you)?

    ii. What activities should be continued to maintain effectiveness?

    iii. What activities should be minimized to increase effectiveness?

    iv. What new activities will increase his/her effectiveness over the next 12 months?

    v. Has the performance of this employee under the above review period met the stated team objectives? Why, why not?

    vi. In your opinion, has this employee performed as a team player under the above review period?

    vii. What skills should be further developed?

    viii. Is this employee meeting his customer's requirement? Explain.

    ix. Should his/her role change in order to better meet/exceed customer requirements over the next 12 months? Explain.

Exhibit 1   Peer Review Sample ADP Template

Name of manager to be assessed: _____

Period under review: From _____ To _____ (DD/MM/YY)

Please answer the following questions as objectively as possible with reference to the above employee's performance under the review period.

   i. How has your immediate manager helped you in meeting your performance expectations during the period under review?

   ii. How have you helped your immediate manager in meeting his/her performance goals during the period under review?

   iii. What would you like your immediate manager to do more of in the next 12 months in order for you to be more effective?

   iv. What would you like your manager to do less of?

   v. Other feedback.

Exhibit 2   Subordinate Review Sample ADP Template

Name: _____   Date of ADP Review: _____

Period under review: From _____ To _____ (DD/MM/YY)

The questions given below are intended to help you clarify your ideas about your job in preparation for the discussion. For your past year's performance, please prepare a document covering the following areas. This document must be returned to your manager by

_____

(to be completed by appraising manager)

A. BACKGROUND
 i. Career background (hire date, position(s) held).
 ii. Education/training background (company training and external training).
 iii. Other elements of your background (optional).

B. PAST YEAR'S PERFORMANCE
 i. Performance versus stated objective.
 ii. Performance versus on-going accountabilities.
 iii. Key achievements.
 iv. Key strengths.
 v. Areas needing further improvements to achieve maximum effectiveness.

C. JOB FUNCTIONS
 i. Brief summary of major job responsibilities.
 ii. Brief summary of other secondary duties.
 iii. What frustrates you?
 iv. What do you enjoy doing most?
 v. Do you see among your main activities any that should be modified, supplemented, or adopted?
 vi. Do you think that the scope of the job itself should be reconsidered?
 vii. What do you consider should be the main targets and tasks for the next review period? List clearly any new targets, priorities and methods or means to achieve them. Consider any training or course required.
 viii. What kinds of support, special skills and experiences do you need to do your job?
 ix. Where do you see yourself progressing in the job?
 x. What can I (we) do better as your manager to help you do your job or achieve your goals?

D. OTHER FEEDBACK

Exhibit 3   Self-Review Sample ADP Template

for the year. *Fourth*, the appraising manager reviewed all of the submitted forms and prepared a formal assessment of the employee. Managers considered 14 different performance dimensions in assessing each employee (achievement orientation, interpersonal communication, conceptual thinking, analytical thinking, initiative, decisiveness, job knowledge, teamwork, customer-focused, focus on quality, organization commitment, leadership, developing others, and adaptability). After preparing a written assessment, the appraising manager then destroyed all peer and subordinate reviews. *Fifth*, the manager and employee met together. During the meeting, the manager discussed his/her written report with the employee. Then, the manager and employee agreed in writing on the employee's performance objectives, measurement criteria and weights, and future career development plans. *Sixth*, these written objectives and plans were summarized in a separate short form that also included comments from the employee, manager, and the manager's boss. These summary forms were kept on file in the local human resource manager's office. The entire ADP process ran from November 1 to the end of February each year.

ADP's Acceptance in the U.S.

ADP was generally well received when it was introduced in the U.S. Bill Lancaster was a big fan.

> After ADP was introduced in the U.S., reviews became something I looked forward to. With all the feedback I got, I could add real value in the review sessions. I was very impressed by what ADP did for people in the U.S.

> ADP was designed as a tool to develop people. Another big benefit that came from ADP was the potential to build a highly functional, high performance team. ADP encouraged people to work together, to build one another. People who were good at managing ADP also got noticed. People wanted to work for them because they saw how successful they were at building people and strengthening a team.

Nicholas Levan, Vice President-Marketing for the Eastern Hemisphere, was one of the senior expatriates in the region and a member of the MAC. His experience with ADP in the U.S. was also positive.

> In the U.S., managers understood that peer reviews were invaluable. They made the job of doing assessments much easier. The reason is that managers don't see their subordinates as much as their peers do. Under the ADP, about 80 per cent of evaluating subordinates is done for the manager. As a manager, I like that. But it is also good for employees. For example, the emphasis on self-assessments and career planning is a great development exercise and tool for building future leaders. Peer feedback and employee self-assessments add significant value to ADP as a development tool and ease the evaluation burden on management.

Despite the benefits of ADP, there were detractors. Bill Lancaster explained:

> At the senior levels, ADP was embraced quickly. This was less the case the further down you went in the organization. I think it safe to say that there were real concerns when ADP was first introduced in the U.S. Some people were very worried that 360° feedback would open up the evaluation process to bias. If they weren't popular, some managers feared that perhaps subordinates would gang up on them. There was also real concern about the amount of work involved in filling out, collecting and processing the forms. If you managed 10 people, you might have 120 forms to go through. Finally, people complained that there was no reward for doing a good job at ADP. What was the payback for spending so much time on a HR function?

Notwithstanding these concerns, ADP had earned wide support and acceptance in the U.S. by 1996. Worry over potential abuses diminished over time, and the process was gradually refined to accommodate the additional time required to make ADP work.

ADP in the Eastern Hemisphere

When Lancaster arrived in Singapore, the Eastern Hemisphere was using its own MBO system. A hybrid of the system which ADP had replaced in the U.S., the Eastern Hemisphere's MBO consisted of a simple rating scale that was completed solely by the appraising manager. A little digging convinced Lancaster that most managers in the Eastern Hemisphere were not using the MBO for joint goal setting. Instead, most were using it only as a simple performance evaluation instrument.

To test out ADP's potential in the Eastern Hemisphere, Lancaster met with Anita Lim, the Singapore-based Manager of Human Resources. Lim, age 32, had been with Black & Decker for six years, longer than almost anyone else in the office. She had risen from an entry level human resource position to one of considerable authority in Asia Pacific. Her insight into the mindsets of Asian workers was viewed as critical.

Lim was opposed to the introduction of the U.S. version of ADP in the Eastern Hemisphere. She had three primary, inter-related concerns. First, she argued that Asian people might not willingly open up the way Americans do. "If you ask them to provide candid feedback on their boss, they are likely to say something polite but won't be critical." Second, she asserted that Asians might not believe in the confidentiality of the ADP system. "No matter what a boss says about feedback being anonymous, Asians won't believe him or her. Somehow he or she will find out who said what about whom and there will be negative consequences for that person." Third, she believed that a change from MBO to ADP might be too radical. In her words, "Asians will not support radical change of this nature."

Sharon Seng, a Singaporean who reported to Lim as a Human Resource officer, had her own views. Seng had recently joined Black & Decker after having worked for the Singapore Broadcasting Corporation and Sony.

> As a HR professional, I have always wanted something that allowed people to increase communication and set objectives. When I arrived, I was quite shocked by the existing performance appraisal and development tool we were using.

> Many of the people being hired at Black & Decker are young. We are the MTV generation. We can be a lot franker than the earlier generation. For example, if I have a problem with my boss, I'll tell him or her. I don't need an annual review to raise concerns. I think if you have gone to university or spent much time overseas, you are much more likely to accept ADP. For me personally, it would not be that big of a deal.

> My biggest concern is the staff. Some of the managers have been here a long time and have rigid views. If their boss has been afraid to tell them something negative for five years, he or she is not going to change because of ADP. Another concern is over language. The ADP booklets from the U.S. are all in English. Many lower level employees don't speak English. Even some of our more senior people in Korea, Taiwan and China don't speak good English. What do we do for them? Even if we translate the material, you have to wonder if they are translating the words or the meanings. It will take a lot of time and energy. I wonder if it is something we should be spending all of our time on right now?

Lancaster decided to talk to more people. He approached other members of the MAC for their reactions. Lancaster summarized their input:

> Those who had seen it work in the U.S. were excited and supportive. Those who had come to the Eastern Hemisphere from Europe [where ADP had not been adopted] were less convinced. I found that those who were opposed to ADP were mostly concerned about maintaining confidentiality. I heard someone say that only "an act of God" would convince people that the ADP results would be confidential.

Lancaster pressed on, meeting with other managers in Singapore and wherever he travelled. Their reactions were mixed. Eric Ang, Commercial Director for Black & Decker in Singapore and Malaysia, explained his perspective:

> In this part of the world, we have three per cent unemployment. Because of this, growing people and building people are essential. ADP, as I understand it, forces your boss to look at your career path. What are your gaps and how do you fill these gaps? In theory, this should help us build the next generation of managers. But the problem is that in Asian cultures, people don't tend to open up. They will never say that their career's ambition is to have their boss's job. As a result, while ADP is designed to build commitment and develop managers, it may backfire. People may quit if they are pressed to open up in ways that make them uncomfortable.

Kevin Ip, Finance Director for China and Hong Kong, was concerned about the ability of ADP to assist in developing people.

> Here in the field, I think ADP will be much more difficult to implement than in Singapore. Although I am based in Hong Kong, I work with three representative offices in China. Trying to effectively communicate ADP to these people will be very difficult. For one thing, virtually none of these people speak English. But also, most people in the representative offices are working very hard. We are so focused on building sales, that I wonder if it is important or even possible to really develop people with broader skills. If you are making the numbers, some people believe that's all that is important.

It is one thing for HQ to use ADP, but another for the country offices. There are not many developmental opportunities in China. If you want a promotion here, where do you go? You can change someone's title, but that's about it. They are still going to be doing the same things with the same colleagues.

Casey Chan, a Singapore-based Senior Brand Manager for Black & Decker, commented on the amount of time required to make ADP work:

ADP seems to have a lot of open-ended questions that are general. It will take a lot of thinking to fill out the forms for an individual. I think it will likely take me three to four hours per person to do an appraisal. And I have five people who report to me. That's almost twenty hours of work. And it comes at the end of the year when we are busiest.

Liew Mee Salamat, Methods & Process manager and a Malaysian national, was concerned about cultural barriers to implementing ADP:

I used to work for a large Japanese MNC. There, we didn't use a formal evaluation system. I didn't know how I was evaluated. The only way I found out I was doing a good job was by the size of the pay raise I got. There, if you question your boss, it is a lose-lose situation. You lose because you question him. He loses because he loses face.

My worry about ADP is that if, in your peer review, you criticize someone whom your boss likes, you are really criticizing your boss. I think if my boss were American, I could be more open in an evaluation session. But if he is Japanese, I don't think I could open up. I could never disagree with him or criticize someone he likes because he will hold a grudge against me. Having said this, ADP is an American system and American systems are generally regarded here as being fair. I would like to give it a try.

Milind Kapoor, Group MIS Manager for the Eastern Hemisphere, was an Indian national who had been at Black & Decker since mid-1995. He also had some interesting insights into ADP:

What I like about ADP is that it promises to give me feedback from in-house MIS customers. I want to know how we are doing and ADP promises to be much better than our existing performance appraisal system.

Despite this positive point, I think that in India, ADP would need to be modified. In my opinion, peer reviews won't work in India. If you have a job opening in India, 10,000 people apply. It is very different than here in Singapore where it is difficult to hire strong information technology people. Because of the tight labor market, I just can't seem to find or retain good people in Singapore. In India, there is so much more competition between peers that peer reviews would be very suspect. Everyone is competing for that one job. We are also so busy in India. We are very put off by the paper work. I am afraid that over time, ADP might not work in India.

If ADP were implemented in Singapore, my guess is that everyone would get an average rating. That is how people seem to do things. So if everyone gets an average rating, what kind of raise do you give people? I believe that the job market in Singapore is so tight right now that whether we do ADP or not, everyone will get about the same raise. In Singapore, if people don't get a seven to eight per cent raise, they'll quit and take another job. So, is all the work associated with ADP really going to be worth it?

The feedback for Lancaster was sobering.

Here I was, relatively new in the job, wanting to change the culture and more effectively develop our people, and everyone was telling me that ADP may not be the way to go at the present time. I really believe in participative management. You can't railroad people. And yet, I still thought ADP could work wonders in the Eastern Hemisphere.

Lancaster had become increasingly worried about the lack of management strength in his organization. The brutal competition the company was facing throughout the region made him particularly sensitive to the need for more and better managers. For him, ADP was an ideal tool for developing these people.

As I contemplated a course of action, I took a closer look at our management needs in the Eastern

Hemisphere. The intensity of the competition over here has surprised me. Our big competitors view Asia as the last frontier. To win the battle here, we need excellent management. I was convinced that ADP was one the best tools we had.

A HYBRID PLAN IS PROPOSED

In March 1996, Lancaster asked Anita Lim to develop an ADP implementation plan. One month later, in April 1996, Lim presented a hybrid performance evaluation and management development system to Lancaster. Her plan was similar to the ADP in terms of its emphasis on career planning and goal setting, but without 360° feedback. Instead, Lim's plan relied on 180° feedback only (no peer or subordinate feedback). She suggested assessing the hybrid plan for a year. This would let people try it out and get comfortable with it. After a year, if it had been accepted, they could then add peer reviews, and then after another year, go to the full 360° ADP plan by adding subordinate reviews. Lim believed that a step-wise introduction of the plan would allow people to gradually buy into the change while at the same time allowing revisions where called for by cultural realities.

Betty Rong Rong, Human Resource Manager for Training, worked with Lim in developing the hybrid proposal. She commented on Lim's proposal:

> Anita put in a lot of work developing the hybrid model. We didn't know a single other company in Asia that had been successful with 360° feedback. IBM came the closest, but eventually shifted to a 180° plan. Most Asians don't like criticism or praise. Peer reviews are particularly unpopular because we are competing with each other for the same promotion.

MOVING FORWARD

With Lim's new hybrid plan, Lancaster began to have concerns about moving forward. On the one hand, he was convinced that ADP could provide significant benefits in terms of management training and development. On the other hand, he knew

he would need the human resource staff's full support if ADP were ever to be successfully implemented.

As he contemplated a course of action, Lancaster was also feeling increasing pressure from Jim Barker to improve results in the Eastern Hemisphere. The Eastern Hemisphere Group's year-end results for 1995 were disappointing and Lancaster needed to ensure that the breakeven point for the company's investments was achieved on schedule.

By late April 1996, Lancaster was considering three different options involving ADP. The first option was to do nothing. Despite the need for action, Lancaster appreciated that this option, like the others, required serious evaluation of its benefits and consequences. Perhaps the cultural gap between East and West was so great that ADP should be put on hold and they should just stick with what they were already using. Implementing ADP would require a huge effort that perhaps would be better spent building sales and focusing on figuring out the external market place.

Part of Lancaster's concern was that for ADP to be most effective, it would have to be accompanied by a huge new commitment to training and development. As a result of ADP sessions, many bosses would almost certainly encourage subordinates to take additional university courses or in-house training programs. Unfortunately, the money and infrastructure to arrange outside courses or design and put on in-house programs were limited. Whereas in the U.S., managers could put much of the onus on the employee, Lancaster realized that such an approach might be problematic in Asia. Lee Kwang Chian, Engineering Manager at the Eastern Hemisphere Design Center, explained:

> The problem is that in an Asian culture people believe that it is up to the company to look after them. If I suggest to one of my subordinates that he or she take a certain university course, he or she will take the course, but only after we arrange it all for him. People take what you give them but complain when it's not given to them on a spoon. With ADP, their expectations may only rise.

These issues were very real to Lancaster. By waiting, he would be able to ensure that the right infrastructure and follow-up programs were in place, and he would avoid shaking up such a delicate organization.

A second option for Lancaster was to go ahead with Lim's hybrid ADP. Clearly, she understood the culture better than he did. By moving forward more slowly, ADP could evolve over time. Iterative change was always less threatening, particularly when the perceived change agent was viewed by so many as an outsider. As he reflected on the input he had received, he had a growing realization that the Eastern Hemisphere was not one culture but many cultures. While he knew this intellectually before, he now had a much better "feel" for the cultural morass he was now working in. Could a single program work in such a diverse part of the world? Perhaps Lim was right and the step-wise introduction of ADP was the best way forward.

Lancaster's final option was to go forward full speed ahead. This had been his initial plan. His logic seemed impeccable. The region clearly needed shaking up. He wanted a new high performance organizational culture in the Eastern Hemisphere. He wanted to hire and support the type of employee who embraced rather than shunned change. He needed management strength now and ADP was the best tool he had. If ADP was imperfect, so be it.

With these arguments swirling through his mind, Lancaster was facing one of the toughest decisions in his career.

> Building managers here has been difficult. In part, it is because there is a limited supply of truly talented managers available. Our people need business skills, leadership skills, and industry knowledge. How do you get this in an organization that is really only a couple of years old? We must grow our people. But how should we begin and what role should ADP play?

SANDALIAS FINAS DE CUERNAVACA, S.A.: TOTAL QUALITY MANAGEMENT (A)

*Prepared by David Ager
under the supervision of Professors
Henry Lane and John Kamauff*

Version: (A) 2002-03-08

In June 1989, John Kortright, president and owner of Sandalias Finas de Cuernavaca, S.A., walked through the sandal manufacturing plant he had purchased nearly 13 years earlier, and contemplated its future and the future of its employees. Competition in Mexico had intensified over the past three years since 1986, when the Mexican government, in a move to strengthen the domestic economy, had relaxed tariff barriers allowing for the freer flow of goods and services into the country. The result had been an increase in foreign manufactured products, many of which were priced competitively and were perceived by domestic consumers to be superior in quality. Industry analysts estimated that by 1989 imports accounted for nearly 20 per cent of all footwear sales in Mexico, compared with 1986 when sales of imports were insignificant relative to total footwear sales in Mexico.

The local trade association, in response to the changing business environment in Mexico, had sponsored a seminar on Total Quality

Management (TQM) to assist its member companies to become globally competitive. TQM, as the concept was taught in the seminar, focused on such elements as customer satisfaction, supplier performance, measurement and assessment, and team development. TQM initiatives had been credited with the renewal and improved competitiveness of many successful American and Japanese business enterprises.

John commented on his situation:

> Sandalias Finas de Cuernavaca, S.A., had always been competitive relative to other companies in the domestic footwear industry. Yet, it was clear that for the company to survive in the future we would have to judge ourselves relative to foreign rather than domestic companies. The company's most glaring problem was its in-process inventory level which had averaged close to 8,000 pairs of shoes or 13 per cent of total annual production of 60,000 pairs of shoes. Although such levels were not unusual relative to other domestic footwear manufacturers, they were unsustainable if the company expected to survive in the future. Introducing a TQM initiative appeared to be a way of correcting the inventory problem while at the same time improving quality and productivity levels, and reducing manufacturing costs and response times. However, despite the potential benefits of TQM and its record of past success, I was uncertain how to proceed and whether the Mexican employees would be able to implement TQM, a system that appeared to be based on different norms and values than those of Mexican workers.

John also had thoughts of exporting to the southern United States where the Hispanic market looked as if it had potential for the company. However, to do so he realized that it would be critical for Sandalias Finas de Cuernavaca to run as efficiently as its foreign competitors.

THE MEXICAN FOOTWEAR INDUSTRY[1]

In 1989, there were 5,480 shoe and leather industry establishments throughout Mexico. Footwear was the most important leather good produced in Mexico, with more than 185 million pairs of shoes manufactured in 1988 valued at over US$1.3 billion.

The footwear industry was fragmented, although concentrated regionally. The key geographical areas for the production of shoes were Leon, Guadalajara, and Mexico City. Exhibit 1 presents a map of Mexico. Leon accounted for the great majority of footwear exports and half of the country's annual production of shoes. The main product of this area was men's shoes. Guadalajara manufacturers principally produced women's shoes with more emphasis on fashion and design. Athletic footwear production was concentrated in Mexico City.

The industry was characterized by a large number of small scale producers (in excess of 5,500), family management, a longstanding dependence on domestic markets, and much lower productivity levels than those found in the world's major shoe manufacturing regions. The structure and production levels of the Mexican footwear industry according to the National Association for the Mexican Footwear Industry are presented in Exhibits 2 and 3 respectively.

Although wages in Mexico were among the lowest in the world, higher fixed and operating costs rendered the country's cost per pair of shoes similar to that in many other countries. Exhibit 4 presents the breakdown of manufacturing costs in some of the world's major shoe manufacturing countries.

Prior to Mexico's becoming a member of the General Agreement on Tariffs and Trade (GATT) in 1986, Mexican footwear manufacturers experienced steady growth in sales and profits except for economic downturns that had been experienced throughout the country after the 1976 and 1982 devaluations. After economic liberalization in 1988/1989 tariff rates were reduced from 100 per cent to 20 per cent and foreign manufactured footwear began appearing in Mexico at price levels that were alarming to the domestic industry. By 1989, John estimated that imports accounted for in excess of 30 per cent of all Mexican footwear industry sales.

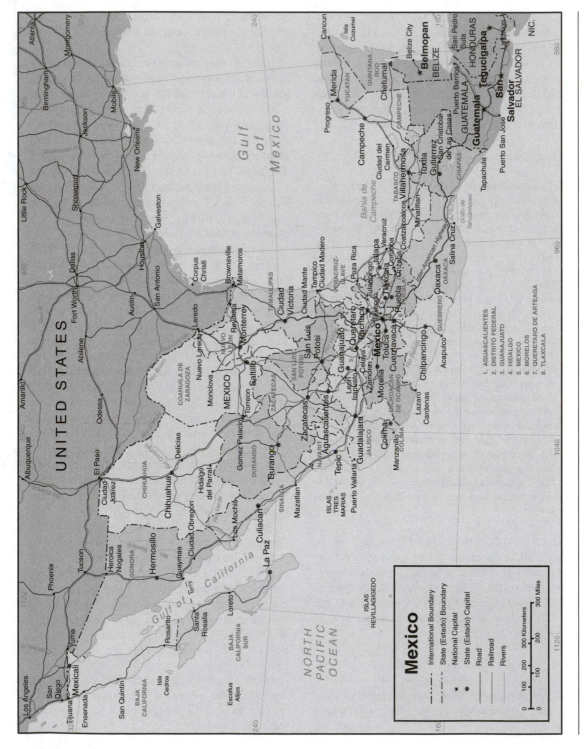

Exhibit 1   Map of Mexico

272

Per Cent of Industry	Category	Pairs of Shoes per Day
75%	Micro manufacturers	Less than 50
21%	Small manufacturers	50 to 500
3%	Medium-sized manufacturers	500 to 2,000
1%	Large manufacturers	More than 2,000

Exhibit 2   Structure of the Mexian Footwear Industry

Source: Camara National de la Industria del Calzado (Mexico).

Level of Production	Type of Production	Daily Production (pairs of shoes)	Number of People Employed
Artisans	Manual	10 to 80	5 to 15
Moderately mechanized	Machines and professionals for cutting	100 to 400	20 to 50
Fully mechanized	Mass production that guarantees quality	400++	500+

Exhibit 3   Production Levels in the Mexican Footwear Industry

Source: Camara National de la Industria del Calzado (Mexico).

The two main factors that had contributed to the success of foreign imports were lower prices and the perception by many Mexicans that imports were a better quality product. Although John agreed that inefficient production and low productivity levels had led to Mexican prices being higher than those of imports, he insisted that Mexican manufacturers were capable of producing footwear that was comparable in quality to that being imported. He also recognized that the influx of imports had given consumers a new point of reference and had increased their level of sophistication.

A third factor that plagued Mexican shoe manufacturers was the purchase of top quality shoe components such as heels, lifts and insoles, which played an important role in the quality of the final product. The lack of low-priced quality components made it difficult for Mexican manufacturers to offer consumers a final product that could compete with imports on the dimensions of price and quality.

Finally, Mexican shoes usually were not exciting in design and often did not reflect current global fashion trends. Like many shoe manufacturing countries in the world, Mexico relied on the main fashion centres such as France and Italy for design ideas. Unfortunately, because of the low level of footwear imports permitted, Mexican shoe manufacturers seldom were exposed to the most recent trends and even when they were, what they saw represented a narrow selection of available designs during a particular season.

SANDALIAS FINAS DE CUERNAVACA

John had grown up in Toronto and had completed an undergraduate degree in modern

Country	Material Costs	Labor Costs	Operating Costs[1]	Capital Costs[2]	Energy Costs	TOTAL
China	$4.00	$0.18	$0.18	$0.25	$0.10	$4.71
Brazil	$3.80	$1.25	$0.18	$0.25	$0.15	$5.63
Korea	$3.80	$1.45	$0.15	$0.18	$0.20	$5.78
Taiwan	$3.80	$1.40	$0.18	$0.20	$0.20	$5.78
Mexico	$4.00	$1.25	$0.60	$0.70	$0.25	$6.80
Italy	$3.75	$4.25	$0.20	$0.25	$0.18	$8.63
U.K.	$3.75	$4.25	$0.18	$0.30	$0.15	$8.63
United States	$3.75	$5.50	$0.20	$0.15	$0.05	$9.65
Germany	$3.75	$8.25	$0.25	$0.30	$0.10	$12.65

Exhibit 4   Breakdown of Shoe Manufacturing Costs (U.S. dollars/pairs of shoes)

1. Operating Costs include: Executives' salaries, office payroll and office expenses, sales representatives' salaries and commissions, advertising and promotion, and travel.

2. The structure of the Mexican industry was comprised predominantly of small and job shop operations that led to lower overall volumes and high capital costs per unit.

Source: Camara National de la Industria del Calzado (Mexico).

history and a master's degree in international affairs from Carleton University. Between his undergraduate and graduate degrees, he had spent some time in Mexico studying Spanish. It was during this time that he had met and married his wife, Martha, who was born and raised in Cuernavaca, a city of approximately 500,000 inhabitants located 90 km. south of Mexico City.

In 1975, in response to a desire to own his own company and to challenge himself to use what he had learned about developing countries, John and Martha returned to Mexico and settled in Cuernavaca. Shortly after their arrival, John purchased a 50 per cent interest in a local sandal factory, Sandalias Finas de Cuernavaca. A year later, he purchased the other 50 per cent of the company from his partner.

John described the original company:

When I first arrived, Sandalias Finas resembled an artisan shop rather than a factory. The people manufactured sandals whose style and decoration were representative of the Cuernavaca region of Mexico.

The sandals were distributed throughout Mexico, although Mexico City represented the largest market for our product.

By 1989, he had transformed the "artisan shop" into a series of departments that mirrored the sequence of steps involved in the manufacture of a pair of sandals. The company sold in excess of 60,000 pairs of shoes a year and had revenues that exceeded US$1 million.

The Product

Sandalias Finas de Cuernavaca, S.A., designed and manufactured dressy sandals intended for women in the 40- to 50-year-old age group who wanted the support of a wedge heel and the comfort of a padded sock.[2] Although the sandals were dressy, they were casual enough that they could be worn every day.

John, along with Martha who was responsible for design, marketing and sales, relied on attendance at trade shows in Mexico and the United

States and on fashion magazines to furnish them with ideas for the more than 50 styles of sandals that constituted their product line. Samples of the product line are presented in Exhibit 5. The Kortrights developed two product lines every year to correspond with the two annual shoe fashion seasons: spring/summer and fall/winter. In designing the product line, they worked closely with their pattern maker in order to ensure that it was physically possible to manufacture their creations and that each style was economically feasible to produce.

Exhibit 5   Product Samples

Marketing and Sales

In addition to attending shoe trade shows and fairs where they received orders for sandals, the Kortrights made several trips a month to meet with buyers from upscale department stores and finer independent shoe stores in Mexico City and Guadalajara. Some of the company's larger customers were Sears (described as being more upscale than in Canada), El Puerto de Liverpool (department store), Salinas y Rocha (department store), and Albano (independent). Although the company sold the majority of its footwear under the John Robert brand name (the manufacturer's label), Sandalias Finas de Cuernavaca also manufactured shoes under private labels for Albano and El Puerto de Liverpool.

Small orders could be for as few as 50 pairs of sandals, while large orders often exceeded 2,000 pairs of sandals. Both small independent shoe stores and some high-end image stores were responsible for placing the smaller orders. Either because of their size or their fashion image, they preferred not to carry a large amount of inventory. In addition to using quality and style as criteria for selecting suppliers, these specialty stores also based their buying decisions on a vendor's ability to complete an order quickly. Although small orders were very disruptive to the manufacturing process, they represented a significant percentage of the company's sales and could not be ignored.

John explained:

> The sandals sold for approximately US$20 wholesale and US$42 retail, which positions them as mid-range priced products being purchased by the middle-class consumer. I believe that Sandalias Finas de Cuernavaca has captured most of the Mexican market for comfort sandals in the mid- and upper-priced ends of the market.

Administration

The administrative area was located in front of the plant and included the Kortrights, two executive secretaries, a building superintendent, one accounting clerk, two customer service representatives, two store clerks, and the plant manager. The main contact between the administrative offices and the plant was through John, the foreman or the customer service representatives. Although the Kortrights received orders for sandals through direct sales, the customer service representatives handled most of the re-orders and emergency orders. Very often, they were responsible for organizing and presenting information regarding a particular order to the employees in the plant.

The Manufacturing Process

The company employed close to 70 people in its manufacturing process including five supervisors and four coordinators. John and the plant manager oversaw the entire operations. The plant was organized into five departments: cutting, sewing, heel and insole preparation, lasting, and final inspection and shipping (the supply room was part of this department). Exhibit 6 presents a floor plan of the plant. Each department was headed by a supervisor and employed anywhere from eight to 25 people. The departments operated separately from one another and the only time people from one department came in contact with those from another was when an order was being moved from department to department.

The four coordinators were responsible for moving emergency orders and re-work through their respective departments and they had the authority to interrupt the manufacturing process so that the order or re-work material they were carrying received priority treatment. Two coordinators were assigned to the sewing department and one each to the lasting and final inspection departments.

Cutting

An order document for the "batch" or "lot" originated in the administrative office, indicating the style, color, size and number of pairs of shoes that were required. This document was passed to one of the six leather cutters who were located on the second floor of the plant. The orders were

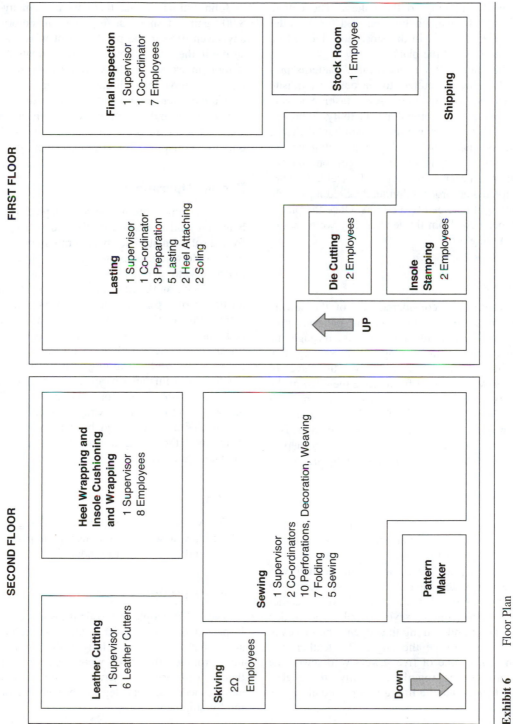

FIRST FLOOR

Final Inspection
1 Supervisor
1 Co-ordinator
7 Employees

Stock Room
1 Employee

Shipping

Lasting
1 Supervisor
1 Co-ordinator
3 Preparation
5 Lasting
2 Heel Attaching
2 Soling

Die Cutting
2 Employees

Insole Stamping
2 Employees

UP

SECOND FLOOR

Heel Wrapping and Insole Cushioning and Wrapping
1 Supervisor
8 Employees

Leather Cutting
1 Supervisor
6 Leather Cutters

Sewing
1 Supervisor
2 Co-ordinators
10 Perforations, Decoration, Weaving
7 Folding
5 Sewing

Skiving
2Ω Employees

Pattern Maker

Down

Exhibit 6   Floor Plan

277

assigned randomly to the cutters. The cutters collected the leather they required for an order from the attendant in the stockroom located on the first floor of the plant.

The leather cutters used metal patterns prepared by the die cutters to cut out the requisite pieces as per the order. As a fashion season progressed, the cutters' productivity improved because they became more familiar with the patterns and they developed a technique for laying the various patterns pieces out on the leather in order to maximize the yield. A cutter completed an order individually. Seldom was an order split between two cutters. Once the pieces had been cut from the leather they were sent to the skiving area.

Skiving

Skiving was considered part of the sewing department. Depending on the pattern, most leather pieces would have to pass through the skiving area before moving into the sewing area. Skiving was a process whereby a thin layer of leather was removed from along the edge of the underside of the leather. This process made it easier for the sewers to fold the leather underneath itself, thereby creating a strong edge. Two people were employed fulltime and one person was employed halftime in the skiving area.

Sewing

Twenty-two people worked in one of three areas of the sewing department located on the second floor of the plant. Ten people worked in the "preliminary" area where the leather was either perforated, decorated, or woven according to the particular style of sandal. Next the leather pieces were sent to seven people who folded the leather under along the edge of the pieces in order to reinforce the edge. The leather was then sent to one of five sewers who sewed the various pieces together. Finally, the pieces were trimmed and a lining was placed along the underside.

John estimated that there were as many as 8,000 pairs of shoes in in-process inventory at any given time in the plant, half of which were sitting in the sewing area. He also estimated that it took in excess of 10 working days for the leather to move through the sewing area.

Matters were complicated further by emergency orders and re-works. Very often projects were set aside in order to deal with priorities, only to be misplaced in part or completely.

Parallel Operations

At the same time as the leather pieces were being cut and sewn, the insoles were being cut from a roll of material. This operation employed two people who used a piece of semi-automated machinery to perform the task. These people were located on the first floor of the plant. Once all the insoles for an order had been cut, they were sent to the second floor, where extra padding was added to the insoles before the upper side was covered with leather. In addition to padding and wrapping the insoles, the employees in this area wrapped the plastic shoe heels in leather. Eight people worked at padding and wrapping insoles and wrapping heels. When the insoles and heels had been prepared, they were sent to the lasting area where all parts of the sandal were assembled.

Lasting

Twelve people worked in the lasting area, where they assembled the leather uppers, the insoles and the heels into sandals.

Final Inspection

The seven people in the final inspection area inspected the sandals for defects and returned shoes that required reworking to the production line. Provided the shoes were acceptable, they then moved forward where they were retouched and cleaned. The final step was boxing and packing for shipment.

Human Resources

Education

John explained that there were major challenges in dealing with his Mexican workers:

> In 1976 the average level of formal education of the workers in the plant was less than five years. I now insist that any new people hired have at least nine years of formal education; the average level of education in the plant is approximately nine years.

> Unlike in Canada or the United States where public education is provided until the end of high school, in Mexico it is only recently that the government has expanded education. Prior to President Salinas coming to power in 1988, the national goal was to give everyone in Mexico six years of education. Only under President Salinas did the government feel that it had the resources to try to provide nine years of education to everyone. The quality of the public school system in Mexico still is not satisfactory and it varies from school to school.

John explained that many bright students who had the capacity for further education left school after grade nine. Their families could not afford to send them to school for more education, nor could they afford for them not to be working and contributing to the family income.

> When I arrived in Mexico in the 1970s, I believed that I could take people with any level of education and train them. I came to realize that this belief was idealistic. I found it difficult to train people, even if they had six years of education because very often they couldn't concentrate on work; they couldn't reason and they lacked discipline. This realization led me to adopt the new hiring policy. I had found that there was a marked difference between people with six years of education and those with nine years. At the same time, I was leery about hiring people with too much education. I found that those people with 12 years of education were over educated for the job I was offering and unless I continued to offer these people better jobs, they left.

In the rare cases where employees have finished high school, they move into supervisory positions in the factory. Supervisors are encouraged to recommend changes to improve the system.

A second challenge was convincing workers to accept responsibility. Exhibit 7 provides a brief discussion of some of the cultural traits of Mexicans. Mexican tradition was one of hierarchical structures in which senior managers took a paternalistic approach to management and problem solving. The top directed the middle and the bottom. Middle managers concentrated on implementing rather than planning, and employees remained silent about a manager's errors or omissions. Correcting or questioning a superior was considered rude. Similarly, accepting a superior's orders or suggestions without asking questions was a strong norm. In the case of a conflict, employees referred to authority and hierarchy rather than to resolving the problem through consensus or on their own. Employees were reluctant to assume responsibility because of their fear of punishment in the event of a mistake. As a result, it was very difficult to encourage decision making at lower levels. As well, it was uncommon for employees to make suggestions about how a work situation might be improved. John commented:

> Mexicans respond to what they hear and see. People bring their attitudes and beliefs from home. At work they expect to follow orders, although very often they don't do what they are supposed to do. They respond well to being treated humanely and appreciate the concept of fairness.

Compensation

The plant workers were paid on a piecework basis. Although wages were low relative to those in other newly industrialized and developing countries, fringe benefits, including labor law benefits were significantly relative to total payroll costs. John explained that in his company benefits represented an additional cost of from 50 to 60 per cent of the basic wage. Exhibit 8 presents some of the benefits stipulated in Mexican federal labor law.

This information is reprinted from *Management in Two Cultures: Bridging the Gap Between U.S. and Mexican Manager*, Eva S. Dras, Intercultural Press, Inc., Yarmouth, Maine, Copyright 1989. It is reprinted with the permission of Intercultural Press and Ms. Kras. Ms. Kras has lived in Mexico for 20 years where she has taught business administration and operated a management consulting company serving Mexican and American companies.

Family

The traditional family remains the foundation of Mexican society, taking precedence over work and all other aspects of life. As one Mexican executive said, "Our family is our first priority and must remain so for the future stability of our country." Within the family unit, the father is the undisputed authority figure. All major decisions are made by him and he sets the disciplinary standards. The mother is subservient, seeking the advice and authority of her husband in all major matters. She is expected to be a devoted mother and obedient wife and is revered as such. The Mexican executive's wife has not usually worked outside the home before marriage and has little knowledge or understanding of her husband's work. Their two worlds meet, however, in their dedication to the family, and especially to their children, who are protected and loved, accepted and enjoyed. The normal weekend recreation consists of entire family units, including a variety of relatives and friends, visiting each other or going out together. Growing up in these circumstances, children feel secure but are very dependent on the moral support of their families. Likewise, children respect their parents and grandparents and care for them in their old age.

Upon reaching school age and having been conditioned by the home environment, children tend to accept school discipline as an extension of parental discipline. This does not necessarily mean that they are all well-behaved, but their resistance to discipline is often clothed in deviousness rather than overt rebellion, a trait sometimes carried into adulthood. The child usually becomes conformist, accepting the rigidity of the school system in which the teacher is the undisputed authority and in which the development of a questioning mind is inhibited.

As a result of his upbringing and education, a young executive appears obsequious to his superior and accepts instructions unquestioningly. He is unaccustomed to solving problems that arise and feels little sense of personal accountability. Since all authority resides in his superior, the subordinate's responsibility is limited to carrying out instructions.

In addition, because of his strong emotional attachment to family and friends, he demonstrates considerable resistance to moving away from them; the need for that attachment and support is simply too strong. The Mexican executive is therefore not as mobile as his U.S. counterpart and will not happily move to another city, let alone to another country (though Mexicans of course do move when economic necessity forces it).

Pedagogy

Mexican pedagogy is based on traditional French and Spanish patterns of deductive reasoning, moving from the general to the particular, from the abstract to the concrete. In practice this translates into the rote learning of abstract concepts, usually long before they can be understood. Ideas and concepts are introduced in early primary grades and children are required to memorize them and reproduce them verbatim for examinations on which all grading is based. Little credit is given for classroom work; students therefore become very examination-oriented. As a student progresses through high school to the university, the method remains basically the same, though the concepts are better understood and related to concrete reality as students become more and more intellectually sophisticated. But the next step, learning how to apply ideas in practical situations, is hardly ever taken. It is not surprising, then, that Mexicans often have difficulty developing problem-solving skills essential in the workplace.

Students generally accept the rigid conformity demanded by the school system, in part probably because of their exposure to an authoritarian father figure during childhood. Children with quick and inquisitive minds are pressured into conformity. Original thinking is discouraged, and students of above average intelligence generally either lapse into boredom and become lazy, or possibly rebel in subtle ways.

Exhibit 7   Some Mexican Cultural Traits   *(Continued)*

Great importance is attached to the attractive presentation of student work, to the point that it is sometimes valued as highly as the quality of the content. As regards subject matter, emphasis is placed on the acquisition of general knowledge in subjects such as world geography and history, sociology, literature, languages and the basics of the natural sciences. A person with this breadth of knowledge, combined with the good breeding that is the norm in upper-class families, is considered a "cultured person" (*una persona muy culta*) who is highly esteemed. Thus, the average university graduate arrives in the business world with a good grounding in general knowledge and an interest in the world at large, but may lack depth in his field of specialization.

Direction, Supervision and Delegation

Mexican executives have great respect for authority. Their upbringing has inculcated in them an acceptance of absolute authority on the part of parents and, at times, elders. As a result, young executives never question or even comment on a decision of their superiors, even if they totally disagree with it. Nor do superiors normally accept such questioning from subordinates. Typical comments by Mexican executives are: "Subordinates are expected to accept unconditionally what their boss says, even through they might disagree," or "If the boss says the paper is green, then it is green," or simply, "The Mexican does as he is told."

In Mexico there is no tradition of delegation of authority; the concept itself is alien to most people. The boss is an extension of the autocratic, authoritarian father image. As a result, delegation of responsibilities normally takes the form of assignment of specific tasks which are carried out in constant consultation with one's superior. Most subordinates prefer this approach, since it saves them from errors and from losing face. This is summed up by a comment from a Mexican executive: "Subordinates feel insecure and are afraid of making mistakes."

The smaller firms are nearly all completely autocratic. The larger companies, on the other hand, have become so complex that the delegation of responsibility for an area, and even some actual authority, has become a necessity. Nevertheless, even in the largest companies today, authority is, for the most part, still vested in a very few at the top. One finds considerable delegation or responsibility but rarely the authority to go with it.

It must, nevertheless, be pointed out that a new generation of managers is growing up in Mexico who, on the basis of their university training and modern attitudes, strongly support the practice of delegation of responsibility together with the accompanying authority, backed up by the necessary accountability. Where this more participative approach has been introduced, it has generally met with success. The shift is slow in taking place, but it is widely felt to be essential for business success in an increasingly competitive economy.

Mexican senior managers generally find it difficult to effectively delegate responsibilities and to develop the full potential of their subordinates. As a result, junior managers are not accustomed to working independently, shouldering responsibility and handling authority. The whole area of effective delegation and supervision techniques thus requires considerable development in Mexico. The junior executive needs the knowledge and the self-confidence to take on heavy responsibilities, while the U.S. manager has to develop the rapport necessary for guiding the transition. This is not a rapid process. It must be understood that the subordinate wants to please his boss and thus prefers to stop and ask for advice rather than make a mistake. Therefore, it is important that explanations be unambiguous and fully understood. On the other hand, the young executive should be brought into the decision-making process as early as possible and be convinced that accepting responsibilities is to his benefit.

Author's Note: These observations represent traditional Mexican culture which has influenced practices in the workplace, however, some companies may be adopting new practices as the Mexican economy changes.

Exhibit 7   Some Mexican Cultural Traits

Item	Description
Minimum daily salary	Established for separate regions of the country. Varied from N$¹12.04 to N$14.27 per day.
Vacation days	After one year of employment employees were entitled to six days' paid vacation, increased by two days for each of three subsequent years of employment and by two more days for each additional five years.
Vacation bonus	A bonus of 25 per cent of normal pay during vacation period was mandatory.
Aginaldo (Christmas bonus)	Employers were required to pay each employee the equivalent of 15 days' pay.
National Workers' Housing Fund	Employers were required to contribute five per cent of their payroll to this fund.
Profit sharing	Employers were required to distribute 10 per cent of their pre-tax profits to their employees.
Seguridad Social (Social Security)	Contributions/premiums incurred by both the employer and employee. It was estimated the employer contribution equalled 17 per cent of the employee wage, and the employee contribution was eight per cent of his or her wage.
Severance pay	Employees dismissed for cause (incompetence/disciplinary problems) received 12 paid days per year of service computed based on a maximum of two minimum daily salaries of the general economic zone. Employees dismissed for other reasons received three months' pay and an additional 20 days' pay for every year employed. Generally severance pay was negotiated and most workers received one and a half months' severance pay. Workers also had the option of contesting their severance pay if they believed they were being treated unfairly.

Exhibit 8 Worker Benefits (as outlined by Mexican federal labor law)

1. N$ = New Peso. To help simplify foreign exchange transactions the Mexican government introduced a new peso on January 1, 1993. The new peso was worth 1,000 of the old pesos. U.S. dollar–Mexican peso exchange rates since 1989 were as follows: June 30, 1989, US$1 = N$2.491; November 26, 1994, US$1 = N$3.44; November 21, 1995, US$1 = N$7.70.

Sources: Doing Business in Mexico—Information Guide, *Price Waterhouse,* USA, 1993.
   Doing Business in Mexico—International Business Series, *Ernst & Young International, Ltd.,* New York, NY, 1993.

DECISION

For some time John had been thinking about how to solve his inventory problem. As he explained:

I realized that the amount of work-in-process inventory that was spread throughout the factory was hindering the company's ability to grow. I kept asking myself how we were going to grow, because I knew that we needed to grow in order to survive into the future. But if nothing changed, and the company grew, it was inevitable that more and more work-in-process inventory would accumulate. It dawned on me that I was never going to get enough money to finance that inventory.

It was clear to me as well that we were not meeting our objectives. We were not achieving the quality levels we wanted and we were not getting the shoes out on time. Things just weren't working. It was at this time that I heard about TQM, and while in principle it sounded like the answer to all my problems, in reality I was sceptical about whether or not Mexico, and in particular the workers in my factory, were ready for a solution made in Japan or the United States.

After reviewing the literature he had received at the meeting on TQM, John visited all the work areas of the shoe plant trying to decide if and how this technique had a place in Cuernavaca,

Mexico. Was it worth the risk and effort required to implement TQM into his factory? If so, how should he go about doing it? If not, what alternatives existed so that this company could survive the influx of foreign imports?

NOTES

1. The information in this section is taken from "Strategic Planning '95—The Mexican Marketplace: Analysis and Forecasts," American Chamber of Commerce of Mexico, A.C., August 1994.
2. The sock is the part of the sandal upon which rest the ball of the foot and the toes.

VICTORIA HOSPITAL REDESIGN INITIATIVE

Prepared by Karen Fryday-Field under the supervision of Professor Al Mikalachki

Version: (A) 2002-02-27

Dr. Linden Frelick, president and chief executive officer of Victoria Hospital, knew that the organization would have to make major changes if it were to continue its role in providing health care to the community. Recognizing that conventional hospitals were no longer able to respond effectively to the problem of reduced resources, he estimated that there was approximately an 18 month window to make major gains in efficiency before the government imposed even more significant economic constraints. In January 1995, he had presented a restructuring vision which he had determined would lower costs, improve patient care, and utilize employees' full potential. His plan required a far-reaching reorganization of the hospital's services: to replace the traditional hierarchical structure of function-specific groups or "silos" with a flat structure of streamlined interdisciplinary and self-managed clinical teams.

Several months later, with no clear consensus among the board of directors and with varying degrees of support from the administration, doctors, nurses, and other professionals, Dr. Frelick had to take action to get his proposed redesign plan back on track.

VICTORIA HOSPITAL

The Public Hospitals Act of Ontario regulated the hospital, which was owned and operated by the Victoria Hospital Corporation, comprising approximately 130 corporate members. In 1995, the hospital had 650 in-patient beds designated for acute care and rehabilitation. In addition, it operated a network of ambulatory services including clinics, day surgery and one-day medical stays. The hospital's areas of specialty included:

women's and children's care, cardiac services, cancer care, and life support/trauma services.

The mission of Victoria Hospital was "to provide excellent, compassionate health care for its community; to provide comprehensive health education; and to seek answers through health sciences research." Victoria Hospital, which employed about 4,000 people and delivered the bulk of general care to London and area residents, was indispensable to the people of southwestern Ontario. Staff treated nearly half a million patients from across the region and the province each year. Commitment to education was strong, with training provided annually for more than 1,100 students from over 20 health related disciplines. The spirit of inquiry was alive through the Victoria Hospital Research Institute which administered over $7 million in research grants on an annual basis.

ENVIRONMENTAL
FACTORS DRIVING CHANGE

Economic Pressures on Hospitals

After many years of expanding their services before 1990, hospitals were facing funding declines which resulted in many years of cost cutting strategies. The health care system would continue to undergo further profound change and budget cuts over the next two years.

Ontario hospitals were currently funded through the provincial Ministry of Health. Faced with a provincial deficit exceeding $10 billion, a downgraded provincial credit rating and reduced federal transfer payments to health care, the ministry had significantly cut hospital budgets. Because funding would be reallocated amongst existing hospitals based on factors such as efficiency and utilization patterns, as reflected by case costs, hospitals were feeling pressure to demonstrate their cost effectiveness. Teaching hospitals, which traditionally received higher levels of funding than community hospitals, would lose this benefit and receive a standard fee based on the type of service provided. The government was also setting policies designed

to drive down the number and length of hospital stays by promoting the provision of more services on an outpatient basis. In addition, the ministry's "delisting" of several health services would result in patients paying the fees for these services that previously had represented a potential revenue source for the hospital.

Operational costs for hospitals continued to be influenced by inflation. Significant cost increases resulted from legislative requirements relating to pensions, pay equity and employee benefits. Seventy per cent of hospital budgets represented salaries and wages. There was pressure for salary increases in 1996 when the Social Contract legislation was due to expire. Hospitals also faced escalating expenses resulting from clinical and technological advancements that required ongoing capital expenditures.

External Forces Affecting Victoria Hospital

Because the city of London had three acute care, teaching hospitals all within a short distance of each other, many services were duplicated. Therefore, the Ministry of Health and the District Health Council indicated that rationalization of the London system must occur. Efforts for joint planning had not yet been successful at creating significant change in city-wide co-ordination of health services. However, in September 1995, a committee proposal for a city-wide rationalization of clinical services recommended a relocation of cardiac surgery and neurosurgery from Victoria Hospital to University Hospital.

Another factor was the changing role of health care patients. In the past, doctors and experts analysed, diagnosed and prescribed treatments with little involvement or input from the patient. However, patients were increasing their demands with respect to health care delivery. They and their families wanted more detailed information about the status of their health and the treatment options available, and insisted on participating in the decision making process.

In the face of changing patient expectations and improved technologies and medical practices, the health care system was attempting to reduce the need for overnight hospital stays and to deliver care in an ambulatory mode. As a result, hospitals were shifting many diagnostic tests and therapeutic procedures to services that they could provide on an outpatient basis. In addition, procedures and therapies historically done in hospital were being done in physicians' offices and walk-in clinics. The perception was that ambulatory care was beneficial for the patients, who generally could sleep at home, as well as for the hospitals, which saved money on a cost per patient basis. Hospitals continued to develop ways to reach into the community to promote health and to deliver health services.

Victoria Hospital's Competitive Position

Conducting Victoria Hospital's operations on two separate sites created a significant operating cost disadvantage. The hospital was working toward a long standing objective to consolidate on the Westminster campus in order to reduce operating costs, enhance co-ordination of service delivery, and improve the morale of the care practitioners. Estimations were that consolidation would cost about $100 million and yield annual operating savings of $2 million to $4 million.

Victoria Hospital's 1995 annual budget was roughly $250 million. During the previous five years, government funding of hospitals had been gradually declining and Victoria Hospital had responded by implementing incremental cost cutting strategies each year. In fact, the hospital had achieved a balanced budget for the past 13 years. However, it expected that the Ministry of Health would remove 15 per cent to 20 per cent of the current operating funding over the next three to five years. Because Victoria Hospital had the highest case costs in the province, further drawbacks in funding would be inevitable if the ministry implemented the plan to reimburse hospitals based on a standard case cost. Therefore, Victoria had developed an economic model that produced the projections shown in Exhibit 1: Given a set of status quo operating assumptions,

the overall financial shortfall would total $64 million by the year 2001.

INTERNAL FACTORS DRIVING CHANGE

Functional Organizational Structure

For decades the hospital had been organized along traditional hierarchical lines with various professional groups linked through functional departments. The chart in Exhibit 2 illustrates the administration's organizational structure during the past three years. The numerous medical functional departments received support from 60 other service departments, such as pharmacy, nursing, physical therapy, social work, finance, human resources and building services (see Table 1). The functional departments conducted department specific training and development, selection criteria and performance evaluation of their department members.

These function-specific groupings tended to operate in silos and focus on the needs of the silos. However, in the current rapidly changing health care field, Victoria Hospital's clinical services had to be more flexible, and adaptable to evolving patient needs and reduced resources. In certain ways, these silos inhibited the capacity of Victoria Hospital's clinical services to respond to the environmental changes of the decade.

Under this system, groups of health professionals delivered care to patients with similar needs within designated areas of the hospital called clinical units. For example, patients with heart problems would receive medical care in the cardiology unit. Each health professional belonged to a particular functional department, such as nursing, internal medicine, or surgery, which generally hired, fired, set targets, assessed performance, determined procedures, and controlled the resources which affected the clinical units. A weakness in this system occurred in some clinical units when the health professionals worked side by side to deliver patient care but did not function as a team. In this situation, the overall goals for the clinical area and even for specific patients were often unclear, and

	1995/96	1996/97	1997/98	1998/99	1999/00	2000/01	TOTAL
Operating Results	11.7	(5.0)	(19.8)	(34.3)	(48.5)	(52.3)	(148.2)
Regular Capital Expenditures[1]	(6.7)	(7.2)	(7.2)	(7.2)	(7.2)	(7.2)	(42.7)
Commitments[2]		(2.5)	(1.0)				(3.5)
Cash Shortfall	5.0	(14.7)	(28.0)	(41.5)	(55.7)	(59.5)	(194.4)
Redesign Savings	3.5	29.5	31.5	31.5	31.5	31.5	159.0
Redesign Costs	(3.5)	(12.3)					(15.8)
Information Technology[3]	(1.0)	(2.5)	(5.2)	(2.5)	(1.0)	(1.0)	(13.2)
Remaining Shortfall[4]	4.0	(0.0)	(1.7)	(12.5)	(25.2)	(29.0)	(64.4)
Regional Savings, etc.[5]	0.0	0.0	0.0	0.0	0.0	0.0	0.0
Net Results	4.0	(0.0)	(1.7)	(12.5)	(25.2)	(29.0)	(64.4)

Exhibit 1   Five Year Financial Projection for Victoria Hospital Operations ($ millions)

Source: Victoria Hospital (CEO's office).

1. Regular capital expenditures were reduced in 1995/1996 as part of the budget balancing strategies.

2. In 1996/1997, Victoria Hospital was committed to building a veterans' park ($0.5) and purchasing a magnetic resonance imaging (M.R.I.) ($3.0).

3. Information Technology cost estimates are based on the original I.S. Strategic Plan Document which is currently being reviewed.

4. The $4.0 cash surplus in 1995/1996 represents the achievement of the Board Mandated Savings Plan.

5. Pending outcome of LACTHRC and merger feasibility.

inefficiencies existed where tasks were duplicated by staff. A failure in communication could also cause health professionals to feel torn between the goals of their functional department and the perceived goals of their clinical unit.

Often, the successful acquisition of the hospital's limited resources was based on the historical power base of the functional groupings rather than through justifiable requirements based on patients' needs or good business planning. Work processes which flowed horizontally across the functional groups were often disjointed and did not evolve effectively because of the vertical barriers built by the functional departments. Technology and better understanding of the horizontal nature of clinical processes afforded opportunities to re-engineer these procedures.

The degree of success afforded by this system varied. Sometimes a silo was inflexible, and resisted changes that it perceived would affect it negatively even if the overall effect for the hospital might be positive. For example, a silo could stall or prevent the implementation of a decision to move resources from one area to another, based on patient need. On the other hand, in some clinical units, groups of health professionals worked to develop methods and processes that allowed them to work as interdisciplinary teams. However, the success of these teams in achieving efficient and effective care delivery processes varied significantly.

Changing Care Delivery Models

One change in the delivery of health service was the movement toward following Patient

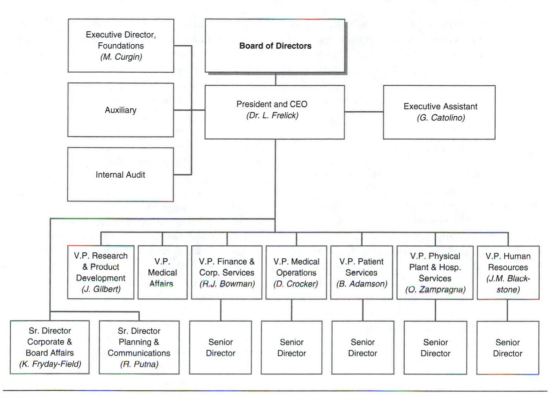

Exhibit 2   Organizational Structure

Source: Victoria Hospital.

Table 1   Functional Departments (Partial Lists—Examples Only)

Professional Services	*Medical Services*	*Physical Plant/ Hospital Services*
Audiology	Anaesthesia	Finance
Nursing	Internal Medicine	Housekeeping/Building
Physiotherapy	Nuclear Medicine	Services
Occupational Therapy	Dentistry	Physical Plant
Social Work	Critical Care	Planning
Psychology	Surgery	Nutrition and Food Services
Speech Pathology	Rheumatology	Transportation
Pastoral Care	Neurosciences	Portering
	Orthopaedics	Sterile Processing
	Nephrology	
	Emergency	

Care Guidelines and Pathways, a series of research-based recommendations for the delivery of care to patients diagnosed with similar medical conditions. The guidelines were often supported by a plan of care that generally standardized the essential elements of care for approximately 90 per cent of patients in any one diagnostic category.

The development of a standard plan of care caused the clinicians, as a group, to examine every step of the care process and identify the value-added components. As a result, staff could dramatically reduce unnecessary variations in ordinary diagnostic tests and therapies.

Information Technologies

The use of on-line clinical information could result in reaching informed clinical decisions both for groups of patients and for individual patients. Victoria Hospital information technology had historically focused on administrative systems such as finance and payroll, rather than on clinical information such as providing lab information at the bedside or tracking patient statistics. However, the health care industry was rapidly moving to the provision of on-line co-ordination of clinical information.

Physicians

In the past, two main health professions existed to deliver the care—medicine and nursing. Physicians were highly trained in the necessary skills for performing diagnostics and prescribing treatment. Nurses had been developing increasing skills and a body of knowledge on delivering care to patients in a holistic sense. Historically, physicians were the gatekeepers to the system and were the overall planners and co-ordinators who determined the treatment and then designated the actual delivery of care to nurses or other professionals. Physicians traditionally had not been required to function as team players.

Six hundred physicians, who were essentially independent contractors in the health system, worked at Victoria. Physicians were usually affiliated with a hospital by contract and were governed by a medical advisory committee to the board of directors.

As Victoria was a teaching hospital, the affiliation of many of the physicians was through a formal contract with The University of Western Ontario, where they usually had teaching

responsibilities. As well, they had the duty residents completing their practical experience. In addition, the university evaluated them for promotion through the system, placing a high weighting on their research publications. Hence, these physicians had dual loyalties to the university and the hospital.

Dr. Mike Lewen, past president of the medical staff, recently provided insight into the physician relationships. He indicated that:

> In general, academic physicians are compelled to progress through the professional advancement system of the university. This requires peer reviewed research and publication. Academic physicians' allegiance is often greater to the university than to an individual hospital, including Victoria.

> Most physicians do not hold any particular interest in the administrative activities and initiatives of the hospital. The announcement from the hospital that it is planning to redesign patient care delivery systems will be met with indifference or scepticism by physicians as to whether the hospital is capable of changing.

> Many initiatives that particular interdisciplinary teams undertake are perceived by physicians to be thwarted by home department (functional department) decisions. Interdisciplinary teams should be able to work independently, within certain parameters, to achieve their goals.

Nurses and Other Professionals

The health care system responded to external demands with more innovation, new technologies, and a new group of applied health sciences professionals. Many of these people emerged from the nursing profession and acquired unique bodies of knowledge based on science and skill. The development of experts in many expanded fields led to pressure from patients, some of whom, at times, wished to access the health care system through professionals other than physicians. The Ministry of Health responded in January 1994 by implementing the Regulated Health Professions Act, which allowed 22 categories of qualified practitioners, such as midwives, chiropodists, audiologists, to perform various functions once only provided by a physician. These developments were challenging the traditional hierarchy of health care services.

Nurses and members of applied health professions were accustomed to performing as members of teams. An organizational change would result in the need to re-evaluate and address how health care providers could work together to provide integrated and efficiently delivered care.

Jennifer Jones, director of nursing, indicated at a recent focus group that nurses were very interested in "where the hospital is going" in the future. She indicated that she was aware of the hospital's desire to move toward interdisciplinary teams. She had a number of comments and concerns about the situation, including:

> Nurses have historically been the co-ordinators of inpatient care and we see this as something that is unique to their function. We are concerned that, in an interdisciplinary model, others may be given this role. It seems logical that the nurse managers who currently manage a nursing unit would, in future, become managers of interdisciplinary teams.

> We are also concerned about the ability of nurses to maintain their nursing practice standards in an interdisciplinary environment. A strong affiliation with the department of nursing is perceived to be important to foster professional growth and development of nurses.

> Personally, I am not at all sure that any kind of organization change is required. The hospital may be overreacting to the economic environment. The downsizing the hospital has done to date should be sufficient to address Victoria's financial problems.

A VISION FOR REDESIGNING THE HOSPITAL

Dr. Frelick recognized that Victoria needed to respond to the challenges it was facing. During the fall of 1994, when he undertook an assessment of the pressures facing the hospital and the many strengths within the hospital, he engaged in significant consultation with senior management,

hospital staff, and the board of directors. In January 1995, Dr. Frelick, through a series of meetings, shared a vision for a newly designed hospital with these groups.

This new vision was to provide a positive environment with effective results for patients, who would move through the various phases of care (prevention in the community, pre-admission, ambulatory, in-patient, etc.) in a seamless efficient fashion. Victoria would achieve this vision by empowering self-directed care teams to:

- develop care plans across the continuum of care;
- develop new work processes to streamline operations and reduce costs; and
- focus on delivering quality care directed at meeting patients' service needs.

The vision also included re-engineered hospital-wide administrative processes that would maximize the use of technology, thereby increasing hospital efficiency. In addition, Dr. Frelick envisioned new entrepreneurial initiatives that would create additional revenue streams as government funding decreased.

Strategies to Achieve the Vision

Many Ontario hospitals which faced similar situations were developing a variety of approaches for coping with increasing economical cutbacks. The most straightforward strategy was an upfront massive downsizing of the organization, i.e., a "slash and burn" strategy. Dr. Frelick believed that, although this method would produce immediate financial results, it was only a short term solution. He concluded that hospitals would have to undergo a fundamental change in how they delivered care, in conjunction with carefully planned restructuring. Therefore, he developed a plan which called for three fundamental business strategies to achieve the new vision.

The first strategy included bringing the organization structure into line with the way the hospital cared for patients. The goal here was to realign the organization with the primary production centres by developing highly capable interdisciplinary care teams which could meet the demands of their ever changing environments. The care teams would be clustered in groups forming "product-lines" (see Exhibit 3). The hospital would also have to build strong linkages and partnerships with other providers of services and supplies in the community. In its restructuring, Victoria would need to determine what work could best be done by others and then form strategic partnerships to achieve these efficiencies.

The second strategy involved the redesign of the "system of production" to bring work processes into line with current technology, expected patient outcomes, patient needs and resource constraints. For example, a project was launched to redesign the admitting process so that patients could go directly to the specific unit without going through an admitting department. The projected impact included significant dollar savings as well as improved patient/customer service.

The third strategy required the development of entrepreneurial strategies to support the vision. Opportunities for significant revenue generation through the provision of services that were no longer covered by provincial health insurance, through services which could be marketed abroad, and services for physicians and other health care practitioners affiliated with the hospital, must be devised.

The first step was to develop a few prototype interdisciplinary care teams. Support would be available in areas such as project planning and measurement development, and a corporate framework of targets would provide direction. These new teams, which could then assume self-direction within those guidelines, would have the following goals:

PATIENT GROUPS			
	In-patient	Ambulatory	Outreach
STRATEGIC PROGRAMS — Life Support Services	T1 T2	T3 T4 T5	T6 T7
	(Work Teams)		

INFRA-STRUCTURE	Support Systems (Across Groups and Across Programs)		
	Some Support Resources in Team		

DEVELOPMENT	Disciplines		
	MAC	Management	Professionals	Workers

Exhibit 3   General Redesign for Care Teams

- defining and clarifying targets to establish world class capability;
- developing a game plan to achieve the targets;
- planning for patient care, related education, and applied research;
- determining what resources are required to achieve their goals;
- developing patient care strategies with good outcomes at reasonable case costs; and
- developing measurement systems to determine progress.

Once the initial methodology for care team design had been tested and enhanced, other related or linked care teams would be mandated to launch the change process. Gradually, groups of care teams would be linked together to form product lines; for example, cardiovascular services, children's services or cancer services.

Careful evaluation of the infrastructure required to support the care teams would also be necessary. Some of the support systems such as porters and cleaners might be decentralized and assigned directly to each care team or program, while other services such as information systems would remain centralized. Health professional disciplines would be assigned to the care teams but would remain grouped together in some form to address certain discipline-specific concerns.

IMPLEMENTATION—THE ORGANIZATION'S RESPONSE

Financial Targets

Task forces were established to design and implement the specific initiatives. Each was led by a member of senior management or a member of the senior medical staff, and staffed primarily with middle managers and some physicians, all of whom were conducting their regular duties in addition to the new challenges of the redesign initiative.

The task forces were to achieve several goals. Their initial financial targets, based on economic forecasts, had been developed to ensure that the savings achieved would be sufficient to meet the

annual economic shortfalls projected to 1999 (see Exhibit 4). They also had qualitative targets, such as reduced waiting time for patients in the admitting process. The CEO asked them to validate the assigned initial targets, to develop specific implementation strategies, and to integrate their redesign plans with other key initiatives, including consolidation of operations on one site.

Board of Directors' Response

Early in the process Dr. Frelick had presented the goals, the strategy for implementation, and the financial targets to the board of directors for information and support. He spent significant time discussing the difference between a "slash and burn" type of downsizing and the participative approach he had chosen. The board shared initial enthusiasm for the redesign initiative by indicating support for the values, the vision and the strategy.

However, during subsequent meetings, debate arose regarding whether or not the plan put forward by the CEO could actually meet the economic challenge facing the hospital. Friction began to develop at the board table. Some members indicated that they did not really understand the redesign initiative and were concerned that the approach might take too long to deliver the required cost savings. On the other hand, others believed that if appropriate care were taken, the organization could achieve more fundamental change through redesigning patient care teams than by "slash and burn" downsizing. Rather than give the CEO the mandate to achieve results, the board members sought more detailed financial projections to ensure the feasibility of the project. Eventually, they asked the CEO to provide a detailed implementation plan prior to the task forces' presentation of their unit based strategies.

Tension continued to grow at the board level. Members debated whether consolidating the hospital from two sites to one site was more important than the redesign initiative. At times, it was unclear whether some of the specific tensions

Overall Dollars Required (Total Target)	1995/1996 $8.3 M	1996/1997 $18.9 M	1997/1998 $16.7 M	1998/1999 $16.5 M
Task Force Cost Cutting Targets				
Overhead/Fixed Costs (Operations Benchmarking Task Force)	(2.0 M)	(1.0 M)	(1.0 M)	—
Clinical Resource Management (Optimizing Case Mix and Length of Stay)	(3.8 M)	(5.5 M)	—	—
Leadership Design (Organizational Structure)	(0.5 M)	(0.5 M)	—	—
Patient Care Innovation (Self-directed Teams and Major Clinical Processes e.g., Care Paths, Admitting)	—	(6.0 M)	(8.0 M)	—
Consolidation (to one campus)	—	—	To Be Determined	To Be Determined
Task Force on Revenue Enhancement				
(Ambulatory Care, Preferred Accommodation, Land Leases)	2.0 M	4.0 M	10.0 M	10.0 M
TOTAL IMPACT (Improved by)	$8.3 M	$17.0 M	To Be Finalized	To Be Finalized

Exhibit 4   Financial Target

Source: Victoria Hospital (CEO's office).

were directed generally toward the administration and concerns about their capabilities to lead the organization through major change or toward internal conflicts among board members.

The Administration

From the beginning, the CEO had involved the vice presidents in his vision of building a new hospital organization and a new way of conducting business. He conducted a series of planning sessions with the senior team to seek their input and counsel regarding strategies for change. However, after several months of discussion, there remained varied amounts of "buy-in" from the senior team members. At this point, Dr. Frelick asked for the support and leadership of each team member. To use their skills and to ensure the active involvement of each individual in sponsoring the initiative, he placed each vice president in charge of a major aspect of the plan.

Once the initiatives had been launched, the vice presidents worked at different levels of enthusiasm and speed to lead their part of the change. In some cases, commitment was unclear and other priorities occupied their attention. Some thought that consolidation should be the single agenda for change; others appeared to avoid change by moving their task forces into endless cycles of analysis.

One of the significant aspects of the redesign involved breaking out of traditional silos and moving to an interdisciplinary team organization. Some members of senior management were hesitant to embrace this new design, as it required taking significant risks. A great deal of discussion took place, but designated leaders did not appear to rise above the traditional discipline tensions.

The External Community

The Ministry of Health continued to put direct and indirect pressure on the hospitals in the region to come to terms with the apparent duplication and perceived waste in the system, and continued to press for system-wide change. The ministry withheld support for some of Victoria's specific change initiatives, such as specific program shifts in collaboration with other hospitals and consolidation to one site, on the basis it would not support changes at one hospital without a city-wide plan for change.

The Problem

Dr. Frelick realized that he had a significant problem on his hands. He was firmly committed to his redesign vision. He believed that, although a downsizing strategy coupled with a single focus on consolidation to one campus might prove popular to some board members and staff, it would not serve Victoria Hospital's long-term needs. He needed to implement a plan for his vision and find a way to acquire a reasonable level of support from board members, vice presidents, physicians, professionals, and workers.

About the Editor

Gerard H. Seijts received his Ph.D. from the University of Toronto in 1998. He joined the Richard Ivey School of Business in 2000. He has taught undergraduate and MBA courses in organizational behavior, human resource management, leading change, managerial negotiations, behavioral decision making, staffing, and performance management. He has also delivered workshops to mid- and senior-level managers on topics such as organizational design, leading change, strategic interviewing, managerial negotiations, and behavioral decision making.

His research activities, spanning numerous journal articles, book chapters, and conference papers, cover a wide range of topics, including goal setting, leadership, training and development, organizational justice, performance appraisal, and team processes. His research has been published in the *Academy of Management Journal, Academy of Management Executive, Journal of Organizational Behaviour, Human Performance, Journal of Business Ethics, Employee Responsibilities and Rights Journal, Canadian Psychology,* the *Canadian Journal of Behavioural Science, Applied Psychology: An International Review,* and the *International Journal for Academic Development.*

He is a member of the Academy of Management, the Administrative Sciences Association of Canada, the American Psychological Association, the Canadian Psychological Association, and the Society for Industrial and Organizational Psychology. He is on the Editorial Board of the *Journal of Organizational Behaviour* and the *Canadian Journal of Behavioural Science.* He is an ad hoc reviewer for numerous other journals in the field of organizational behavior and human resource management. He is past division chair of the Human Resources Division of the Administrative Sciences Association of Canada.